The Missing Link in Our Understanding of Man

"Mind-broadening. . . . A significant contribution."

> —Shimon Peres, Vice Premier
> and Minister of Foreign
> Affairs, Israel

"A work of major importance."

> —Charles R. Kelley, Ph.D.
> author of *Education in
> Feeling and Purpose*

"An optimistic and reassuring book. . . . He sets human beings
well above what Freud allows."

> —Senator Eugene J. McCarthy

"Clearly and persuasively identifies the role played by irrational
fear . . . in the living and thinking of individuals and societies."

> —John Silber
> President, Boston University

Thinking in the Shadow of Feelings

A New Understanding
of the Hidden Forces
That Shape Individuals
and Societies

REUVEN BAR-LEVAV, M.D.

A Touchstone Book
Published by Simon & Schuster Inc.
New York/London/Toronto/Sydney/Tokyo

Touchstone
Simon & Schuster Building
Rockefeller Center
1230 Avenue of the Americas
New York, New York 10020

1   3   5   7   9   10   8   6   4   2
1   3   5   7   9   10   8   6   4   2   Pbk.

Library of Congress Cataloging in Publication Data
Bar-Levav, Reuven, 1927–
Thinking in the shadow of feelings.

Includes index.
1. Fear.   2. Emotions.   3. Critical thinking.
4. Fear—Social aspects.   5. Critical thinking—
Social aspects.   6. Psychotherapy.   I. Title.
BF575.F2B27   1988   152.4   88-4521
ISBN 0-671-60631-X
0-671-68266-0 Pbk.

I would like to thank the following writers, publishers, and copyright
holders for permission to reprint the quoted material listed below.
"The Anatomy of Angst." Copyright © 1961, Time Inc. All rights
reserved. Reprinted by permission from TIME.
"Sunny" by Bobby Hebb. Copyright © 1965, 1966 by Portable Music Co.,
Inc.
"The Independent Variable" by Frances K. Conley, *The Runner*, June,
1983.
"Notes and Comment." The Talk of the Town, *The New Yorker*, May 6,
1985. Reprinted by permission. Copyright © 1985, The New Yorker
Magazine, Inc.
Leon Altman, "Some Vicissitudes of Love." *Journal of the American
Psychoanalytic Association*, Vol. 25, No. 1, 1977.

Contents

Dedication   9

Introduction   15

  1. A Working Theory of Man   15
  2. A Brief Outline of the Book   17
  3. Wanted and Needed: Better Relief from Anxiety   19

ONE FEAR   23

  1. The Fear of Abandonment   24
  2. The Fear of Engulfment   40
  3. The Fear of Non-Being   50
  4. Self-Coupling vs. Self-Love   59
  5. How Do We Know What We Know about Man?   61

TWO THE ORIGINS OF DEPRESSION   64

  1. The Many Masks of Fear   65
  2. Anomie as a Curable Illness   72
  3. Our Dramatic Beginnings   74
  4. Viewing Adults as Grown-Up Infants   78
  5. A Brief Note to the Reader   80
  6. Objective Sources of Knowledge about the Earliest
     Life Experiences   81
  7. Man's Yearnings for Physical Closeness   84
  8. Viewing Humans as Part of the Animal Kingdom   86
  9. The Physiologic Basis of Character   88
 10. The Depressive Position   91
 11. Is There a "Right" Distance in Close
     Relationships?   93

12. Life from the Infant's Perspective 95
13. The Inevitability of Disappointment and Dread 98
14. Is Emotional Dependency Dangerous? 103
15. Current Treatments of Depression 105

THREE FEELING AND THINKING 113

1. Rationality as a Goal in Need of Fulfillment 113
2. What Are Feelings? 116
3. A Personal Note to the Reader 118
4. Why We Downgrade Feelings 119
5. Man as Part of the Animal Kingdom 122
6. The Fascinating Model of Our Human Brain 124
7. The Delusional Idealization of the Intellect 128
8. Brain Development in the First Two Years of Life 130
9. The Basic Qualities of the Basic Feelings 133
10. Feelings as Our Guardians 138
11. A Most Common Hidden Disorder:
    Confusion in Thinking 140

FOUR LOVE AND HATE, ANGER AND HURT,
      SADNESS AND HAPPINESS 144

1. Love: An Introduction 144
2. The Love that Children Have for Others 147
3. Romantic "Love" 148
4. Sexual Aspects of Love 155
5. Real Love 158
6. In Defense of Sensible Selfishness 160
7. Free Gifts and Some that Are Not So Free 161
8. Hate 164
9. Anger 170
10. Hurt 180
11. Sadness 189
12. Happiness, "Happiness," and Contentment 191

FIVE HEALTHIER CHILDREN IN A SANER WORLD 194

1. A Personal Word to the Reader 195
2. How Far Must We Go in Saving the Lives of the
   Seriously Handicapped? 197

3. One More Personal Note to the Reader 198
4. The Tragic Results of Overidentification 199
5. Natural Selection vs. Human Selection 202
6. The Urgent Need for a Dictatorship of Reason 204
7. The Consequences to Humanity of
Overpopulation 205
8. The Golem of Prague 212
9. Should Childbearing Be Licensed? 212
10. A Brief Guide to Good Parenting 217

SIX THE TREATMENT OF EMOTIONAL
DISORDERS 220

1. Objectives and Basic Principles 220
2. The Growing Value of Patients' Consent 227
3. The Real- vs. the Therapeutic Relationship 229
4. The Therapeutic Setting and Contract 231
5. Mothering and "Holding" as Part of Healing 234
6. The Need for Fathering and for Limit Setting 238
7. The Yearnings for Dependency and the Fear of It 246
8. Individual, Group, and Marathon Sessions 249
9. Cost Considerations 251
10. The Urgent Need for More Competent Therapists
and What Limits Their Number 253
11. Using This Chapter as a Guide to Therapy 254

SEVEN NOTES ON THE FUTURE OF THE WEST 259

1. The Root Problem: The Dictatorship of Feelings 263
2. The Basis of Civilized Existence 267
3. The Law of the Jungle 269
4. Fighting Domestic and International Terror
Successfully 274
    Principle I 275
    Principle II 279
    Principle III 280
    Principle IV 285
    Principle V 289
5. A Personal Note 292
6. The Expertise of Experts 293
7. Liberty in New Hands: The Media 294

8. Idealism and Naivete:
   From William Jennings Bryan to Cyrus Vance   302
9. The Dangerous Fiction of International Law   306
10. On the Need for Truth and the Current Necessity
    for Lies in Democracies   307
11. A Sensible Code of Conduct for International
    Relations   311
12. Three Practical Suggestions   315
13. A Concluding Personal Note   316

EIGHT   A UNIFIED THEORY OF GENERAL HUMAN
MOTIVATION AND BEHAVIOR   318

Introduction   318
The Theory   322
   Man's Earliest Beginnings   322
   The "Pull of Regression" and the "Push against
     Progressing"   326
   The Boundaries of the Self   330
   Observations on Personal Power and on
     Powerlessness   336
   The Basic Wants of Infants and of Adults   338
   Feelings vs. Thinking   342
   Dangers and Opportunities for Free Societies   345

Acknowledgments   351
Index   353

Dedication

A totally unexpected long-distance phone call woke me one morning not long ago. The caller, an old friend, told me in a broken voice that on the following day "We will be burying Norman," his son. To Norman I dedicate this book.

I had known him since infancy. He became a cute little boy, a bit naughty, and even then sort of lost. As long as he was a young child it was easy for me to be with him, but he changed when he became a teenager, as many teenagers do. He was openly unpleasant, sullen, and rebellious. I remember him challenging anyone he perceived as an authority, and he usually acted as if someone had just wronged him. Eventually he dropped out of college, worked only sporadically, and showed no interest in pursuing a career. Luckily he was never on drugs.

He was still likable in spite of his troubles, and I worried about him and tried to reach him from time to time, but to no avail. He approached me one day when about twenty years old and asked for a loan of $150, promising to repay it a couple of months later. I don't remember what he said the money was for, but it made some sense, and besides I wanted to lend him a hand. So I gave him a loan without many questions. I expected no interest, but I did expect to be paid back.

For eleven years I heard nothing from him. I barely remembered the debt. But I did remember Norman, and whenever I did I was saddened.

Then the mailman brought me a completely unforeseen letter on official-looking stationery with Norman's name on top as one of the partners of a small law firm. I was surprised and very happy and I eagerly read what he wrote:

Dear R.,
   Enclosed please find my check in the amount of $256.55 which represents my repayment to you of a debt long overdue.
   I hope that you will accept repayment of the $150.00 originally

9

lent me in 1971, with five percent interest, compounded an-
nually over the past eleven years, as some measure of my
intent to honor my obligation to you over this long period of
time.

I hope that this short note finds you and your family well
and that the new year will bring all the best to you and the
rest of the family. Again, thanks for your patience with me
and here's wishing you the best in the coming year.

Cordially,
Norman

I was overjoyed. My faith in Man's basic goodness was restored. Without delay I wrote him a reply:

Dear Norman,

I was flabbergasted and elated at receiving your letter and
the check. I use these words very sparingly. The surprise of
unexpectedly receiving such a letter from you and its enclosure flabbergasted me, and I was elated because it was such
good news from you. I had assumed that you were lost, and
am so very, very happy that you found such a good avenue to
express yourself as an adult.

I will cash the check and spend the money with great pleasure because it is a measure of your achievements. The repayment signifies that you are on a good road and I truly rejoice. I
open my heart and my arms to you and would like to welcome
you in person. Please write to me again and tell me what has
happened to you, whether you are single or married, alone or
with a friend. If it is easier, pick up the phone and say hello.
Let's get reacquainted.

Please give regards to your parents. I hope they are well, too.
Your father and I are not as close as we used to be, but I hope
I can yet be a true friend to his son.

Be well,
RBL

The exchange of letters took place a couple of years before I
received his father's phone call. I had wondered many times afterward why he had not written again, or at least called. But I
respected his need to keep his distance until he was ready. I had
welcomed him with an open heart, and that was all I could do.
What was left was to wait. So I waited.

I shall wait no more for his call, nor for his visit. He was buried the next day at 1:00 P.M. His father had told me that Norman "had backed out of his depression too late." He had been found asphyxiated in his car. He was thirty-three years old.

Perhaps another Norman, somewhere, will find this book of help.

*The unleashed power of the atom
has changed everything save our modes
of thinking, and we thus drift
toward unparalleled catastrophes.*

ALBERT EINSTEIN

Introduction

1. A Working Theory of Man

Primitive man must have faced the mysterious forces of nature in almost constant terror. Insignificant and vulnerable, he assigned magical meanings to the unknown and began to appease it with gifts and strange rituals, thus lessening his fear. To us such efforts appear not only pathetic but also heroic. They were Man's first clumsy attempts to come to terms with the overwhelming forces that shaped his destiny. Now we also know how erroneous these attempts were, and how ineffective.

Since then we have learned to tame nature and even to unleash some of the tremendous energy that is locked up in atomic and in subatomic particles. Yet, though we understand the cosmos and can even manipulate our satellites at unimaginable distances, fear is still as close a companion for many of us as it was for our ancient forebears.

Our eyes look outward and away from us, and it follows that in our search for security we first looked in those directions. Only recently have we dared to acknowledge with much trepidation that hidden forces inside us may be as fierce and powerful as those outside us. They determine the destiny of individuals and the fate of nations. But we are only beginning to really understand these forces. Till now they have been described crudely, and our attempts to control them have failed almost totally.

The very tool that enabled us to conquer the physical forces of nature—our capacity to understand, to infer, to make connections, in short, our power of reasoning—has been the main stumbling block. We insisted that we were rational beings capable of looking after ourselves no less well than we could manage all other things around us. Even Freud viewed Man as a special being able to cure himself by understanding his unconscious. As a result, we know a lot about things, very little about people, and almost nothing about ourselves. The affairs of individuals, families, and societies are still tangled.

Technologically, life at the end of this century is altogether different than it was at its beginning, when we did not have radio, telephone, television, air traffic, mass education, antibiotics, space exploration, atomic energy, lasers, and the microchip. The natural sciences have changed the very essence of our lives in a very short time. But loneliness, despair, and the search for meaning continue. They have become, in fact, more central concerns of modern existence. We live better and longer and our sophistication is much greater, but we are not happier. We do not conduct our affairs rationally.

It is well known that the social and psychological sciences are lagging behind. We still need a set of principles that will help us use the many new facts about people that our extensive research has unraveled. This book attempts to provide such a master key, and Chapter 8 offers such a set of unifying principles.

If valid, a theory of human motivation and behavior should enable us not only to bring order and harmony into our personal lives but should also help us run our institutions and governments much better. It must be applicable to all human experiences, past as well as present, regardless of geography or cultural differences; it should be capable of predicting the future behavior of individuals and of societies and provide the tools needed to increase industrial productivity and morale. Above all it must enhance our chances of survival in a nuclear age. Like all new keys, such a theory is likely to have some sharp edges at first; new things seldom work smoothly without at least minor adjustments.

The basic motives of our behavior are relatively easy to understand, like the other laws of nature. The general outline of what follows, if not every detail, is comprehensible by any thoughtful and intelligent person. Still the danger of a temporary loss of objectivity exists, because readers are likely to see themselves repeatedly in this book. Our nature is such that we tend to follow our hearts rather than our minds, and we must repeatedly overcome this tendency if we wish to increase our understanding of anything.

Scientific discoveries often consist of no more than careful descriptions of the reactions of materials, phenomena, individuals, groups, or societies. Any single such observation is rarely useful in itself. Our understanding of the universe is only expanded when we discover and uncover general trends and patterns that apply even to things that we have not yet observed directly. Men had always observed that objects fall to the ground, but it was not till Galileo's experiments and Newton's law that gravity was understood. Previously disparate phenomena then began to form a connected system in which future behavior could be predicted. Man could henceforth plan better and improve his methods. Even new observations cannot be usefully gathered except on the basis of a tentative working theory. The search is otherwise as effective as looking for berries in a wheatfield.

Further observations and research will validate and invalidate various parts of the theory that is presented here, but any thoughtful reader is really capable of assessing to what extent its basic themes make sense. By virtue of being alive, we are all somewhat expert on the subject: We have acquired intimate knowledge of human nature and assembled a rich treasure of observations about it. We can often recognize familiar facts even if we cannot elucidate them ourselves.

2. A Brief Outline of the Book

The central importance of irrational fear in the lives of humans is still generally underestimated. It dominates all other feelings and limits health and achievement. Chapter 1 describes the three basic types of fear that torment people: the fears of abandonment, of engulfment, and of non-being. The last of these, which is not the same as the fear of death or dying, has never been described this way before.

Chapter 2 traces the origins of irrational fear in early life, when character is shaped and lifelong expectations and attitudes are formed. This chapter also explains why depression is practically universal. It takes the reader into the world of the newly born, a space in time that each of us has occupied once but that none of us can remember cognitively.

Chapter 3 addresses the all-important differences between thinking and feeling. Most people are at least vaguely aware of the powerful influence of feelings. They not only shape "opinions," but often they are also responsible for "decisions." But true deciding can never be impulsive. It depends on a thoughtful consideration of all the issues involved, yet this is often hard to come by, since "learning to really think requires first that we make room for it by diminishing the domain of feelings."*

The fascinating story of the development, functioning, and limits of the human brain are also described in Chapter 3. We shall see how we have always tried to escape fear by using rationalizations, downgrading the enormous power of emotions. Yet feelings dominate the affairs of Man both individually and collectively. Potentially a blessing, they are very often the cause of the things that people unwittingly do to harm themselves and others.

Chapter 4 considers in detail the six other basic feelings that exist in addition to fear: romantic and non-romantic love, hate, hurt, anger, happiness, and sadness.

Chapters 5, 6, and 7 address some of the important implications of our new understanding, both for the individual and for societies. It might perhaps be possible now to avert the early decline of democracy, an imperfect system of government that nonetheless offers Man's spirit more freedom and dignity and his body more material comforts and security than any other system in the long history of our species.

Chapter 5 is concerned with the quality of life in a world that is quickly becoming overpopulated. We examine here some of the painful moral dilemmas that we have no choice but to face. How do we rationally reconcile the sanctity of life with our need to maintain its quality? How do we raise healthier children in an unhealthy world?

Chapter 6 outlines a new and different approach to psychotherapy that is capable not only of ameliorating the horror, hurt, and pain of depression but also of curing the illness. This chapter can serve as a guide to the perplexed seeker of help for such diverse conditions as addiction and smoking, obesity and social isolation, alcoholism and phobias, the tendency to fail or the obsession to succeed. These are all symptoms of anxiety and of depression, as we shall see. Man stands a chance to become truly free not on barricades but in therapeutic settings that are effective. The way out of meaninglessness requires much work, courage, expense, and time; but easy or not, such a way clearly exists.

In Chapter 7 an alarm is sounded that is meant to awaken

---

* The above quote appears in Section 80 of Chapter 8. Quotations from this chapter are integrated in the text throughout the rest of the book without specific citations. The purpose is to facilitate reading without interruption. The interested reader will always be able to find the source of the quoted phrases in one or more of the ninety-nine Sections of Chapter 8.

Western societies from their delusional slumber in the domain of feelings. We examine ways to defend ourselves better against international terrorism and focus upon the urgent need to discard the old fictions of an international law based on wishful "thinking." Also included are several practical suggestions that might improve the chances of democracy in its struggle against barbarism.

Chapter 8 is the culmination of the book. It is a systematic presentation of the many separate observations about Man's nature found in earlier chapters. This unified theory of human motivation and behavior explains how we got to be the way we are, what we want, what interferes with our plans, and how we might break out of our characteristic habits of existence.

3. Wanted and Needed: Better Relief from Anxiety

Most people today are at least superficially aware of unconscious motives, but few realize how powerful and how prevalent they are. Man is not what he claims to be. The talking mouth is probably the least trustworthy organ of our body. It obfuscates as much as it clarifies. What we are and how we feel are expressed much more faithfully by other parts of our body: by facial expressions and by muscle tension; by the glint or dullness in the eye; by the pain in our posture; by how we sit, stand, walk, smile, eat or drink, sleep, and even smell. Our mouth lies to save our face. At least unconsciously, words and "thoughts" are often designed to mislead, ourselves as much as others.

Observant individuals can learn to recognize their facial and bodily expressions; they can be seen even more readily in others. These physical phenomena reflect experiences in our distant past, when each of us first adjusted to extrauterine life. "Nothing is lost in the universe. Even though we have no conscious memory of [such] early experiences, our body remembers." We can find traces of such long-past experiences not only in our bodies but also in our behavior and in our habits. If we come upon a tree that is grossly bent in one direction, we can safely assume that it was subjected to recurring winds or other pressure for a long time. In the same way, we can understand people's strange and seemingly inexplicable reactions and behavior. Everything makes good sense in some framework, even if it looks "crazy" in the context in which we first observe it.

It will become increasingly clear along the way that Man is

essentially *not* a rational being, merely one capable of rationality. He is fully rational only rarely, for relatively short periods of time, mostly when the social expectations of him are clearly spelled out, well understood, and voluntarily accepted. In the bosom of his immediate family and in intense emotional involvements he repeatedly acts and reacts "on the basis of feelings, not rationally."

Man, we are told, has been created in God's image, with the capacity to choose between good and evil and between rationality and impulsivity. His high potential is, however, not very often realized. Although capable of existing just below the angels, irrational fear condemns most of us to living far below, among all the other crawling creatures. Living consciously, without dread or distortions of reality, is the glory of human existence. We shall soon see, however, that we are commonly diverted from this lofty state by senseless and yet very real panic.

Billions of dollars, marks, pounds, yen, and even rubles are spent every year to alleviate anxiety. Medicine, psychology, social work, religion, business, government, and many others offer help; but they usually succeed mainly in distracting sufferers from their pain. The despair and the need are so great that many useless and even damaging "remedies" find willing customers. New drugs and procedures as well as self-help books and belief systems are regularly touted as "the answer"—but not many people get more than temporary relief. Yet it is possible now to actually cure most types of emotional stress and illness.

Why is this such a secret then, and why are such approaches not more commonly used? Mostly because irrational fear—the greatest human limitation of all—has hindered both sufferers and those who would help them. Freud understood correctly that psychoanalysts must first be analyzed before they are competent to analyze others. But even he did not know that the cognitive and intellectual process of analysis is essentially irrelevant to eliminating irrational dread. Gaining insight is fascinating, and it is somewhat reassuring, since it sheds light on the frightening darkness of the unknown. But it does not cure illnesses. A person's body must change before dreams-that-cannot-be are slowly and reluctantly given up. Changing perceptions is not enough.

The basic fears of Man that are discussed in Chapter 1 are subjectively so terrible that we failed to fully understand their nature till now. But understanding them is not enough. The fear must first be eliminated within the person who wishes to help others effectively. This cannot be attained by book learning and by being smart, nor even by having clinical experience. Prospective helpers must actually dare to face their own fears and essentially rid themselves of them. But practically everyone is too afraid even to look at them directly.

Therapists generally rationalize that other less frightening, easier, and simpler ways exist. There are nine ways to skin a cat, they often claim, probably innocently. As we shall see in Chapter 3, Man has repeatedly erred by idealizing his wonderful brain, causing his own tragedies. His error is understandable, since the brain is as close to a true miracle as we ever come. But the price of this delusion has been very high. Many millions have perished because they failed to see that they were being led astray by feelings that are usually irrational. They ignored thinking, which might have saved them. Fear, the most powerful of all feelings, commonly numbs us; and it frequently interferes with our capacity to reason.

Millions of disappointed, disillusioned, and disgruntled ex-patients of psychiatrists, psychotherapists, counselors, ministers, and various "morale builders" continue to suffer misery and pain. Still others turn to occupational therapists, art therapists, music, movement, and dance therapists, gurus and cult leaders, wasting not only money but also human dignity, hope, and life itself. Acute symptoms are often ameliorated, but the lifelong illness continues to fester underneath.

Standing on the shoulders of Zen masters and other giants like Martin Buber, Sigmund Freud, and Wilhelm Reich, just as Einstein stood on Newton's, we can now see awesome vistas altogether different from the landscapes they described. Our view is clearer and we can see much further, not away from us but deep inside us.

A swelling market demand for effective therapy may be the only force strong enough to bring about change, pushing prospective therapists through the rigorous process of self-transformation, the prerequisite for really helping others. Marketplace pressures might thus transform psychiatry into a more useful branch of medicine, and psychotherapy from an endless crutch into an effective system of healing. It is a formidable goal, but the task must be undertaken, since the welfare and lives of millions hang in the balance.

To benefit from this book and enjoy it does not require previous expertise or knowledge, either in psychology, political sci-

ence, or other fields. It requires only the flexibility to see ourselves in a new way.

Although of interest to professionals, students, and experts,
these observations are within the reach of every literate person.
Although it offers no easy solutions, the book is meant to have
practical applications. Strange as it may sound at first, I regard
the general human predicament as a condition which is literally
curable.

ONE

Fear

Be not afraid of sudden terror . . .
PROVERBS 3:25

The whole wide world
Is but a narrow bridge—
And one's main task
Is not to fear at all.
RABBI NACHMAN OF BRATZLAV
1772–1811

Fear not, my servant Jacob . . .
JEREMIAH 46:27

Fear has many names but only one sensation, which ranges in intensity from mild trepidation and restlessness to terror, panic, and a sense of impending doom. Fear is more often referred to by less threatening labels, because they evoke less of the frightening sensation: anxiety, jumpiness, tension, being upset, rattled, troubled, or lost. It causes people to be extra cautious, shy, retiring, or diffident. As we shall see in the next chapter, the origins of this irrational fear go back at least to the time we take our first breath, but traces of it normally remain in us for life. Two main types of fear haunt most men and women from time to time: the fear of abandonment and the fear of engulfment. A third exists at the root of these two, and at the core of all other anxieties: the fear of non-being. This, the most terrible and profound manifestation of dread, is still relatively unknown except by its effects.

All these fears are irrational in the sense of not being evoked by dangers in the present. They are residues of long-past experiences that occurred in one's life soon after birth. Yet the long-term effects linger on, and the first step in the process of becoming free is to know exactly what enslaves us.

Fears caused by realistic dangers in the present usually steel us to meet them effectively, as long as they are not so large as to overwhelm us. Stage fright and other forms of signal anxiety, all being lesser threats, make us more alert and enable us to do well what we must or wish to do. A car accident in which we are not harmed may bring out the best in us—clear thinking, good judgment, and courage. During such moments we often act appropriately without being distracted by irrational fear.

A catatonic, withdrawn, and chronic backward patient who was hospitalized for over twenty years without speaking to anyone suddenly snapped out of his catatonia during a fire. To the surprise of all, he took charge of the orderly evacuation of his fellow patients. For a little while he reverted to his competent old self as fire chief. As soon as the realistic danger was over, however, he became catatonic again, and all attempts to reach him were in vain.

When we must suddenly face danger of catastrophic proportions, on the other hand, we are likely to be overwhelmed. Since we are powerless to do much, we often either panic or become numb. The same happens when a lesser danger stimulates, gives rise to, and ties in with suppressed fears of old. The combination is usually too much for most people to cope with successfully. When all avenues for flight are closed, or even when they only seem to be, we escape from reality. We become immobilized, temporarily or permanently, physically or emotionally. Many people become confused and unable to think clearly when they get scared. This aggravates the original fear. Without acceptable and rational reasons for a fear that holds us in its grip, we become more terrified: Are we also losing our mind? Anxiety thus often begets panic.

1. The Fear of Abandonment

We sometimes enjoy being alone, but we never enjoy being lonely. We at least have our own company to give us solace when alone, but we are only in the company of fear when lonely. The essence of loneliness is emptiness, and the essence of emptiness is terror. In loneliness a person often behaves as if he or she were drowning, grabbing at anything or anyone. The emptiness of a lonely weekend can be more terrifying than any real danger in the real world. A gaping nothingness. Two days without work make the three nights around them very long, black, and bleak.

Too much time for rest and recreation is a severe punishment for those who are very restless inside: It provides almost endless opportunities to experience panic.

Many single people rush to congregate in crowded bars at such times to establish some form of human contact. The dominant mood at T.G.I.F. (Thank God It's Friday) pubs is hardly thankfulness. It is anxiety. It is only superficially true that the very nervous young men and women who mingle there are looking desperately for sex partners. In fact they are looking for something much more important, although not necessarily knowingly: at least short-term companionship to relieve the frightening anxiety of loneliness. A warm body is the classic antidote to the cold grip of panic.

The fear of abandonment is present in men and in women, in the young and the old, in heterosexual and homosexual relationships. Divorced or widowed men and women often rush into a new marriage essentially to avoid this fear, although they usually deny having it in the first place. Yet, without it, nobody would get entangled so quickly in a new serious relationship.

People marry, they have children, they join clubs and causes, they mix socially, and they form alliances and friendships with other people as well as with dogs, cats, birds, and other pets—all to avoid loneliness, or at least to lessen it. Those who have not consciously known the fear of abandonment are often amazed at its intensity and how quickly it is relieved by company. One young woman never dared to go down alone into the basement of her house, even during the day or when it was well lit at night. To her own amazement, she suddenly found herself free of this fear as soon as she brought her new baby home from the hospital. She would now take the newborn in her arms and confidently walk down the steps. She felt safe in the physical presence of another live human being, even her own totally helpless infant. Feelings do not necessarily make sense, as she understood, and it required both candor and courage to admit to such senseless behavior. People normally hide embarrassing views of themselves, for embarrassment itself is a mixture of fear and shame. It is common for people to fear being abandoned because of such imperfections.

The nature of the fear of abandonment can be well illustrated by analogy: If an orange is cut in half, each of its halves has a large exposed and oozing surface. Since each is open to the air and not covered, drying soon begins. Before long each half-orange completely dries out and shrivels unless its open surface is protected. A whole orange is so well packaged in its peel by nature that its vitality and juice are not quickly lost.

Not so a half-orange. It would immediately experience a sense of foreboding if it had conscious awareness, and it would be overcome by panic. Such half-oranges are indeed really in "mortal" danger, their future and continued existence precarious. Their juicy center would soon be no more without corrective measures, and they would cease to exist. Like all non-whole objects, each cut orange faces the early prospect of emptiness.

The ideal covering for a half-orange would be another half of similar diameter and with physical properties resembling its own. It would fit best with its own other half. Neither would dry up very quickly as long as the two halves were superimposed upon each other and provided that they remained tightly attached. The same words and images are also used for lovers when they pine and yearn for each other. They also cling for dear life and embrace tightly as if they too were two cut halves of one whole. This is why the mutual pull is so strong. Union means survival and salvation, for oranges and for people who are not emotionally whole.

Although every person is physically self-contained, most people do not experience themselves as emotionally whole. They sense themselves as if they were cut in two, and sometimes even refer to their spouses as "my better half." What makes such spouses "better" is not their superior human qualities. Rather, simply by existing they help their mates "feel" whole, thus lowering their terrible anxiety. This makes such spouses very important indeed, though they are often rather deficient as human beings in reality—needy, angry, unreasonable, unpleasant, moody, or bitter. They may leave much to be desired, but all this hardly matters, for they relieve the sharp fear of abandonment by their very existence. Being "in love" brings similar relief. Non-harmonious aspects of a relationship are ignored or played down if the romantic attachment fills the gaping internal hole.

People sometimes commit suicide or murder, or they have nervous breakdowns and other serious troubles when a lover or a mate dies, deserts, or divorces them. Why? Not because of the pain that is associated with any important loss. Pain is bearable, but the fear of abandonment often is not. The breakup of a central relationship is often experienced as leaving a hole in the middle of one's abdomen, as if something were torn out from there. Many of those suddenly left by an important person sense themselves without any attachments, in danger of drifting into outer space forever. The fear of non-being, described a little later in this chapter, is often activated at such times. It bubbles just below the fear of abandonment.

Losses always cause pain, even when a person is emotionally whole, though they do not always elicit fear. In the relative absence of fear the pain is only transitory, because time helps heal the agonies of mature mourning. Millions of people "out there" are reasonable candidates to replace the ones lost, though new relationships are not formed easily, and they rarely fit immediately as well as the old ones did. Like newly planted flowers that must be helped to take root, so new relationships must be carefully cultivated. But with effort and time, mature people normally fix their lives.

The situation is basically different when people use each other mostly for emotional shoring-up. A breakup then causes panic, which results from the sense of having been abandoned. The term itself contains the explanation for that panic: Adults and even older children can be left, but only babies can be abandoned. Leaving causes hurt and anger; abandonment—fear and possibly death. But adults often experience being left as abandonment, exactly as if they still were babies. Although actually safe, they have a sense of real, extreme, and immediate danger. Many people experience such moments as if their umbilical cord had never really been sealed shut: Their life substance might just ooze out through it, and they would be no more. Emergency help is needed *now*, they fear, before all vitality is totally and irretrievably lost. Most sudden marriages and suicides occur under such circumstances.

Those in panic are positive that "others" simply do not understand the dimensions and the urgency of the danger that confronts them. Why else would "they" still be so calm? When a security-providing relationship is lost, the result is pathologic mourning that consists of terror and panic and that appears endless and empty of hope. Death often seems highly preferred to bottomless agony. Physical illnesses often develop at times when the will to live is at a low ebb.

Our cortex learns much faster than our physiology, as we shall see more clearly in Chapter 3. Many adults continue to react therefore in ways they know make no sense. They cannot gain control over their reactions or feelings, even though they understand that the fear of abandonment is a useless leftover from another age, much more troublesome, however, than the intestinal appendix. We are at the beck and call of this fear, proving once again that our feelings are much more powerful than our thinking and will. This further deflates our sense of being powerful, because we must acknowledge in spite of our posturing that we are not really in charge.

The existence of the fear of abandonment is often denied by those who find it very frightening to accept the fact that each of us is all alone in the universe, forever unattached once born. Although existentially true, this is often a source of much anxiety. The physical and emotional rootlessness of people in highly mobile societies adds to this sense of belonging nowhere. Families are smaller, supercities larger, and anonymity is the rule. Many fear that without some identifying documents on their person at all times they might collapse somewhere and nobody would know who they were. More than ever we live in a Kafkaesque world: Many have a sense that they are faceless, nameless, and with no connections. Such people are desperately eager to hold on to somebody and they are hungry to be held. Many fear being left, forgotten, abandoned. This is why many people want to see their names on plaques or in print, to be "eternally" remembered by others. This is also why some people are so driven to have children.

Those who have not consciously experienced this horror may think that these descriptions are merely metaphors. But the fear of abandonment is very real, and this is its real content. Grownups can obviously fend for themselves, but "most adults are physically grown-up children of various emotional ages. They typically act and react on the basis of their earliest life adaptations as reflected in their feelings."

How does an intelligent and otherwise competent adult finally accept the fact that he or she may be desperately afraid of being abandoned? With great difficulty. It sometimes helps a little to realize that few people are totally exempt from such anxiety, although not all people suffer equally, and almost everyone has periods of relative tranquility in life. It sometimes helps to remember that a profound fear of abandonment is a symptom of a real illness, not a sign of weakness. But most people continue to hide their fear as if it were a mark of shame. Days continue to be too stressful and too busy, nights too long and too silent, and weekends too empty and too meaningless—and all this must remain hidden. Such pain is almost too much to bear. Those in the grip of this fear are sure that everyone else has someone close nearby and that others are content.

Partial denial of reality is often the only option left to those with much fear of abandonment, and it involves a partial but chronic loss of sanity. This is an extreme solution but not an uncommon one. Otherwise sane, intelligent, and competent men and women often distort themselves grossly to maintain their relationships with spouses or with lovers. Dignity and self-respect are usually the first, but not the only, casualties. People appease and please endlessly to insure that they will not be abandoned. They may be giants in the office, on the job, or at the club, but crawling dwarfs at home. The thought of abandonment rarely crosses their mind, but their behavior reveals these hidden concerns and worries.

The unseen fear of abandonment also has a tendency to escalate. Will this relationship continue as one gets older, less attractive physically, less potent or desirable sexually, weaker, less exciting? Is this job secure? The cost of appeasement is always greater appeasement. More and more of a person's interests are given up in the effort to please the other, to maintain the status quo. At rare moments of relative sanity people realize that their "adjustments" are degrading; but this further lowers self-esteem and aggravates the fear as it adds to the pain and to the hidden rage. This is when peace-loving and docile people sometimes break into murderous rampages. Those in the degrading prison of fear frequently warn their children and others not to follow in their footsteps, but they cannot themselves break out.

The well-educated and sophisticated are obviously not exempt, although many people still naively believe that more education is somehow directly related to better mental health. The well-educated are sometimes even more reluctant to accept their irrational fears. But this only insures that they bear the fear less well. As we shall see in Chapter 3, the visceral brain that is in charge of our emotional reactions is really not willing to accept commands from its younger neighbor the cortex, even though we fervently wish it would.

Separation from Mother is not really completed when the umbilical cord is cut. Emotional separation is achieved in fact only with great efforts over many years, and most people never complete the process at all. This is why the fear of abandonment is so common. Overcoming the emotional need and wish to be attached to others is hardly ever accomplished without pressure, because separating goes counter to Man's tendency to follow the path of least resistance. It is, however, the major necessary step in the process of individuation, our becoming emotionally whole individuals, not merely detached parts of someone else.

People in whom the fear of abandonment is especially strong become more frightened when their spouse or child begins taking steps toward individuation. Knowingly or not, they often sabotage the process, although it is in the best interests of those whom they claim to love. Parents sometimes hold on to their growing children too long, and they retard their legitimate attempts to become emotionally independent. Spouses or children of people in serious psychotherapy often try to stop it, for fear that those who become free would leave. Such frightened relatives have probably never known good relationships based on cooperation and mutual regard. They often act as if fear and guilt are the only forces that can hold people together. How would they know otherwise if they have never experienced anything else?

Those with little or no fear of abandonment can indeed no longer be held prisoner, but they stay in essentially good relationships by choice. The freedom to leave destructive, degrading, and damaging relationships is obviously not exercised in mature and decent ones. Such relationships are highly valued, protected, and nourished.

The boundaries of the self are like a psychological skin. They are well defined and reasonably intact in individuated persons. Such people survive well emotionally by themselves when they have to. They are no longer pushed by terror to find someone in a hurry in order not to be alone. Even without others they can exist without panic, although no sane person would want to live without the company of others. It is not only helpful but also truly enjoyable when fear is not involved.

Choosing to be with someone is basically different from clinging to a person. The former is based on free choice, the latter is an effort to lessen panic. But clinging does not insure emotional closeness, and it almost guarantees in fact that the partners will remain emotionally distant. The fear of being all alone often serves as a strong glue, however, which holds people even in poor relationships. But those driven against their free will, in a car or in a relationship, do not enjoy the scenery very much. They may smile bravely to hide the embarrassing fact that they are powerless prisoners, but they are in pain and degraded even when they hide their status from everyone, including themselves. The self-delusion is rarely total. Many husbands and wives, lovers, children, parents, and others know that they have secretly wished at times to be able to leave everything and everybody behind and just go away.

The optimal distance between partners in a relationship can be determined only by those free of the fear of being abandoned. The need for relief of this fear is seldom exactly the same for any two people. One may complain of being crowded, while the other is experiencing neglect. "Conflicts, divorce, and even violence are common in romantic 'love,' because the closeness eventually exceeds the tolerance for it by one of the partners while insufficient for the other." Hurt, anger, disappointment, bitterness, and more fear often result, although the one with the greater fear of abandonment generally yields on all matters and normally keeps these sentiments well hidden. The freedom to express such feelings does not exist when any fear is strong. Only bitterness then trickles through.

Ideal conditions exist only during or before the honeymoon of relationships, when the yearnings are most alike in both partners. The anxiety of each is lowered by the presence of the other, and both usually expect that the other will cause it to disappear altogether. The inevitable disappointment that follows most honeymoons springs from the painful realization that the partner failed to bring such happiness, though even this disappointment is sometimes denied for years. Hope springs eternal when nothing more concrete can be relied upon. The realistic adult need for distance is often overlooked by those who fear abandonment. But even the formal pact "till death doth us part" does not guarantee non-abandonment.

The basic assumption in romantic love is that the lover will always be perfectly attuned to all our open and hidden wishes for closeness. The secret and mostly unknown hope is for a replication of the infant's experience in the womb. The same yardstick is used, in fact, to measure both the "love" of a lover and the devotion of a pregnant woman to her unborn child: how much either is willing and able to satisfy the needs of the other before his or her own. Pregnant women must indeed deny their wishes and needs sometimes to protect the unborn fetus, but perpetual demands for such sacrifices are clearly unreasonable and damaging in adult relationships. The fear of abandonment is often so sharp, however, that to allay it people become emotionally enslaved. Those with extreme fear are often willing to demonstrate their readiness for self-sacrifice as a proof of their "love." Emotional cowering indeed lowers fear, but only for a short while. The partner whose presence is not assured must be appeased again and again, without end. Many people still expect their happiness to come from outside themselves, although it is really impossible for anyone to produce feelings in others, or even in oneself, as we shall see later. All we can do is evoke reactions that already exist. When the capacity to experience happiness, rage, and pity is blocked—hardly anything will bring them up.

The processes of separation and of individuation are practically never completed automatically, because the fear of abandonment continues to hold us in its grip till it is forced to yield. "The wish to remain psychologically attached . . . co-exists with an opposite wish for self-sufficiency. . . . But since all children encounter situations that they are unable to master, fear often overrides the wish for independence. Really letting go of all mothering figures is therefore a very scary prospect, analogous to, but much more frightening than, letting go of the side of a deep swimming pool for the first time and daring to venture into its middle." Even unfulfillable dreams are not given up without fierce struggles. As long as we are only half whole, terror always lurks nearby, and an extreme sense of fragility is often present. When we fear abandonment, we desperately seek someone who is sure never to abandon us. Since no man or woman can ever fulfill such an impossible wish, we frequently turn to God.

Those without enough innocent faith in God or in something else withdraw like newborns into their individual shells for comfort. Here they "couple" with themselves, as described later in this chapter. They live here emotionally much of the time, venturing out only rarely for brief moments of contact with other people. Their retreat is as real as physical withdrawal. They speak little and they make no waves. They have given up. They have accepted the life of depression, isolation, and silence. Their quiet withdrawal is usually filled with a deep sense of futility, which can even exist in the midst of a whirlwind of social activity. Yet the price of not experiencing the fear of abandonment is to feel little of anything else, and cynicism is the inevitable result: "Is this what life is all about?" they wonder.

The sad story of the handsome Prince of Wales is a good example. He was forty-two years old in 1936 and the most popular member of the British royal family when his heart became entangled with Wallis Simpson. She was still married at the time to her second husband. Nobody took this affair very seriously, because the prince surrounded himself with many beautiful women. Besides, as soon as he became King of England and Emperor of India, he would automatically become the head of the

Church of England, and Parliament would forbid him marrying a divorced woman. Everyone understood these plain facts, including the prince, who was carefully groomed from early childhood for his duties as king.

The prince ascended the throne as Edward VIII in January 1936 after his father, George V, died. Hitler was already making threatening noises just across the English Channel, and the empire was not holding together so well. It was hoped that the young king would provide a new spirit of energetic leadership. But he was busy with other things. He became involved in Wallis's divorce from Ernest Simpson, a colorless but respectable businessman. Only then did everybody around the new king recognize that serious trouble was brewing. They tried to reason with him, but to no avail. The great "love affair of the century" was clearly interfering with the king's ability to think coherently. Reason took a back seat, as usual, at the height of feelings. Stanley Baldwin, the prime minister, also tried to talk sense to the young king, but concluded, "It seems that certain cells in his brain have not developed properly. This whole thing does not seem to cause him much anguish or internal struggle."

King Edward VIII abdicated on December 10, 1936, and became the Duke of Windsor, telling the British people and the world that he simply could not live without the woman he loved. Only in fear, not in true love, does one experience such a complete absence of choice, such a confusion between subjective and objective reality. People commonly make serious errors while in the grip of strong feelings.

According to the strict laws of those days, Mrs. Simpson's divorce would become null and void if it could be shown that she had relations with someone other than the husband within six months after the decree. So Edward lived alone for these six months in a castle near Vienna. He appeared as a pathetic child —lost, torn, desolate, and in constant need. It was obvious from his demeanor that he was inextricably caught in the iron grip of fear, since he was temporarily "abandoned" by Wallis. He was emotionally so dependent on her that he phoned her repeatedly, day and night. The newspapers reported that he "worshipped" her.

"He was like a child in her hands, the poor man," said a friend, Lady Alexandra. "He suffered so very much. Wallis was able to rule him without restraint. From the moment that he fell under her spell he seemed to have fallen apart altogether. But close friends like us knew that he would repeat the same scenario all over again, without hesitation. I don't believe that he was sorry about what has happened."

Edward VIII was raised to be king, but only intellectually. "The young usually receive insufficient as well as incorrect guidance or help in the difficult task of maturation. The central role of feelings, and especially of irrational fear, is usually ignored." Emotionally he remained forever a boy, living in a dreamworld and never understanding the concept of work or the moral dilemmas of his day. He admired Hitler and liked cocktail parties, gardening, and golf.

Those who were given unlimited means, ample time, and almost every imaginable opportunity to make a man and a king out of this boy failed grossly. Their basic flaw was in their assumptions about the nature of Man, and their understanding of the educational process was therefore wrong. But these same assumptions remain essentially unchanged even today, and they still are being used throughout the world.

The duke became somewhat interested in public service years later, but it did not amount to much. His belated willingness to serve was only a response to his increasing awareness of the pathetic emptiness of his existence, although rich, well connected and well educated, a charming celebrity, still handsome, and married to the woman of his dreams. He learned very little and much too late. His life was essentially wasted.

Wallis Simpson was often described as a scheming social climber, but she was also an insecure and spoiled child who discovered that her femininity and looks gave her the power to command what appeared to be security. This is a well-traversed path, wide as an avenue, and very commonly used by beautiful and sexy women everywhere from the beginning of time. Both of her previous husbands probably failed in "making her feel safe." A dashing and popular prince would surely use his swift sword to slay the dragon of fear that taunted her mercilessly. It is the stuff that fairy tales are made of, but these two children acted as if it were real. "Most adults are physically grown-up children of various emotional ages." Both Wallis and Edward merely tried to survive, and they had very little choice in what they did.

Wallis liked partying. The highlight of her day was her appointment with her personal hairdresser. The couple had very few intimate friends, but they were always busy attending clubs, shows, and private parties. Edward went along with her, but night life, daily calls to the Swiss stockbroker and banker, and

golf were not enough to fill the next thirty-six years. Disappointment was inevitable. Although they remained together, the duke
was clearly miserable. It was said that he never drank before
seven in the evening but that he drank a lot afterward. A photograph taken before his death at the age of seventy-eight shows
him as a broken and pathetic figure. He probably never understood what happened to him or why.

Those who knew the couple intimately agreed that, tragic as
the whole affair was, everything fit. They were like two little
orphans lost in a dangerous forest. Each idealized the other as
someone powerful enough to allay the fear of abandonment. The
duke needed a strong woman who would rule him, and she was
drawn to him because he was a king, and therefore supposedly
powerful. Tragically, neither was able to do for the other what
each of them needed and wanted. They had no choice but to
cling to each other and to their public facades. Even if they had
understood what had happened, they would have had to continue denying it. He gave up position, power, prestige, and personal dignity for a mirage; she was lost in a dreamworld. They
acted out a fantasy, and then they were stuck in it for life. Their
lives were empty of joy and full of disappointment and pain, in
spite of all the glitter.

No cells were underdeveloped or missing in Edward's brain,
contrary to Baldwin's conjecture. The cortex is simply an irrelevant organ where panic is concerned. Edward's subcortical pathways and his physiologic patterns needed altering. "The
characters of free men and women capable of governing themselves [must be shaped], since no one ever is born free, nor is
anyone free of fear before he or she is freed from it." Edward
could not rule others before he could govern himself.

The struggles of famous men and women with irrational fears
exist in the public domain, and they can therefore be easily examined. What is true for them is equally true for others. We are
all human beings who had a physical life-sustaining attachment
to a mother before we were born. Each of us also had an almost
equally intense emotional attachment to her, or to someone taking her place, during the first hours, days, weeks, and months of
life. These attachments made it possible for us to survive. It
would be unnatural and unlikely for anyone to give up such
important connections willingly or easily at any time.

We may not always want to be near Mother once we do not
need her for actual survival. We may fight her when she dominates our lives. But at any age when we experience anxiety we

normally want someone with the qualities of an ideal mother to stand by us and to comfort us. She comes in many shapes and forms, and is not necessarily an individual or a female. A cause or a male often fulfills the mothering function very successfully. We may be embarrassed by our strong wish to be supported and cared for, and we may also fear not being in complete control, which is why we may deny such wishes. But we really learn to depend upon ourselves only with the greatest of efforts and against the most persistent resistance.

A more ordinary example than Edward is the intelligent, forty-four-year-old, handsome, and competent professor who became involved in a health fad which included a vigorous daily aerobic exercise program. Financially comfortable, professionally successful, and happily married, he was the proud father of three children, "sitting on top of the world." But then, during a routine physical examination, some previously unnoticed irregularities were seen on the electrocardiogram. This could merely be a result of his exercising, he was told. Still he was advised to take it easy for a few days until a stress test confirmed the benign diagnosis, since more serious heart trouble had to be ruled out.

The man panicked. What would he do if he had to be hospitalized? What if he needed a coronary bypass? He was at the prime of his life, he thought, and just beginning to really enjoy himself. His wife and children were still young and full of life. Would he have to slow down and be forced to limit his career and social activities? Would his pretty wife stay with him in his deteriorated condition? Could he still satisfy her sexually? Would she seek the company of others? Would he end up lonely and forgotten, if not dead? Everything was suddenly becoming bleak and dark. The fear of abandonment activated the underlying fear of non-being. He was already busy mourning for himself.

It became more important now than ever before for him not to appear weak. He hid all his fears from everyone, including his wife, even the questionable EKG findings. All went well during the physical examination, he lied to her as he tried to smile. She did not notice his perspiration, the extra tensing of his vocal cords, or his frightened look.

Wishing to maintain his image as powerful, he joined her the next day for their usual exercise class, even though it was stupid, he knew, to take such risks with his heart. But "fear is often responsible for major errors in judgment, since it greatly interferes with the capacity to evaluate what one sees." Losing his life seemed less frightening than losing his wife. Their relationship was solid, but he would take no chances in his panic. She might leave him! The taste of abandonment he knew well from his early beginnings, and he was not about to risk experiencing it again. But the horror of death was only a fantasy, and it appeared less horrible.

His story is in no way exaggerated. We humans can indeed exist without others, but we are reluctant to discover this. Emotional freedom is objectively an advantage; but we are usually not so eager to seek it, since it requires us to give up once and for all the dream of ever finding someone as perfect as an ideal mother. The thought of standing all alone in moments of loneliness and fear generally provokes intense anxiety. Yet by giving up our delusions we make room for our real strength in the real world. We are more powerful and less vulnerable when we are able to look to ourselves for reassurance and for support. Most people pretend that they have already reached this state, but in reality they experience the dread of loss, not the possibility of gain.

Individuation is the *active* process of mourning for dreams that cannot be, without passively becoming resigned to futility. Individuated people have not only more real power but also more energy and more interest in fulfilling possible dreams of their choosing. The process of making oneself whole is outlined in Chapter 6. It will become clear why this process can practically never be finished spontaneously and why it does not occur naturally in humans as part of growing up.

Young animals, by contrast, can fend for themselves soon after birth. But we humans do not run in herds, nor do we swim in schools. We are usually born singly and raised one at a time. Each of us is unique. Man alone among all living creatures was endowed with a "new mammalian brain" that continues to develop during the first two years of life, as we shall see in greater detail in Chapter 3. In a sense we humans are all born prematurely. Not only Macduff was "from his mother's womb untimely ripp'd." Each of us is expelled from the uterus when our body becomes too large to be contained in it. But our cortex becomes fully functional only much later. We can breathe immediately after birth, but many months must pass before we learn to stand tall; much more time must elapse before we begin to understand and to speak. A baby abandoned is a baby dead. Our physical dependency on our caretakers is much longer than that of most other species, much more important to survival, and much more encompassing and complex. It is therefore much more difficult to give up. Most people hold on to various mother substitutes forever, unless such attachments are pried away from them. Subjectively, such emotional attachments are Man's ace in the hole, an emotional insurance policy that he holds on to for as long as possible.

Although we humans are born before we are really ready, everyone is nonetheless immediately regarded as an individual and given a name all his or her own. Each of us has a separate identity, and before long we also develop unique personality characteristics. We have an address, fingerprints, and our own Social Security number. Having been created in God's image, each of us is, like Him, one. We alone among all living creatures must learn to choose right from wrong. The task of becoming a mature adult is infinitely more complex than physically growing up. Humans are very reluctant therefore to ever admit that they have reached the point of full competence. They frequently try to postpone assuming their human responsibilities, and many appear always eager to seek guidance from others.

Sparta stands out as a symbol of hardiness and fortitude in the history of civilization and as a warning against the excessive wish for endless dependence upon others. The actual number of Spartan children that were thrown off the rock to test their mettle was undoubtedly much smaller than the number of people who have learned from this story that one must be stoic and self-disciplined to survive. In part it is metaphor: No child, Spartan or otherwise, was likely to survive such a harsh test; self-indulgence itself may have been the target. Even the Spartans would not let go of Mother's apron strings without pressure; even they had to be forced to become independent. The story condemns the yearning to be cared for beyond childhood.

Many non-Spartans have probably been scared by this story into resisting their push against progressing. "We know our mothers and we . . . hold on to them tenaciously and refuse to let go. In some primitive cultures mothers paint their nipples with a black and bitter substance when their babies are old enough, to force them off the breast." The wish for endless clinging to overcome the fear of abandonment is given up only forcibly, and the harsh example of Sparta serves this purpose. The regressive wish to not grow up can be seen all around us, even if we cannot see it so clearly within us.

The fear of abandonment is as old as Man, but it was more obscure when he lived a simpler and slower life in small communities. The presence of relatives and acquaintances in the immediate vicinity provided relief and prevented this fear from surfacing. Modern transportation, high technology, and affluence made us mobile. We now enjoy ever-expanding horizons and encounter an endless series of new people and new situations. But with all this came anomie and alienation, a sagging sense of identity, loneliness, and the sharper edge of the fear of abandonment.

Physical isolation was not as oppressive when someone related or known to us could be counted on to be nearby. It was easier then to maintain the delusion that we were not all alone in the world. Today suburban life in big and often half-empty houses surrounded by sprawling lawns emphasizes our separated status. Even neighbors are often strangers. Life in apartment complexes with hundreds or even thousands of identical units above and below us, to our right and to our left, is not much better. Those living in such deserts of concrete often experience isolation and fear very acutely. Even though we live among many people, only a few of them have faces. Gray anonymity is modern man's mark of recognition. Desolation and a vague sense of danger are the rule.

Maurice Ravel fought his fear of abandonment by living much of his life in fantasy. He composed his second and final opera, *The Child and the Sorcerers*, in 1924 to a libretto by Colette. It was a story of enchantment, warmth, and surrealism. The director of the Paris Opera and others all agreed that Ravel was the ideal choice to write the music, says a biographer, since "He moved all his life in a world of children and animals." Ravel apparently suffered all through life from being undersized. But unlike Napoleon, who was also physically small, he remained tiny in his inner identity: "The worship of his mother was the center of his life until his 42nd year." Such idealizations generally result out of fear: Only the vanquished sing songs of praise and pay tribute to those who lord over them. Ravel's mother may have meant well and she may have done nothing wrong except to permit such worship. His biographer tells us that Ravel cherished Spanish folk songs and folk dances because of his "devotion" to his Spanish mother, and that he was so fervently attached to that "tender" and "lovely" woman that "no sentiment for any other woman could ever fill his heart. This attachment embraced all the characteristics of his personality, psychological as well as musical."

Some mothers encourage or even demand to be worshipped, and they can enforce compliance because their withdrawal would elicit the terrible fear of abandonment. Ravel lived much of his life in this emotional prison, and that is why he overidentified with the mythological characters of his opera. His throat, we are told, "choked up with tears as the creatures of the opera bent over the child, whispering forgivingly in phrases hardly formed into words." This is what he too was hoping for. His term of imprisonment was lifelong. Yet this seems not to have bothered him, for he was freed in return from having to experience his horrible fear.

Many adults stagnate in destructive relationships because they provide at least minimal protection from the fear of abandonment, while others simply refuse to leave their parents to establish lives of their own. They live with them as fully grown people until one or both parents die. Then they have no choice but to leave. Such middle-aged, or older, men and women often react as if they have indeed finally been "abandoned." Overwhelming panic that shakes a person's entire being often sets in very quickly. In such cases the battle to hold the horrible fear of abandonment at bay has been lost.

2. The Fear of Engulfment

The very same panic that characterizes the fear of abandonment is also found at the root of the fear of engulfment. It is triggered, however, from the exact opposite direction. With every fiber of our being we fear that we will surely cease to be, or at least cease to be ourselves, unless we immediately escape. Safety exists only with enough distance to insure that "they" cannot "swallow," choke, or control us, and that we will not be manipulated, directed, or tricked. Such are the strange images and thoughts, usually co-existing together, that we associate with this fear. A basic protective readiness always exists to push away those who are experienced as coming too close. The fear of engulfment can be held in check as long as control is maintained of all relationships with others.

Salvation appears in the form of physical or emotional isolation. This does not always mean living alone, as William Holden and Howard Hughes did near the end of their days. Many who fear engulfment marry or become involved in other relationships, and they can have acquaintances and even friends of a sort. Social activity often hides the fear, both from those who have it and from others, since such contacts can remain forever superficial and formal. But something is fundamentally wrong in such relationships, which becomes evident sooner or later because the wives, husbands, or partners sense that their mates are "not there," even when they are present. Such involvements are usually devoid of real intimacy and trust. Emotional isolation can be more insulating than real walls. People who greatly fear engulfment experience intense anxiety whenever their threshold of safety is trespassed by anyone, and they will go to almost any length to avoid needing others, which would render them vulnerable. Almost more than anything else, they have an excessive fear of becoming old, poor, or debilitated, a burden upon anyone, even their own children. This is why they tend to be stoic and why they want to be known as strong. Not necessarily believing it consciously, they act as if they know that all people are essentially unreliable or self-serving, capricious and possibly even malicious. They often prefer the company of pets over that of humans.

This fear sometimes shows in the fanaticism with which such people dismiss tenderness, sensitivity, and honest self-disclosure —which invite others to come closer—as signs of weakness. They often most distrust their mates, friends, lovers, and therapists—the people who could hurt them most. People are presumed guilty unless they have proven themselves innocent, meticulously and repeatedly. The fear is easily recognized by the excessive and endless worry about being controlled. Those fearing engulfment understandably tend to be very suspicious of and hostile to all authority. They are the perpetual rebels, even when they seem to conform. Their typical response to a friendly invitation is a cold or impatient shrug, if not a withdrawn silence.

The fear of engulfment is much more widespread than is commonly known. Like the fear of abandonment it is universal, but not generally quite so devastating. It is likely to beget endless emptiness and fatigue. "Loneliness is the best friend I ever had," said one such person who eventually committed suicide. Even death seemed preferable to close involvement with others. He remembered hearing repeatedly as a child that "a boy's first duty is to look after his mother." He learned his lesson very well. "She is a good, hardworking, and modest poor woman," he used to say of his mother, and "nobody out there takes care of her." So he did. Unable to free himself of the enslavement that he hated yet feared to let go of, he drank. This, he hoped, would drown his hopeless rage. He was trapped. He would immediately experience the panic of abandonment when he distanced himself a little from either mother or wife, yet he felt "sucked dry" by their quiet but incessant demands when near them. They appeared so weak, meek, and suffering that he felt guilty for even wishing to escape. His suicide note read: "I was born to a mother without a vagina, but with two mouths. The demands are unsatisfiable. Someone like me is hopeless. Goodbye."

For such people, existence is always at the margin, and "home" always lies beyond the next minefield. Fear keeps them from moving, and this condemns them to stay out in the cold. Practically everybody is regarded as a threat. Those suffering from extreme fear of engulfment often live as if they actually sense that their psychological "skin" is incomplete. Without such a self-containing layer, all closeness is felt to be dangerous, since the possibility of fusion with another is a constant threat. Separateness is never assured. "They" are always more powerful and expect us to merge with them and to become their mindless appendages.

This stunted ability to trust others regularly interferes with the formation of lasting relationships, except with those who are equally scared. But the unseen fear often surfaces even in more casual contacts and it shows when such people must entrust their bodies to physicians, their possessions to financial institutions, or their secrets to friends and associates. The fear also keeps them from really relaxing: They customarily work so hard at it that they are more tired after they try. Vacations aren't enjoyable either when it is unsafe to lower one's guard at any time. Even yielding to sleep is sometimes too frightening, and chronic insomnia results. They find it very difficult to take it easy, since it would prove them to be mortal, not supermen and superwomen as they like to appear.

To be a little weak, vulnerable, welcoming, or friendly is to expose oneself to the danger of being taken over. Those busy with evading this fear of engulfment are usually driven therefore to seek more power, more money, and more influence in order to strengthen their position. Yet none of these are ever enough, since the hidden purpose of getting "more" is to conquer irrational fear. Rational explanations of the irrationality and futility of such pursuits by parents, prophets, or psychotherapists never make much of a difference. The hidden fear is recognizable also in stinginess, in hoarding, and in the inability to give generously of oneself, even to oneself.

When the ability to give food, enjoyment, or respect to oneself is badly damaged, such conditions as anorexia nervosa and its apparent opposite, obesity, may be the result. Both are character-ized by an angry holding out against and by the tenacious thwart-ing of the efforts of those who wish to force a change, even in the direction of survival and health. Both are dangerous and sometimes actually self-destructive solutions to the problem of having to fight back all intruders. They are but two examples of the many ways people find to overcome the fear of engulfment. Those who experience themselves as basically powerless and small really do not know that adults have more effective meth-ods of asserting themselves.

An unwillingness or inability to accept gifts given freely is another sign of this debilitating fear: One should never be in-debted. From this perspective, it appears that gifts are never really free. Even legitimate help is often regarded suspiciously and rejected.

Difficulties in reaching orgasm, especially in women, and pre-mature as well as retarded ejaculation can also be traced to this fear, which causes bodies to tighten up under such circum-stances. Being on guard and on constant alert obviously inter-feres with the ability to welcome anyone gently. Psychogenic infertility may sometimes result. If symptom-oriented sex ther-apy fails to bring relief, then the fear of engulfment must be tackled directly, as explained in Chapter 6.

Two opposing forces are in powerful confrontation within each of us, probably even before birth: the wish to remain safe within the womb, where all our physiological needs are con-stantly met, and the wish to break out and exercise our own will. These same two forces are in even greater competition once the young child becomes mobile. It resents being held when it wants to move and explore the world. Yet whenever something frightens the child, it rushes back to Mother to be protected. The range of movement expands with the child's curiosity and con-fidence, but then the cycle is repeated again. To frustate either of these two forces arbitrarily or insensitively is to cause lasting damage, as we shall soon see.

Weaning from the breast or from the psychological protection of a mother must be gradual, though perfect timing is rarely achieved. As a result, some people continue to have a powerful lingering desire to be seen at all times, and guided, even as adults, which reflects their fear of being abandoned. Other peo-ple have more fear of being manipulated, and they are forever preoccupied with protecting their freedom to choose and to de-cide, as if someone were always eager to rob them of it. People who fear engulfment the most are fanatic in their defense of "human rights."

The fears of engulfment and of abandonment are flip sides of the same irrational panic-in-existence, an ill-defined but real sense of dread that must be attended to. Most people work hard to keep it out of awareness. They dare not stop to find out whether there is a better way to handle it. Few of us wish or dare to face the ghosts of the past that torture us in the present, especially when we experience them as threatening our very existence.

For the newborn it is said to be good when the mother's nurturing breast is available and bad when it is absent. But this is a gross oversimplification. In reality, the available breast is only a source of comfort when the infant is hungry, either for food or for the security that sucking provides. The breast that is not withdrawn soon after the baby is satiated, or the one that blocks the infant's breathing, is also experienced as bad, and sometimes as deadly. It elicits anger, terror, or both. The helpless infant may actually learn to associate closeness with choking, thereby establishing "pushing-away" pathways in the visceral brain. The basic quality of our earliest experiences with mothering determines our lifelong susceptibility to the fears of abandonment and of engulfment. One or the other of these two forces is typically predominant within each person. "But the proportional strength of each changes from time to time, depending on later life experiences."

Anger and fear do not exist as distinct feelings at the very beginning of life, only as a generalized sensation of discomfort or of danger. This grips the baby when it experiences itself exposed and lacking attachments or orientation, or when the huge physical presense of Mother limits its breathing or interferes with its ability to move. Such moments have occurred in everyone's life, and they result from Mother's own anxiety, tiredness, or insensitivity. When frequent enough, they condition the baby to reject physical closeness itself. Mothers who are inadequate and very anxious tend to hold on to their very young babies too tightly and for too long in order to comfort themselves, thus making future closeness seem dangerous to the child.

Such early experiences also determine the baby's basic attitudes about power. An insensitive and overbearing mother raises children to be powerless victims who throughout life automatically overempathize with the downtrodden. They tend to favor the consumer and side against the manufacturer. They are usually vocal in their opposition to strong central leaderships and meticulous in assuring that enough checks and balances are in place. They are anarchists at heart, if not in mind. They see a scheming cult leader lurking behind every legitimate authority. Even as grownups they have relatively little freedom to make real choices. They continue to experience the world from the perspective of powerlessness, and in elections they generally vote their fears, not usually knowingly. They are against big business, big government, big labor. They are against organized religion, even if they belong to a church. These are the people who are most vociferous in protesting the death penalty and who see the evil influence of the military-industrial establishment everywhere. They often support conservationism and the preservation of endangered species because they overidentify with those who are threatened. The fear of being engulfed is at the root of their strong conviction that invariably "power corrupts and absolute power corrupts absolutely."

Are we humans really so predictable? Generally, yes. Do we really have so little choice? Again, generally speaking, yes. Many of our attitudes are determined by our earliest experiences with power and with powerlessness. Such a view of Man is not flattering. We want to see ourselves as masters of our lives and as capable of making real choices. Yet the power of our earliest fears is so great that unless we free ourselves of them they will determine most of our political, economic, and moral values.

Mothers whose main fear is of abandonment raise children with more than the usual fear of engulfment, while those who most fear engulfment raise children with more than the usual fear of abandonment. Mothers who fear engulfment often experience even the demands of their newly born children as unreasonable and excessive, and they attend to their babies only poorly. Grossly inadequate mothering is not necessarily the result of evil intentions, and even extreme fears in children are no proof of parents' malice. More often they are merely evidence of deep pathology. (Chapter 5 addresses some of our difficult dilemmas in this regard.) Pathologic cruelty and uncontrolled violence are always inexcusable for any reason, since they are so destructive; but they are probably not as common as it appears these days. Fear magnifies any horror. Even average people with good intentions who really try to be good parents often produce emotionally damaged offspring, since nobody is able to exceed the harsh limits imposed by fear.

Life often resembles a balancing act between these fears of

being abandoned and of being engulfed. The first pushes us to be near, the second to be far. The first is alleviated when others come to us and cater to us, the second when they leave us alone and don't intrude. Everyone has experienced physical closeness as a source of security, inner peace, and pleasure—but also of pain, rage, and fear. We long to be taken care of but also to be the masters of our own fate. We proclaim ourselves weak so we may be helped, but also strong so we will not be taken advantage of. The balance we seek is for these two fears to interfere with our freedom the least.

If we had unlimited power and unlimited wisdom to use it, we would adjust our environment continuously to fit all our changing contradictions. Since we do not possess either, we must forever adjust ourselves—with or without awareness—a time-consuming, strength-depleting, and difficult task.

The pushing away that minimizes the fear of engulfment typically takes the form of angry, unfriendly, impatient, bitter, hateful, threatening, loud, disoriented, or violent behavior. People are sloppy, dirty, or smelly sometimes for the same reason. We usually assume such behavior automatically, without realizing how effectively we convey our subliminal messages.

Daredevil acts are also used to ward off this fear. To appear invincible and even unafraid when others cower demonstrates strength and shows that we need no one. Being subordinate or dependent, by contrast, is intolerable and therefore to be avoided at all costs. Even career "choices" are made to avoid this possibility. An independent businessman, contractor, or farmer is not told what to do by others. New recruits in the armed forces often get into trouble because of their fear of being submissive, as some graduate students do in highly regimented professional schools such as medicine and law. Many of the brightest flunk out despite years of painful, tedious, expensive, and dedicated preparation because they fear being engulfed in a highly competitive struggle.

When yielding is experienced as submission or as a defeat, chronic difficulties must be expected in marriages and in other long-term relationships. These require a mutual willingness to compromise, an impossible goal for those who fear engulfment. Marriages may last if the fears of the spouses are somehow balanced, but such relationships typically become an arena in which power is constantly being tested. In this tragic struggle, partners fearing engulfment often use the open or the implied threat of abandonment as a powerful weapon against mates who are affected by it. This is an effective tool with which to control the distance in the relationship. Those who fear engulfment generally find mates, friends, and acquaintances who simply are too weak, too needy, or too scared to pose any threat. Unconscious choices cleverly satisfy both parties' pathologic needs. Both healthy and unhealthy relationships can continue to exist for many years as long as the emotional needs of both partners remain essentially stable and balanced. In this narcissistic era of affluence and sexual permissiveness, they tend to disintegrate, however, much more frequently than before. Still, the glue of fear can hold people together for a very long time, even today.

Fear of being hurt and perhaps even destroyed is usually one potent factor contributing to male and female homosexuality. Homosexuals perceive the opposite sex as less kind, less sensitive, less loving, and more abusive. The fear of engulfment is increased by close encounters with members of the other gender. Although homosexuals are labeled by sexual preference, sex is only a minor consideration in their choice of partners. Neither love nor sex draws people into serious relationships. Many would deny this, because otherwise they would have to accept and to acknowledge the centrality of fear in their lives. Like heterosexuals, homosexuals also form partnerships to lessen fear and to maximize human satisfaction. Most would readily admit that the non-sexual aspects of their lives with their mates are the more important. In this sense homosexuality is no different from heterosexuality. When the initial flurry of any sexual excitement is over, practically all stable relationships must provide some degree of comfort: Lowered anxiety is the most important component of this state.

The presence of this fear of engulfment also explains some of the strange paradoxes of sado-masochistic relationships. When closeness itself is experienced as a threat, sexual gratification that depends upon loving intimacy and trust is not possible. Intimacy requires that we disarm ourselves before approaching others, yet those with ill-defined personal boundaries often feel extremely vulnerable when in close proximity to anyone. The prospect of intimacy seems self-destructive. But sado-masochistic relationships do not require such vulnerability: Here pleasure is largely derived from having a sense of power. Close contacts involving physical pain are not experienced as a threat. Psychological and real arms and armor have a place in relationships of dominance or submission. Closeness of this type is not only tolerable but also enjoyable. The sadist experiences power in the relationship directly, the masochist indirectly by tolerating and even by seeking gross physical abuse. The sense of power nullifies the fear of engulfment for a while. The sado-masochistic relationship permits a distorted form of closeness that is guaranteed to permit no merging.

The masochistic partner is usually thought to be the victim of the sadist, but in reality both are. Neither dares to be tender and trusting in a relationship based on mutual love and respect. The sadist becomes sexually excited from having the power to inflict pain, the masochist from enduring it. Both escape their sense of powerlessness while hiding their extreme fear of engulfment.

Power-hungry political aspirants seeking support for their cause often exploit the fear of engulfment, a specter so frightening to so many people that it has often swept dictatorships into power. The fear has also been fanned to divert rage and frustration away from rulers who would otherwise have been overthrown. An internal or external group is first designated as an enemy, and it becomes the focus of hate, anger, and physical abuse. As in sado-masochistic relationships, the abusers feel less anxious and more potent once they vent their hate on those who are unable to protect themselves. Mobilizing against any enemy minimizes fear in personal relationships as well. Husbands and wives often use each other this way, employing anger to hold their own fears in check. Imaginary enemies or grievances are quickly invented to serve this purpose when real ones are not conveniently available.

Even poverty, disease, and injustice can be used as common enemies in societies that would not tolerate hatred of racial or religious minorities. As long as hate of something can be fanned, internal turbulence can be temporarily ignored, as we shall see more clearly when we examine "hate" in Chapter 4. Hitler selected Jews and gypsies as his target; Joe McCarthy, creeping Communism. The most visible group or the most powerful can easily be made to look like the greatest danger. This is why the Soviet Union, the Ayatollah Khomeini, and Fidel Castro vilify U.S. "imperialism" so consistently. Still, many Americans naively fail to understand this classic device of political survival, and they try to prove their goodness and fairness, even to terrorists and outlaws, as if these were the issue.

When a common enemy disappears, rage that no longer has an

outlet becomes generalized and fear increases. Dictators are therefore usually in a hurry to find a new enemy as the focus of hate and terror. Internal minorities are obviously the best target, since they are present where needed and easily reachable. Khomeini's mass executions of Iranians and the Khmer Rouge's genocide of Cambodians not only changed the composition of each society but they also served to channel the hate that was previously directed at the Shah and at the U.S. The Russian intelligentsia was designated as the new Enemy of the People once the Bolsheviks had eliminated the Czar and the bourgeoisie. Ethnic minorities and Jewish doctors came next on Stalin's hate list, followed by the small neighboring Baltic states. Territorial expansions by force of arms are usually explained as measures taken to insure relief from the danger of engulfment.

Hitler used propaganda as if he understood the deep and primitive roots of the fear of engulfment consciously. Strict upbringing in the Prussian tradition probably sensitized the Germans to this fear, and Hitler regularly incited his followers by fanning it, using powerful sexual imagery. A young, blond, blue-eyed, buxom but innocent German maiden was often portrayed as the target of scheming, greasy, dark-eyed, long-nosed non-Aryans who would contaminate her unless all Germans united to preserve racial purity. In this context his exhortations sounded almost virtuous, an appeal not only to self-defense but also to decency.

No election campaign is ever totally free of appeals to this and to other primitive fears. Though Western democracies usually shun crass appeals to base emotions, at least traces of them are found here also. The readiness to react to the fear of engulfment is never far from consciousness.

Why was or is the United States eager to deploy MX missiles, to develop a "Star Wars" defense, or to station Pershing missiles in Western Europe? Why have the Soviets marched into Afghanistan, Czechoslovakia, and Hungary? Why are they threatening Western Europe, China, and the U.S.? Why do both superpowers spend such a large percentage of their gross national product on defense, at the expense of urgent social programs? Because their people fear engulfment by others, militarily, politically, and personally. We respond so readily to the manifestations of this fear in the outside world because we know its power inside ourselves so very well. But while essentially irrational in personal affairs, it often is valid in the reality of international relations.

3. The Fear of Non-Being

Of all the fears of Man, the fear of non-being is the first to appear, the most horrible to experience, and the most prevalent. It is so terrible, however, that it has remained basically unknown as a separate phenomenon till now. Yet it leaves its traces everywhere.

Proof for the existence of this fear, as for the curving of space postulated by Einstein, cannot generally be obtained by direct observations with our senses. Much of it must be deduced by inference, based on the many clues that we find in the lives of most people. It is the most primitive of Man's fears and it exists at the root of the two others.

If we did not succeed in warding off the fears of abandonment or engulfment, we might sense a trace of the vague, featureless, cold, black, and totally silent fear of non-being. We cannot pinpoint its beginning and we always wish its end, but without ever being aware of it consciously. The fear of non-being is not experienced as a presence but only as an absence, a void with an ill-defined outline, a hovering possibility of dread. Although these descriptions sound poetic, the sensations are real.

The fear of non-being is not the same as the fear of death. Death is a clearly understandable state, even if our legal definition of it is changing as our sophistication about it increases. Death is irreversible, incurable, finite, and associated with specific and predictable physiologic changes. It is followed by rituals such as funerals and mourning. Our understanding of death is a source of comfort to us, since we fear the unknown infinitely more. The horrors of non-being are not anchored in any known reality, and they are therefore wild and limitless. Man has always sought knowledge because certainty diminishes the domain of the unknown, where his most terrifying fears dwell. Even the most horror-filled conscious fantasies are preferable to the terrifying non-images of the unconscious fear of non-being.

How do we know that this fear actually exists and what its nature is? We used to have to infer it from observations of infants; we can now directly observe traces of it in adults who panic in psychotherapy sessions and temporarily lose their capacity to "know" reality as it really is. Without totally losing contact, they sometimes find themselves unable to think for a few minutes. They shake; they sweat profusely or become faint; their eyes widen and dart rapidly in real terror; and they have an almost irresistible urge to run for their lives, even though they are in no real danger. Such reactions can be observed directly, photographed, and examined soon thereafter. They occur only in environments that are very safe and that are perceived as such. Under such circumstances the body can risk dipping into this horrible fear for a few moments. At other times this fear causes us to freeze and to react as if we were totally powerless. A smell, a sound, a long-forgotten gesture, or a motion can elicit traces of this fear; but it is never cognitively experienced and identifiable when one is all alone.

The existence of the fear of non-being is also confirmed in daily life. Just about everyone has sometimes experienced an "unexplainable" sense of suddenly falling from great heights, as if the earth itself were not solid enough to hold us securely. Most people have also known a sense of impending doom, "for no reason at all," as they have had dreams of dropping into emptiness. The images in such dreams vary, but the sensation is always dread. Our hearts pound very rapidly, we suddenly flinch, and only then can we sleep more peacefully. The bodily reactions are often all that we remember upon awakening: We still shake a bit or sweat, and our heart rate may still be faster than normal. Happily, the frightening images are usually forgotten quickly.

Man has always invented graphic details about the unknown to minimize the sense of danger. He attempted to "know" through his fantasies that which was not repressible and also not reachable by his limited knowledge. This is what mythology consists of. It was easy to determine what happens to the body after death, but is was too terrifying to contemplate the mystery of what happens to our personality, our "human essence." To assume that it also decomposes and vanishes was simply too dreadful a possibility. All civilizations have "discovered" therefore the details of "life" after death, and many have developed elaborate and expensive rituals to ease the "passage."

The hidden treasures in the tombs of the kings of ancient Egypt are the best known example of this preparation for the unknown. Today ultra-Orthodox Jews in Jerusalem riot against archaeological digs that might desecrate 2,000-year-old graves. According to their tradition, when the Messiah comes to redeem mankind "at the end of days," the dead shall live again. Every morning these God-fearing people rise to watch whether the Messiah's entourage can already be seen in the distance, and they fear that the dead may miss the revival if their "rest" is disturbed. The stone-throwing protesters in Jerusalem believe such details with a fervent but childlike innocence, even if their acts are fanatic. The digs are fought with as much fury as one would muster in an attempt to prevent the murder of innocents. Those irreverent archaeologists might doom the dead to remain dead forever just as they are about to rise again! How is it, they must wonder sometimes, that non-believers fail to understand the obvious logic of their virtuous acts of protest?

Poor and simple folk everywhere have often slaved extra hard throughout life to assure that they will "rest in peace," at least after they die. This fantasy about the good life after death anchors the otherwise horrible and featureless images about what might happen later on. The emotions evoked by the possibility of nothingness after life, and after death, resemble too much the dread and more dread that we actually had to endure in the nothingness before we knew that we existed.

The newborn does not know what life is or that it ends in death. Since it knows nothing, it is also unable to give any meaning to its many sensations of being groundless, disoriented, and filled with the precursors of dread. (Chapter 2 will describe the origins of this seemingly endless absence of constancy.) Any sudden change in the internal or external environment of the newborn reawakens the barely slumbering fear of non-being, which squeezes, pressures, pulls, and tears at the infant as if it were a powerful giant and not merely a fragile little organism. Such experiences have many causes but no regular rhythm, so the newborn cannot brace itself physiologically in anticipation. It must be ready to respond to the unexpected at any moment. It also has no notion of time and therefore no capacity to anticipate a better future. No choice exists but to be constantly alert with only brief moments of relative relaxation. The subjective sense of danger at the beginning of life was titanic indeed. Man must not allow such a fear ever to reappear.

Our bodily reactions in adulthood "remember" the confusion and the terror from the time when only feelings existed and no thinking. Thought was not "knocked out" by our panic, it simply did not yet exist then. Even decades later as fully grown people we continue to dread the possibility of helplessness and we dare not let go of understanding and thinking: We normally use these to protect ourselves. But what about the things that we cannot know? We construct delusions about the unknown future and make them up to look like facts, to save us from the physiologic "memories" of the past. When faced with much uncertainty, our body tends to react as if it were still in danger of experiencing those old horrors again. Many people "worry" that even thoughts about non-being might bring the faceless terror back. This is too much to risk. Early infancy was so full of dread because it happened before we had any tools to help us get oriented. Our conscious capacity to understand and to think is indeed the basis of our sanity and of our power to control things within and about us. It is obvious why Man has elevated thinking and knowing to a height even beyond what they deserve. Since we do not do well without understanding, we also invented explanations for the unknowable nature of God in every age and in all civilizations. Such beliefs dispelled non-knowing, which always had been associated with this fear.

People generally hope that when death comes it will be swift, involving no torture, fear, or pain. We wish to end our journey on earth suddenly, like Moses or old Indians on their mountain-tops, as if by a kiss. We dread some things even more than death, such as continuous suffering without the ability even to die. It is not uncommon to harbor a secret wish that some loved one would help expedite our last ordeal if needed. Suicide only occurs because it appears as a way out of a horror worse than dying —a life seen as a curse, whatever its actual content. Those lost in an endless black tunnel pray for death to free them. Free them of what? Of living with hopelessness, at the bottom of which, lurking in hiding, lies this most horrible of all fears, the fear of non-being.

It is a terrible fear, perhaps best described in the following dream: "I was very small, the size of a fingernail, and very light in weight, like a petal of a flower, and I was floating on the surface of a huge bathtub filled with water. It was not like swimming in a lake, because I was totally unable to move and did not have any power at all. I could not even thrash about and play with the water. I was just floating, unable to determine my course in any way. Suddenly someone had removed the plug from the drain, and the water level began to recede quickly. I could still move my eyes, so I watched with horror what was happening. My eyes soon got transfixed on the huge gaping hole, which was fast growing bigger and which sucked everything in very hungrily. I found myself soon at the edge of a large whirl-pool, twisting and turning faster and faster. The speed increased as the circle became smaller, and I became dizzy. It was like being driven crazily at speeds of several hundred miles per hour in an open convertible, without anything to hold on to. Everything turned gray, then white, or maybe black. Surely I was but an eye-blink away from being swallowed up. My heart seemed to stop beating and I did not breathe. Then I woke up. Cold sweat was running down my forehead."

Floating helplessly on top of a fast-emptying bathtub evokes, in a weakened form, the same feelings that one might have in endless outer space, suspended in total darkness, emptiness, isolation, and silence. All sense of direction is soon lost. Time quickly becomes indistinguishable and continuous, filled with the unending expectation that every next moment will be worse than the one before. An unseen "black hole," in which everything disappears forever without leaving any trace, is constantly coming nearer. Yet we never quite reach even that. The dream at least provided the dreamer with intelligible content, that of horrible engulfment. The fear of non-being that was evoked by it does not have even that. No conscious images are conjured up by it. It lies below them.

A sense of helplessness and hopelessness is associated with all irrational fears, but it is worse with the fear of non-being. It is totally disabling. Anyone in such a position would surely try to find some attachment to hold on to "for dear life." Mates, lovers, charismatic leaders, cults, and causes—anything will do at such desperate moments. This in fact is the soil from which cults sprout, and the continuing anxiety is what sustains them. Lesser fears always yield to greater ones. The fear of engulfment takes a back seat whenever the fear of non-being becomes the driver. First of all we must be. Second we must not be abandoned. Only last must we not be engulfed. All three fears often co-exist, although one or another is usually dominant.

Newborns do not know of bathtubs or of engulfment, and they cannot make up lesser horrors to comfort themselves with. Their terror is faceless and meaningless; and their sense of dread and doom is pervasive, everlasting, and totally out of control. And yet babies often seem to be carefree and even "happy" before they begin to be conscious. Such contentment is the result of contacts that babies make with objects, with other people, or with themselves. A sense of orientation and of being grounded brings with it relatively brief absences of fear. This pattern of recurring internal instability alternating with short moments of contentment often remains true throughout life. Physiologically, the neonate "expects" danger and pain even before it "expects" any pleasure from the nipple or from the thumb, both of which appear equally external, often unreachable, and generally uncontrollable. The sense of dread associated with the next unknown stimulus is the fear of non-being.

The first few hours, days, and weeks are the crucial period in the life of the newborn. With time, every little bit of knowledge gained diminishes dread. Babies are the fastest learners: A whole new world is literally emerging for them. They are actually flushed with the excitement of discovery as they gain consciousness. The fear of non-being is quickly forgotten as it recedes. As the years pass, we even push the memories of the old horrors out of consciousness, thus "hoping" to rid ourselves of the vulnerability to them. It is a neat and courageous attempt to do the undoable.

Though no images of the fear of non-being exist in us normally, it evokes recognizable sensations in practically everyone alive. These produce measureable changes in many of the body's functions, and they can be observed in sleeping infants, for example. They sometimes suddenly shake violently, as if they had just lost their footing, and they often awaken with a cry of fear. What settles them down most quickly is being held by someone calm and competent. Such physical closeness is similar to the intrauterine experience of being snugly embraced. Very young infants exist in a state known as "normal autism" all the time, except for the fleeting moments when they have such security-providing physical contact. This brings temporary relief from the ongoing dread and it enables them to begin exploring the external world. The newborn also gives solace to itself automatically by rubbing, rocking, socking, pulling, or pushing one member of its body against another, or against an external object. These are obviously not purposeful activities but only random contacts made when two separate parts find each other. Although both may belong to the same body, the parts do not "know" this, and they seem as glad to couple with each other as two lost orphans would in a dark forest. The sensory stimulation temporarily relieves the emptiness of disconnectedness and of total isolation.

Young babies suck their thumbs, for example, because the act brings about a sensation of physical wholeness. A circle is completed, an open circuit closed. The exposed thumb covers and protects the exposed palate, even as it is simultaneously covered and protected by it. Such experiences have been observed in utero. They represent the biological basis of the "knowledge" that close physical contact provides a sense of security. The forms and means of coupling become much more complex later in life, but the sense of security provided by the experience remains basically the same. Holding and touching also relieve the sense of dread in adulthood. In the absence of another person we attempt to do our own comforting by touching or by rocking ourselves, by filling our internal emptiness with food or with alcohol, and by numbing ourselves with drugs. Failing in all these, we hold on to an imaginary reality with the help of ruminations, hallucinations, and psychosis. Somehow we try to survive.

The newborn lives in its own little internal world. The experiences of sensory-deprived adults offer us reliable clues about the nature of that existence early in life. Even well-adjusted and sane grownups become disoriented in a very short time. They begin hallucinating not much later. Even after receiving regular external stimuli for decades we still need a constant flow of auditory, visual, and other contacts to maintain our sanity, our orientation, even our ability to recognize people well known to us. Apparently we cannot store such experiences for more than a few hours. We need frequent reminders as to our current situation. The newborn has none, and in its "mindlessness" it is unable to receive any.

Daydreams and hallucinations may well be desperate efforts by withdrawn or autistic people to restore contact with some "reality," even if it is one only invented for this purpose. The organism apparently seeks even imaginary stimuli to help it orient itself. (Night dreams may serve a similar function for anyone asleep, although they also have other purposes.) To regard hallucinations merely as expressions of insanity, rather than as extreme and unsuccessful attempts to restore sanity, is a leftover from a less sophisticated past in which we classified emotional disturbances according to observable behavior. Most professionals grossly underestimate the power of irrational fears even today, and thus they pay most attention to behavioral disturbances rather than to these forces. But psychosis really is an attempt to cope with crippling fear that is experienced as threatening survival itself, just as inflammation is a reparative attempt by the body to fight threatening infection. The swelling accompanying inflammation may cause brain damage and even death when in the tight confines of the skull, even though it normally heals rather than kills. The same with psychosis: It helps cope with the horrible fear of non-being. Hallucinations may be jumbled, distorted, or confused pictures of reality; but even if they make only crazy sense, they are much more desirable to the one experiencing them than the absence of any sense at all.

Only the fear of non-being is terrible enough so that insanity and even death are preferred over it. People do not generally know how to protect themselves against this fear in a less extreme fashion because it has no recognizable features. How does anyone fight an unknown, unseen, and faceless enemy? It is impossible to determine at whom and where to strike, when to escape, or even where to. The ghosts we fear have describable features; darkness teems with creatures that have imaginary outlines, and phobias relate to specific dangers. Not knowing who stalks us or from which direction we might be hit is how we experience the nebulous and terrifying fear of non-being, the ultimate in vulnerability, "unknowability," and danger. Even cancer, which most people fear so much, has a known development and outcome.

Knowing correctly that we are who we are, where and when we are—as well as what, where, and who we are not—is what sanity consists of. A correct assessment of our self—where we begin and where we end, what is now, what was before and what comes later, what is outside of us and what is inside—allows us to relate to others sensibly. If we do not sense our own boundaries clearly, we must create distances between ourselves and others. We might not remain distinct otherwise. A fuzzy definition of oneself breeds generalized confusion about others. Are we who we are, or Napoleon? Are we here or in heaven, human or frog, awake or asleep, alive or walking-dead?

Yet even the confusion of psychosis does not obliterate the fact that there is something we call "ourselves." A person may believe that he is Jesus Christ, but at least he "knows" that he is somebody. The newborn infant does not possess even such a confused, but in many ways reassuring, picture of reality. It knows nothing.

Since the newborn experiences without comprehension, it is not like a psychotic person but more like a fish. Even worse, unlike the fish it is oblivious to real danger but not immune from the physical sensations of imaginary danger. A sense of imminent doom almost continuously "alerts" its tissues. But unlike the brain of the fish, the visceral brain of the newborn that is being "programmed" to respond to perceived danger, eventually becomes part of a conscious, reasoning being. In spite of the cortex, this visceral brain will continue to exist, and to control the automatic or autonomic functions of the organism in later years also. The highly developed new mammalian brain will eventually integrate all phenomena that it can recognize.

But how can even such a miraculous organ integrate faceless phenomena that it has no knowledge of? The "programmed" reactions to the fear of non-being were "registered" only in the visceral brain, and the nebulous outlines of this fear were never "seen" by the eyes that are controlled by the cortex. This explains why the cortex is blind to it. Knowledge of the fear of non-being, unlike the fears of being, is not obtainable by direct observation. We can know it only by piecing together the puzzle from the many fragments that we have collected.

What happens as infants come out of their normal autism? They are usually eager to discover the world when they dare, thus liberating themselves from the nothingness of non-relationships and diminishing their fear of non-being. Their subjective experience is that they have survived forever without any help from anyone. They do not know that anything or anyone existed before them. Slowly they are discovering an emerging mothering figure, but they must regard her with mixed emotions. Dependency on her is wonderful. Even an imperfect mother provides many satisfying, reliable, and consistent experiences. She sometimes responds with warmth, solidity, softness, and nourishment, and also with reassuring, pleasant, and rhythmic sounds. In addition she provides a nipple to couple with—almost as good, but not quite as reliable, as the thumb. She is not always present at moments of panic.

But if Mother is infantile, inconsistent, or grossly incompetent, we do not trust too much of ourselves into her care. We remain much of the time within the subjectively safe, if confining, shell of our shut-in selves, at least partially withdrawn and autistic. We tend to continue coupling with ourselves as before. We are much more experienced by then and can find our thumb with greater ease and speed. Sucking, rocking, rubbing, pulling, and pushing all provide us with autistic opportunities for coupling with our own body or with our favorite blanket or doll. Without any consciousness, each of us had to face the most critical existential dilemma of all: Whither security?

Although we are poorly equipped to make such "choices," they are nonetheless made by everyone alive. Very few people remain completely autistic throughout life, but the tendency to remain withdrawn in lesser degrees is the rule rather than the exception. Many withdrawn children and some adults who appear as organically retarded eventually develop normally, if late, proving that they were never really deficient, except functionally. Other organically intact children of very immature and disturbed mothers remain forever at the margin of existence. They may thrive physically but not intellectually, emotionally, or socially. They are practically indistinguishable from the organically retarded.

Why would anyone pay the high price of autism? Because something more valuable than all the gratifications from the outside is obtained in return: the avoidance of fears, especially the fear of non-being. The autistic shell isolates the organism from experiencing reality in general, and it protects it from experiencing fear. It is an extremely expensive solution, but those who know of no better way to survive are often willing to pay even this price. "The push away from fear or dread supersedes everything."

4. Self-Coupling vs. Self-Love

Basic concepts of dynamic psychology must be revised in light of these observations. The avoidance of "unpleasure" is obviously not a main motivating force of human behavior; avoidance of fear is. Freud did not really succeed in explaining why anyone would ever give up the "pleasure principle" in favor of reality. Heinz Hartmann tried in 1964 to fill this gap by claiming that "if the infant finds himself in a situation of need, and if attempts toward hallucinatory gratification have proved disappointing, he will turn toward reality; and the repetition of such situations will gradually teach him better to know reality and to strive for those real changes."

But hallucinations are not necessarily disappointing for infants or even for adults. They helped the infant survive when it had to face, alone, the most horrible of all fears. Besides "striving requires much self-control" and a taste for mastery, and no infants—or even many adults—possess either. There is a much better explanation for our turn toward reality. The Spartan children mentioned earlier in this chapter are a good illustration; even they had to be forced to leave delusions behind.

Most people give up autistic living, but only slowly, hesitatingly, cautiously, and seldom totally. We do retain the capacity to live in unreality, and we often use it—when we are lost in our thoughts, when we act according to our feelings, and when we ignore reality temporarily while awake and during sleep. Above all, we keep the option of living in delusions full-time when we experience externality as intolerable. Man has always been comforted by the knowledge that the exit doors of suicide and insanity are never too far away.

If the competition between pleasure and reality were totally free, the outcome would clearly favor the first. As a species we are well known for indulging "the desires of our heart" at the expense of our real self-interest. What else did the prophets of old warn against, and why do preachers today still exhort us from every pulpit? It is necessary to remind us again and again that the rewards of a mature and thoughtful life are greater. We do not give up the natural tendency to live by pursuing pleasure unless we are forced to do so by consistent, fair, and unrelenting fathering.

Self-coupling comes easier. This is how we all began life. In this mode of living—popularly known as narcissism—unpleasant or painful aspects of external reality do not affect us much, since we are exclusively preoccupied with ourselves. This is the "pleasure" of infants and of many adults, and it must be given up in order to live non-autistically in reality. Narcissism does not provide genuine pleasures; it only lessens the fear of non-being by providing room for existence in a delusional shell. The growing child gives up self-coupling only to the degree that it is persistently expected to adhere to reality in a context that provides sufficient encouragement, security, and support. No striving is involved in the early years of life. This will beome clearer when we discuss fathering in Chapter 6.

Narcissism or self-coupling is the opposite of self-love. The latter requires that we avail ourselves of the many real blessings of life; very few of these can be ours within the shell of delusional withdrawal. When newborns couple with themselves they are merely trying to survive. Since they know nothing cognitively, they also have no concept of self, and so they cannot love "themselves." Besides, the capacity to love develops much later, if it develops at all. As we shall see later, loving requires that we give of ourselves. Newborns, young children, and narcissistic adults can only grab, take, accept, or reject. They cannot give.

Even the term "narcissism" is ill-chosen. Narcissus was not an unconscious neonate but a young man, even though he too was exclusively preoccupied with his self, like an autistic infant. We are told that he lived as if he were "in love" with his own reflected image, spurning all others. Yet those commonly called narcissistic spurn no one. All the newborn can do is couple with itself, and this is why "narcissism" is normal and inevitable for it. But the "love" of a grown Narcissus for himself was a sickness, indicating a serious developmental block. Emotionally he remained a suckling. Like all adults, he must have known cognitively about the existence of others, but nobody existed outside of himself emotionally and behaviorally. For such people, others merely serve as objects to couple with, like a favorite blanket, or as things to be used and discarded, like a towel.

The price of such autistic living is always very high: One can have only a limited existence, more like a plant or a primitive animal than a human. Narcissus became a flower, and thus he felt fear no more. His suicide is so pretty that we almost fail to recognize it for what it was.

Narcissistic people often embarrass themselves because they normally act in a crude and uncivilized manner, like infants. Unreasonable and endless demanding comes naturally to them, and they see nothing wrong with it. What others try hard to avoid, they pursue. When on rare occasions they are able to observe themselves and their behavior, they are humiliated by it. This causes them to retreat quickly into their autistic shell again, a safe haven that excludes most pain. Although a horrible prison, this is where they experience most safety. They emerge only reluctantly when reality leaves them no other choice. Superficially, such behavior resembles that of people driven by the fear of engulfment. The end point of both is splendid isolation. But those who fear engulfment actively push away, while people who fear non-being just fade away, leaving all others behind.

Man has always tried to hide the existence of his irrational fears, both from himself and from others. Perhaps he believed naively that the unseen might magically disappear. Besides, he was too scared to be seen as afraid, for this would increase his vulnerability. Although ineffective and irrational, such behavior was the best he could come up with. The attempts to delude himself naturally failed, and he had no choice but to pay the high price in pain and in trouble again and again. No one knew that irrational fears, including the fear of non-being, could actually be eliminated. It is finally possible for men and women to live consciously now with dignity, pride, joy, and inner peace—but only after they vanquish these hidden enemies that exist within.

5. How Do We Know What We Know about Man?

Western science is generally based on empirical observations and experiments, and it is rightly suspicious of abstract formulations that cannot be tested directly. Social and psychological scientists have thus narrowly pursued lines of research that are essentially quantifiable, mimicking the natural sciences and reflecting their professional sense of inferiority and inadequacy.

Although a tremendous pool of quantifiable data has been accumulated by social scientists all over the world, it has not made us much wiser. It is time to wonder if our dependence upon this approach has failed us. The principles and methods that work for physics may simply not be adequate to gain a real understanding of Man, a miraculous creature capable of observing and of examining his own workings.

Clinical observations and conclusions derived from them may be the only source of the clues that we need. Yet such observations have been viewed in the past as necessarily biased and therefore as unreliable and irrelevant. Clinical findings are indeed subject to major distortions resulting from the interpretations and misinterpretations of observers, and they are not easily duplicable or verifiable. People frequently do not even agree on what they observe. Two individuals watching a movie at the same time and from adjacent seats usually see at least somewhat different versions of it: The angle of viewing anything is always at least slightly different for any two people, but in addition, eyes have biases built into them. These must be recognized fully and adjusted for accuracy before agreement is reached on what is being seen.

Clinical data can be of great value if meticulous care is taken to correct their biases. We can no longer afford the luxury of simply dismissing such observations, even though they are far from perfect. We will probably have to correct our findings again and again, but whether we like it or not the gray area of clinical findings seems to be where the missing pieces of the human puzzle are hiding.

Even in the exact sciences the position of the observer affects the nature of his or her observations. The theory of relativity complicated the study of distant stars and galaxies at first, but it also made it possible to explore previously unreachable worlds and concepts. The problem is even more complex when we ourselves become the subject of our observations, because our fears of what we begin to see interfere with our seeing. But we discover fascinating new views once the central role of fear is recognized and its distortions corrected for.

We humans are and always will remain the ultimate instruments of our observations in any field. All our determinations and measurements are really subjective, since by nature we are incapable of absolute objectivity. Not even our most finely calibrated instruments are totally reliable: We use Greenwich mean time as a fixed standard because even the most accurate clocks do not always tell time correctly. Subjectivity confuses us only when it is claimed to represent an objective reality. The construction of theories is always a subjective effort, based on human observations and assessments. No better building blocks exist. Try as hard as we can, absolute and total objectivity will forever elude us.

As we shall see more fully in Chapter 3, emotions or feelings are usually misleading and unreliable yardsticks of reality, and they often masquerade as thoughts. We must discount them therefore when we attempt to discover the hidden outlines of our real nature, which is only knowable when observed dispassionately. Events and facts that are charged with emotions can usually be evaluated reliably only after enough time passes for those feelings to become diluted. Likewise, difficult choices and important life decisions are best not made at moments of great enthusiasm. It is wise to become suspicious when we have very powerful reactions to what we observe or read. Feelings reflect past experience; they propel us to trust too little and to stay distant too much, or else they turn us into true believers and cause us to forget that honeymoons are not forever.

Our capacity to evaluate critically what makes sense and what does not often remains unused. Our wish for guidance from others is frequently so strong that we substitute the judgments of critics for our own, and not only in evaluating movies and plays. Many people are always eager to hear what pundits have to tell them about the meaning of things that they can easily understand without help. It is hardly necessary to recapitulate a president's remarks, but commentators do so regularly. The opinions of experts are frequently given excessive weight, as if such opinions are not also colored by feelings. The almost blind acceptance of the words of experts is considered more fully in Chapter 7.

Readers can trust their own evaluations of the material presented here, provided that "gut" reactions are excluded. These are often based on hidden fear, which can be recognized by the intense emotional heat that it tends to generate.

TWO

The Origins of Depression

A vague but powerful sense of impending doom in the face of the unknown that was us and everything about us is every person's first experience after birth, always completely out of consciousness. Since we exist in that situation before we have any comprehension of anything, including time, it is a timeless experience. It is felt as eternal. The entire experience has absolutely no meaning for us, no direction, no framework, only dread.

CHAPTER 8, SECTION 1

Across the dinner table sits a reasonably attractive woman in her thirties, politely refusing each of the choice wines offered her. "I'd rather eat my calories than drink them," she explains matter-of-factly. "I'm sticking to my diet," she continues, "now that I've lost eighty pounds." Why did she gain all that weight in the first place? Why did her handsome and trim husband prefer her to be fat? Why does he say openly that he does not like her as much now? What pushes other men and women to act and to behave as strangely as these two, and worse?

My dinner companion did not know that she was riddled with anxiety. For years, I eventually discovered, she had been eating compulsively as soon as she started to sense that vaguely defined pain. She dreaded those disabling "attacks" so much that she would often begin stuffing her mouth in anticipation, "noshing" like an alcoholic reaching for a drink, often without realizing what she was doing or why. The separate episodes soon merged into almost continuous munching and she eventually convinced herself that she was simply physiologically insatiable. Her husband married her when she was already obese. The hidden truth was that he had been seeking a woman who was not likely to desert him: Desertion frightened him the most. He had lived with its bitter taste since early in life, and without realizing it he sought a woman that most other men would ignore. As his wife was becoming more attractive he became increasingly restless and critical. He experienced her changing as a real threat and, completely without awareness, he resented it.

Are these people unusual or just more obvious than others? Are anxiety, stress, and depression more common now than they used to be? More people seem to suffer from a sense of rootlessness these days, and they live without much contentment, happiness, or meaning. What is life all about? they ask, after the struggle for material comforts and security has been won. Throughout history the dream of the good life consisted of peace and of freedom from hunger, pestilence, and natural disasters. This dream is not yet fulfilled for most inhabitants of the earth, but to an ever larger number of people material success no longer brings either joy or peace of mind. The restless soul is left in agony. Right in the middle a gaping emptiness still remains. The desperate search for meaning that spawns religions, fads, and cults, after love affairs and fancy cars have lost their magic, is not yet so evident in China or the Sudan, but only because more pressing needs have a higher priority there. In more developed and richer countries, the gnawing pains of doubt and free-floating anxiety commonly lurk in the background, much too close for comfort. At least secretly almost everyone knows loneliness that weighs heavily on the heart even when all seems well. Many tear ducts are clogged with a pressure that dampens joy. Why?

1. The Many Masks of Fear

One word exists in German, *Angst*, for both fear and anxiety, since they are really the same. But while fear is often felt as such, anxiety is also manifested through bodily sensations. It shows in the gaping eyes and in the terrified faces of Edvard Munch's well-known paintings, in twitches and in repetitive movements of hands, legs, or feet, and in every starved drag on a cigarette by a tense smoker. Man has recognized anxiety at least since biblical days by an unsteadiness in the knees, a queasiness in the stomach, a dizziness in the head, and a blurring of vision. Anxiety can affect almost any organ or system in the body, and it often does.

Sometimes the brain temporarily ceases to function in its presence and even intelligent people cannot think, remember, or
reason then. The genital organs fail to be aroused; palms become
cold and clammy, hearing selectively impaired, and vision unreliable. Anxiety causes generalized perspiration, pallor or blushing of the face and neck, tremulous fingers and shaky vocal
cords, skin disorders, high and low blood pressure, hypersensitiv-
ity of the teeth and gums, general limpness of the musculature,
and a perpetual lack of energy that is not relieved by sleep or by
relaxation. Obesity results when anxiety is felt as an insatiable
hunger in the pit of one's stomach, promiscuity and unrequited
nymphomania when the turmoil is displaced to the genital organs. Remember Richard Burton? The search is endless, and it
usually fails to bring the yearned-for contentment.

Anxiety wears many masks. It may appear as loneliness, as
despair, as an endless busyness, as a gnawing unsteadiness. In
one form or another it is present at the core of practically everyone, except those relative few who have faced the demons within
them, flinching perhaps but not escaping. Man can live freely
without fear, as the story of the patriarch Jacob demonstrates
poetically. The lad Jacob became a man only after he prevailed
in his encounter with the angel of the Lord. Only then was he
ready to assume leadership. The new man that emerged from
Jacob's heroic struggle required a new identity and he received a
new name, Israel. Similar struggles are commonly found in the
literature of many languages and in folklore, and they show that
close and courageous encounters with danger or death sometimes help people discover their real power: Darkness always
precedes the dawn of a new day. But the average person is not
required to fight under such stark and dramatic circumstances,
and change is normally not as swift. Under normal circumstances, fear is merely "overcome" by denial, "conquered" by
suppression, "mastered" by will, or "managed" by medication.
Existence without fear is indeed possible, but reaching it is rare.

"Anxiety seems to be the dominant fact—and is threatening
to become the dominant cliché—of modern life," according to a
cover story in *Time* (March 31, 1961), an example of the periodic
coverage of anxiety in popular magazines. The story continues:

It shouts in the headlines, laughs nervously at cocktail parties,
nags from advertisements, speaks suavely in the board room,
whines from the stage, clatters from the Wall Street ticker,
jokes with fake youthfulness on the golf course and whispers

in privacy each day before the shaving mirror and the dressing table. Not merely the black statistics of murder, suicide, alcoholism and divorce betray anxiety (or that special form of anxiety which is guilt), but almost any innocent, everyday act: the limp or overhearty handshake, the second pack of cigarettes or the third martini, the forgotten appointment, the stammer in mid-sentence, the wasted hour before the TV set, the spanked child, the new car unpaid for.

The story succeeds in evoking the tense horror that is the essence of anxiety:

The automatic elevator stops with a jolt. The doors slide open, but instead of the accustomed exit, the passenger faces only a blank wall. His fingers stab at the buttons: nothing happens. Finally, he presses the alarm signal, and a starter's gruff voice inquires from below: "What's the matter?" The passenger explains that he wants to get off on the 25th floor. "There is no 25th floor in this building," comes the voice over the loudspeaker. The passenger explains that, nonsense, he has worked here for years. He gives his name. "Never heard of you," says the loudspeaker. "Easy," the passenger tells himself. "They are just trying to frighten me."

But time passes and nothing changes. In that endless moment, the variously pleading and angry exchanges over the loudspeaker are the passenger's only communication with the outside world. Finally, even that ceases; the man below says that he cannot waste any more time. "Wait! Please!" cries the passenger in panic—"Keep talking to me!" But the loudspeaker clicks into silence. Hours, days or ages go by. The passenger cowers in a corner of the steel box, staring at the shining metal grille through which the voice once spoke. The grille must be worshiped; perhaps the voice will be heard again.

This is not a story by Franz Kafka or by one of his contemporary imitators. It is a recent dream remembered in precise detail by a successful New Yorker (one wife, three children, fair income, no analyst) who works with every outward appearance of contentment in one of Manhattan's new midtown office buildings. Whatever Freudian or other analysis might make of it, the dream could serve as a perfect allegory for an era that is almost universally regarded as the Age of Anxiety.

. . . It speaks of man's dreaded loss of identity, of a desperate need to make contact with his fellow man, with the world and with whatever may be beyond the world. Above all, it speaks of God grown silent.

Although he died in 1855, the great Danish existentialist Soren Kierkegaard described the effects of anxiety in terms that are strikingly apt today. He spoke of his "cowardly age," in which "one does everything possible by way of diversions and the Janizary music of loud-voiced enterprises to keep lonely thoughts away." Yet all the noise is in vain: "No Grand Inquisitor has in readiness such terrible tortures as has anxiety, and no spy knows how to attack more artfully the man he suspects, choosing the instant when he is weakest, nor knows how to lay traps where he will be caught and ensnared, and no sharp-witted judge knows how to interrogate, to examine the accused, as anxiety does, which never lets him escape, neither by diversion nor by noise, neither at work nor at play, neither by day nor by night."

When a fact is as universal as love, death or anxiety, it becomes difficult to measure and classify. Man would not be human were he not anxious.

The sensitive writer of this piece describes the condition much better than he can explain it. The probable reasons he offers for this profound and widespread distress are commonplace, and far from convincing:

> ... There is general agreement among psychiatrists, theologians, sociologists and even poets that in this era, anxiety is indeed different both in quantity and quality.
>
> Other eras were turbulent, insecure and complex—the great migrations after the fall of the Roman Empire; the age of discovery; Copernicus and Galileo's tinkering with the universe, removing the earth and man from its center; the industrial revolution. But in a sense, the 20th century U.S. is the culmination of all these upheavals—itself the product of a gigantic migration, itself both champion and victim of the industrial revolution, itself faced with the necessity not only of accepting a new universe but of exploring it.
>
> The American today is told without pause that the world is up to him—war or peace, prosperity or famine, the welfare or literacy of the last, remotest Congolese, Tibetan or Laotian. And he is facing his demanding destiny in a state of psychological and religious confusion.

No real explanation was available several decades ago, and nothing very new has been added since. Anxiety is still with us as always, and so are confusion and a lack of clarity about its causes. We shall soon see that the root of all this trouble is to be found within the individual person, and yet the search for causes usually focuses upon developments in society.

Freud focused his attention in the right direction, but he was wrong about what was to be found there. Rollo May interpreted the presence of existential anxiety more accurately, but he and others also had difficulties in reconciling "Weltschmerz," that global suffering and pain, with the original fear of losing Mother's "love." Otto Rank, Erik Erikson, Karen Horney, Harry Stack Sullivan, Erich Fromm, and other psychologists, historians, philosophers, and theologians have all tried to solve the mystery. Each came up with plausible explanations for this universal malaise, but we are still puzzled. Explanations such as "the infant's fear of disapproval" are obviously not sufficient.

Although anxiety, stress, and depression are often used interchangeably, they are really not the same. Anxiety is a feeling—fear. Stress occurs when conflicting demands, wishes, and needs clash with each other: They cannot all be satisfied or dismissed. People experience a sense of inner pressure then, often accompanied by anger and dread, as if they were about to be punished, censured, ridiculed, or rejected. Fear is the predominant sensation in stress, although it is not always experienced that way consciously. Depression is an illness, at the core of which fear and hurt but not sadness are always present. It is commonly characterized by a sense that all attempts to change things for the better are futile and by the expectation that total defeat is inevitable. Repeated episodes of subjective hopelessness and helplessness are common in it. Depression is often associated with stress, which is one reason why the two are often thought of as being the same.

Depression is the basic and by far the most common illness of all. Like the anxiety at its core, it can and often does both mimic and trigger other physical and emotional illnesses. Since traces of depression are present in practically everyone, it is repeatedly claimed to be an integral part of Man rather than a curable illness. "Man would not be human were he not anxious," says *Time*. But depression and its irrational fear are, as we shall see, a pathologic condition of which Man can cure himself with effort.

The traces of depression that are more or less present everywhere are merely subclinical. The nature of Man and his vulnerability to depression are the same now as they have been in the past, but more trouble shows on the surface today. The clinical form of depression is what we see more of nowadays. Affluence has freed many people from the distracting struggle for existence, even in less developed countries and behind the Iron Curtain, where the standards of living are lower but no abject poverty exists. More room exists for overt expressions of the illness when we have the leisure to wonder about the meaning of life. The stress of modern existence is not really at fault.

When we must concern ourselves with survival itself, anxiety usually recedes from the surface and it does not generally bother us. This powerful remnant from each person's individual past is pushed aside for a while when he or she must face life-threatening danger. This alerts us, as it does all living things, and for as long as our adrenaline supply lasts all our resources are mobilized for fight or flight. When primitive man was busy hunting or foraging for food, and when he had to be almost constantly on guard lest he become the hunted one himself, death from illness, accidents, and other "natural" causes usually occurred long before he had much time to interest himself in the meaning of his existence. His life span was short. The more sensitive ones, those who suffered "neurotic" anxiety and depression even under those brutal conditions, were also the ones least successful in insuring their survival. This is still true in wars and during violent disturbances. Some died more quickly than others in the death camps of Hitler, and some of the less essential physiologic functions were often suppressed: Many women failed to menstruate. The efforts to avoid the immediacy of death always supersede the concern with the quality of life. The need for food, shelter, and physical security takes precedence. We become concerned with our emotional safety and well-being once these are satisfied. This is when anxiety surfaces.

Depression can manifest itself as alcoholism and as low morale and decreased industrial productivity; in drug taking and in most family discord and interpersonal conflict; in suicide and in business failures; in the silence of withdrawal; and in the shattering noise of rock music. Capitalism, socialism, and communism share in it equally, since it is not a result of societal organization but of Man's individual fate. No country except Utopia has ever been free from it.

Man's nature is such that he quickly forgets that life was not always so good as it is today. We tend to take the dramatic improvements in our standards of living and health for granted and soon regard them as minimum base lines. We are acutely aware of and always troubled by the many imperfections and difficulties of our complex lives and tend to overlook the many blessings that are ours. We indeed live in the shadow of a nuclear holocaust, with family disintegration, crime in the streets, and drugs on the job and elsewhere. But we are nonetheless much better off than our ancestors. At least in the advanced societies, some poverty continues to exist but actual starvation is rare. Life expectancy is markedly longer: Only one hundred years ago, most adults expected to live less than thirty-five years, not the seventy that we do now. Old cemeteries are a good reminder of the high rate of infant mortality in the past. Families used to be large because parents wanted to insure that at least some of their children would survive. Disease, exposure, and malnutrition took a heavy toll, and relatively few reached puberty.

We evaluate our experience in comparative not in absolute terms. In spite of frequent breakdowns in law and order today, the system basically holds. We complain bitterly about thefts, muggings, and other crimes against the person because nothing less than complete security has become our standard. War also used to be much more horrible without rapid evacuation of the injured or modern surgery; peace was less stable and life much harder and much cheaper. Man had fewer rights and many more responsibilities to God and to church, to family, tribe, and society. Work used to reward Man with fewer of his necessities for a much greater effort. Our many mechanical servants did not exist, and only the very rich had any help at all. Horses are much slower and more difficult to handle and to keep than cars, and besides they stink. The freedom to choose values and life-styles was practically nonexistent for most people in the past. The anonymity of our huge and impersonal urban centers raises anxiety, but we also find in them more room to be ourselves. Our expectations are so much higher at the end of the twentieth century precisely because we have come to expect the vastly better quality of our lives. But now that so many wild dreams of earlier generations have been fulfilled, why are we still not content and why are we not yet free from anxiety and loneliness? Because "joy and peace of mind are findable only in the absence of irrational fear." Depression is not changed by changing external circumstances, nor does it disappear with the passage of time.

Nostalgia is at the root of every generation's belief that the "good old days" were better. The tendency to idealize what used to be is one of many manifestations of our irrational nature. We use our personal experience as if it were a reliable and objective yardstick. People often naively think of the past as having been painless because they know the suffering of earlier generations only from historical accounts, but not so their own fear and pain. These are known by the anguish in the flesh.

All people automatically engage in a wide variety of activities to escape anxiety and hurt even before they become aware of their existence, as was the case with the woman who had gained and lost all that weight, earlier in this chapter. Most people really do not know consciously how much they are troubled by fear and by hurt, and often they do not even know that such feelings exist. Fear especially is repressed, suppressed, and hidden, automatically and almost instantaneously. The first tinge of panic usually mobilizes a person's primitive animal nature in an effort to contain and to neutralize the monstrous horror. We often act as if we believe that what is kept out of sight and out of mind will actually disappear. The power of anxiety is such, however, that it usually finds some unsealed opening and then pushes through.

2. Anomie as a Curable Illness

Existential philosophers have named it anomie, a sense of profound alienation from others, even when in close physical proximity. But they have no real explanation for it beyond stating that it is a consequence of existence and of our being-in-the-world. They are obviously correct in claiming that we are doomed to live with anxiety unless we learn to live fully in each moment of existence, yet this desirable state of "being there" is not achievable as long as anxiety interferes. So we are back to square one. This is a fancy example of circular thinking that leaves the original question unanswered: Why are we anxious?

The existentialists did not realize that anomie is best understood from the perspective of a physician, not that of a philosopher. Anomie is a mass expression of the anxieties of many individuals. Medicine requires its practitioners to look at each person as an individual, each an independent system, diseased perhaps but self-contained even when in need of repair. Specific clinical observations of people in agony—not speculations about our species as a whole—enable us to understand anomie more correctly now and to explain it more fully. Most importantly, they lead us toward the possibility of eliminating it altogether.

Our traditional ways of explaining economic, political, and social behavior must be revised if it is true that the attempts to evade anxiety and panic are central in motivating people to do whatever they do. Many of the lessons of philosophy and sociology must also be re-evaluated as we notice that group behavior in general reflects the many typical ways of coping with anxiety. Societies are not basically different from the individuals that make them up. Mass behavior has some unique characteristics, but it is based on the needs, wishes, and fears of individuals.

Much of what Man does alone or with others can be understood most easily as part of his desperate search for emotional security. He is not propelled by higher ideals as much as we used to believe, though he wants to give the impression that his motives are lofty. Essentially, we all try to survive—emotionally and physically—without losing position or face. Public behavior is sometimes a little more refined than behavior in private, but only in societies that expect adherence to high standards of mutual respect. Otherwise Man often acts in a base and inhuman manner. Millions of Germans were directly and indirectly involved in the systematic extermination of other human beings, in large part because they were safer under Hitler's regime if they committed such acts. But whether individuals behave nobly or like barbaric animals, whether in private or in the public eye, Man's nature remains the same. Only his actions change from time to time and from place to place, depending on what lowers anxiety the most.

Almost all of Man's constructive and destructive efforts—his pursuit of peace and his going to war, anything that he does and that he is, even his receptivity to illness—derive from his efforts to cope with anxiety. There should thus be one set of principles that can explain both individual malaise and social turmoil. Modes of existence helpful in the prevention of disease should also prove useful to societies in organizing themselves for good government.

Illness, except when it results from normal aging, is often an expression of the continuing wish of individuals to be cared for by others, since such human closeness generally is reassuring. This, more so than genetic determinants, explains why some young and relatively fit bodies are much more susceptible to disease than others. A sudden aggravation of a subclinical depression often triggers a physical sympton. Such cases are common, and folk knowledge confirms them in many cultures. Overt physical sickness often summons helpers whose mere presence is often sufficient to relieve extreme fear.

The same principle holds true for societies. Gurus, charismatic political leaders, and dictators often exploit this desperate search for security to advance themselves and to maintain their power. Societies in turmoil or in decline often welcome authoritarian rule because their anxious citizens are usually glad to render total obedience in return for stability, security, and the promise of protection.

What is the source of all this anxiety? It is the direct consequence of Man's existence as a separate organism. Otto Rank claimed that the trauma of birth was at fault; but although difficult and dangerous, it is merely one relatively short shock to the newborn's system. What happens to each of us as soon as we are born is much more fascinating and significant; it is truly miraculous, in fact. Organisms like fish or amoebas, which normally live in water, quickly shrivel and die when taken out of the environment that sustains them. The opposite is true for creatures that breathe air; they drown in liquid. Unlike some species, we humans cannot survive both on land and in the sea. But at birth the newborn human is suddenly thrust from a liquid into a gaseous environment, and its remarkable physiology adapts to it swiftly and normally without difficulty. A great deal of anxiety is involved, however, in accommodating to this dramatic change, which is merely the very beginning of a long and subjectively most dangerous adventure.

3. Our Dramatic Beginnings

Everything is totally new immediately after birth. Light, most sounds, rapid temperature variations, food intake by mouth, and even the feel of a breeze on delicate skin are all new experiences for an organism that was already viable for many months. It understands nothing and expects nothing, since it has no sense of time. Every moment brings completely fresh sensations. Past experience is basically irrelevant for the newborn, with the possible exception of the body's recognition of muffled sounds and rhythm. And yet the organism "knew" safety before. The quarters in which it existed were cramped but snug, a pleasantly warm and steady "home." The womb once enveloped each of us in its consistent, constant, and careful hug. Then, after a sudden disturbance that we later know as a painful and rough squeeze, we suddenly experience a sense of being physically rootless, as if we might fall at any moment and break into many pieces.

We shudder at this experience. The benign, assuring, and engulfing presence that was Mother (although we obviously didn't know even that) suddenly is no more. Somehow we must survive or not survive in a totally new environment. Knowledge that most organisms survive this subjective horror would obviously have helped, but this adult reconstruction is not known to an infant at that point. Everything was feeling, and nothing was thinking. We experienced it all as overwhelming because nothing made any sense. "Nothing is lost in the universe. Even though we have no conscious memory of our early experiences, our body remembers."

If only we could have had some understanding that all these major upheavals were merely temporary and that they usually are compatible with life! But from one moment to another the newborn is thrust into radically different settings without any capacity to understand what is happening to it. Every stimulus that is strong enough to affect it causes the entire little body to shake, often violently. Most of these unknown and unknowable new experiences are part of normal development, and they "should" not realistically be shocking, but they are.

The more powerful reactions of the newborn are visible to adults; many of the lesser ones are internal and therefore invisible. Although fear as a concept, or even as a distinct feeling, does not yet exist for a newborn, its life is nothing but a series of extremely frightening events. It experiences fear only as a huge and powerful physical wave. We adults are usually so fascinated by a new baby that we enjoy its wide open eyes and cute features and pay relatively little attention to anything else. Our wishful "thinking" causes us to interpret its indistinct facial expressions as the beginnings of a conscious smile, long before it learns to smile in order to please its all-powerful caretakers. Those old enough to know are always intuitively very eager to please the ones believed to be capable of bringing relief from panic, but newborns do not have such knowledge. What we normally overlook are the newborn's long periods of withdrawal into its self, its lost look, and the ease with which it breaks out crying.

Every newborn is like E.T., far away from "home" and powerfully yearning for its safety. The great success of the movie is based on people's hidden identification with that helpless and perplexed extraterrestrial creature. Each of us must have craved with our total being to be firmly cuddled and thus protected during moments of fear, to be physically shielded from this elemental force. No baby actually remembers the relatively tranquil conditions that existed before, but everybody's body "wished" to be restored to them. This wish persists in later life. The newborn knows none of these cravings, but they nonetheless shape its expectations, its character, and its life.

We know this not only from observing the reactions of newborns but also from the many adult reactions that can be explained only as reflecting a desire to regain such security. Babies become less tense, more peaceful, quieter, and less jumpy when held calmly, steadily, and tenderly. We have seen in the previous chapter that many adult "decisions" and "choices" are also made merely because they promise similar relief. We shall see the force of such desperate cravings to be protected and cared for again and again. Even the sight or the sound of an approaching caretaker reduces panic. Language itself reveals the nature of such desires: The Hebrew word for "longing" actually consists of baby sounds: "ga'a-gu'a"; and "pining," which is derived from the Latin *poena*, means to suffer and to yearn. Infants indeed reach out and strain to be comforted as pines reach up toward the warming sun.

But language fails us in accurately describing this experience of suddenly having to live as a separate organism no longer attached to another. What actually happens lies beyond our usual formulations about newborns. It is inaccurate, for instance, to say that newborns experience the earliest moments of existence outside the uterus as very precarious, for the term "experience" implies some conscious comprehension, and no newborn is ever conscious of anything. The physiology, not the person, experiences whatever it does. Anthropomorphic terms applied to physiologic processes are misleading. But how else are we to describe the situation from our adult perspective?

Much time passes before we can stand on our feet and before our thinking brain becomes functional, but our lungs are called upon to supply us with enough oxygen immediately. Since we survive, we slowly begin to "know" that our physiology can adapt even to experiences that are most dangerous subjectively. Many of these events never become "known" as objectively safe. Subjectivity, not objectivity, is the determining factor of all our bodily reactions. Our physiology often distorts reality, but our body follows its dictates nonetheless, even later in life when we know better. We eventually realize that many of our physiologic reactions make no sense, but they persist in adulthood in spite of such knowledge. We react with our entire body to perceived danger, even when nothing dangerous exists nearby. Yet most people still try to deny the existence of reactions that they cannot explain rationally. "Our view of ourselves as rational beings depends on . . . " our rationalizations being valid.

The real task of good psychotherapy is not to teach the cortex but to alter the physiologic reaction patterns that do not conform to objective reality. This difficult task is described in Chapter 6. People are commonly ashamed or frightened when they react in ways that they cannot explain or approve of, and it helps only a little to convince them that such reactions are unnecessary. Explanations and interpretations are interesting but they do not change behavior significantly. People continue to react as before, perhaps with a little less shame. The crippling reactions must be essentially eliminated if real relief is to be achieved.

We have already seen that all of us must have "wished," long before we knew what a wish was, to regain the sense of security that was ours before we were suddenly thrust into the cold world. But "hopes" and "yearnings" for perfect caring are repeatedly dashed, because no caretaker is perfect. No one can anticipate or satisfy all of the newborn's needs at exactly the right time, before panic takes hold. Even if that were possible for a while, the moment of truth would eventually have to come anyway. Long before the young organism is capable of really understanding why, it cannot always have its way. Frustration, anger, and a sense of helplessness are inevitable. It is easy to see why we resist accepting external constrictions at any age. The old cravings for a perfect world that fits our ever-changing needs and wishes are not simply given up just because they are unfulfillable.

Unexplainable panic, deep despair, futility, and profound disappointment—the precursor of hurt and rage—all have their roots in such moments of terror when help failed to arrive in time. Young babies naively "believe" that every disappointment will surely be the last. This is why they are so very angry each time they are disappointed again. The sense of futility does not take over until we have reached for relief many, many times in vain.

Most people have denied such wishes consciously for so long that they have forgotten them. The fear of being disappointed and hurt again causes many to recoil from ever reaching for help or even for wishing it. But even when the impossible dream of a perfectly sensitive loving presence remains a deep secret, it continues to shape the destinies of many people. At least a few small remnants of those early yearnings continue to be a part of our expectations throughout life.

4. Viewing Adults as Grown-Up Infants

Newborns acquire understanding as they grow up. They eventually know that they exist. With money or marriage, with a lover or with learning, with a God or a guru on their side, they channel their old yearnings and hope in new directions. Is there someone or something "out there" waiting for us? Even most adults find it much too frightening to accept the existential truth that, once born, we are all alone in the universe. We really live alone and die alone, even if others are near us. They are not part of us. Two people can be emotionally and physically very, very close—but they never become one. Such observations do not elicit fear in those who are no longer at the mercy of the yearnings of early infancy. Yet most adults are not so fortunate, at least not until they are very old. Not having faced their archaic fears, they continue to reach for the impossible time after time. They expect their great effort to be finally rewarded both in personal affairs and in public life.

Whatever we attach our infantile yearnings to is bound to disappoint us in the long run. These yearnings really are unfulfillable. Relationships come to an end; nothing is forever. When this realization proves to be too scary, we make unrealistic promises in the hope of diminishing panic, and we expect the same from others: "I will never leave you" or "I will love you forever." Hurt, disappointment, and anger result when such impossible promises are broken. The associated fear commonly assumes panic proportions and it is often totally disabling. Since "they" promised undying faith and loyalty, how could they be so fickle? Not surprisingly, violence sometimes occurs when such rage and fear are evoked. It is nearly impossible for most people to accept emotionally what they know intellectually—that they are all alone in the universe, once separated from Mother. Above all we aim to evade the immobilizing and sickening effects of panic, but true acceptance of our aloneness might give rise to it. So most people continue living somewhat delusionally; they are not choosy when rushing to escape panic. We eagerly take whatever road we can find to get us out of this darkness.

Job's unwavering faith in God in spite of his many ordeals and tragedies may indicate more than mere steadfastness. To curse God would also have meant to abandon the source of his personal security, which would have been much worse than blasphemy. For similar reasons we often cling not only to good partners in marriages and in other relationships but also to bad ones. Even after their deficiencies have become obvious, we still tend to hold on to invalid belief systems as tenaciously as we do to those which make sense. The alternative is to face our aloneness, which might activate our sense of loneliness, the essence of which is profound fear.

Fear or dread is the closest companion of newborns and of young infants, and it remains a very close companion of most people throughout life. There was no good escape from it early in life. Not knowing anything, we were unable then to construct fantasies with which to help ourselves. Our first well-formed dreams and imaginings, perhaps after we had survived a very long first year, were often ghoulish ones, based on our isolated existence before consciousness. They could hardly provide very young children with much solace, since such dreams routinely consist of ghosts and of unreal devouring multiheaded creatures with huge, deformed, and dangerous features. But even such terrible imagining is more comforting than the featureless, meaningless experience of nothingness that was described earlier as the fear of non-being. We have learned about the existence and nature of such fantasies from the questions that children ask about them later. They want us to reassure them that such monsters are not real. Science fiction books and movies interest many people for the same reason. They anchor nebulous but horrible fears that exist beyond description in some definable, if terrifying, reality.

Very young organisms that have no way to escape dread also become numb and remain so for a while to avoid panic. This response of being insensitive often becomes typical for life, and it is used not only when the emotional stress is extreme. The sense of danger disappears when our perceptions and thinking are separated from reality, when we become psychotic, even for a moment. Panic suddenly disappears. We can thus exist even in situations that would have been too frightening to tolerate otherwise, although not without paying a very high price. Such momentary escapes from reality may eventually become habitual. Many "normal" people take such brief trips. The damage caused by such excursions may not be gross, since the psychosis is well encapsulated and short in duration. Though our judgment in other matters may remain intact, the price of being insensitive even under minor stress is to lose much of the ability to relate emotionally. Relationships become wooden and constricted then, and their intensity is diluted.

Physiologic reactions to perceived danger are direct bodily equivalents of emotions. Without ever sensing any anxiety, some people develop ulcers or colitis, headaches and other aches, arthritis, skin conditions, high blood pressure, low energy levels, and a variety of other diseases. Help then comes automatically. The attention of a physician or a healer becomes focused upon us when we develop physical symptoms in an attempt to bind our anxiety or as we "accidentally" injure ourselves. The nebulous sense of dread becomes tolerable once bound to something real that we can understand and explain. But this obviously is a dangerous way of asking for—and of getting—help, yet not an uncommon one. Often it is not only the best but also the only way available to those who find it too embarrassing or too frightening to ask for a helpful hand directly.

Emotion-laden periods in life—passages—are merely the peaks of the swelling waves of anxiety that are also present before and after. Puberty or middle age may disturb the old equilibrium that kept panic at bay, and so can a marriage or a divorce, the death or departure of someone close to us, or simply our own aging. Panic surfaces then. Recent stresses thus trigger old and hidden fears, especially those that were barely kept from erupting. "Suddenly" we find ourselves in a crisis, faced, as we were early in life, with the urgent need to somehow reduce anxiety. Seeking professional help is one of the many ways available to adults. More generally we "choose" what we already "know" from previous experience, using what became typical for us long ago. We generally overlook distinctions between constructive or destructive measures at such moments. Like a drowning person, we reach for the straw that is nearest at hand, whether or not it can support our weight.

5. A Brief Note to the Reader

It is difficult to verify these descriptions of the newborn's experiences directly, since they always occur before memory exists. But one good indirect way is to check your emotional and physical reactions as you read this material. How engrossed or bored have you become? Are you sleepy even though not tired, or excited beyond what the material deserves? Are you excessively warm or cold? Have you become fidgety or otherwise uncomfortable? When we read about infants we also read about ourselves, since we are all grown-up newborns. Although we cannot remember, we can often recognize certain unknown situations when they are sensitively described for us by others.

Any discomfort or anxiety that reading this material may have aroused in you is likely to be an adult re-experience of some of the old helplessness of the infant within. We enjoy the advantages of reason and of understanding now, and with their aid we can usually restore our adult view of reality quickly. Focusing on our adult competence is always a helpful, if short-lived, way to combat anxiety.

No perfect way exists to piece this picture together, since every person has had at least a slightly different experience from all others. No single description is ever likely to be completely accurate in every detail for every person. But the basic essentials should be recognizable if true. Such recognition may, surprisingly, not be instantaneous; it may come only hours later, if at all. I invite you to remain aware of this possibility. My claim is that the basic experience of dread is universal and that no one could have escaped it totally. The experiences described here should therefore be verifiable by everyone if only they are patient enough and as long as calm and thoughtfulness continue to prevail.

6. Objective Sources of Knowledge about the Earliest Life Experiences

More objective findings about the first experiences of life also exist. The information obtained from studying adults in long-term intensive psychotherapy at first only supplemented the knowledge that we gleaned from observing infants directly. But it turned out to be a primary source of understanding early-life phenomena, greater in value than infant observations. These leave much to be desired, since we must always interpret what we see and our conclusions cannot therefore be fully reliable. For instance, reasonably healthy infants shake or twitch violently when exposed suddenly to a strong noise, a bright light, or an unexpected motion. So we assume, probably correctly, that such reactions are caused by these stimuli. We can also test this hypothesis by repeating the stimulus. But what of similar reactions that result from other less obvious causes? Is the stimulus internal or external? We can observe directly only the latter.

Babies tense up physically and scream when they are hungry, too warm or cold, and when they experience other discomforts. Since they lack a framework to assess the relative importance of their experiences, they react to them all at first with equal ferocity, not necessarily related to the degree of the discomfort. Trying to alter subjectively disturbing situations, they redden like a beet and they arch their entire body like a bow. Their effort is always total at the beginning. When all is felt to be well, on the other hand, the musculature of young babies is completely relaxed, their breathing deep and regular, and their general demeanor pleasant. Newborns know only a generalized sense of well-being or of disquietude, the forerunner of anxiety. We cannot easily prove or disprove our assumptions about the exact cause of their discomfort.

Not so with adults. We are what we were free to become. By observing the present we can reconstruct the past with a high degree of accuracy. Most important, we can test the validity of our reconstructions directly by producing a reaction, using the same approach as that used in chemistry. Just as we note a color change during titration, so we obtain clear physiologic confirmations for our reconstructions in intense therapeutic work with adult patients. Unlike very young children, adults normally modulate their social behavior to fit the circumstances, but their physiologic reactions remain qualitatively the same; only quantitatively are these altered somewhat. The size of our body increases markedly with the passage of time, and so does our comprehension of reality, but the typical ways of reacting to fear and to hurt are normally fixed within us. Memory and understanding of the new circumstances that exist in adulthood modify our automatic reactions, but only slightly; they do not reverse them. (This can be achieved only with much effort, as shown in Chapter 6.)

An immediate, distinct, and visible physical change often occurs in a patient who is confronted by a verbal statement that disturbs the emotional status quo: Facial and other muscles tense or relax, the chin may start to quiver, the jaw shuts tight or it finally loosens, the color of the skin in the face or neck often changes abruptly, breathing becomes shallow or deep, the eyes may widen as if seeing a ghost or they soften, pressured protests may be uttered very rapidly, or tearing follows in short order. Verbal agreement or disagreement does not count for much; the talking mouth often lies, usually unintentionally. Deep sobbing "without reason" is not an unusual response to a well-timed and sensitive intervention. A host of other reactions, too many and too varied to enumerate here, also occur regularly. Much of what is described in this chapter was garnered from repeated observations of such reactions.

Adults commonly report dreams of falling endlessly into black space and, when awake, of having a vague but powerful sense of anxiety and dread, without an overt reason for it. Apparently anything can stimualte such frightening experiences at the oddest moments and unexpectedly. It would be reassuring if such fear were related to something specific, for we would not have to worry then in addition about going crazy. The fear is multiplied when such anxiety is aroused by something one is totally unaware of. A familiar but forgotten smell, sound, sight, or ambience can elicit feelings that emanate from a world into which we no longer have direct access except with the help of a good and trusted guide. A full-blown panic attack often follows unexplainable anxiety of lesser intensity.

It is impossible to know all the strange emotional leftovers from our earliest experiences as fragile new organisms. But whenever a powerful physiologic experience is made coherent in the light of adult observations, some of its emotional charge is reduced and the scope of rational living is slightly increased. The validity of the reconstruction that has stimulated the physiologic reaction is thus confirmed. Knowledge in this area is advanced only slowly, and assembling it requires much patience.

Phobias are also helpful in expanding our understanding of that earliest period of life. No phobia ever makes sense from the adult's point of view, but everything fits in some context. Phobias can be seen as marvelously inventive and sensible expressions of a person's forbidden needs or yearnings, remnants from an earlier period of life. Their existence justifies our demands for understanding and for acceptance of behavior that would otherwise not be tolerated, such as our "inability" to go to school or to work. The pathologic "push against progressing" that is described in Chapter 8, Section 22, thus gains undeserved credence. How can anyone be held responsible for acts committed under the influence of a supposedly overpowering force?

When something restimulates any of our old, primitive, and previously dormant fears, we automatically try to attach them to something concrete in the present. Unknowingly, we hope to bring the irrational under conscious control by making it appear coherent and rational. Its chances of overwhelming us might thus be lessened. We anchor our free-floating anxiety to a place, a condition, a situation, a circumstance, or a person to help us maintain our view of ourselves as sensible creatures. We can now claim to have a reason for our otherwise "crazy" feelings. For a while we are also distracted from the real but unexplainable trouble, since we busy ourselves with self-"protection." As long as we maintain that heights, elevators, close spaces, or flying are our problem, we can hold on to the view that we are otherwise sane. Even paranoia makes sense from this perspective. The hidden wishes of the infant within the adult can be detected by observing the end results that phobias produce.

7. Man's Yearnings for Physical Closeness

Fetuses appear to experience, even in utero, occasional hunger-like pangs and other forms of physical discomfort as well as momentary experiences of unsteadiness. But these are dwarfed by comparison with the routine adjustments required of everyone once born. Above all, no fetus ever experienced the sense of being untouched or non-enveloped, yet this suddenly becomes the norm of existence after birth. Physical separateness is an altogether new experience, shockingly different from anything known before. The long-term effects of this early shock linger in us, since it leaves permanent imprints. These determine the way we relate to externality.

Normal daily life yields reliable clues about the typical responses of infants to such a sudden and dramatic change. People generally wish to touch and to be touched and cuddled. So fine restaurants often have muted rather than stark lighting, and seating is arranged to convey a quality of warmth and soothing privacy. The designers may not know why the public responds positively to such arrangements, but they do know that those who go out to dine often seek a sense of secure and comforting intimacy. Most people relax best in chairs that embrace them, in nooks and crannies in which they can hide, and in rooms with low ceilings that make them feel cozy. They cover themselves with soft clothes, with blankets, and with "comforters" in part to lower vague and unexplained anxiety, and they find solace in sexual and in other forms of physical contact. Many become nostalgic when they look at postcards that show a softly lit and warm little hut nestling against a snowy mountain on a dark and cold night.

The wish to be held snugly in a tender, safe, and comforting lap or enclosure is never far away, and fantasies that satisfy it are common. These are all normal remnants of the early yearnings to be enveloped and thus to feel safe and protected, longings that remained unfulfilled by the necessity of a separate existence. The relief that follows orgasm indicates the depth of gratification obtained when such yearnings are even momentarily satisfied: "Complete" union with another person was achieved for a moment. Crying sometimes occurs at such times, since very profound bodily tension is suddenly released. We have just dared to be very close to someone who also risked being very close to us. For that one blissful moment at least we can accept the painful realization of our separateness and aloneness without panic.

The hunger for touching is not common, however, to everybody. The earliest experiences after birth leave some people with such powerful residues of fear that intimacy is thereafter regarded as dangerous. This is especially true for those with a history of actual physical abuse. They literally recoil from physical contact, especially if it is intimate; they associate it with a sense of choking and with pain, and they go to great lengths to avoid it. But if their fear of intimacy is ever lessened, perhaps as a result of falling in love or because of successful therapy, a previously denied hunger soon emerges as an actual starvation. These are the people who tend to cling endlessly when they have a chance. In fact, some try to avoid all close contact because they sense the immensity of their hunger. Without understanding it consciously, they fear being devoured by it. Such people are tragically stuck: They consistently and automatically reject that which they desire and yearn for the most. Many of these unfortunate individuals become driven workaholics, others find nonhuman objects such as pets to satisfy this deep need for physical closeness. Sexual frigidity and other forms of sexual malfunctioning often result from this fear.

The body always reacts to touch and to close physical contact in adulthood on the basis of what it knows from before. We can reconstruct the distant past reliably therefore from the typical reactions in the present. We are all newborns—twenty, thirty, forty, or fifty years later. Our *understanding* of the universe changes greatly, but our sense of solace and safety normally remains associated with physical closeness to an accepting, reliable, warm, and tender person or object. When young babies develop the power of motility they tend to push themselves into the corners of their cribs, where they can press against not one but two sides of something solid; they feel least vulnerable there. Up to a point, the more an exposed organism is covered and touched, the greater its sense of physical and emotional security.

The very young human organism, like a kitten, is calmer when it rests comfortably against a live pulsating body, and it normally seeks petting, contact, touching, warmth, and being held. Full breasts or a firm shoulder serve this purpose equally well. Such yearnings and wishes are part of our nature. Humans are generally embarrassed about being part of the animal kingdom, and they try to forget and to deny that they are. But what is true for animals is also true for babies and even for grown humans: They all like and need to touch and be touched, unless they are too afraid even of that. This need is often satisfied only poorly in humans, because touching can lead so easily to sexual involvement. Even innocent physical contact has been severely restricted in the Judeo-Christian tradition because of the zeal to regulate sexual mingling.

8. Viewing Humans as Part of the Animal Kingdom

Man has suffered in shame for a very long time because he tried so hard to rid himself of his animal nature. In vain. He became somewhat civilized in his behavior, but as the Hitlerites and others have shown, the primitive beast within was barely harnessed. Moses only forbade the freed Israelite slaves to *act* as if they were impulse-driven animals, but Christianity later went one better in expecting Man to renounce his beastly qualities altogether. Even some of his thoughts and many of his secret wishes were declared sinful, dirty, and forbidden. In a well-meant effort to ennoble and to improve us, our kinship with all other animals was played down and even denied, as if it were a failing and not a fact.

Man began to have totally unrealistic expectations of himself in the process, believing that he had to deny many of his fears because they were irrational, and many of his real needs and wishes because they were forbidden. Realizing that he was capable of existing just below the angels, Man pretended to have already reached that goal, since he did not know how to get there. He wished so much to make sense that he drove his irrational feelings out of sight and into hiding. This did not solve the problem, however. Without an open channel to the surface, these powerful forces tended to accumulate and, like underground movements in general, they pressure us, terrorize us, and oppose our will. We often punish ourselves with shame and we look down upon ourselves with disdain when our false cover is blown. Tragically, we feel humiliated for being what we really are. The wealthier and the better educated we become, the more guilt we normally experience and the more we are eager to wear a fancy mask of phony reasonableness.

As a result, an endless series of skirmishes between his rational-thinking part and his irrational-feeling part occupies Man constantly, since face-to-face confrontation between the two are not possible: Only the first one is said to exist. Internal conflict multiplies, and guilt about falling short of his unrealistic expectations plagues him daily. Feelings always win, and they usually rule him. Man named the wonderful mental functions of his cortex "higher," hoping to thus lift himself above the "lower" animals—an admirable but pathetic attempt to better himself. It was bound to fail, and it did.

In reality, most of our *reactions*, like those of a dog or a cat, are essentially instinctive and autonomic, and they occur much too fast to involve either thinking, understanding, or knowledge. (This will become clearer in Chapter 3.) But with hard and patient work we can alter our animal nature slowly till thoughtfulness plays a much more significant role in our lives. The first step is to separate acting from our feelings and to slow down reactions that normally are automatic. This is hard to do, and it cannot be achieved without help, for reasons explained in detail in Chapter 6. Our characteristic ways of responding physiologically are eventually modified also. The intensity of the underlying fears and the differing capacities of people to withstand internal pressure determine how long and how difficult the process will be. The subjective sense of danger and the objective degree of safety are obviously never exactly the same in any two situations.

Is it correct then to characterize the newborn's experience of sudden separation from mother as horrible? Not really. This is only true when we consider it from our adult perspective. The newborn knows nothing, and it cannot know anything as "horrible" either. The experience could be described more accurately as a physiologic sense of severe, sudden, and continuing disequilibrium and shocklike disquietude. Take a fish out of water or try to trap a small animal and observe their bodies. What they experience is terror, although they do not know it as such. Experience is independent of knowledge. Fish and Man often fail to understand the nature of their happenings. The nervous system of a fish is less complex and it is probably experiencing its fear with lesser intensity, but the quality of its reactions is the same. The newborn's experience soon after birth resembles that of the fish taken out of water, except that our miraculous physiology generally adjusts to the new conditions: We usually survive.

Most people can easily recognize panic in an injured bird or dog from the way they look. Such animals do not know the concept of panic, but they surely know the experience of panic. Like them, we are often in the grip of fear without realizing it. In spite of all their sophistication, humans at any age generally react physiologically in the same way that other creatures do. Adults have a capacity to comprehend the meaning of their experiences, but even this is often lost, since profound fear usually overrides this capacity. Terror, panic, and dread, the extreme forms of anxiety and fear, generally immobilize anyone, at least for a short while; and they interfere with the ability to think, to understand, and to reason. At best, understanding can dilute fear a little, but it cannot alter it basically.

9. The Physiologic Basis of Character

We have already noted that language itself is misleading when the experiences of newborns are described. Since they lack conscious understanding and intent, it is not accurate to say that they withdraw from externality and into themselves: No conscious sense of externality or of self exists yet. Even so, adult tendencies to withdraw have their roots in such early experiences. The characters of adults are largely shaped in early infancy. One of the most common ways to cope with hurt and fear is to withdraw inside. Here we have ourselves to couple with and to receive solace from. We lick our wounds. Our heart rate slows then, our breathing deepens, and muscular tension lessens. Withdrawal is characterized by a glazed and somewhat distant look, by a fitful attention span, and by non-involvement with others.

Whatever helps the organism lower its anxiety and its excessive physical tension soon becomes habitual and integral to the physiologic character structure. But lowering anxiety through withdrawal causes us to lose out on much of life, since the constant effort to avoid anxiety saps energy and limits the capacity to enjoy and to learn. Harry Stack Sullivan observed correctly that anxiety acts as a brake on intelligence. The I.Q. of people who have benefited from good psychotherapy often rises twenty to thirty points.

The physiologic basis of the character structure determines achievement limits that can be expressed in simple and practical terms: how far people go in school, how much they enjoy their work and their leisure, how well they take care of themselves physically and emotionally, how close and how meaningful their relationships, and even how much money they will earn in a lifetime. The typical patterns of coping with anxiety established in early infancy are reactivated and used again and again when needed throughout life. The real limitations on the freedom of most individuals are not those imposed by objective external circumstances. The walls of our individual prison cells are constructed by the subjective sense of danger. Even oppressed slaves eventually free themselves and throw off their yoke once they are free of fear.

Much of our collective trouble stems from individual enslavement to fear. Political leaders, judges, teachers, parents, and those in the media who shape public opinion are all ex-newborns also; their typical ways of coping with anxiety mold their sympathies and influence their values, opinions, and decisions. Like everyone else, they too see the world through the prisms of their past experience. The personal boundaries of socially prominent people are often nebulous and ill-defined, and their inner confusion is frequently reflected in public acts and policies. Even so, those in positions of authority customarily speak with a great deal of certainty, as if they were completely sure of themselves, to enhance their influence and the weight of their words. Although no malice or evil may be intended, the public is usually victimized and misled when blindness replaces clear vision and a mixed-up jumble is portrayed as order. Fear that is evoked and fanned "often paralyzes the ability of [individuals and] free societies to pursue policies of reason in their best interest." Overidentification and self-righteous or non-reflective attitudes in those with the responsibility of leadership are obviously extremely dangerous "to democratic societies in the age of mass communication."

The tendency to be sickly is another aspect of the physiologic basis of character. Some people typically respond to subjectively unbearable stress by developing physical symptoms, the direct bodily equivalents of emotions. Asthma and various skin disorders commonly develop when such overflow occurs early in life; gastrointestinal difficulties, high blood pressure, and rheumatic disorders are more typical later on. But increased susceptibility to anything, including the common cold, infections, and injuries, is often a sign of intensified stress and anxiety. Dependency upon alcohol or drugs, the compulsive pursuit of money or sex, excessive work or play, gambling, and a large variety of other preoccupations are also symptoms of trouble, as well as means of coping with intense fear. Symptoms bring attention, first aid, and helpful healers—in short, relief from empty loneliness. Besides, they provide relief from adult responsibilities and freedom to regress without loss of face.

Symptoms like phobias are ingenious devices that help us survive, even though they extract a high price in pain. They are usually best treated not as independent entities but merely as representatives of the underlying anxiety. It is much more economical and least painful in the long run to eliminate the source of the trouble. Near the end of the twentieth century few would recommend that illness be treated by prayer alone or by moralistic incantations. Instead we aim at reversing the pathologic process. But drugs to suppress anxiety, or interpretations to increase understanding of the reasons for it, are still used widely, although basically irrelevant and ineffective as cures. They are, in fact, the mainstay of current-day psychiatry. Drugs and understanding do help in temporarily lowering destructive anxiety, thus enabling sufferers to function somehow, but they also hold out false hope, since they never cure.

Although terrifying, anxiety is not in itself damaging. But alcoholism, bad marriages, physical illnesses, and suicides—all methods of escaping from anxiety—are destructive in reality. Even panic attacks would pass without causing actual harm if it were possible to wait them out without seeking immediate relief. But "the push away from fear or dread supersedes everything."

In the grip of panic the entire body, not the mind alone, is in extreme turmoil. Even though we idealize the brain in our culture, much more than "peace of mind" must be found before relief is obtained. It is confusing and incorrect to regard body and mind as separate entities split from each other, since they react together, as parts of a whole usually do.

10. The Depressive Position

The depressive position represents the social outlook determined by the subclinical depressive core. It is characterized by an attitude of futility, an all-pervasive sense that things do not really matter, since it is only a matter of time before we and everything about us disintegrate. It is the pessimistic view par excellence. People in that position sometimes try for a while to hide their misery from themselves and from others: They smile too often and at inappropriate moments, they become loud back-slappers or glad-hand everyone, and they are always busy socially. Such people tend to drink too much and to talk too much, and usually they are much too jolly and too eager—all components of the effort to hide what lies just beneath the surface. A black heaviness often envelops such people in spite of all their endeavors, and it hovers close by even in moments of relative joy. Many people know of the depressive position and sometimes they live there, even if they never develop the full-blown clinical syndrome of depression. This happens less often, and only when important enough losses later in life tip the scales.

More people than ever before live today with a depressed outlook, which explains why these last few decades have been named the Age of Anxiety. The cornerstones of the Judeo-Christian value systems have been eroded by overpopulation, affluence, and urbanization. Two world wars and modern technology destroyed the innocent order of old and caused mass destruction, mass population transfers, and large-scale mobility. Tradition, close family ties, and the work ethic used to provide stability even if they were also oppressive. They have all been weakened and their influence eroded. Everything is, or at least seems to be, in a state of flux. Individuals with poor personal boundaries used to have more steady support in the past from familiar surroundings in smaller communities and from family members who could always be found nearby. No longer. Widespread confusion about sex roles, personal and professional responsibilities, and self-identity now exists everywhere. Many people are interested in discovering their roots or in defining them more clearly. Identifying with a favorite ball club can shore up diffuse boundaries a little, but this is hardly enough. Fragile identities become even more shaky when most contacts are superficial in nature and short-lived. Many seek confirmation of their own worth from relative strangers, since anxiety is often no longer containable.

A profound sense of doom often appears on the surface now. The distance between the depressive position and overt clinical depression is often dangerously short.

People sometimes get temporary relief from anxiety by joining with others in worthy, and not so worthy, causes. Even temporary entanglements with others can relieve the pain of loneliness. The rhythmic pounding of rock concerts also serves this purpose well. Individual pain and confusion are easily drowned while the electrically charged mass of humanity shrieks enthusiastically. In the same way, various protest movements are often much more effective at allaying personal anxiety than they are as influences in the political process. Their aims are only secondary and therefore easily changeable; the same marchers walk the same routes, only with new slogans. Being a part of a "movement" promises solace by temporarily dispelling the fear of abandonment. Here finally is one socially sanctioned avenue through which anger and hate can be mobilized and openly expressed with almost no restraint.

Many protesters are half-knowingly eager to be confronted by the police. This provides a chance to rage against a powerful adversary with an assurance of being stopped before all control is lost. Many have never had any opportunities to define their personal boundaries within their families, and they find it emotionally helpful, desirable, and reassuring to be firmly handled, even if they are physically dragged into a police van. A sense of power is gained when one can exercise strength in an open challenge to the establishment. Besides, anger serves to hide fear, and a sagging sense of self-worth is always boosted by participation in a fight against injustice. We become "good" by rallying against "evil." Racism in South Africa, nuclear proliferation, oppression, famine, pollution, some ethnic interest, or the defense of human or gay rights all serve the cause of combating anxiety equally well. In an almost constantly changing world, injustice and evil seem to be almost blissfully permanent. The fight against them is guaranteed to be never-ending. Not only is the commitment of protesters usually marginal and transitory, but their political goals are often also very unrealistic, utopian, and naive. This is as expected, since the hearts of activists are almost always elsewhere: They are trying, above all, to survive in the midst of the depressive position.

The losses that can precipitate an overt depression are varied and numerous, since it is so easy for most people to lose their footing in any event. A loss may consist of no more than merely growing up or growing old, a relatively minor injury to one's self-esteem, or just one more instance of losing hope. Losses need not consist of such obvious events as a divorce or a death of someone close.

Many people devote most of their energies during their lives to keeping their panic safely under wraps. The endless pursuit of happiness is merely one form of this very tiring, demanding, and ineffectual effort. Paradoxically, the hopeless pursuit may itself bring about an inability to continue, causing a deep sense of exhaustion and an early burnout. The overt clinical depression that these efforts are designed to forestall is often precipitated by such an endless and fruitless endeavor.

People in the depressive position go through life without spontaneity or joy and with great caution, as if they were living in a minefield. Sermons about loving others or about God's love for us cannot affect this sense of futility, fear, and fatigue. Since the basic message of sermons and of psychologic advice is that prayer, willpower, resolve, or insight can cancel the hurt and dread, they often add insult to old injuries and aggravate them. Something must be wrong with us if we do not heed all those good and wise words and still fail to leave our depression behind. We must be weak, "bad," or not determined enough. If guilt is not increased by such well-meaning interventions, despair usually is. This also is the danger of the promises made by self-help books. These promises prove empty before long, and those who try sincerely and hard to pull themselves up by their bootstraps are left even more discouraged than ever. Remember Ernest Hemingway, William Holden, Richard Burton, Maria Callas, and a host of others, in and out of the public eye.

11. Is There a "Right" Distance in Close Relationships?

The panic-knowing core of relatively healthy or well-defended people is not usually exposed in superficial relationships. But it commonly gets touched in more lasting and more intimate relationships where enough attachment and trust develop for our sense of security to become intertwined with another person. A mate or a close friend often fulfills in adulthood the same function that a teddy bear or a security blanket did in childhood: We reach for them in bad emotional weather. Most people are hesitant at first about getting deeply involved, wishing to minimize their risk of loss, but eventually they become emotionally attached and depend on the other to provide solace and support. Popular songs express this situation most graphically: "Sunny, yesterday my life was filled with rain. Sunny, you smiled at me and really, really eased the pain. You gave to me your all and all. Now I feel ten feet tall."

In this context it is easy to understand why a major emotional crisis is often precipitated by the breakup of a marriage or of an important "love affair." The sense of safety that is derived from the approval, the physical presence, and the emotional acceptance by another is suddenly in jeopardy. Mates who become so important pathologically must constantly be appeased and mollified. The fear of abandonment that is held in check by such relationships is mercilessly unleashed when those bonds fail to hold. The threat of being overwhelmed by the fear often casts an ominous shadow upon everything in sight.

The difficulties commonly encountered in marriages are generally inevitable because many are based on the expectation that the partner will allay such a powerful fear, all in the name of "love." Besides, the wish for intimate risk-taking and the capacity for it are usually not the same in any two partners, and this imbalance often triggers panic. The more anxious partner is typically the appeaser. We have already noted in the previous chapter that those fearing engulfment are usually less at the mercy of their partners than those fearing abandonment. The roles may change with time, but one or another of any two marriage partners is normally much more apprehensive about the possibility of its dissolution. Those fearing abandonment usually complain that the other is "too distant" and therefore always in a position of readiness to leave. Those fearing engulfment generally experience their partners as coming "too close," as wanting "too much," and as potentially choking. Both fears often masquerade as anger. What the one experiences as desirable, safe, and necessary frequently appears as an unreasonable demand to the other, or even as a threat. Many people avoid long-term and intimate relationships altogether, to insure that they are never exposed to such disappointments and panic. Their subjective vulnerability dooms their close relationships to certain failure.

Each of us had to face the most profound moments of terror all alone when we were least ready for them—at the earliest period of life after birth. We are left with deep scars from such experiences. Our bodies often react as if they know that all other people are somewhat unrealiable. The impact of such impressions can be lessened by hard therapeutic work or by fortunate circumstances, but long before we understand or remember anything we have already become cautious and somewhat leery about closeness. Without being conscious of it, people usually devote a great deal of their time and much of their energy to insuring that they will not be too vulnerable again. Everyone "knows" how horrible terror is. Our built-in caution and our distrust of others and of the unknown commonly interfere with our ability to really "let go." How can we trust, since "they" have failed to protect us? Against our own wishes and contrary to our better judgment, we may even hold ourselves back from those whom we like the most and know to be trustworthy. The ability to be with others and to depend upon anyone else emotionally is quite often very seriously impaired. Some people are unable even to accept gifts or other loving gestures, fearing the strings that may be attached.

Difficulties with closeness may show only in important relationships that are emotionally involving, but any physical closeness or sexual contact is impossible in extreme cases. All these difficulties may remain totally hidden for a very long time if the two partners in a relationship are more or less evenly balanced in their fears and equally damaged in their capacity for trust. It is possible with luck to find a suitable distance sometimes so that neither partner is crowding or crowded.

The purpose of social and business etiquette is to insure that such issues of deep distrust do not play themselves out in public. In formal living rooms and at the conference table we usually see only the acceptable facade. We are often surprised therefore when someone we thought we knew well but knew only officially suddenly behaves in a manner that is totally unexpected and to us way "out of character."

12. Life from the Infant's Perspective

Our first physiologic adjustments to panic usually sensitize us for life. If we overreact to losses and to traumas later, it is a result of what we were disposed to earlier. Let's look a little deeper into what happened then, but this time from the perspective of the infant. We have already noted that adult concepts and language do not fit such experiences very well, though they are all we have. Romain Rolland and a few other gifted writers have tried to describe life from this vantage point, but even though we have been touched by their descriptions, they were usually taken as having fictional value only. We did not even attempt to draw universal conclusions from them. Patient and keen researches have since confirmed such speculations by actual video recordings. Our early beginnings were indeed most trying and our circumstances most difficult.

Having just been born and having just survived a difficult passage to a mysterious unknown, the newborn was immediately subjected to a long series of unexplainable sensations that impinged upon it rudely again and again. They shook its entire being. This is how we humans "know" of cataclysmic experiences. It was all so overstimulating that the organism soon sank into a shocklike state. The changes were all sudden, forceful, and unexpected; none were gradual, pleasing, or reassuring. The little body was powerfully squeezed, its bottom was sharply hit, its eyes were flooded and the other parts of its body were rubbed, wetted, dried, pinched, smeared, powdered, covered, and uncovered. A cold and sharp scalpel may have cut into its live flesh, sharp needles may have been forced into its tiny veins, probably in the scalp. Light was shining brightly and harshly into its eyes, and loud clattering sounds intruded upon it uncontrollably. Pangs of hunger also started to pull mercilessly on its empty stomach like pincers, as if sharp teeth suddenly bit its insides. Unexplainably, it experienced a sudden sinking feeling from time to time, sensing that it was about to fall and fall and fall. Naturally, instinctively, it screams for its life. This is all it can do. No relief. Nobody seems to be out there. Is there an "out there"? With all its remaining strength it screams more, and it continues screaming "forever," endlessly: Time is not known as such. The attempts to scream pain away and all that panic are to no avail, yet screaming is its only option, the only way to stave off the hosts of mortal enemies who do not cease to intrude themselves. This description was not meant to resemble the earlier one from *Time* about the man caught hopelessly in an elevator, but it evokes in me, the writer, the same sensations.

Something happens from time to time and all the horrors suddenly vanish "for no reason at all." What is a "reason" anyway? The organism is still blind to everything, including reason. An eternity passes before relief "happens," a timeless and endless time of total helplessness before any knowledge of "help" exists. This happens repeatedly, but since even rudimentary memory is barely beginning to come into existence, each episode represents an altogether new and unexpected jolt. The panic and pain are experienced each and every time as new horrors. Each time is the first time. The little organism screams with all its might for dear life literally, till it is relieved by comforting and thus quieted, or until it collapses in an exhaustion of futility. What is this all about? What is happening? What has happened? No questions are possible yet and no comforting answers. Each time the newborn's entire strength is totally spent in a desperate attempt to stop the meaningless horror, whatever it is. What is it? It craves comfort, fullness, solid grounding, non-exposure, warmth, attachment, safety—without knowing what craving is or what anything else means. Solidity and attachment had existed before the abrupt change, before emptiness, groundlessness, and pain replaced them, although it does not remember this either.

The screaming is the prototype of all protest. No more nothingness! More warmth! Peace now! Stop the burning of wet diapers! Stop whatever! Stop! The newborn "wants" desperately to be held, to be given to, to be cared for, right now. Whatever it wants it wants urgently. It must feel safe immediately, without delay. Alternately it begs and demands—in rage, in hurt, with pain and with fear—not to be forgotten, not to be neglected, not to be left. It knows nothing, or anything, of either its begging or of its demanding. It simply runs out of steam when it can continue no longer, it does not even know how to stop. All that is left is to fold in, to give up, to check out. Its thumb arrives by chance sometimes to couple with, or it bumps into the reassuring solid side of the enclosure which is its bassinet. Relief and comfort often arrive, or perhaps nothing happens.

Moments such as these are the roots of the sense of deep hopelessness, helplessness, powerlessness, futility, and resignation, the taste of which is somehow known to everyone. Since no mother or caretaker is ever totally perfect, moments like these are unavoidable. The residues of such experiences linger on for life in the autonomic physiologic responses of our bodies, even if they affect overt behavior only relatively rarely. Here we have the obvious roots of the *Time* dream, quoted at the beginning of this chapter. Here also is the dynamic source of all the rage of students and of their teachers, of children and of their parents, of the young and of the old, at any age and in any place. The mass protests of the 1960s, the terrorist acts of the '70s and '80s, all the wars, the crusades, the revolutions, and the coups d'état were fueled by it, no matter what additional reasons in reality also propelled them. A more current rationale always existed, but this basic built-in propensity for rage and for protest was the engine that drove them all. Contemporary causes unite protesters and revolutionaries, but the urgent need to banish the personal sense of impotence is almost always present. The causes are often real and sometimes only fabricated, but the rage and the fear are always genuine. On the ramparts and in the crib the feelings are basically the same.

Practically everyone tries desperately at one time or another to escape from or to overcome their fears about personal defeat and powerlessness. The concern is universal. It is understandable why "the push to gain power has such a tremendous force." "All excessive pursuits of wealth, pleasure, political influence, and territorial dominance—even the pursuit of happiness itself —are attempts to minimize vulnerability and the possibility of being hurt by others." Early in life we often had to lie there resigned and unable to move, "waiting" for the inevitable, the end. The meaningless sounds in the midst of a shrieking silence must have been much more horrible than any sensation an adult may have while waiting for death to strike the very next moment. The fact that there was no comprehension then was both the reason for the horror and the blessing that enabled us to survive.

The possibility that we might be returned to a state of total powerlessness—in sickness, with aging, or otherwise when we are rendered helpless—is a terrifying prospect. The degree of disturbance from such a possibility yields reliable clues about the basic quality of our earliest beginnings. Our original stress was never of the kind portrayed in the movies and in folklore. No single big calamity occurred, no one big dramatic event that traumatized us and that needs "uncovering."

13. The Inevitability of Disappointment and Dread

Even a parent who would wish to anticipate any and all of the newborn's needs would surely find it impossible to do so. Besides being unrealistic, such a goal is in fact undesirable. It would merely postpone the inevitable disappointment, and the eventual despair would be even more profound. At best, parents can only respond to the overt and covert demands of their babies, but from the unreasonable perspective of the needy newborn this is simply not good enough. It "wants" and demands more of the "ideal" conditions of intrauterine existence.

But once born, we will never be fed automatically again unless we settle for the intravenous drip method. Eating, drinking, and even seeing require some effort. From the subjective perspective of the newborn this is an unjust requirement that deserves the loudest and the strongest of protests. Temperature regulation is likewise no longer automatic, and it requires work and attention to covering and uncovering oneself. Even so, optimum conditions are hardly ever achieved again. For the struggling infant all this is an unwelcome and unfair change, a true deprivation. The common sense of being unfairly and unjustly treated has very deep and early roots indeed. These are the primitive precursors of preverbal rage. Frustration is inevitable. Try as hard as one will, the newborn's unreasonable expectations are bound to remain unfulfilled. It will surely get hurt, and fear is bound to be a part of its experience. Newborns and "old-borns" simply cannot always have their way. We cannot always prevail.

Depending on its genetic heritage, its intrauterine experience, and Mother's physical and emotional health, the greater the newborn's strength the more powerful are its demands and the more intense its eventual disappointment. Weaker babies demand more meekly, withdraw more readily, and settle for less. But whatever the intensity and persistence of the demands, they will not always be satisfied, and almost never fast enough.

Some physiologic routines such as breathing become established in the first few seconds of extrauterine life, and as soon as this happens they also become a part of our past experience. We now have some proof that we can survive even under the new conditions. This "realization" helps the new organism calm down a bit, for a little while at least. But the turmoil continues, and so does the loud and angry demanding that often serves to cover up the panic. As we have seen in the previous chapter, even adults, like newborns, fear sometimes that they might simply evaporate. They often help themselves by becoming outraged.

A residue of having "given up" or "given in" always follows such episodes of screaming and demanding that are not satisfied soon enough. Although this tendency is common, some people have more of it built into their personalities than others. A basic sense of futility and bitterness weighs some people down from early childhood, while others experience it only later.

Here is a graphic example from a morning newspaper:

A man of 51 was found dead by one of his eight children, crouching on a chair in the family kitchen. It was a most unusual suicide: he choked himself to death by tightening a thin nylon thread around his neck. They thought it couldn't be done, but it was. A few weeks earlier he was cornered by two assailants after he left his job as a diamond cutter. Believing him to be the owner and not just a low-paid worker, they forced him back into the shop and demanded the combination for the safe, which he did not have. For half an hour they tortured and beat him, cutting him superficially with a knife on his face, back, arms and legs. They then held a pistol to his head and threatened to kill him . . . but let him go when they finally found a bus ticket in his pocket and realized that he was merely a worker. He needed 11 stitches and was bruised —but safe—at least physically.

Emotionally, the incident shook up a host of fears that were barely held in check before. . . . He . . . was a survivor of Hitler's death camps. His parents and all members of his family were gassed and burned. Only he survived. This is why he wanted so many children: each was named after someone close who was exterminated. "He was always against suicide," said his wife afterwards. But he lived with a sense of futility even before the robbery. Now he knew that he was defeated and helpless and that one cannot prevail. His family struggled financially and the last holiday was celebrated very modestly. "We didn't have much money and many things were missing on our table," she said.

The man left two notes. In one he placed the responsibility for the family's welfare on the shoulders of the 21-year-old son, the oldest. "I ask you children to always stick together and help each other. Do not ever ask for charity or hand-outs. Share in everything justly and according to the urgency of needs. . . . " In the other note he wrote about himself: "I ask your forgiveness, my wife, and also that of yours, my children, but I must say goodbye forever. As you saw, I have become half a person. I grew a beard to hide the scars on my face, but they remained in my heart. I can't take it any longer. I lost all interest in life. Depression has taken over and rules me since those evil men attacked me. I could not imagine that such a thing would happen in a civilized society. I hope the police catch them and that they pay the price. Goodbye.

Such sad people distance themselves emotionally even from those they love. They live as if they must always stay behind a protective barrier beyond which no one is ever allowed. Sneak attacks are best prevented by trusting nobody. But this poor man failed even in that. His body already "knew," long before Hitler existed, that life was precarious and that defeat was inevitable. His existence later confirmed this beyond doubt.

Franz Kafka, who described these horrors best, knew hopelessness, dread, and disappointment intimately from personal experience. "I have been writing and once more I am able . . . not to gaze into utter vacancy," he wrote in a letter to a friend. "Only this way can I hope to find improvement." Thomas Mann, who knew Kafka and liked him, understood the depths of his friend's despair: "He might almost have said 'salvation' instead of 'improvement,' " he commented. Myth makers and other perceptive writers were also able to describe this dread in terms that man could recognize and respond to emotionally, but the real cause of the despair and disappointment was left unexplained. The basic questions remained essentially unanswered: Why the deep hurt? Why do we expect so often not to be heard, not to be answered? Not seeing the true nature of our yearnings, we were not ready yet to accept the fact that paradise was a myth. It may be a part of the world to come, but here it exists only as a dream of little children yearning for the impossible.

We are told that Man was expelled from the Garden of Eden just for eating from the Tree of Knowledge. Why was the price of knowing so high? Something was always missing in the traditional explanations, but now we can make good sense out of that story. By knowing reality we lose our childlike innocence and our expectations that we may be cared for by others perfectly and forever. We can no longer live in the fantasy that God, or anyone, will always look after us and watch out for our welfare. Even believers know that God helps those who help themselves. The Garden of Eden is a metaphor for the womb: We cannot live there again once we see and understand. Not only Adam and Eve but everyone is expelled from that place, not because anyone has sinned but because we are too big to live in a confined space without the freedom to move. We are not really falling from grace but rising to our human potential. Primitive man was so full of fear that he was unable to accept his expulsion with thanks instead of trepidation.

Living consciously means that we recognize fear and pain as unavoidable, even as we appreciate our many blessings. The Garden of Eden is a utopia, like the perfect welfare state in which every child has the right to grow up painlessly into happy adulthood. Not only had we no freedom in the uterus but also no choice, no knowledge, no companionship. Such an existence may be a sweet fantasy for very young children, for spaced-out acidheads, or for a primitive Adam, but it is a dubious blessing for thoughtful and mature individuals.

Every mother responds to her child's cry in her own way. In general, such responses are objectively either a little too quick or a little too slow, too abrupt or too hesitant, based on too little or too much self-confidence. Very little in life is absolutely perfect. Her reactions are a function of Mother's concept of herself as a person and of her emotional readiness for her role, more so than they reflect her understanding of her duties and responsibilities. Parents with newborns are generally young, inexperienced, scared, pressured, financially struggling, and self-doubting. Many more mothers and fathers than one would expect are actually jealous of the attention, time, love, and money that are devoted to their pampered newborns, and they often resent them. Babies make such extreme, persistent, and unreasonable demands upon their parents' strength, patience, and resources! Mothers who are themselves bitter and dissatisfied about their own earliest beginnings experience this even more sharply. Knowingly or not, a mother might wish to be cared for herself rather than care for anyone else; the needy little creature in her arms often stimulates the mother's own yearnings to be held.

Children of such mothers are not necessarily abused. The great majority of adults control their angry impulses, especially toward their own young. But such mothers tend to become inhibited with their infants, so careful not to be wrong that they are rarely right. Mothering can become either overprotective and smothering or else too cautious, cold, and formal. There is too much of Mother as often as there is too little of her. A mother does not have to avoid her child for her not really to be there.

At least occasionally every newborn feels dissatisfied and disappointed. From its "view," all mothers and fathers fall short, since they fail to protect it from dread. Even so, its very life is in their imperfect hands. So fear is unavoidable, even if the infant has no comprehension of it. Its experience is like that of a deep-sea diver who is dependent for survival upon an oxygen supply controlled by someone in a boat above. What if that person happens to fall asleep sometimes, or if they just leave for a little while, perhaps because they are annoyed? Such a diver would be in a constant state of panic unless he knew beyond doubt that his support crew was utterly reliable. Panic would always be present, even if he was in actual danger only very rarely. Fortunately, newborns are unconscious of their situation, but they cannot escape the subjective experience, and it leaves traces in them for life. This is the source of unexplainable anxiety attacks and of anxious dreams. Competent women do not really panic just because they encounter a mouse, and competent men do not fall apart just because of a business failure. Sensible people obviously do not break into a cold sweat suddenly for no other reason than driving past a cemetery. Young, handsome, and intelligent men are sometimes completely lost when their girlfriends leave them, but only because leaving activates a dormant anxiety of old. A rich variety of incidents trigger the old panic. Why are such simple and self-evident observations not yet known to all? Because too much anxiety is evoked even in intelligent observers once they begin to acknowledge the existence of such terror. Many people, including experts in the field, do not dare even now to see the obvious.

14. Is Emotional Dependency Dangerous?

Consider the tremendous fear many people have of being dependent upon anyone, even a mate, a friend, or a surgeon. We often fear to trust others. We want a second opinion when we can have it, and a third, to check on the first and the second. Of course, if we put our life in someone else's hands, we better make sure that they are not only competent but also sane, responsible, ethical, and physically healthy. Naturally we are very careful, since not all mates, friends, or physicians meet all these qualifications. But we were actually even more totally dependent in early infancy, though we had no assurances at all about the quality of our caretakers. We have already noted that they must have been less than perfect, and everyone's experience must have been therefore less than fully joyous. So we are very wary now, because once was more than enough.

But why does the idea of an *emotional* need for someone, or of emotional dependency, evoke so much fear in adults? Because even in adulthood such losses often trigger reactions similar to the horror that we experienced early in life. Actual dependency differs greatly from emotional dependency, as we have seen, but both are often experienced as one. We prefer therefore to be involved only with those who have proved themselves to be totally reliable "forever." Since this is obviously impossible, many people try to avoid long-term or intense relationships in which emotional dependency normally develops. Many relationships remain devoid of intimacy to insure that no subjectively perilous loss becomes possible. The willingness to pay such a high price merely to maintain the subjective sense of safety is one more proof of how unsafe we "believe" the past to have been.

The very strong emotional dependency that develops in relationships between non-individuated people is generally experienced as if it were an actual dependency. Remember the story of the Duke of Windsor in Chapter 1. A loss of such a relationship is perceived as actually endangering survival, evoking much fear of abandonment. When mature adults sustain important losses, they experience pain but not usually fear. Yet "Many intellectually mature adults are often emotionally not much older than toddlers." "They typically act and react on the basis of their earliest life adaptations as reflected in their feelings and physiologic reaction patterns." Emotional involvement and dependency can indeed be dangerous as long as one's personal boundaries are ill-defined. These boundaries can and must be repaired for real closeness to become possible.

Under the influence of the women's liberation movement some women have proudly begun to claim that they are invincible and self-sufficient. This is important to them for the same reason that many men want to appear strong, quiet, and steady, never shedding a tear. Remember John Wayne or all those motorcycle gangs that are so eager to challenge everybody, those who "never" are afraid of anyone? Why do they want to be feared? Why does anyone wish to be seen as invincible? Because the oldest way of banishing fear has always been to whistle in the dark and to appear unafraid. We hide the fear and hope that it will not affect us. Those most afraid are usually most eager to show themselves as supermen and superwomen. It is not a very effective way of finding safety, but it is the best way that many people know.

In general, the more one fears vulnerability and weakness, the more one denies them. The more one craves a helping hand, the greater the shame and the fear of reaching for it. Losing face is dreaded because it often means losing position, which in turn can make a person seem more vulnerable.

Many people do not dare to be emotionally dependent in the present because actual dependency in the past was so very frightening. Before individuation is achieved, adulthood is often experienced as being similar to early infancy. Even being sensitive is often regarded as a liability rather than the asset that it really is, because those who appear insensitive can more easily maintain that they need nobody and cannot be influenced by anyone. Such people usually feel scared, small, and vulnerable, and they dedicate themselves to hiding and to denying it so nobody can take advantage of them. They poke at others to prove that they have the power to do so and to get away with it, though they commonly damage their most important relationships in the process. But denial does not change the reality that we are all somewhat interdependent, both as individuals and as societies, even if admitting the truth causes much anxiety.

15. Current Treatments of Depression

Major "breakthroughs" in anti-depressant drug therapy are announced every few months with much fanfare. Many people are, or know someone who is, clinically depressed, so such news is good copy for TV and magazines. Much rides upon such hopes—the profits of pharmaceutical companies and of their advertising media, the budgets of universities and hospitals looking for greater financial support, and the advancement and prestige of those who spend their lives trying to find new and better drugs.

The well-being of those in need of better treatment is least affected by such news. All these drugs, old and new, alleviate some of the horrible pain for shorter or for longer periods, while producing some unpleasant or dangerous side effects. None cures or changes the illness itself. They usually do not touch the underlying problem, and it remains unattended. Most "experts" nowadays hold that depression is merely a biologic aberration like sugar diabetes. As long as they can entertain this possibility seriously, they need not look at their own hidden anxiety. "Intellectual . . . achievements tend to confuse and to conceal the marked discrepancy that often exists between the emotional and the chronologic age." Perhaps the panic that is so painstakingly denied will just fade and go away.

Drug therapy under the supervision of physicians is obviously preferable to self-prescribed drug dependency, but the benefits are the same: Both lower the anxiety and dull the hurt by masking the symptoms. If drugs are not used to bring a little relief, compulsive traits become activated, physical illnesses develop, or drinking, overeating, and smoking are resorted to to control the bubbling panic and to block it out of consciousness. Gambling, the endless pursuit of material things or sex, and burying oneself in work are other devices to maintain some control over the anxiety. Although dangerous and occasionally deadly, all these must be regarded as efforts to survive. It is obviously better to lose money, health, or even some self-respect than life itself. The measures used to dull the sense of dread are not equally destructive; compulsive reading, which causes a person to withdraw from adult involvements, is obviously much less damaging than criminal activity or dependency upon alcohol. Anti-depressant drug therapy, like psychiatric hospitalization, can be helpful and even lifesaving when used sparingly and judiciously. But it never cures the illness.

To merely treat the symptom is to neglect the patient. Yet this is the current norm in psychiatry. A major conference was recently held in a leading teaching hospital in the United States on "Diagnosis and Treatment of Anxiety and Panic Disorders." The many physicians and medical students who attended were told that "if a patient has three panic attacks in a three-week period" he needs treatment, and that "the diagnosis should be made if a patient has any five of the following nine findings: insomnia, dizziness, dyspnea [difficulty in breathing], ringing in the ears, palpitations," etc. What causes anxiety and panic? A whole lecture was devoted to a common and essentially non-harmful inborn disorder of the heart—mitral valve prolapse—which was featured that day as the main cause of anxiety. The rest of the half-day program concerned itself with "Pharmacologic Management of Anxiety and Panic Disorders" and with "Behavioral Therapy in the Management of Anxiety and Panic Disorders." This is the state of the art. Many millions of patients really have no place to turn, even in the U.S., with its otherwise advanced medical facilities.

To "manage" means to control, to administer. It does not mean to eliminate or even to ameliorate. The implied message of that conference was obvious: Since nothing can be done to cure these conditions, we must at least learn to manage them more efficiently. It may not reduce suffering much, but it may at least reduce costs. No one even suggested or mentioned the possibility of a cure. (For the contrasting view see Chapter 6.) One of the lecturers stated flatly, as if it were an established fact, that "panic attacks are genetic and run in families, as proved by twin studies," adding that the "usual procedure for the treatment of a panic attack is to flip a coin as to which of the anti-anxiety agents we used, since they are basically all the same." The vulnerability to anxiety and to panic was claimed to be an "inborn error" of development, "like having a tendency to have a trick knee."

Ignorance in this area is still the rule, not the exception, because any increase in understanding requires that the observers first note and then work to eliminate their own anxiety. Only then might they dare to see the depths of panic in anxious patients. But "the push away from fear or dread supersedes everything," and this applies as much to experts as it does to others.

Since the anxiety at the core of the person existed since birth, he cannot "revert" to a panic-free existence. Patients treated symptomatically are condemned to a precarious existence that is lifelong. But the condition is curable in the majority of cases, although not without consistent and dedicated efforts over several years. Those who reach an anxiety-free state live freely for the first time ever.

It is extremely costly and wasteful to merely treat the symptoms, since restorations to the "pre-morbid" status quo are usually short-lived. The panic tends to bubble up again and again, repeatedly interfering with normal living. Depression weighs like a heavy stone on a person's neck, pulling him or her down. Every task is twice as hard as it should be, takes extra effort and time, and is done less well. No reliable figures exist, but economists estimate that the gross national product is substantially reduced because of the widespread effects of this malignant condition, which affects productivity and morale, the incidence of accidents, the frequency and severity of illnesses, and the inventiveness and initiative of all. Like defective motors, depressed people function with only two or three of their eight cylinders working. The car with such an engine is usable for short distances, as long as the weather is not extreme and the landscape is flat. But it becomes useless in the cold of winter, in hilly countryside, for long journeys, and when it gets a little bit older.

New episodes of the lifelong illness usually reappear in patients who are merely "managed." These are often regarded as "new" and therefore compensable illnesses by insurance companies as long as six months or more have elapsed between successive attacks. Expensive rehospitalizations costing almost a thousand dollars *a day* follow one another, draining public funds and private hope. What needs to be treated is the core panic itself, not just the overflow that shows on the surface. This is very hard to do, but it is doable nonetheless.

In the meantime, while confusion and lack of understanding abound, avoidable tragedies multiply without end. The symptoms are regularly mistaken for the illness. Worse yet, most symptoms are not even recognized for what they are. An innocent reach for a cigarette or a sudden and unexpected decision to get married may both seem normal. But both are well-established devices to lower excessive anxiety.

Symptoms of depression do not generally exist in isolation; they are usually part of a larger pattern. Fear of flying, for instance, may be but one manifestation of a person's unconscious plan to remain at home, where it is subjectively safer. The hidden wish to regress to a childlike existence is often not consciously acceptable to those experiencing it, and they may deny such wishes in good faith. It may nonetheless exert a tremendous influence on their lives. The fear of flying is a symptom of a real illness, just as fever or swelling is associated with infection. It does not result from any lack of understanding about the safety of air transportation, and it is not affected by reasoning with the person. Thinking, understanding, and will are irrelevant when pitted against anxiety and panic. The purpose of most symptoms is to bind the otherwise free-floating anxiety, which is achieved as long as the symptoms continue. Symptoms often disappear by themselves when the level of anxiety is lowered sufficiently.

It is relatively easy to desensitize a person against a limited fear, such as that of flying. But this hardly solves the real problem and often worsens it. The unbound anxiety must find a new outlet, or something else is likely to break down before long. Symptom substitution is a reality, regardless of how many people still fail to see it. Merely treating symptoms is not only an unkind but also an inefficient way to approach suffering human beings. One would not treat a broken mechanical device this way. Each patient also deserves to be treated as a system in need of repair.

Pathologic symptoms such as the fear of flying result from the body's growing big before the person matures emotionally. People who never felt secure enough cling to outer symbols of safety throughout life—financial or political advantage, job seniority, old routines, a woman's bosom, a man's physical strength or size. Anxiety always rises to the surface and a new symptom develops when such established arrangements are suddenly dislodged. To eliminate the symptom without reducing the anxiety is to ask for trouble, as is apparent from the following memoir by Frances Conley in *The Runner* (June 1983) of one man's struggle to balance life and death through the discipline of running:

I always promised, John, that someday I would write your story. . . . I don't remember exactly when you came on the scene, but you rapidly joined the small group of people with whom we spent our increasingly precious time. . . .

You were a resident in internal medicine, I a medical student spending my requisite time with your team. . . . The residency is a difficult time in the training of any physician, a relentless 24-hour-a-day job, and one is always on hand to witness the immediate effects of one's judgment, to see a wrong decision reflected in a turn for the worse or even the death of a patient. You rapidly became my hero. . . .

I did not find it very peculiar that you should go about your doctoring chores wearing a 20-pound weight vest under your clean, pressed, and buttoned-up professional white coat. . . . It seemed that running was your game, not just a podunk few laps around a track, but real distance running, five, ten, 20 miles at a time. Since you began your rotation as senior medical resident, time for running had vanished. The weights were your attempt to maintain fitness and keep in shape. . . .

At that time I could not have begun to understand how important running was to you. . . .

Winter rolled into early spring. . . . Whenever I met you in the hospital I would jab at your ribs to see if you were still wearing that silly weight vest. If you weren't, it meant you had already run five to seven miles and had plans to go out for an additional joyous jaunt at the end of the work day. You were at peace. . . .

It was you who . . . encouraged our group to join the 300 zealots running the Bay-to-Breakers race. As we finished those 7.6 miles through the streets of San Francisco, we too finally understood the exhilaration and sense of accomplishment you got from your sport. . . .

For me, as for you, running had become a very important component in the equilibrium of my life.

Our friendship broadened beyond the spheres of medicine and running and we began to see you often socially. . . . You were then at the last stage of medical education, having decided to specialize in hematology/oncology . . . an intellectually challenging specialty that is also often filled with despair. So many of the patients an oncologist sees are those with incurable diseases, for whom a physician can do little but

give compassion and comfort. It seemed a fine choice of career
for someone who could give so much of himself to the an-
guished needs of others. Your sense of humor would serve you
well. We applauded your obvious professional success and saw
none of the sadness and torment. . . . The steadily increasing
mileage, the weekly road races became a necessity for you, a
diversion for us.

After you moved a short distance away to establish a private
practice, we no longer ran together regularly, but our social
events often included a run or athletic games before a party.
To one such affair you brought a woman friend, a lively, sympathetic person and an accomplished pianist. After the run you
abruptly, inexplicably, departed alone. "Not to worry," your
friend explained, this had happened before. You would return.
And you did, but you were quiet, preoccupied, unable to capture the spirit of the party. You left, along with your friend,
early in the evening.

This was a new John. We discussed the event and decided
that something must have happened to one of your patients. . . .

We heard about the accident in which you totalled your
beloved red Chevrolet convertible and chuckled to learn that
you had bought an indentical car that same afternoon. . . . Still
the news carried an unspoken undercurrent, a disturbing question. We wondered whether drugs had been involved. . . .

The true situation became manifest with jarring clarity. . . .
A mutual friend . . . asked if I could house you for the night.
You were manic, and while rational, couldn't be trusted with
the care of patients and were in need of psychiatric help. Unfortunately, a hospital bed on the appropriate inpatient psychiatric unit would not be available until the following morning. . . .

You paced about chattering happily and restlessly exploring
the apartment you had been in a hundred times before as if it
were completely new. I suggested we go out for a run. At this
you abruptly stopped cold and told me very deliberately that a
broken bone in your foot had not allowed you to run for the
past month. You would not be with me now had you been able
to maintain your running, you insisted—not being able to run
had deprived you of an essential release for your pent-up "energy." . . .

After I took you to the hospital your psychiatrist treated you
with a drug called lithium, and while it did calm you, it provided you little comfort. . . . Watching young persons die of

incurable disease plunged you into intolerable depths of despair. Drugs were handy—you used them to quiet the pain of
cancer in your patients and found, in time, that the same drugs
could lessen the agony of your own paralyzing bouts of depression. . . .

With treatment you did improve, enough to return to your
home and to a limited medical practice monitored by concerned peers. You even began running again, slowly and painfully. But somehow you could not, perhaps would not, allow
running to assume the place in your life it once had occupied.
Maybe you were afraid to become dependent again on that
activity, which in the past had so totally consumed your physical and psychic being.

Yet a means of escape from the traumas of your world became as vital to you as sleeping, eating and breathing. Other
activities were tried and rejected, each proving inadequate to
tame your terrors into peaceful submission. Tranquility continued to elude you, and you found that without running you
were unable to continue living. Your suicide told us that, for
you, running had been everything.

John's tragic living, suffering, and dying cannot fail to touch
us. His agony did not result from his inability to halt the process
of a terminal illness, or from watching young people die. He had
a terminal disease himself, and he actually died from it—depression. The many other millions everywhere who share his fate
remain faceless and nameless, and they fail therefore to stir us.
But their pain and their struggles are no less real and no less
tragic. They usually have nowhere to turn, except for first aid.

The proper treatment of depression requires undoing the tendency to fold in and give up. This is a formidable task, since
sufferers do not allow themselves to hope again. They fear opening up very deep and old wounds. It is nevertheless possible to
help such people become involved in dependable long-term therapeutic relationships that are based on real human contact and
commitment. The task requires persistence, patience, sensitivity, skill, and dedication, but it can be done.

Chapter 6 describes the quality of sane, consistent, and dura-
ble therapeutic relationships that permit the uninhibited experience and expression of all feelings, including the fear, hurt, and
rage that otherwise choke or even kill. Dormant yearnings are
slowly reawakened in such a setting, and hope is rekindled. The

person is helped to legitimately claim some place in the world as his or her own.

My dinner companion did not just "gain" the eighty pounds that she eventually "lost"; she grabbed them out of fear that she would be blown away otherwise and be no more. She felt herself as insignificant and acted as if this were actually a fact. Yet such an explanation, although true, would have made no sense to her. She had other, more "reasonable" explanations for her condition. Her husband failed likewise to recognize his hidden panic. Their anxiety was of such a magnitude nonetheless that it determined major aspects of their lives. Denial does not change reality. The fears of abandonment, engulfment, and non-being often remain unseen, but when present they eventually exert themselves with a powerful force that shakes people to their very foundations.

THREE

Feeling and Thinking

... most of our knowledge about the universe is subjective, and subjectivity contaminates practically all objective observations. The way we are is the way we survived, so we tend to hold on to our basic convictions and views about reality with the greatest tenacity. It is often obvious that what we claim as rational is no more than a poor rationalization, but we are usually the last to notice it.

Achieving objectivity requires the courage to critically examine cherished positions and to abandon those that no longer make sense, even though they may have been important sources of our security in the past.

CHAPTER 8, SECTION 64

1. Rationality as a Goal in Need of Fulfillment

Why is it often said that religion and politics are best not discussed with friends? Because these, more than most other subjects, generate strong feelings that interfere with the ability to reason. When feelings intervene, conflict rather than clarification is the probable result. Feelings cannot be reasoned with, even when they appear in the guise of thoughts. Cautious men and women therefore usually avoid discussing controversial issues except with people known or suspected to share their basic convictions and assumptions. They don't dare expose themselves to views that might cause them to boil over. Should we have been in Vietnam? Should there be prayer in public schools? Should government finance abortions? George McGovern and Barry Goldwater used to elicit powerful reactions and not only

113

because of their political positions. Their personalities alone evoked strong feelings. Most people disliked at least one of them almost instinctively, regardless of what they stood for. All such immediate reactions are expressions of basic attitudes anchored in feelings; only rarely can attitudes be substantiated on the basis of rational considerations.

But we like to think and to speak of ourselves as rational beings, and any suggestion that we may not be is usually met with indignation. What makes us different from and better than all other animals, we claim, is our ability to be rational. We generally expect ourselves and others to make sense, but nonetheless from time to time we defend the indefensible because we have a strong urge to prevail. What propels this urge? Feelings. Such a stance obviously makes no sense, but this rarely deters us. We are often willing to be flexible at the expense of reason when emotionally charged issues become involved. We may even claim at such moments, in good faith, that we are still eminently sensible.

People are generally willing to submit without protest to arbitrary dictates such as traffic lights as long as they are convinced that they are not being singled out unfairly. But some regard even such normal obstacles as personal insults, proving the world's insensitivity to their preferences, which they often experience as urgent needs. Not everyone accepts the constrictions of reality as inevitable, and constraints that are not so clearly neutral are often met with resistance based on anger against all authority. In general, unpleasant reality is more acceptable when it is not excessively charged. Charged with what? With feelings.

Everyone sees the world from his or her own perspective in a unique and special way. Although reality is whatever it is, one and the same, people generally see at least slightly different versions of what they look at, even when observing the same thing at the same time. Individual views of reality are merely approximations. The physical position of the observer is responsible for some of the differences but not for all. Feelings cause our eyes to see through distorting lenses, producing images that are a little bigger or a little smaller, a little closer or a little more distant, but usually somewhat different from what they are objectively. In a sense, each experience of seeing leaves an imprint in our eyes, affecting the accuracy of how we see next.

Feelings thus limit our ability to see, hear, smell, touch, taste, and evaluate things objectively. Since they also interfere with the ability to think clearly, they are powerful enough to bend our perception of reality, sometimes to an extreme and amazing degree. Even so, most people innocently assume that the stronger their convictions about the world, the more they are right. In the heat of an argument, even very intelligent men and women often fail to note that others, equally thoughtful and knowledgeable, are equally convinced that their opposing views are at least equally correct.

Feelings routinely push even sensible people into making wrong choices. We often marry people who are not really right for us because we are blinded by love. Sometimes we divorce reasonably compatible partners because fear, anger, hurt, or hate interfere and mislead us. Some tend to distance themselves from all people, others pursue them relentlessly even in hopeless situations; feelings determine what they do. We may understand that it makes no sense to follow such a course, but only rarely can we reverse ourselves in spite of good advice and the suggestions of many self-help books. Some people become obese, others worship at the altar of physical fitness because of feelings. Many of the hard-to-name aches and pains and the symptoms that remain forever vague result from feelings. The list is practically endless. We make money and friends and then lose them; we try hard in life or refuse to; we succeed and we fail; we are cautious or reckless—all because of feelings. Propelled by their force, we "choose" values and life-styles, make political decisions, and embrace causes. Public policies and editorial positions often reflect their hidden influence. A high-sounding statement such as "very deep concern exists about disturbing developments" is often no more than an expression of someone's disguised fear. Feelings distort objective reporting and they introduce a bias even into scientific observations. Overt or covert, feelings are everywhere.

Man makes relatively few decisions freely, without the hidden coercion of his feelings; because of their pressure he often overlooks his best interests. In general, people are led by their feelings and then they unknowingly invent rationalizations to explain their actions or decisions to themselves and to justify them to others. No one wants to be seen as irrational, in the grip of forces bigger than oneself.

This is why people commonly delude themselves that they are thoughtful, when in fact they are merely preoccupied with thinking. Such ruminating is to real thinking what busywork is to real labor. Lacking direction, ruminating is unproductive and wasteful. Its main purpose is to bind anxiety to its busyness, thus keeping the anxiety under control. It is extremely time-consuming and tiring but leads nowhere, like driving a car several hundred miles, all around the block. The scenery is painfully boring; the work is hard, long, and tedious; the effort is real. But the car ends up exactly where it started. "Much thinking is circular and ruminative and leads to conclusions already arrived at by our feelings." Ruminating enables us to live by the dictates of feelings without losing face; we appear to be thoughtful.

People in general are unaware of the tremendous power of feelings, and they do not guard themselves against their disturbing influence. Even when we acknowledge their existence we usually deny that their power over us is so great. The first step toward lessening our relative powerlessness is to recognize our feelings much more than we do.

2. What Are Feelings?

Emotions or feelings are the residues of our lifelong individual experiences. Physiologic patterns are established very early in life, and those that help the organism survive become part of its habitual way of responding to stimuli. Some of these patterns are already established in utero, others become functional soon after birth. But once established they become characteristic and they determine the quality and force of our automatic responses in the future. Such early programming limits a person's freedom, since normally no one acts "out of character."

The typical reactions of a person thus yield reliable clues about the specific nature of one's past and about the experiences that shaped his or her character long before memory existed. Rather than reflecting current reality, feelings express our expectations based on what we already know from before. They are therefore totally unreliable as a guide to actions in the present. Falling in love is a poor reason for getting married, and being angry or hurt is not in itself a good cause for getting divorced. Normally we respond emotionally with little consideration of the real circumstances that confront us. Deep convictions in matters of trust, for instance, may have very little to do with the real qualities of the person we are involved with now. The nature of our most important relationships early in life determines to a large extent how we relate to others later on.

Remnants of feelings that have been denied and suppressed accumulate within us, since they find no legitimate outlet, and their pressure increases with time. These hidden forces remain powerful influences in practically every life, though conscious awareness of what exists within us is usually lacking or incomplete. Education, intellectual growth, and other achievements do not reduce this internal pressure. Much energy must always be spent on assuring that such forces remain under control; even so, leaks are unavoidable.

Fear and hurt are the two feelings that most commonly live underground, and from there they influence our relationships, our thinking, and various body parts and functions. Many people really do not notice that their breathing is always shallow, their musculature always tense, and their ability to see, hear, or even think always greatly constricted. Since they have never been completely free of fear or hurt, they understandably assume that how they are is not only normal but the only possible way to be. The pressure of these feelings causes chronic tension, which invariably brings about considerable damage. The stress that is associated with this tension is seldom the result of current difficulties alone. Although most people still ascribe it to their job or personal life, it is a reflection of suppressed fear, hurt, or anger. The body of a tense person is like a car whose accelerator is pushed down and stuck with the engine in gear and the emergency brake tightly on. The tense body, like that car, also tends to tremble, to shake, and to break down too soon. The extra burden of internal pressure shortens the life spans of motors and bodies alike.

We have the potential to be guided in life by the two modalities that can be ours: thinking and feeling. But this double-pronged tool is not dependable before we correct the biases and distortions that are reflected in our emotional reactions. These can be slowly eliminated, though only with consistent and patient help from another person. In the meantime we repeatedly end up in deep trouble when our actions are stimulated by feelings without being corrected by our thinking. In spite of an endless supply of examples to prove that reliance upon intuition, impressions, hunches, or feelings is disastrous, most people fail to examine carefully enough that which their heart is set on. Individuals as well as societies pay a high price for this tendency.

The problem is compounded because people tend to masquerade their feelings as thoughts, without being aware of doing so.

Since they do not realize that they are being swayed by irrational forces, they do not guard themselves against being misled. People often claim in good faith that they have considered matters thoughtfully even when they have not done so. We generally dare not admit even to ourselves how little room we have to maneuver when strongly gripped by any of our emotions.

3. A Personal Note to the Reader

If these observations are valid, they apply to all. Neither you the reader nor I the writer are exempt. It is possible therefore that in reading this book you might react, even strongly, as I have on occasion when some ideas disturbed my inner status quo. Were you unexpectedly impatient or excited, unusually pleased or displeased, eager or restless? Were you suddenly tired, energized, or bored? If so, do such reactions reflect the quality of the material or mostly your physical state and feelings? You may be pleased if your reading confirms what you have sensed all along. On the other hand, some anxiety and even annoyance may be expected when one considers the possibility that the yardstick used for daily contacts with others may be faulty. Whatever your reaction, these ideas probably deserve to be evaluated thoughtfully. This note is meant as a reminder in the service of maintaining objectivity.

I recognize that my calling attention to the desirability and need for self-observation may strike a sophisticated and sensitive reader as condescending, as a justification for dismissing the whole thing. Yet, surely not every reader would immediately notice that his or her impatience may only be a concealed form of anxiety. This is something all people would rather avoid. It has the power to block clear thinking and patient consideration. Anxiety often causes people to escape from or condemn whatever elicits it. I have to face this difficult problem somehow, and addressing you directly is the best solution I can find.

In any event, the charged nature of many of the ideas in this book involves us in the exciting but difficult process of checking how our emotions sometimes trip us. We cannot examine our basic assumptions about people and things unless we remain objective and thoughtful. You the reader and I the writer have a relationship through this book. Its strength and worth are tested by its capacity to remain relatively constant, regardless of any momentary strain.

4. Why We Downgrade Feelings

The more sophisticated and educated we are, the less likely we are to express strong feelings openly. We have too high a stake in remaining rational at all times, even under stress. Although it makes no sense, many people try to pay as little attention to their feelings as they can, hoping that somehow this might lessen their effect. We still tend "to hide even from . . . [ourselves] the fact that many of . . . life's most important choices and decisions are made on the basis of feelings, not rationally." The entire educational process is geared toward thinking, even if it fails to produce many truly thoughtful individuals. Having such a heavy investment in rationality, we obviously want to assure its safety. We do so in strange and ineffective ways.

By now it comes naturally for many people to modulate their voices and to moderate their arguments in the Anglo-Saxon tradition, regardless of how vital the issues are. The civilizing veneer is paper-thin, however, as the bitter infighting and backbiting in marriages, in academia, and elsewhere strongly suggest. Raw and unrestrained anger and irrationality are not uncommon in political protest and in labor and other disputes. Too many conflicts in public and in private life exist only because "the central role of feelings, and especially of irrational fear, is usually ignored. . . . Yet feelings obviously do not simply disappear when their existence is not acknowledged." As a result, often no rational resolution of disagreements is possible, even though the conflicting interests may be objectively reconcilable without much difficulty. Bar brawls are not recommended, but they are much more efficient than are intellectual disagreements and debates that ignore feelings and lead nowhere. If a covered pot boils over, it still boils over.

Paradoxically, the greater our investment is in always appearing rational the less successful we usually are. Maintaining thoughtfulness under all circumstances is not assured by avoiding controversial issues or people, nor by taking only middle-of-the-road positions. Rationality can be preserved only after we have accepted our irrationality, and not before we have taken pains to eliminate rather than to deny it. We can maintain a rational mask otherwise only for as long as we avoid everything and everyone with whom we might disagree. We associate then only with those who are "like us," read only what reflects our "good" beliefs, and obviously vote only for the "right" candidate, never for anyone from the "wrong" party. Truth and the freedom to think for ourselves are the victims. Although we may assume a haughty air of superiority to justify our being so exclusive, we are not really free. We live narrowly in very small and confining spaces, and we tread most carefully. We cannot really consider positions other than our own before we trust our capacity to remain thoughtful even under the pressure of strong emotions. This always requires preparatory work.

People who do not need to be always refined and rational demonstrate more openly what happens when their strong "convictions" clash with those of others: Voices and blood pressure rise; speech becomes faster, sharper, or less coherent; reasoning is fuzzier; and in extreme cases physical violence erupts. More sophisticated people tend to view such expressions with disdain, as if they prove the primitive nature of others. But no one is totally exempt from the possibility of having such irrational outbursts.

Generally people wish to hide the fact that much of what they stand for and believe in is influenced by feelings and is not necessarily the result of thoughtfulness. Decisions do not result often enough from consideration of the various alternatives. Yet the words "I feel" occur frequently in daily speech, in spite of the common denial and downgrading of feelings. This strange linguistic twist, which is customary by now, may have started as an unconscious slip, but it makes sense anyhow. It is in the nature of feelings to change quickly; those in the habit of saying "I feel" may sense somehow that positions can be given up more easily if based on feelings. This is desirable when it is important never to offend or displease anyone; firm points of view must be avoided then. "I feel" leaves more room for hedging than "I think" or "I believe," and it is much easier to retreat from such a position without losing face.

In general, the presence of fear increases the value of retreat as an option. Wishing to avoid conflict, reasonable people often yield to those who appear to be irrational. But under the guise of being reasonable, people with fear often give in too quickly. Those who really are unable to control their rage often prevail, and so do the others who merely succeed in conveying the impression that they might lose control. Irrationality is fast becoming an increasingly effective tool. Not so long ago retreat was a mark of shame, and we honored those who had the courage of their convictions. While still paying lip service to this ideal, we have adopted the habit of retreating, both in domestic relations and internationally. Indeed, orderly existence in societies is not possible unless all parties yield momentarily whenever strong feelings are aroused. But modern man went further: He elevated yielding and assigned it a value all its own . He downgraded feelings and hoped that a unilateral commitment to living by reason would make him safer. Naively, he also must have expected that his example would be sufficient to sway those living without such a commitment.

Since we are proud of our ability to compromise, we often fail to realize that only in the realm of feelings is give-and-take always justified. In matters involving thinking, compromise is often morally indefensible and it frequently leads to appeasement of others, to degradation of oneself, and eventually to extinction. It often involves the sacrifice of principles, vital interests, and friends. Truth does not necessarily lie somewhere in the middle between two extremes. Right and wrong do not have equal value, and they do not deserve to be given equal time on the evening news or anywhere else.

Moderation, which is desirable in the realm of feelings, is often the first victim when powerful emotions are given room and license to prevail in actuality. This is never safe. But it is safe to experience feelings and to express them openly with full intensity, as long as no physical action or decision-making is ever associated with such expressions. Even panic, storms of rage, and powerful yearnings to be loved are safe under such conditions, without harm coming to anyone. Relationships are not necessarily disturbed by feelings; even when stimulated by others, they reflect first and foremost internal pressures in the person who experiences them. Children who are allowed to express their feelings without hindrance while required to assume responsibility for all their actions grow up with little fear of ever losing control. Without suppression, denial of the power of feelings is unnecessary; hardly any remnants accumulate in the body. Emotional appeals have only slight influence then, and both personal and public affairs can be managed steadily, without sacrificing either principle or integrity. This ideal situation has never yet been achieved on a societal plane. It is still rare even among individuals.

The denial of feelings and the rejection of emotionality do not indicate enchantment with rationality but rather a secret recognition that thinking is normally no match for feelings. It is obviously naive to act as if denial changes anything, but this is exactly what Man has generally done and is still doing in regard to feelings. This denial is rooted in old traditions that hold that the flesh is weak and the spirit susceptible to sin and to lust. It assumes that to have a feeling is the same as to live according to its dictates. It sees Man as having even less power and even less will than he actually has.

Yet even though it is widely used by almost everyone, denial is an extremely poor method of self-help. In the short run it helps in warding off painful and frightening realizations, and hence its popularity; but the ability to cope with reality remains grossly impaired. Many intelligent and knowledgeable Jews and others paid very dearly for denying the danger of Hitler's rise to power, yet this is how we often react to extreme fear. The eventual awakening, which cannot be postponed forever, is always more rude and more painful than it would have been otherwise.

People also deny their feelings because they are embarrassed by them. From an adult point of view they are indeed irrational, since they no longer fit the new circumstances of adulthood. Yet we all want to be rational, and we desperately wish to be known as such. Our experiences early in life, before we were able to understand anything or to reason things out, were subjectively so terrible that we cling even to the appearance of rationality. We naturally cherish and jealously guard the view of ourselves as rational beings.

But if Man were as rational as he claims to be, he surely would settle his many disputes rationally. Peace and harmony would reign, and neither riots nor rebellions would ever plague us. It is no secret that violent conflicts, suicides, divorces, unemployment, strikes, and wars are all wasteful of scarce human and natural resources. But they are part of life everywhere, now and throughout history. Man repeatedly proclaims himself to be a thinking creature, even though his actions prove that this is often not true.

5. Man as Part of the Animal Kingdom

Like all animals, Man is first and foremost guided by his feelings, and he too gets trapped or damaged when they misguide him. Feelings are biologically designed to help creatures in their struggle to survive. They enable animals to react automatically, and therefore very quickly. But the inflexibility of feelings is also the basis of all hunting and fishing. Predators learn how their prey is likely to behave, and this is how they succeed in trapping it.

We humans are the best hunters and fishermen of all because

our reasoning capacity can assess reality more reliably, though more slowly, than our feelings can. We have a second guidance system to warn us against dangers not perceived correctly by the first. We alone have the potential use of two complementary systems, feeling and thinking, with which to acquire knowledge about the universe. With their aid we have gone further than all other known species in exploring our environment.

Traditionally we have devoted much time and energy to teaching the subjects that can be learned by understanding, but we have neglected feelings, the more powerful system. Never knowing till now how to master it, we simply ignored it. Yet feelings must also be "educated," though using a totally different approach. Our emotional reactions can be calibrated to fit the new realities of adulthood; then they become reliable as a tool with which to assess reality. Although this need to calibrate our feelings is usually ignored, we nevertheless depend upon them heavily and use them daily. Here is the cause of the trouble everywhere. We are repeatedly being misguided by a defective system. Since feelings helped us survive long before we could think and reason, we automatically turn to them again and again for guidance and help.

Like other creatures, we humans react physiologically by seeking experiences that we have known as safe and by avoiding situations that we recognize as sources of discomfort and pain. In a sense we are not basically different from very hungry fish who swallow both a real and a man-made fly with equal fervor. We err too. When not propelled by the pain of hunger or by the fear of starvation, fish might be a little more cautious and bypass a suspicious-looking lure. But a desperate fish, like a person in panic, throws caution to the wind in the pursuit of relief. It is easy to see why any creature would overlook hidden hooks in bait while in the midst of a hurried and compulsive escape. Man has devised ingenious traps using this principle, even for the largest and most powerful animals. But he also gets trapped when "the push away from fear or dread supersedes everything." We ourselves are not very successful in avoiding dangerous pitfalls when we act in accordance with our feelings and when we fail to pay attention to our judgment.

An amoeba automatically propels itself away from a noxious environment and toward one that is more compatible with its continued existence. The same principle applies to all other creatures in the animal kingdom, including Man. The reflex arc is the simplest, fastest, and most primitive of our warning systems.

Several other intermediate information and regulation systems help us with our complex existence: the nerve centers in our brain stem that govern such functions as breathing; the pivotal areas of the autonomic nervous system in the midbrain and elsewhere; and the relatively unknown system that mediates our feelings. The nuclei of this system are believed to lie adjacent to but below the cortex, which is the center of thinking and understanding. Even anatomically, feelings are independent of rational considerations. Although feelings are slower and more complex than the reflexes, they are much faster than our thinking. Based on past "knowledge," feelings enable us to react to stimuli that are perceived as threats much more quickly than we could if we depended upon thinking alone.

As we have seen, Man likes to look upon himself generally as a creature altogether different from and better than all others. This belief in his exalted status provides him with a sense of power that reduces his anxiety. He often prefers therefore to minimize the importance of the links that unite him with the rest of the creatures in the animal kingdom, which is why some people resent any comparison with an amoeba. But Konrad Lorenz and other leading ethologists are probably right in claiming that the comparative study of animal behavior is best carried out across the broadest possible range of species. Feelings would misguide us again if we allowed them to limit the scope of our observations.

6. The Fascinating Model of Our Human Brain

A few decades ago, Paul MacLean, a neuroanatomist, elaborated a theory about Man's overall brain structure, sometimes referred to as the triune or tripartite model. It holds that the brains of humans and of other advanced mammals consist of three evolutionary parts that *ideally* act together and complement each other.

The first and most primitive part of the human brain he called "reptilian." It concerns itself essentially with instinctive and repetitive behavior. (The typical behavior of lizards and birds is essentially repetitive because their brains are mainly of this type, hence the name.) MacLean called the second and more recent evolutionary part of the human brain "old mammalian." It is chiefly concerned with feelings and roughly corresponds anatomically with the "limbic system," a term also coined by

MacLean. This central neural network stores the "knowledge" that determines how we react emotionally, and it regulates the specific nature of our reactions. The third and last part to develop is the "neocortex" or the "new mammalian brain," the crowning glory of evolution. It is responsible for all the complex and unique capacities of Man, the so-called higher mental functions such as thinking, understanding, conceptualizing, and communicating.

MacLean's model of the brain won almost universal acceptance, although it is still unclear whether it is accurate in all its details. Its widespread attraction comes from its ability to explain many of the strange manifestations of human behavior that are not easily explainable otherwise. Why do we persist in reacting emotionally in the same old ways, even after we have learned that certain things are not in our best interest? Why is understanding not a powerful enough factor to alter our typical ways of being?

Using the tripartite model as a starting point, we can now come up with very plausible answers to these questions. Our experiences in the first few hours, days, and weeks after birth, and probably even earlier, during the later phases of our intra-uterine life, make deep impressions in the neural pathways of the reptilian and the old mammalian parts of our brain, collectively known as the "visceral brain." From then on, our body continues to react basically in the same manner that it already "knows" to be compatible with survival. The engraved "footprints" determine how we respond to any stimulus that activates our characteristic modes of reacting.

Subcortical firings are at first sporadic and random, but not for long; connections that help us survive soon become preferred pathways. The more a pathway is used, on earth and in the brain, the sooner it becomes a highway; and highways are preferred because travel on them is quicker and the chances of getting lost are smaller. Repeated use and reuse of the preferred pathways of the visceral brain reinforce them to the point that all other possibilities nearby functionally cease to exist. They are rarely if ever used. The established pathways soon determine our characteristic ways of automatic behavior. Those who take care of an infant can soon predict how it is likely to respond in any given situation.

The outline of the physiologic basis of our character thus begins to become clear very early. Before long, every new experience of dread automatically and instantaneously calls up all the information that the organism already has about similar stimuli. When we are only hours old, our body already reacts on the basis of what it "expects" to be most adaptive, least painful, and least damaging to it. Unlike the simple reaction patterns of the amoeba, ours are already influenced by a rich storehouse of past experiences. No consciousness or memory exists yet, but our feelings mediate our reactions quite efficiently even then.

As newborns we become essentially what we are as adults. Each of us will react emotionally in typical and specific ways throughout life. Since many billions of possibilities exist when the neurons of the subcortical (visceral) brain first become activated, no two people ever react exactly in the same way emotionally, even if their earliest experiences were nearly identical. This is what makes us humans so fascinating.

Our capacity to store the lessons of past experience is greater than that of "lower" animals because our subcortical brain is relatively large. It has many more neurons and it can hold much more information about our experiences before consciousness existed. But our muscles, like theirs, also tense from fear when we perceive danger, our eyes and pupils also widen under such circumstances, our heart beats more strongly and faster, and we suddenly forget all other pain and discomfort. We too mobilize for fight or flight. We too withdraw in hurt and in defeat and explode in anger and sometimes in fear.

We humans are blessed in addition with a unique cortex that enables us to ascribe meaning to things and to communicate in speech. This truly wonderful organ is capable of performing marvelous feats that even our most advanced computers connot come close to matching. Yet, though it can integrate new data without difficulty, it is not in command of the old knowledge of the body. Those aspects of our existence known as "autonomic" are essentially not affected by anything we learn intellectually later on. We may fully understand, for instance, that a gun is not dangerous in itself, that it must be used to cause harm, yet most people nevertheless experience a rush of anxiety when they suddenly notice that a gun is present. The body does not regard the newer information that is stored in the cortex as superior to its own. Since it already "knows" what is safe and what is not, it "refuses" to accept commands from higher up. It relies instead on what has worked for it in the past, before the cortex was functional to aid it in the task of survival. Thus, sometimes even relatively minor incidents that cause us some anxiety activate the old pathways of the visceral brain. Our feelings are not usually upgraded, so they are quickly triggered and repeatedly get us into trouble.

Feelings can be deprogrammed, but not as easily or as quickly as we can change our thinking. Even this requires a great deal of effort. To change our feelings requires that we alter the subcortical pathways that regulate them, a task believed impossible till now. Although our typical ways of emotional response may mellow a little with time, such spontaneous changes are relatively small and extremely slow. Proper psychotherapy as described in Chapter 6 accelerates this process and makes room for essentially new ways of reacting. Our perception of what is dangerous must be thoroughly changed. When successful, this is a truly liberating process that frees people by enabling them to live fully without irrational fear.

The development of each person's brain parallels the historical evolution of the human brain in general. The cortex becomes fully operational much later than the two more primitive parts. This is why we can breathe on our own long before we can speak, think, or recognize ourselves and others. Although nonintentional grasping is reflexive and occurs early, intentional grasping, like walking, requires an accurate gauging of distances —a function of the cortex—and it is therefore later in coming.

We are obviously much less fragile by the time we learn to walk and when we begin to understand. We have learned much about life by then, and we begin to know that even if our situation is less than perfect, most of the time we are not in real danger. The young child has already undergone powerful and important experiences by then, but it has no memories whatsoever of events that occurred before its new mammalian brain became functional. This explains the strange fact that even intense fear or the most powerful yearnings are often evoked by something or somebody without our knowing what, who, or why. Finding no reason for such unexpected reactions, people often naively conclude that no reason exists. Even physicians are likely to tell a patient that there is "nothing wrong," simply because they cannot diagnose the trouble with their usual expertise and instruments. Emotional pain is often regarded even now as unreal. But even when there is no memory and when no physical findings exist, the body "remembers."

Most people know that we humans tend to repeat our mistakes and that we are often powerless to reverse our pathologic tendencies even though we try. Now we can see why this is so. Insight and increased understanding, being functions of the cortex, are powerless to affect behavior patterns that are governed by other parts of the brain. New Year's resolutions are not generally kept: The reptilian part of our brain is simply not impressed by sincerity. The cortex, which is what we normally have in mind when we think of our brain, is irrelevant in the efforts to alter repetitive or ingrained behavior. Using this understanding allows us finally to devise effective methods to eradicate our self-damaging and self-destructive tendencies.

The capacity of our will is also limited. Man's tendency to indulge himself and to follow the path of least resistance is so strong that usually he does not even exercise his will fully, making the common excuse that he is powerless to do anything else than what he is already doing. Yet will alone really cannot change character. Basically we are not the masters of our fates until we are freed from the dictates of our feelings; we only pretend that we are, to save face. "The suggestion that Man is essentially guided not by rational thinking but by irrational feelings . . . endangers [that part of] our sense of power . . . [which is derived from] the delusion that we are more in control than we really are."

The old established pathways of the visceral brain must be loosened before more adaptive ones can be formed. Behavior change that is not the result of such alterations is only temporary. Character modification that enables a person to live essentially without panic is very difficult to achieve, but it is finally within reach as we shall see in Chapter 6. Rationality is, even now, a promise waiting for fulfillment.

7. The Delusional Idealization of the Intellect

It is easy to understand why we idealize the cortex even beyond its real importance. Since the intellect gave us power, we crowned it king. It provides us with the capacity to reason, to think abstractly, to deduce, to organize phenomena, and to communicate in speech—all functions that elevated us above the "lower" animals and that enabled us to harness many of the forces of nature. Our intellect established our position on the top of the evolutionary totem pole. But no matter how much we idealize the cortex, it remains the youngest part in the evolution of our brain. Like most youngsters, it does not always fulfill the hopes of those who love it and who believe in its potential. We can be rightly proud of our wunderkind, but we have become so enamored of it that we ignore its youthfulness, its failings, and its weakness when compared with its two older neighbors.

In reality, we depend even now mostly upon our feelings to lead us and to guide us. It would be much better for us, individually and collectively, if we could actually live the way we pretend we do, by reason and thoughtfulness. But this goal still eludes most people. Historically, only a little time has passed since we lived in the darkness of our prehistoric past, before the cortex enabled us to change our lives. We try to live in a civilized way, but as our private and public behavior proves, our nature is still basically primitive. The goal of living just below the angels has not yet been reached.

We frequently refuse to accept these facts because they are deflating to our self-concept. We like to believe that we are in charge and in control of what we do, and since the internal forces that pull and push us are not plainly visible, we can succeed in forgetting that they exist. We are thus saved from facing our relative powerlessness.

At the dawn of history we reduced our fears by assigning magical meanings to the mysterious phenomena that surrounded us. Only as we began to understand more did we slowly dare to stop worshipping deities that never existed. Naturally we do not want to risk losing the hard-won position of apparent rationality, whether it reflects reality or not. We are reluctant to discover that our belief in the power of understanding and in the intellect may be delusional.

But the promise of rationalism was not fulfilled. From the marble facades of great buildings we proclaimed that "knowledge is power," but even so, strong feelings rendered us powerless. The sudden eruptions and storms of powerful emotions still cause us to lose our bearings. We are driven by fear, and our judgments are confused by it in spite of our intellectual sophistication and technological advances. By filling ourselves with wishful fantasies about our power to control our lives we do not really become stronger, only bigger, like a balloon. Even a painful reality provides more real power than the most comforting delusion.

Freud's formulations about the unconscious threatened to deflate our fantasied sense of power, but not for long. He and his followers soon deluded themselves into believing that the lost power could be won again by gaining insight, by analyzing the unconscious, and by making it conscious—all functions of the cortex. Psychoanalysis has helped many people become wiser, and the relationship with the analyst usually lowers anxiety somewhat; but it basically fails to cure, because it attempts to change reactions and attitudes under the control of the visceral brain by working with the new mammalian part. The physiologic roots of anxiety remain essentially untouched.

Even if intellectually we accept the idea that we are not really in charge of many of our decisions, it can be frightening to consider it as applying to ourselves. We can find comfort by dismissing the disturbing ideas and by putting them out of our mind, but it really is unwise to do so: Up to a point, knowledge is power. Understanding cannot alter physiologic processes, but it can lessen that small portion of our anxiety that results from not knowing what plagues us. It can help us know which way to turn when we attempt to gain control of our lives.

8. Brain Development in the First Two Years of Life

Neuroanatomists, psycholinguists, anthropologists, psychologists, and others have studied the behavior of mothers and children in many cultural settings in order to discover what causes children to begin speaking when they are approximately a year and a half old, and why humans eventually learn to walk erect. After all, their ancestors walked on all fours and they too begin life by crawling, like other animals. Standing up is the physical basis of our special perspective which allows us to be taller and to see farther ahead.

Several studies suggest that the number of nerve cells in the cerebral cortex, and probably throughout the brain, is fixed at birth, but that much of the maturation of these cells occurs in the first two years of life. This apparently is unique to our species; in others, a sudden slowing of brain development takes place roughly at the time of birth. It explains why we can learn such complex and totally new activities as walking erect, thinking, and speaking long after we are born.

Although the human brain does not form new nerve cells, it does develop new dendrites, those armlike extensions by which a nerve cell makes contact with axons, the branches of adjacent cells. Observers have also noted that non-neural cells continue to proliferate in between the nerve cells, thinning out their dense bunches and doubling the weight of a child's brain in the first year of life. These cells consist largely of myelin, a fatty white matter with insulating qualities. They eventually make up sheaths of myelin that surround each nerve fiber and separate it from all others, very much like the plastic sheathing around the metal core of electric wires. Insulation facilitates *selective* conductivity in both cases. A wire will conduct electricity with or without insulation, but without it, any current that passes through one wire is also transmitted through all others that touch it, causing a generalized reaction.

This is a somewhat gross but not really inaccurate approximation of what happens in the brains of newborns as they experience strong stimuli. In the absence of adequate myelination, all stimuli that are strong enough to activate the system cause a generalized shudder reaction. Newborns shudder at the sound of a loud noise, when a bright light suddenly shines into their eyes, or when a noxious smell disturbs their equilibrium. Such reactions are at first total, involving the entire body. Even internal stimuli are often experienced as major threats, as if suddenly the newborn were falling into an abyss. These non-specific reactions look like the typical bodily response to intense fear at any age.

Although the newborn does not yet know danger as such, it fully experiences dread. Because it cannot yet distinguish between minor and major stimuli, everything strong enough to arouse it is experienced as titanic. The new mammalian brain does not become fully functional until the myelin sheaths around the cortical nerve cells are fully formed. The visceral brain is in charge of everything before that, and it regulates all responses to internal and external stimuli. This is when the typical pathways of physiologic response become established by repeated use.

Becoming automatically numb is one typical way by which the newborn helps itself survive, despite the flood of stimuli that impinge upon it. One reason why newborns sleep so much is that they need protection against overload; sleeping shuts out stimuli. Such periods of relative non-receptivity serve exactly the same purpose that fuses do in an electric circuit. Since neonates, unlike amoebas, are not mobile, all they can "do" is fold in, physiologically and psychologically, as if life were only possible in a cocoon.

As their myelin sheaths form, the functional capacity of the cortical nerve cells increases dramatically. Impulses are channeled as nerve cells become capable of conveying specific and discriminating messages. Although the actual speed of impulses through the nerves is probably constant, it appears faster because specific parts of the body now respond very rapidly. The maximum possible rate of successive firings also seems to increase. Since fewer cells are activated by any one stimulus, less time appears to be needed for rest. Each nerve cell is now protected from stimulation by nearby cells, and it is therefore more often ready and available when needed. The newborn's earliest reactions are the most generalized and therefore the most exhausting. More time is required to regroup from such experiences than from the lesser ones later on.

Neuroanatomists do not yet have experimental proof for the hypothesis that the "higher" mental functions of Man increase proportionately to the increase in myelination, but such a relationship appears to be highly probable. It is obvious though that we begin to distinguish shapes, sounds, colors, and tastes only slowly, after we have managed to survive for a relatively long time. Our humanness eventually begins to unfold, but not before we start to understand, to speak, and finally to experiment with assigning meanings to our various experiences.

This general outline is not in dispute, yet we still tend to think of the cortex as being synonymous with the brain. The visceral brain is not so well known, and it is often overlooked even by experts in favor of its competitor, the cortex. But since experts derive their status and their livelihood from the cortex, their position about its value is not necessarily objective or valid; feelings are often involved, and they tend to color and distort the experts' opinions. Forgetting this, we usually quote experts as if their words necessarily represent unbiased facts.

The troubling but exciting truth is that you the reader may have as much "expertise" on these matters as anyone else. With care, you are in a position to determine to what extent experts make sense in this regard. Impressive credentials in themselves are not enough. We cannot afford to overlook our own emotional reactions when we wish to sustain our ability to think objectively. It is useful therefore to become somewhat suspicious of unexpected fatigue, of temporary difficulties with understanding, or of other unusual reactions. We too ought to be careful not to downgrade the visceral brain.

The face of reality is best recognized by checking its features repeatedly and carefully from several points of view, as surveyors do. It really is best not to trust our immediate reactions when we first encounter new, foreign, unusual, or seemingly unpalatable foods or ideas. The expansion of perception requires time, patience, and courage; but these are richly rewarded when we gain a better understanding of ourselves and of our surroundings.

9. The Basic Qualities of the Basic Feelings

When someone is asked, "How do you feel?" the usual reply is "Fine," "Good," "Okay," or the like. Prodding might produce an answer such as "About what?" Sometimes people even admit that they are troubled or distressed, though usually not in public.

But these are not feelings. They are all non-specific and socially accepted expressions by which people communicate with one another, and they serve to hide how we really feel. People are normally reluctant to reveal their feelings lest such information be used against them. Injured or sick animals in the wild soon become the prey of others, and so they instinctively attempt to look healthy and even fierce. To survive, Man has done likewise. Just a few centuries ago people also lived much more precariously, in cruel and harsh environments, worse than our crime-filled streets of today. The self-protective habit of hiding emotions is as old as Man, and it is interwoven into his nature; many people are almost totally unaware of how they feel. Hiding our inner life may indeed prevent others from hurting us when we are vulnerable, but it also prevents us from helping ourselves when we are in pain and in need.

Relatively few distinct feelings exist. They are love and hate, hurt and anger, happiness and sadness, and—above and beneath them all—fear, the subject of the first chapter. In addition we also feel such direct physical sensations as hunger, cold, heat, pressure, fatigue, and several others. Shame, embarrassment, guilt, envy, or jealousy are either variants or combinations of the basic seven feelings. To feel guilty, for instance, is to feel fear and to expect some punishment such as ridicule or rejection.

We commonly speak of love, hate, or some other feeling, but we do so very loosely. If we really loved ice cream and fish we surely would not eat them. Similarly, we do not really hate getting up early in the morning, we are only disappointed or annoyed at not being able to sleep a little longer. Teachers who "feel" that students should try harder or parents who "feel" that schools are too lenient are really expressing thoughts. The idea of another Vietnam may give rise to fear in those who might get killed or maimed in such a war, or even in those who are close to them, but no anti-Vietnam feeling exists. Politicians some-times evoke the hidden fear of an anti-nuclear "feeling" because they can exploit it to advance themselves, though they would not admit to doing such a thing. Teachers may be angry at stu-dents who abuse and frustrate them, as parents often are at their spoiled sons and daughters, but such anger is often denied under a mask of false reasonableness. Obviously, no feelings exist that will tell us whether unemployment or the value of the dollar will rise or fall. Television is peddling nonsense when its com-mercials urge us not to lose that "good feeling" of buying prod-uct X.

We all have strong emotional reactions, but frequently we do not know it; not always do we feel our feelings consciously. Many people have never had the freedom to emote openly, even as young children, and they were never given sufficient oppor-tunities to learn what they feel. They are either numb to their emotions or blind to them. Yet even feelings that are not expe-rienced as such continue to exist; they affect the various tissues and systems of the body even more strongly. Anxiety, for in-stance, most typically constricts muscles and blood flow, and it speeds up the heart rate. We may nonetheless fail to take correc-tive action for a very long time, since we are often unaware of what is happening. Important relationships and body parts thus break down, without the people involved knowing that they had been under severe and chronic stress. A physical symptom or an emotional crisis occurs when the internal pressure exceeds the holding capacity. "Nervous breakdowns," many industrial and automobile accidents, and most illnesses are the end points of such a process.

But ignorance still abounds. The National Council on Com-pensation Insurance, which sets workers' compensation rates in thirty-two states, still says that "on-the-job" stress accounts for nearly 14 percent of all claims, up from under 5 percent only a few years ago. Depression and heart attacks were said to be the most common "job-related" illnesses in Michigan in 1983. A group of psychologists, working hand in hand with lawyers, ad-vertises in California newspapers for "work stress" and harass-ment complaints, the "in" categories now. A Kentucky seamstress actually won benefits because of her claim that she suffered a nervous breakdown from the stress of choosing differ-ent thread colors!

We have already noted earlier in Chapter 1 that nobody can make anyone else feel anything. We can only evoke that which already is present. We can produce physical pain or even death, but not feelings—in ourselves or in others. It is impossible, for instance, to make others happy. Basic contentment must already exist in those seeking happiness, for it cannot be induced or produced otherwise. Feelings are in fact totally self-made by those who experience them. When others elicit feelings in us, they only awaken them from their dormant state.

Even very strong emotional reactions normally pass quickly if they do not connect with stored remnants of suppressed feelings from the past. The fact that many people react similarly under similar circumstances only proves that we often have similar life experiences. For instance, we all feel somewhat scared of becoming old and physically dependent, since we were all helpless at our beginnings; we "know" a lot about that state. But no two people react to this possibility, or to any other, in exactly the same way.

"You make me feel bad" or "I feel hurt by you" are examples of attempts to induce guilt, the most insidious tool of oppression in existence. It is meant to force another person to apologize, to cower, or to behave in a way that would please us. Some parents and marriage partners use such strategies to prevail, exploiting the fears of their children or spouses to get their way. Youngsters raised in such a fashion often try to "get even" when they grow up by treating others similarly. If others are hurt by our actions it is because we do not fulfill their expectations, which often are unrealistic.

Hurt is commonly kept hidden; otherwise the hurt person is revealed as vulnerable, thus opening him or her to the possibility of being hurt even more. On the other hand, both real and feigned hurt are sometimes used as weapons against others, to elicit guilt, to extract submission, and also to obtain sympathy and succor. Hurt thus often becomes a life-style that some people cling to with great tenacity because it provides the supplies they want or need. Such people sound whiny, they typically complain, and they are seldom satisfied. In return for the rewards that they extract from others they must appear to suffer, a posture that becomes inseparable from them. Victimizers and victims at the same time, they survive on crumbs.

Anger and hate are generally frowned upon in most societies because their potential for harm is so great; they can lead to violence. Uncontrolled eruptions are widely feared, and for good reason. Stories about murderous rampages of people excessively devoted to the cause of peace are well known. Even the existence of these two feelings is therefore often denied and any trace of them kept out of sight, as if such precautions would protect us from being overpowered. We fear the possibility of exploding with rage so much that we even dread experiencing anger as a feeling. Most people expect feelings to be followed by actions; those associated with anger and hate are too dangerous to come near.

Much confusion exists because of this extreme fear of anger. Even psychoanalysts shun the term "anger" and use "aggression" instead, as if the two were one and the same. In reality, anger is a feeling, aggression an act. The first is safe, the second is not. Paradoxically, the danger of exploding uncontrollably is increased when the opportunities for expressing anger openly are decreased. Yet most parents and others, including psychotherapists, try to plug up all verbal expressions of anger, for fear that the caldron will boil over. So the internal pressure that finds no safe and acceptable relief slowly builds up till something "suddenly" happens "out of nowhere."

Tremendous energy is wasted in never-ending efforts to keep anger suppressed, repressed, and hidden. The more complete the denial the greater the danger. Slow-moving, slow-thinking, and slow-speaking pipe smokers and others who can seldom be ruffled and who do not react strongly to anything may not only be boring but also potentially dangerous people. Those who unexpectedly butcher, mutilate, or randomly kill everyone in the sight of their gun are often described as having been quiet, decent, well behaved, and extremely well controlled. Many men and women plan everything in their lives with meticulous care and caution to insure that such horrors won't "happen" to them. But when one feeling is suppressed, all others are squashed also. Such cautious people cannot ever let go; they do not often laugh heartily and hardly ever enjoy anything with relish or delight.

Even genuine love is something that people dare to express only with great trepidation. Loving requires sensitivity, tenderness, and also the willingness and ability to risk close involvement with another person. It is much easier and less hazardous to profess romantic "love" and to gush with phony "caring" and sweetness, since these are only devices meant to impress others, to find—not necessarily knowingly—a protector from the fear of abandonment. We are naturally eager to display our "sincerity," "humanity," "devotion," and "loyalty" when we are campaigning to be chosen as someone's favorite. But we must be open and unarmored to be deeply touched, and also when we reach out to touch someone's soul. We are vulnerable then. To be met by insensitivity or inconsiderateness at such moments may cause us much pain. This is why people generally dare to love others only when they experience themselves as safe.

The same with happiness. People like to give the impression that all is well in their lives, since those envied are often believed to be more powerful. Bragging and exaggeration are not uncommon therefore, but true contentment is. Even though ostentation and conspicuous consumption are everywhere, it is rare to find a person who would openly admit that he is happy and has enough. The rich usually try to avoid full disclosure of their wealth, and they guard these secrets more than the details of their sexual involvements. This preoccupation with secrecy is not merely a result of the wish to escape the attention of criminals, competitors, salesmen, and tax collectors. Genuine blessings are often kept hidden for "fear of the evil eye," and besides, many people still worry about some sort of retribution for having a richer or a better life than they believe they deserve. Like animals, we tend to guard and to hide what we have, lest bigger and stronger creatures take it away from us. Many people also do not easily forget the lessons of childhood, that everyone is entitled only to a fair share.

Depressed people often do not know that they are sick, but they can sense that something basic is wrong. They commonly believe that what is missing from their lives is love, and that happiness would come with it. But neither of these is obtainable from others. Not knowing this, people often spend much of their time and many of their resources on improving their looks and their social skills; they read to sound intelligent and dress up to be desirable. False advertising cruelly promotes the futile search of such desperate people. The pursuit of happiness is a thriving industry of huge proportions based on false promises and encouraging false hope. The poor souls who seek love and happiness this way run till they collapse from exhaustion and a broken spirit.

What really pains these people is not what they miss but what they have: an extra dose of hidden fear and hurt. These unresolved remnants of the past weigh them down in the present. Happiness and love can find no room when fear fills everything. But the empty chase normally continues nevertheless, since most people do not know how futile it is, and they would not dare to accept it if they knew. The yearned-for goal appears always just a step away, but it remains forever elusive, like a rainbow.

Even now most adults still believe like innocent children that "finding" love or happiness means that they would "be loved" or "be made happy." They have never discovered that no degree of love from others ever makes a lasting difference before self-love exists, and that real happiness must emanate from within.

Sadness is usually hidden less. But even then we try not to let others see it unless we sense that they would be sympathetic. Otherwise we just grin and bear it. Those sad sacks who typically advertise their sorrow are usually not so sad as they are scared, and they try to survive by evoking pity, the closest substitute for love that they know.

Real sadness, unlike hurt, is not only painful it also has a tinge of sweetness. We have no need to deny the existence of sadness, because it never threatens the integrity of the self. It exists only beyond hurt, beyond anger, and beyond jealousy, since it signifies acceptance of things as they are. Sadness only surfaces in the relative absence of fear, and it often arrives in the company of wisdom. This is why we often welcome it. It signifies that some of our struggles are over, that turmoil is lessened, and that inner peace is near.

Because of the great importance of these feelings to our understanding of Man's functioning, each is considered in further detail in Chapter 4.

10. Feelings as Our Guardians

Although we may be blind to the existence of feelings and deny their presence, they nevertheless not only lead us but also watch over our body when our thinking is inoperative, such as during sleep. Fear and hurt cause people to become encrusted in a layer of insensitivity that insulates them from all but the most powerful stimuli. But those who remain sensitive often have a premonition of danger before it becomes evident. Feelings that are not distorted by remnants of the past frequently warn us even during the waking state, as dreams do at night. Dreaming represents activity of the visceral brain as it nudges the sleeping cortex to wake us when needed, or to protect our sleep when we become too anxious. Since we are unable to think, reason, or understand during sleep, dream images are usually garbled and

confusing to our cortical understanding. They are meant to produce emotional responses propelling the dreamer to act automatically: Sometimes we need to act on our behalf while not
consciously aware of our situation. Freud was fascinated by the
content of dreams, since he had a strong pro-intellect bias, but
the feelings are the really important component. In the past,
feelings were even more underrated than they are today.

No living creature would survive for long without some alert-
ing mechanism in constant operation. We usually have dreams
that alarm us, like a clock, when the conditions around us become very uncomfortable or dangerous. We wake up not only
when we have an urgent need to empty a full bladder but also
when fire or smoke endangers us, when we get uncomfortably
cold, and sometimes even in the presence of a stranger who
stares at us. Dreams that do not wake us are also our guardians.
When strong feelings from the waking state interfere with our
physiologic need for rest, dreams often help to remedy the situation by allowing the emotional conflicts to be resolved for the
duration of our sleep. The day's residue, consisting of the most
recent incidents, is apparently not so well filed yet, and the visceral brain often reaches for it in its attempt to arouse feelings.

But psychoanalysts still concentrate their efforts on discovering the hidden meanings in the content of dreams, as Joseph did
in ancient Egypt. They regard the unconscious mind as if it were
a part of the new mammalian brain with which their patients
did not yet have the pleasure of becoming acquainted. It is in
fact a function of the visceral brain. It is unrealistic therefore to
expect that analysis of forbidden wishes, dreams, and slips of the
tongue would free Man from the forceful grip of his feelings. The
terms "insight" and "understanding" have been infused with
magical powers that they do not deserve; for many they are new
idols. Yet belief in them does not change the nature of such
graven images; they remain powerless. Feelings continue to
dominate, since analysis fails to change them. Rather than be
guarded by our feelings, we must continue to guard ourselves
against their pull.

Not everything we do thoughtlessly, impulsively, and automatically is governed by the visceral brain, the one we depended
upon before the cortex was functional. Harsh parental prohibitions, for instance, and some other early-childhood lessons are
incorporated by *cortical* learning. These also become part of the
character and they will also be obeyed unconsciously. Such constrictions of the "superego," and the guilt associated with them,

can be lessened by analysis. But this does not help very much. What really cripples most people is their animal nature, the "id." The veneer of civilization only covers some of its gross behavioral manifestation, and analysis does not affect it. Even when we understand the commands of the visceral brain and make them conscious we do not reduce their power over us.

Up to a point we can be "taught" to behave, like an animal, by using the stick and the carrot, which is the way behavior modifiers try to do it. But to eliminate most anxiety, cure depression, and gain freedom to react rationally we must change the physiologic patterns that otherwise determine most of our behavior and much of our thinking. Our automatic reactions normally hold us on a very short leash. Freedom from them can only be obtained through many struggles "in the crucible of no-choice."

11. A Most Common Hidden Disorder: Confusion in Thinking

Our double-pronged tool for relating to reality gives us a double advantage once our thinking and feelings have become essentially independent of each other. We have a unique ability then to correct the errors of the one by the other. But when the two are intermingled and in each other's way, as is often the case, we become confused, lose direction and get into serious trouble. The extent of the problem is illustrated in the following example from "The Talk of the Town" in The New Yorker of May 6, 1985:

> Two men stand in a room looking at the same object. "It's a ferocious lion, about to attack us," says one.
> "No, it's a tiny rabbit that wants to be fed," says the other.
> Thus do the hawks and the doves argue with one another about aid to the Contras, the Nicaraguan rebels. They not only recommend different actions but, standing before one and the same creature, see two completely different creatures.
> "I see an extension of the Soviet monolith. The Russian bear now growls at us from our own front yard," says the hawk.
> "I see a revolution in a small country with a population about the size of Brooklyn's," says the dove.
> "I see a totalitarian state, suppressing all dissent, taking all power to itself, enslaving society—censorship, thought control, the gulag," says the hawk.

"I see a besieged revolutionary government trying to consolidate its power, unsure as yet what political direction to take but still permitting considerable freedoms," says the dove.

"I see" . . . says the dove . . . "I see" . . . says the hawk.

"It's another Munich," says the hawk.

"It's another Vietnam," says the dove.

Quite aside from the merits of the two positions, the extreme disparity is in itself cause for alarm. Even people who disagree are fated to live in one reality. And that reality—the world of actual events, the world of fact—is, like the earth we stand on, the true common ground. . . . Yet now this common ground appears to have been lost. . . . For the time being, the consequences are not dire. . . . But reality—whichever is the reality—is not going to vanish, and graver decisions may soon have to be made. At that point, if our country is not to tear itself apart, we'll have to find our way to a shared understanding of the world from which to take our bearings.

We are often unable to see objectively, think clearly, and reason coherently while pressured by fear. Moreover our difficulties are increased because we generally fail to notice how profoundly anxiety affects us and we try to save face by ignoring its corrupting influence upon our thinking. As a result, many intelligent, sophisticated, and well-educated people encounter serious interferences in their attempts to think. Thought disorders are so disabling and frightening that people hide them for as long as possible, at least from others. Their prevalence is therefore generally underestimated. Once believed to be a sign of schizophrenia, thought disorders are now said to affect two-thirds of any population. They appear as major difficulties in concentration, learning, thinking, and even repeating simple sentences when more than minimal anxiety is present. For many people this is true much of the time. We have already noted that we are unable to rely on our feelings to guide us properly until they are calibrated and corrected; now it seems that most people also cannot really depend upon their thinking. Not only "our country" but civilization itself is in danger of tearing itself apart, as we shall see in Chapter 7.

The mind that is cluttered with yearnings and overpowered by fear is too busy to attend to reality. Normal people are thus paralyzed at times in their ability to think and to reason. Since the condition results mostly from an overload of anxiety, it can be corrected by sharply reducing irrational fear. Not only can this menacing confusion in the head be lessened, it can be eliminated altogether. "Learning to really think requires first that we make room for it by diminishing the domain of feelings." This goal is now within reach.

The urgent need to separate our thinking from our feelings is met by first learning to identify our emotions, then by calibrating them so that they fit the current situation. The stored remnants of repressed and suppressed feelings must also be neutralized, which can be done by eliciting and repeatedly expressing them in a safe setting: All but verbal or vocal expressions must be strictly excluded. The maintenance of control is thus assured at all times. As the internal pressure is lessened, room is created for thoughtfulness to prevail.

The nature of feelings is still commonly misunderstood. They do not represent permanent attitudes but only transient reaction states. They are not excuses for irresponsible action but only swift messengers of our nervous system. Their open expression, even with the greatest intensity, does not necessarily lead to unacceptable behavior.

Our efforts to teach the young how to think are often less than successful because we ignore the fact that little freedom for it exists when powerful feelings dominate the person. "The young usually receive both insufficient . . . [and] incorrect guidance . . . in the difficult task of maturation." As a result, "many intellectually mature adults are often emotionally not much older than toddlers."

Most people do not know *what* they feel because they often do not even know *that* they feel. After many years of inattention to feelings we generally recognize only extreme fear as such. As a result, many people believe that they simply have no feelings, and some are even happy or proud to make such a claim. They have seen sensitive men and women suffer, and they fail to realize that those people are also the ones who have a greater capacity to enjoy life.

Emotions clearly exist in everyone. They show plainly in facial expressions and in body tension; in pallor or in blushing; in nervous and in repetitive movements of the fingers, knees, feet, or eyelids; through changes in the quality of the voice; in sweating, dryness of the mouth, or wetting of the palms; and in the many other bodily manifestations and symptoms described in Chapter 2. Tearing is associated with the overflow of any emotion, not just sadness or happiness. Emotions even change our vulnerability to viral, bacterial, and physical agents, since they affect our natural resistance and our attention to reality. They must be brought under control, so they do not control us. Fear especially cannot be safely ignored, for it regularly sabotages our ability to think clearly.

Much of Zen is concerned with disciplining feelings till they become effective and helpful tools for daily life. Zen students are forced to question themselves beyond the intellect: What *is* the sound of one hand clapping? In the absence of answers from the guru the student has no choice but to come to grips with his continuing wish to be cared for and to be taught forever, rather than becoming a master himself. The pathologic "push against progressing" is never given up without fierce internal struggles.

Yet attempts to calibrate and to harness feelings are uncommon in the West. Emotional anesthesia is the rule. One unusually troubled young woman spoke painfully about her real distress: "I know when something is wrong with me, so I eat, only to find out later that I was not hungry at all, but hurt. Or I take a nap when I really wish to relieve my thirst, or when I am scared. The other day I started crying and didn't know why. I discovered days later that I had been very angry."

Most people are at least aware of their physical sensations, and sometimes they can even identify their feelings in clearly defined social situations—at weddings or funerals, births or divorces, or in encounters with real danger. But how do we feel during all the ordinary moments? Feelings become useful and they no longer interfere with our thinking after they have been altered to fit the present. We can face others realistically once we are masters of ourselves; only then can we attend to our world thoughtfully and with compassion.

FOUR

Love and Hate, Anger and Hurt, Sadness and Happiness

Who is a true hero? The one who subdues his passions.
And whoever tames his temper
is mightier than a conqueror of a city.
SHIMON BEN ZOMA
2ND CENTURY
Ethics of the Fathers
CHAPTER 4, VERSE 1

All . . . feelings are experienced and expressed only
in the space that fear does not occupy.
CHAPTER 8, SECTION 13

1. Love: An Introduction

Throughout the ages, popular songs, ballads, poems, and plays have all extolled the blissful state of being "in love." Why is it said that it "conquers all" and that lovers are "the luckiest people in the world"? Because romantic love takes us to the heights of joy. Jilted lovers find themselves in the depths of despair; but even so, being "in love" jolts us out of meaninglessness and fills us with a sense of heightened intensity. Love is the enemy of dullness. It brings excitement and hope into gray lives. Love "makes us" happy and sad; it brings a glint into our eyes and floods them with tears. Because love can do such miraculous things, men and women have always yearned for and dreamed about it. Yet many people have difficulty in explaining what it really is and why it is so wonderful.

144

Love is a feeling, fleeting like any other emotion. Being "in love" is altogether different. It is being fixed or frozen in what used to be a feeling. Loving must thus be distinguished from being "in love," and we shall use quotation marks when referring to the second. As we shall see later in this chapter, being frozen in love produces romantic "love," as being frozen in anger produces hate. Both are pathologic conditions, dangerous to the self and to others.

Age and experience have a lot to do with how one describes love. A wise observer, Leon L. Altman, writing in the *Journal of the American Psychoanalytic Association*, describes it well:

A very small girl announces firmly that love is "pretty." A slightly older boy scornfully describes it as "silly." The adolescent reports that love "makes you crazy." To a nubile young thing, it is "marvelous." The disappointed middled-aged regretfully conclude that love is a myth. A women's-lib spokesperson will tell you that love is a fiction created by men to keep things comfortable for themselves—a property ploy. The elderly either deem love a solace, regret its passing, or deny its existence.

The capacity for loving reflects the basic quality of our relationship with the person who first cared for us, long before we became small boys or small girls. It develops in Mother's bosom, the matrix of our ability to trust, or not to trust, anyone. Love, more than any other feeling, is in fact based on this ability to trust, oneself first and then others.

By contrast, romantic "love" is unrealistic, its powerful appeal rooted in magic. It is a product of urgent groping for a sense of safety, and it is unrelated to the real quality of the relationship between the lovers. Their "trust" in each other is blind, as the work of cupid usually is. Indeed, "love" is often intensified by rejection or physical abuse. The person "in love" is frozen in that state and unable to leave, hopelessly gripped in a tight vise. What holds people in destructive and humiliating "love" relationships, and what makes them plead and even beg to be "loved," is extreme fear of abandonment. The force of this fear is so great that people degrade and humiliate themselves to avoid it.

Real love and romantic "love" are, in fact, often mutually exclusive. They are related to each other as water is to ice or to steam. Although made from the same molecule, the physical characteristics of each are altogether different. We are in need and not necessarily loving at all when romantically "in love." In return for the many declarations of our "love" we expect the "loved one" to be totally devoted to us. Above all, fear-filled people seek to be reassured that they will not be rejected; this is the central concern of "lovers." Not so in real love. The joy and pleasure of loving are derived from the very act of giving, not from obtaining anything from anyone. The wish to share one's inner plenty is the essence of real love.

Love is neither an obligation based on past performance nor a contract for the future. The words "I love you" always refer only to the present moment, although they are generally misunderstood as a promise for all time. Real love can only exist when feelings in general are neither suppressed nor denied, and it commonly alternates therefore with hurt, disappointment, and anger. They often come and go in quick succession, like bright rays of sunshine on a somewhat cloudy day.

Many people nevertheless still think that love can last till death or for any other fixed period of time. Few know that love's impermanence is not a sign of its fickle nature but a feature of its essential character. The promise of eternal love is always false, always self-serving, and always aimed at deluding the one that it is made to, although usually without conscious awareness of such an intent. Those making such vows and those willing to accept them are engaged in the exchange of bogus promissory notes having no real value. The inevitable crash occurs sooner or later, when the initial fund of goodwill proves insufficient to cover the many demands made upon it.

In reality, a commitment between people can only bind their acts, not their feelings. We can promise to behave in certain ways and not in others, and we can also agree to remain in a relationship for some specific period of time. If such promises are made for life, with no legitimate exit at any point, they are prescriptions for disaster. Marriages were meant to be permanent, at least for the protection of children who need stable environments. But some are bound not to work out well, and the commitment to remain in them anyway is like playing Russian roulette. It may require a person to impose a life sentence upon him- or herself, barely surviving in a self-built jail.

A person capable of really loving is basically content, able to give, to accept, to share, and to be with others. These traits represent a mature state of existence, even in the rare cases when they are exhibited by children.

2. The Love that Children Have for Others

Most of the time children adore and revere those who are good to them, who support them, and who gratify them. The love of children seems so innocent, uncomplicated, and trusting that adults are often touched by it deeply. But since young children depend upon us almost totally, their love is a form of gratitude. Except for occasional moments it is not as pure as our enjoyment of it suggests.

In fact, the ability to really love does not exist in young children. Youngsters in nursery school tend to grab, hit, push, and pull each other without restraint or any consideration of anyone or anything. They climb on top of and over each other as if the other children were inanimate objects, not people. They do not form real friendships before they become civilized, and the only control that makes their behavior tolerable is at first external. Like little animals they can be trained; but still lacking the capacity to be sensitive to others, they neither love nor do they have much compassion till much later.

The "love" that children have for their parents and for other adults is based on romantic idealizations. They believe that parents have extraordinary powers—to take a hurt away with a mere kiss, to answer all questions, and to ward off all trouble, including that brought about by terrifying ghosts. Any threat of losing the love of such powerful figures evokes terror. When adults are "in love" they similarly believe that the "loved" one has magical qualities, capable of assuring peace of mind. The sudden disappearance of such a wonderful creature often throws a person into an emotional tailspin.

Consider the bright-eyed youngster who, running through a field on a lovely summer day, comes across a perfect yellow dandelion. He plucks it and runs home, clutching the precious find tightly in his tiny fist. Exploding with excitement, he presents it to his preoccupied, tired, insensitive, or angry mother and father. They see no more than an ugly, shriveled yellowish weed given by a well-meaning but overeager kid exactly when they have no time or patience to appreciate it.

So the youngster's little heart "breaks" and "sinks," his eyes lose their happy glint, and they fill with tears, which he tries to hide. His gift held an expectation of a reward: returned love, approval, and appreciation. The presentation was a romantic kind of act, since only romantic "love" can be spurned. No gift given with so much delight is really pure. Wounded innocence often turns into self-recrimination for having been so vulnerable and "stupid." Young children often learn early to avoid similar humiliations in the future. Their uncomplicated, receptive openness begins to be enveloped in a tough exterior. Love is dangerous! Repeated experiences of this kind slowly shape future behavior under similar circumstances. To some degree that innocent child is each of us, before we learned to be careful.

The loss of any love relationship is deeply painful, but fear is present only when romantic "love" is endangered. All relationships in life must end sometime, by death or otherwise; but we panic only when the loss threatens our security. The more satisfying and the more central a relationship is, the greater the void when it is lost. The room we have made for others within ourselves suddenly becomes an emptiness, to be filled in time through normal mourning. It follows all breakups and it consists of sadness and of hurt, but not of fear. The empty-nest syndrome that results from children growing up and leaving home is no more than a short-lived disturbance in reasonably healthy families. It is experienced as a desertion only when the previous attachment was pathologic.

3. Romantic "Love"

Being "in love" is essentially a passive state; the goal of lovers, like that of children, is to be loved. By contrast, real love is active. When emotionally mature people love, they extend themselves to others. This is how sane parents love their child, for itself and not for what it offers them in return.

Romantic "love" is characterized by yearning. We are filled with a sense of well-being when near the "loved one," or with jealousy and dread when we are involuntarily separated. Even a voluntary separation can quickly become very painful and evoke a sense of impending doom. Separated lovers expend much energy desperately trying to reach each other in writing, in calling, or in attempts to "get together" as soon as possible. Separation is so intolerably painful that the lovers are often unable to eat or to sleep, to work or to behave normally. Only one goal exists: to reunite. Separation often brings up so much anxiety that many physiologic processes are disturbed, producing clinically acute shocklike disorientation and distress similar to that which follows a major physical trauma.

Sex with the "loved one" is usually exquisitely satisfying since it stills the fiercest emotional yearnings, replacing turmoil with togetherness and upheaval with tranquility. The physical union gives concrete form to the nebulous wish for emotional oneness, bringing with it the wonderful sensation of perfect inner harmony. Finding such peace always was and still is the long-term goal of all men and all women. But it lasts only a short time, if reached. Idylls were not meant to last. So people in this state naturally hold on to each other with the greatest tenacity, hoping never to lose again what they have finally found after so many painful disappointments. Yet in doing so they usually squelch their joy, as one would a delicate flower.

The very high price of such an intense attachment to another person is almost always overlooked. Inner peace is not really reached when the key to it is held by someone else. The never-ending need to worry about the other's state of mind drains energy and produces constant tension. One is constantly agitated unless reassured again and again of the lover's continued satisfaction.

Being "in love" thus impoverishes both lovers, and it robs them of the flexibility to respond freely to changing situations. Fear of losing the lover causes the other to behave in ways that are guaranteed to please, regardless of the price. Displeasing increases the chances of being deserted. Although being "in love" is subjectively experienced as a "heightened" form of existence, it really forces people to lower themselves till they become like slaves, without honor; ingratiation is the typical mode by which lovers relate to each other.

Some claim that romantic "love means never having to say you're sorry," probably because lovers generally anticipate each other's wishes and try to fulfill them even before they are expressed. This is what Mother's body does so perfectly for her unborn fetus. Adults continue to pine for such perfect understanding, and lovers appear able to satisfy such secret wishes, even the most hidden ones. Such total and self-negating attention to the needs and preferences of another is only tolerable because it serves to allay the horrible fear of abandonment. Not love but fear causes lovers to be so sensitive. "In love," said Rilke, "two solitudes protect and touch and greet each other."

Yet bitterness generally creeps in before long, although at the height of their involvement lovers seem to be totally unaware of this almost universal sequence. They only know that they are fulfilled and happy, and they seem to fear nothing but the loss of their "love." This fear is seldom far away, however. The highs and lows of those "in love" alternate in quick succession. Even when everything seems rosy, anxiety is nearby. Since one's happiness depends on the other being satisfied, it is not solidly established. Those "in love" need an outside force to pull them up when they are down; they appear incapable of saving themselves from their despair.

Lovers customarily hold hands in public as well as in private to minimize the dread of desertion. They sweet-talk, peck, look deeply and longingly into each other's eyes, kiss, touch, and repeatedly profess their "love" for each other, oblivious to anything and to all others around them. Indifference or even mutual sniping often replaces this closeness after the honeymoon. But even so, those afraid of desertion remain very careful not to overstep the boundaries of what their partner will accept.

Those with ill-defined boundaries of the self tend to "stick" to others, as if their skins were not intact; in a sense they really become glued together in romantic bonds. Being intimately involved renders them extremely vulnerable, so it is understandable why they fear love in general, even as they desperately want to be "loved." Such people cannot even comprehend the pure joys of real love, since they can only see its better-known and much more glamorous romantic half sister. People with diffuse boundaries commonly fear real intimacy because they half consciously "know" that close involvements may be destructive to them. Intimates are experienced as potentially harmful; they take others over by capturing their individuality, their liberty, and their will. Once captured, one remains "forever" powerless in an unyielding grip.

At least traces of this fear are present in almost everyone because their earliest and most intimate contacts were so similar in terms of power. No mother can ever fit her behavior exactly to the wishes, needs, or tolerances of her child. From the perspective of the infant she is often wrong. Mothers have no choice but to be guided by their intuition and judgment, which reflect both the healthy and the pathologic parts of their personalities. Newborns must often experience the manner in which they are held and fed as objectionable or even as painful; mothers sometimes do not let go of their baby when it has had enough. The sense of choking frequently lingers for life. Most people never really learn that real love is different and that it does not require actual dependence at all.

A person's basic attitudes about physical and emotional closeness are normally determined by such automatic reactions. But the delusional expectations of being "in love" are usually so powerful that they overcome them for a while. With our true "love" we take emotionally wild chances because they suddenly do not appear wild anymore.

The awakening is usually rude and always very painful. New hurts and new disappointments are piled up on top of the old ones. Bitterness and anger follow, because the promise of living "happily ever after" cannot be kept. Lifelong dreams of perfect harmony and of "eternal" love, nurtured through fairy tales since early childhood, are suddenly seen as false and misleading. Parents do not usually realize the many ways by which they innocently encourage such delusional expectations in their young. Romantic novels and films sustain and strengthen them. Yet now the previously dormant fears about closeness are suddenly reconfirmed. Intimacy *is* extremely dangerous! The attitude of distrust is hardened further. At least emotional closeness will be regarded with even greater suspicion in the future, though superficial physical contacts may continue.

Many people regard all loving, trusting, and non-antagonistic involvements as delusional or, worse yet, as designed to lead them down a primrose path and into a dangerous trap. All intimate contacts are avoided when the fear of engulfment is very strong. But even when the fear is less extreme, human associations are often characterized by much tension, caution, and compulsive competitiveness. These interfere with and limit the enjoyment that is obtainable from the company of others. Such disorders as impotence, frigidity, premature ejaculation, and functional infertility are common expressions of this fear when it involves sex.

Hermits, recluses, and confirmed singles tend to blame external circumstances for their socially barren existence. But more often than not they are afraid of serious emotional involvements and commitments. Such life-styles are rarely expressions of free choice. Yet even married people, or those who live with others, are not necessarily free from this fear of engulfment. It causes many people to shun all intimacy. Its roots are so deep and so widespread that emotional isolation often typifies even "happy" married life.

Rather than risk the hurt and fear that are unavoidable in romantic "love," youngsters today, like the Don Juans of yesterday, often find it much safer to have a series of meaningless and superficial short-term relationships. Thus they can support their self-delusion that they are living a full life. But even if they saw the truth it would not change their behavior. The underlying fear must be dissolved before a fuller life is possible.

People "in love" forgive grave and obvious faults in their "beloved" because they believe it imperative to preserve the relationship at all costs. The prospect of being abandoned is so terrifying that they repeatedly excuse, overlook, and deny even the most troubling shortcomings. Since lovers look at their partners through idealizing eyes, they hardly know them as real persons. Besides, they generally refuse to discover the truth. Similarly, parents who "love" their children blindly are often shocked when they suddenly discover what kind of people they really are. Lovers and many parents unabashedly describe the objects of their "love" as the most beautiful, sensitive, or talented, as the wisest, the strongest, the most understanding, charming, generous, or glamorous—in short, as perfect. Although such descriptions are grossly unrealistic and embarrassingly silly, lovers hotly and earnestly dismiss any questions about their objectivity. They themselves may not believe what they say, but it is often extremely important for them to impress others. Very insecure people actually derive prestige, a semblance of power, and at least a tenuous sense of security from identifying with the desirable attributes of their "beloved," even if these exist only in their imagination.

Couples often appear to be grossly mismatched—tall and short, thin and fat, sophisticated and simple, attractive and plain. Some hidden "chemistry" other than those observable attributes must draw people to each other. What causes us to fall "in love" with one particular person rather than with another who is socially more fitting? With the "loved one" we feel the safest. Some aspects in the lover's personality happen to soothe our sharpest and most acute hurts even as they lower our hidden anxiety most dramatically. Since "the push away from fear or dread supersedes everything," all other considerations become irrelevant. Families have often tried to separate lovers by sending one to the opposite corner of the earth—but in vain. Rational arguments go unheeded at such times. Even in an age of rationalism, "love" still blinds people and it deludes them more powerfully than anything else.

The dramatic lowering of anxiety by the mere presence and existence of the lover proves to the partner that the other indeed possesses extraordinary qualities. People marry and divorce, they change careers, jobs, religions, and values, and they move to distant cities and countries to be with their "loved one." Only later do they discover that they have made crucially significant life decisions thoughtlessly, and that their new lives stand on very flimsy foundations. Feelings are indeed a very poor guide to reality.

One can rise to great heights of human compassion and tenderness when truly sensitive and loving, but not when one falls "in love." We often injure ourselves when we fall, and falling "in love" is no exception. It is like falling into a pot of honey, sweet but also gooey and sticky. One's freedom to move and to be is severely curtailed.

Since the happiness of romantic lovers is really nothing more than the balance achieved by two people who help each other hold dread in check, disappointment is only a matter of time. The panic always returns, unless a new lover soon replaces the old one and a new magical bond is formed. This is why forlorn ex-lovers often get married on the rebound. Since being cast off evokes not only the fear of abandonment but often also the more primitive and the more horrible fear of non-being, those who have been jilted tend to become bitterly vindictive, and they eargerly seek revenge. Coming back with a punch helps them a little to feel less vulnerable and not so powerless.

We forget how "fickle common lovers are," as Dryden put it, because the fear that something will break our "love" relationship is so terrible that those of us involved swear that *this* "love" is forever. Lovers understandably consider themselves the luckiest people in the world because their most terrible fears seem to have disappeared and their most profound yearnings seem to have been fulfilled.

Being "in love" is thus synonymous with being "out of fear," and this is achieved here by being "out of mind." Lovers complement each other most perfectly during the honeymoon of relationships, and so they hold on to each other for dear life then. Their anxiety is reduced in exactly the same way that sucking the thumb reduced it in infancy. Rather than couple with a part of one's own body, lovers couple with each other. But even so, dynamically it is still self-coupling. This is why lovers promise, demand, and expect exclusivity and total loyalty from each other. Since survival itself is subjectively at stake, lovers must always be "on call" for their beloved.

The birth of a child who commands, and usually gets, preferential attention from the mother is therefore often experienced as a serious threat by young fathers. The newborn is actually

dependent upon its mother for its survival, but the husband may
be emotionally almost as needy. His subjective sense of safety is
suddenly lost. Unlike the mother, he does not have much physical contact with the baby at that point, not enough to experience himself as attached. The father is literally being replaced,
and he experiences this situation almost as if his wife were having an affair. In a sense she is. It is with the baby that she often
prefers to spend her time in a special and intimate fashion. She
naturally identifies with this physical product of her body that
confirms her biologic competency. Having absolute control over
the young organism, she feels safer by attaching herself to it
rather than to her husband. The baby really cannot desert her.
This relationship is thus ideal for temporarily dispelling her fear
of abandonment.

Power over others still serves many people as the best of all
anti-depressants. "The push to gain power has such a tremendous force because it is the only hope Man has had of overcoming his sense of precariousness." In this sense, a mother's
relationship with the father of her child is less satisfying. It provides much more mutuality and fulfills her adult needs much
better, but her ability to control it is lesser. The new mother
needs her husband much less than ever before to feel secure. She
does not pursue him so much, therefore, and not so urgently,
except at the height of sexual intercourse. Being more secure,
she may finally be free enough to experience more real love for
her husband. But he may have trouble reciprocating because his
anxiety often shoots up to new heights at such times. From his
point of view, he has become an unloved stranger in his own
house.

Romantic lovers therefore often reassure their mates by denying any lessening of their pining for them. Instead they frequently profess to be as helpless and as needy as infants. This
would hardly be a bargain in any sane relationship, because mature people prefer their partners to be self-sufficient and helpful.
But in romantic "love" it is often imperative above all to provide
the other with a sense of power. "How much do I depend on
you?" asks a schmaltzy Valentine Day card. "I only wish you
knew" is the pitiful rejoinder on the inside. Some women are
still taught to appear fragile, cute, and somewhat ineffectual in
order to bring the "big man" out of the little boy whom they
want to marry. But men also compete to seem helpless. They
become whiny, quiet, perpetually hurt, clumsy, and somewhat
lost, often having trouble finding their feet or their socks. Un-

knowingly they look to be adopted by a wife acting as Mother. They are willing, often eager, to become house boys in the hope of lessening their terrible fear. Even in public some husbands call their wives "Mother," meaning it as a compliment, without realizing what it implies about them. Many powerful men in business become pathetic and helpless little boys once they cross the threshold of their home.

"I love you" is, first and foremost, a statement about the speaker. He or she is capable of loving, and love is what that person feels at the moment. But people usually say these words as a romantic promise of "love," and those addressed are reassured by them: They *are* lovable. Rather than rejoice with and for the speaker, the ones to whom such a statement is directed are usually only "happy" for themselves. They feel safer. In general, romantic "love" is measured by how successful each partner is in "making" the other happy, or relatively free of anxiety. The assumption that such a thing is really possible is so widespread that it usually is not even questioned. But the real reasons for the misery of cheerless people cannot be found in others, only within. Finding "love" from the outside is not the solution.

4. Sexual Aspects of Love

Why is the prospect of perfect sex with a beautiful woman so powerful that it sells cars, clothes, deodorants, travel, and all kinds of other products? Because such an encounter holds the promise of banishing loneliness, hurt, and dread. The thought that she would desire, accept, and welcome us creates so much excitement that our troubles temporarily disappear. In the bosom of such a wonderful creature we unknowingly expect to find safety. People may deny the existence of panic, but they nonetheless sense its cold presence; men commonly experience the warm body of a woman as the best shelter in which to hide during dangerous emotional storms. Beyond the biologic urge to reproduce, this is what makes sex so powerfully attractive.

Sex symbols are practically always female because so was the source of everyone's original security: Mother. The curvaceous, dreamy-eyed, and soft-spoken Marilyn Monroe was a terrified child herself, but her many admirers did not see this very well. They yearned for her, and some still do, as if she could provide more than just a moment of pleasure. Her welcome meant security. Male nudity can also be powerful as a sexual stimulus, and for some women it too can evoke a sense of urgent anticipation. But in general women do not buy magazines that feature naked men; other men do. These cannot associate safety with females; sexual women cause their bodies to tense with fear or with anger. They can let go and relax only with other males. Yet even in permissive societies, homosexuality involves only a small minority of all men.

Most men and some women respond to the sight of the female form with excitement. Photographs showing barely covered, soft, and full breasts appear on the covers of so many magazines because this is what sells. What are these buyers searching for so eagerly? Why do they spend their money on these magazines, month after month, as if they wish to finally discover some long-forgotten secret?

More than the expectation of enjoying carnal delights must be involved. People do not get so physically excited about any other form of physical pleasure, such as eating, resting, or non-competitive sports. Sex is unique because it is a proven antidote to the fears of abandonment and non-being. Even if these fears remain unknown to us intellectually, our body knows them well. That which brings relief from these horrors becomes highly valued and desirable, and we seek it with the desperate determination of an addict in search of a fix. But what is so special about young breasts that so many hearts in so many chests beat so much faster at the sight of their mere outline? Why are older breasts not equally exciting?

Because old women do not give birth to babies. Most newborns, male and female, have been comforted at the breast of a relatively young woman. Mother's body is the first and the most important haven of security, the ground of steadiness and the source of sustenance. From it come comfort, warmth, and tenderness when we need them most. The same powerful physiologic yearnings that were satisfied in the newborn by Mother's body are still evoked in grown men at the sight, touch, smell, and promise of acceptance by the female. Women are anatomically too much like Mother to invest any part of their bodies with such extraordinary meanings. They have regular daily contacts with their bodies for years. They see, touch, wash, and dress themselves, and thus possess an intimate and real knowledge of their physical parts. Women do not usually become sexually aroused by the female body, because no part of it is invested with magic. Lesbians are the exception that proves this rule. They continue to yearn for contact with a woman, very much as they did in infancy.

Even in adults, sexual desires are not strictly sexual. They are often little more than adult forms of cuddling with a security blanket. Only in puberty, when the inner pressure and the confusion are the greatest, is any contact with the opposite gender infused with exaggerated sexual expectations. The purely physical release in sex is not basically different from the relief obtained when other forms of physical tension are lessened. Animals in heat eagerly stalk each other till they find a suitable mate, but unlike humans they are not essentially interested in sex at other times. The male wish to release his seminal fluid into the female's receptive body is nature's wise way of insuring the propagation of the species. But sexual pursuits by humans also serve other purposes. Our wonderful cortex enables us to anticipate and to fantasize situations in which we feel welcomed and comforted. This alone can make us a little less tense. We seek sexual pleasure frequently to lessen our anxiety, which we feel as loneliness, not so much to satisfy any biologic drive.

The eager cravings at the height of sex may or may not be a symbolic attempt to become one again as we were before birth. But the peace and relaxation that follow orgasm surely are reminiscent of how contented babies are between episodes of panic. For many people this sense of contentment is the real reward of any sexual involvement, because periods of anxiety and dread commonly precede and follow such moments. Being taken into the female body is so exciting to males because it means coming home and finding peace.

But the basic wish for mothering remains unaltered by anatomic destiny. Now that oral sex is widely accepted, many women find it at least as enjoyable as intercourse itself. The enjoyment that men obtain from fondling, kissing, and sucking on breasts is similar to that obtained by many women from doing the same with a penis. Although a relatively small organ, it too is commonly assigned an exaggerated importance and magical meanings: by men, to deny their anxiety about its smallness and to hide their sense of relative inferiority; by women, because they regard it as men do breasts.

Some women do not really get sexually excited unless they can have the man's erect penis in their mouth. Not only can the act of sucking evoke the old sense of safety that existed with Mother, but often it also gives the woman a sense of power: She is completely in charge then of this powerful symbol of masculinity, the essence of maleness. Now it is within her power to satisfy her mate or to deny his urgent desires. For the moment at least, she is in complete control and therefore relatively free of fear.

"Gentlemen prefer blondes" for similar reasons of power. The stereotype of the blonde is one of innocence and naivete, lacking the wisdom to discriminate and to reject. Not too bright but wide-eyed and bosomy, the mythical blonde is such a delicious male fantasy because she represents a common wish to find a child-woman who will be always soft, sweet, and a little silly, not too sophisticated to compete with him and not too complex in her tastes to challenge him. With her he can see himself as big. She will "love," accept, and welcome him unconditionally at all times. The man who feels like a boy but believes that he must behave like a stud has a chance here. With her he can be powerful and unafraid.

5. Real Love

Real love is altogether different from either sexual or romantic "love." It can exist only in the absence of fear. Before we can love anyone else we must first be able to love ourselves, and this is only possible if others have loved us so that we know ourselves as lovable. People who have not been mothered and fathered kindly or consistently enough are usually unable to treat themselves lovingly; they also cannot really love anyone else, not even their children.

Real love is only possible for those with reasonably intact personal boundaries. They can dare to be vulnerable and to approach others unarmored and unarmed. Basically they trust people to be sensitive and respectful. But even more than that, they trust themselves as competent beings. If others suddenly prove to be different than expected, secure individuals would easily change course. Occasionally they get hurt by the actions or insensitivity of others, but this does not cause them any real harm. Reasonable caution is always called for, but the excessive fear that reflects archaic and long-forgotten injuries no longer interferes with their capacity to be, and to love themselves and others. Such individuated people are aware of their many blessings even without counting them. They are essentially free of old bitterness, hurt, or anger; and they are often filled with a sense of well-being that they are eager to share with others. It really is true that the more real love one "gives" to others the more one has.

A person with essentially intact boundaries is like a well-constructed vessel in good repair. Since it does not leak, such a vessel can hold the liquids poured into it for a long time; fresh supplies are not often needed to fill it, since it loses very little through evaporation or otherwise. Similarly, once the sense of well-being has been established in people with good boundaries, self-love can easily replenish it. Such people need praise from others only infrequently, and they are able to extend themselves lovingly to those around them. The pool of love from which they draw is practically inexhaustible; the walls that hold it are intact. Such people are often eager to give of themselves because their sense of fullness would become a burden otherwise. The capacity to remain receptive and thankful eventually becomes clogged when blessings are hoarded and never shared with others. Loving is not altogether altruistic.

People often behave lovingly, but this does not prove that they actually experience the feeling of love. We can easily learn to act in loving ways, and people often plan everything they do accordingly, to earn loving gestures from others. This usually happens without conscious awareness and surely without an intent to deceive; everyone tries to maximize his or her sense of safety in the world. Such loving-like behavior is obviously self-serving. Recipients generally sense the real purpose of such behavior, later if not sooner. Even so, they may pretend not to see what they observe, for what they get is better than nothing.

But when loving acts are characterized by true generosity and kindness and by genuine sensitivity to the welfare of the other, real love is probably present. The joy of real loving is in offering it, not in expecting a return; in adding to the world, not in extracting from it; in beautifying, not in making oneself beautiful. It requires no reciprocity, although it is not one-sided for very long. One-sided giving without end is associated only with fear, or with saints.

The capacity for loving begins to develop early in life. Those who are well mothered gradually learn to orient themselves to the new reality of extrauterine life. Fear-free moments begin to alternate with the many periods of terror and panic. The young organism eventually develops a taste for safety and an expectation that all will turn out well. Such babies soon discover that their own internal resources are often sufficient to cope with their sense of danger. They are able sometimes to really relax.

The level of their bodily tension is lowered once they gain visceral knowledge about the universe as a non-threatening presence. Fears that do not overwhelm the baby become somewhat less awesome the next time around. The growing confidence in one's ability to survive securely allows the child to begin to love itself, and eventually others.

Real love is free of pining and anxiety. It is self-contained; specific toward some people, not generalized toward all of humanity; temporary even if frequent. Just as hurt and anger embitter, so love ennobles and sweetens. Love that is sought cannot ever be found, yet those capable of loving find objects for their love without ever having to seek them. Since they pursue nothing, they are at peace.

6. In Defense of Sensible Selfishness

Before we can love others we must learn to love ourselves. But most people are taught from early in life not to do so, since this is "selfish." In our culture, being selfless is held in high esteem, even though self-love is the most reliable source of building up stores of self-confidence. Without it we cannot afford to give of ourselves to anyone else. We must first accept ourselves and our emotional needs as legitimate; only then can we be sensitive to the needs and wishes of others.

In reality, selfishness is a necessity for healthy existence. In an effort to protect the growing young from an excessive preoccupation with themselves, a mark of severe pathology, we have downgraded all self-love and practically forbidden its practice. Self-coupling, which is living autistically in an isolating shell, is obviously not compatible with social existence. Diverse civilizations have independently discovered the wisdom of impressing upon their young the danger of retreating into such shells, where nothing exists but endless self-preoccupation. With the passage of time even worthwhile ideas are sometimes bent out of shape; eventually any interest in oneself was damned. This tragic confusion has been a source of untold sorrow and the root of much needless pain over many generations.

Yet condemnation of selfishness did not work. We do not give up what we must have to survive just because others do not approve of it. Man lived with guilt and in shame for being selfish, pretending not to be. Lacking realistic guidelines, he often became so very selfish that he forgot about others; sooner or later they forgot about him. Resisting the efforts to enforce an impossible rule upon them, many people have never learned how to balance their self-interest with the needs of their community. As a consequence, they lead impoverished and narrow lives, barren of friendships and of meaningful involvements. Paradoxically, this is what condemning selfishness was meant to prevent.

Selfishness does not mean self-coupling, any more than narcissism means self-love. It means putting oneself before everybody else, not instead of all others. Although used by the "me" generation, selfishness is not a justification for merely pursuing comfort and fun. Yet confusion is still common in this regard. Most people still find it extremely difficult to accept selfishness openly as legitimate, and they see themselves as thieves when they reach for something they want or need. But self-concern and self-care are obviously not the same as self-indulgence and self-coupling. The first two are necessities for existence; the latter are pathologic aspects of immature personalities, incompatible with sane and sensible relationships. Sane living requires that we be self-centered.

We have no choice in this matter. Mothers who do not properly attend to their own physical or emotional needs become too weak, too tired, or too resentful to care for their babies lovingly and willingly. Neither guilt nor duty can motivate people to come toward others bearing gifts of love and joy; only inner abundance can be the source of such giving. People who neglect themselves chronically in the name of self-sacrifice die prematurely, and not as heroes on any battlefield. True self-sacrifice is rare, because it is an act of people who love life and who love themselves. Only they can value something even more than their existence. No one can give what they do not have.

7. Free Gifts and Some that Are Not So Free

Free gifts are precious and rare. No strings are attached to them and no expectations of a return. They are expressions of real love, not payments of any obligation. Recipients of such a gift are free to do with it whatever they wish, since it is theirs from the moment they accept it. They have the right to accept the gift or to reject it if not desired. This rarely happens, however, since such an act of giving is generally recognized as a free gift in itself.

Since most gifts are not really free, strict codes generally govern the giving and the receiving of gifts, to spare the feelings of givers. We are expected to praise the gift and to thank the giver. But those who give freely do not need this protection. The established codes usually succeed in what they are designed to do, but since they treat all gifts and all givers alike, they also rob free gifts of their special significance. No token of gratitude can match in value that which is given freely from a full heart.

"I love you" is free in real love, but it is only a part of the bargaining process in romantic "love," a self-serving attempt to enlist the loyalty of the one to whom the words are spoken. The uttering of these words is a true joy to the one who really loves another person, because the speaker is overflowing with the richness of loving. But romantic lovers understand such expressions differently. Here the words elicit tremendous relief in those to whom the words are addressed, as if they confirm their lovability. Because romantic "love" is everywhere and real love is relatively rare, people generally hear "I love you" as a pledge of endless loyalty, companionship, or service. They feel cheated when "love" ends, as if they have been unjustly robbed of something important that was theirs by right. This confusion is what tragedies are made of. Yet in real love all is clear and easier. If the "you" were dropped from the magic phrase we would easily see that the one who proclaims "I love!" relieves some of his or her overflowing joy by embracing the world. The identity of the object of such love is a less important consideration.

Much of social behavior is designed to suggest to others that we love them, whether we do or not. The act of giving, for example, is customarily fixed to coincide with special occasions such as birthdays, weddings, anniversaries, and holidays like Christmas. Since the giving is predetermined, a very well defined social obligation, it is not necessarily an expression of love. Not only the time of giving but the value of gifts is more or less fixed by custom. Nevertheless, we are expected to pretend that we are touched. As a rule, the less genuine the experience of loving the greater the pretense that it exists.

Gifts are often given to curry favor with those whom we fear or need, and sometimes they are even offered to those whom we hate or are angry at, to hide our real attitudes. Such "voluntary" tribute is much more degrading than the giving which conquerors used to impose on the vanquished, because it is propelled by a morbid eagerness to appease; the conquered were not required to also distort themselves inwardly. They could maintain their human dignity even in the midst of slavery, since only their public behavior had to be governed by lies.

The greater our hidden aversion for those to whom we offer a gift that is meant to appease, the greater its material value and the more lavish and effusive the "loving" expressions that accompany it. We try hardest to hide that which we believe needs hiding the most. It follows that the greater our fear, anger, or hate, the more severe the damage that we inflict upon ourselves when we nevertheless attempt to appear loving.

The wheels of civilized existence are also greased by other social codes, all designed to minimize interpersonal friction. We greet and we thank each other, we sometimes hold a door open for a stranger, and we tend to be nice to people who have been nice to us, even if we don't particularly like them. "Being nice" involves compliments, kind deeds, and friendly gestures such as smiling. But we also behave in such ways to cope with irrational fear, emotional insecurity, and low self-esteem, to insure that nobody is ever antagonized. Some people are always recruiting potential allies for life's battles. They often become very hurt, bitter, and angry when their friendly gestures, which include gifts, are either ignored or spurned.

False giving is a common practice of people who are desperately eager to lower their anxiety. They spend much time, thought, energy, and money on it. One woman was in the habit of sending over five hundred birthday and greeting cards every year to her many "friends," and she would actually shudder in fear on the very rare occasion when she would fail to remember someone's anniversary. She was always busy correcting addresses and adding names. The more index cards she had, the safer she felt.

The ritual of receiving gifts is clearly delineated to insure its continuation. Future gifts dwindle and eventually they cease altogether for those who fail to follow the rules. We are expected to heap praises upon the giver and the gift over and above what they deserve, unless it is given by someone of lesser status and prestige. We must appear to obtain as much pleasure from receiving white elephants as we would if they were useful and needed workhorses. Approval of the gift and admiration for the giver are both meant to boost his or her self-esteem. This is the return that givers expect on their investment. It is good form therefore to indicate, without necessarily meaning it, that a gift of lesser value would have been appreciated no less.

The bridal shower is a good example. Helping a poor bride get a decent start in her married life used to be its rationale, but compassion is not what sustains it now. This crude leftover from less affluent days is being kept alive because it benefits the many guests more than the one about to be wed. The bride-to-be will open the gifts in public, speak the required impersonal and meaningless banalities, and tastelessly exaggerate her praises. Although givers are pitted against one another in a crass competition that exploits their insecurities, everyone has a chance to show off their affluence and generosity. The gift and the giver will be on display. Since most people are somewhat shaky in their sense of self-worth, many will be impelled to give beyond their means. Tension and anxiety typically fill the room, which generally is empty of true joy, relaxation, and friendship. Loud laughter and much giggling commonly pepper the superficial conversation, in a vain attempt to cover up the discomfort or pain.

So why don't we give up this outdated ritual? Why do we continue to consume this spoiled product which is no longer edible, even though its stench is hard to take? Because it fosters the delusion of happy togetherness. We are willing to endure the anxiety that it provokes, since it lessens loneliness and the fear of abandonment, at least for a few short hours. Everyone present is always so "lovely," so "loving," and so "lovable," and everyone is so "happy" because they have so many "dear" friends.

Many people compulsively "go along to get along." Their self-esteem is almost totally dependent upon a constant flow of approval, which explains why they are always in hot pursuit of it. Since they do not know how to love and mother themselves, they worry and fear that they might give too little to others; the custodians of one's safety must be kept satisfied at all costs and at all times.

8. Hate

Much hate is "love" gone sour. Being "in hate" is commonly the result of having been spurned by those with whom we used to be "in love," a consequence of believing that they are treating us lightly and with disdain. The ugly and dangerous fangs of hate are bared when those still important and dear to us act as if we are not at all important or dear to them. Like romantic "love," hate is not strictly a feeling. Both are states in which a feeling has become frozen, both are often associated with extreme fears of rejection and abandonment, and both tend to produce psychotic-like behavior. Under their influence, judgment becomes grossly impaired and clear thinking is often suspended. Hate is to anger as romantic "love" is to real love.

Hate is sometimes directed against something or somebody truly evil, but even then it often is psychotic-like. In the fixed position of hate it is almost impossible to maintain the necessary flexibility required for fighting an enemy successfully, as the circumstances dictate. The passion of hate, like that of romantic "love," gives off intense heat; it tends to interfere with the ability to assess alternatives coolly.

Like "love," hate is seldom experienced toward total strangers. The involvement with those whom we "love" or hate may be totally in fantasy, but it is experienced as centrally important nevertheless. People commonly attach their "love" or hate to others who are basically unknown, but this very attachment turns strangers into significant and emotionally familiar figures. Political leaders, teachers, and movie stars often serve as focal points for such feelings; the "love" or hate for them is not based on personal acquaintance or on any direct dealings. The Nazis could claim that their hatred of Jews was based on some reality, since they had actual contacts with them. But anti-Semitism is sometimes present in people who have never met a Jew; they attach their hate to the stereotype as if it were real.

The intensity of hate is enormous, but its incidence is not. Unlike "love," hate is relatively rare, unless deliberately fanned and cultivated. It does not lower anxiety as dramatically or as quickly as being "in love" does, but it can so fully preoccupy a person that dread is masked for a while. Both "love" and hate are effective in banishing the fear that is at the root of the sense of powerlessness. "Love" uses the delusion of union with the loved one for this purpose; hate holds out the promise of destroying and annihilating the hated object. This was the formula that made Hitler successful with the German people.

Hate often leads to violent acts that can be almost as destructive to the hater as they are to the object of the hate. But in general, extreme assaults on one's own dignity and self-interest are part and parcel of being "in love"; violent rage against others is the hallmark of being "in hate."

Fresh hate is hot and burning, like a furious caldron. The fear underneath remains hidden by the flames and by the smoke. When hate is institutionalized it becomes cold and calculating. It looks less menacing then, but appearances often mislead. Hate is in fact a usable form of insanity at that stage, commonly called upon to advance political, religious, or other interests. Here the underlying fear is usually more evident. Such hate is extremely dangerous and extremely destructive. The force of hate, being beyond reason and beyond normal human compassion, commonly wreaks havoc and sows tragedy and pain, destruction and death, wherever it reaches.

Hate affects only individuals, but it can spread and infect entire populations, as in Nazi Germany, Iran, and elsewhere throughout history. Unscrupulous leaders have turned fear into hate in every age, fanning it into huge conflagrations that devoured everything standing in their way. The more anxious the people, the more they were in search of something to follow, someone to lessen their dread; hate of others has often been used to divert fear away from the self. It is always associated with a delusional idealization of a leader, a social class, a political movement, or a religious cause. The bond of hate, like that of "love," is very powerful, strong enough to mask one's real interests. Although people "in love" appear to be totally different from those "in hate," basically they are very much alike. Both exist precariously at the margin of reality, and both are dangerous, either to themselves or to others.

Hate is basically different from anger, although both involve the wish to thrust out aggressively against others and both are often feared equally. Everyone is angry at times, but relatively few people hate. The first is usually safe, the second never is. Like hate, anger can be intense enough to grip one's entire being, body and soul. But anger is a feeling that changes rapidly over time, usually without causing lasting damage. Complete self-control and even some measure of objectivity can be maintained even during extreme rage. Only in hate is the hold on reality lost. Even when quiescent, hate is not subject to rationality. The push of hate to obtain revenge may therefore be unstoppable except by chance, by force, or by the fear of force.

Man must have sensed long before he understood it that hate was basically different from even intense anger, and this is why he coined a separate identity for it. Anger is often useful, necessary, and desirable. Hate never is. The label of hate, like a black warning flag on a beach, alerts us to danger: A destructive storm may be nearby. Time to board up our vulnerabilities, to be cautious and aware, to beware. Yet Man's natural tendency is to hope for the best rather than to prepare for the worst. This is how the world and the Jews of Europe treated the gathering evidence of the increasing storm of hate that was first brewed in Munich by Hitler and his henchmen. We are creatures of habit who prefer not to be disturbed. Most people mobilize themselves only when they have to, often too late.

The non-explosive, calculating, and institutionalized form of hate is commonly turned into thoughts, ideas, or plans. Although the slow, meticulous, and deliberate planning gives it the appearance of rationality, the basic underlying push is nonetheless insane. Because such plans are so crazy, rational people tend not to take them seriously. But this kind of psychotic hate often has an awesome destructive power exactly because it is no longer impulsive. All the wonderful faculties of Man's inventive brain are utilized to perfect its mad design.

Hate is dangerous because it is transmittable from one person to another, and even from one generation to the next. It is highly contagious, especially to those with ill-defined personal boundaries. Such people must always cope with a great deal of fear, as we shall see more clearly in Chapter 8; they provide therefore a very fertile soil for transplanted hate. This is why barbarians and outlaws always stand a good chance of succeeding in their eager efforts to destroy the civilized order. They teach their young to hate, to kill, and to destroy on purpose. The Hitler Jugend turned bright-eyed youngsters into murderous hooligans, and the same is happening again today in Iran, Libya, Lebanon, and Cambodia. We forget the experiences of yesterday. Even the Russians who have been victimized by Nazi and Stalinist hate, and who should therefore know better, do not realize fully enough the dangers of supporting terrorism and barbarism: A plague can always get out of hand and devour everybody.

Hate often leads to vicious destruction in cold blood of property and persons. Those propelled by it carry out acts of terrorism and murder that often reach extremes of butchery and brutality. Easily impressionable youngsters with a profound sense of impotence and fear sometimes drift toward hate-filled causes in their desperate search for solutions to their personal torment. Through violence they gain a sense of power, a public identity, and the respect of their terrorist peers. Thus they survive by keeping their underlying panic and meaninglessness in check. Most terrorists have not directly suffered at the hands of those whom they attack and wish to destroy; they hate on the basis of repeated lessons that sensitized and familiarized them with "the enemy," who by then is no longer a stranger.

Yet some potential for hate exists in all of us, and it increases in intensity when all opportunities for a legitimate and safe expression of preverbal and verbal rage are chronically blocked.

Hate can be transplanted because of the existence of this potential. When hate is legitimized by an organized group or by some ideology, when a victim is chosen and repeatedly vilified, and when the social fabric is disintegrating, this potential for evil becomes activated within many individuals.

This explains why Armenians whose parents were not even conceived when the Turkish genocide against their people took place in 1915 committed acts of terror against Turkish diplomats who themselves had to learn that history from textbooks. Iranian-sponsored fanatics who had probably never seen a live American sacrificed themselves in Beirut car-bombings that killed sleeping U.S. Marines who didn't exactly know where Iran was. Hate is regularly passed on in sick families where paranoia reigns and where contacts with reality are insufficient. In general, people learn to accept the constraints of reality only reluctantly, but some never do. From time to time they erupt in sociopathic and hate-filled ways. When anger freezes into hate, all other feelings also become more or less fixed. This is how psychopathic or sociopathic killers can perform the most hideous crimes or the most daring exploits without experiencing guilt, remorse, empathy, or fear.

Hate packs such a powerful punch because punching is a perfect, if temporary, antidote for panic. The more destructive and dramatic the impact of insane violence, the more useful hate is for plugging up the gaping emptiness and the better it harnesses panic and dread. In panic, people are often frozen in total helplessness, waiting immobilized for the ax to fall. The alternative of picking up an ax and hatefully chopping up the enemy generally seems much more desirable at such moments.

Demagogues have always found many ready and eager followers by legitimizing hate. People sickened with it do not usually seek professional help, in part because it is so easy to find a legitimized outlet for it, some group that supports their delusions. The blocked rage and the hidden fear beneath it can thus be externalized, which lessens the sense of choking. Nazism and Khomeini's Islamic fanaticism are only the latest in a very long series of religious, social, and political movements that sanctioned hate and used it. Let "the others" be victims! The eagerness of haters to destroy and to kill can be easily understood: They are escaping frantically from an internal sense of danger. Kill or be killed. They are running for their lives.

But not every murder for political reasons is a result of hate. Rarely it is a rational act based on thoughtfulness and the cool considerations of alternatives. Responsible, sad, and sane people are sometimes willing to lay themselves down in front of the crushing wheels of harsh circumstances in order to save institutions and people dear to them. They agonize about their choices and about the situation around them; this distinguishes them from those driven by hate. Inflammatory words from magical figures clothed in myth only fill them with sadness and fear. Unlike hate-filled fanatics, such plotters are emotionally awake, thoughtfully present, and fully aware of the tragic consequences of violence, for themselves and for their targets. A place in history or in heaven is neither assured nor expected. A horrible task must be performed, and someone capable enough must perform it. Personal integrity triggers an internal command which dictates the need for such an act. It cannot be performed by emotionally labile or immature people, nor by those lacking self-discipline. When rational thinking, self-examination, and moral considerations are present, hate never is.

Hate separates and disengages. We often continue to be involved even with people toward whom we feel extreme anger, and we do not always withdraw permanently even from those who evoke deep hurt in us. But hate distances us not only from reality but also from those toward whom it is directed. Hate is a slamming of a door, a final departure without saying goodbye. Hate leads to unbridgeable chasms of estrangement beyond which no new beginnings are found. This in fact is one way by which hate is helpful to some people, though not without extracting a high price. Children and adults who cannot separate from those with whom they used to be "in love" sometimes accomplish the impossible with hate. One form of craziness supplants another.

Relationships between parents and their children, between lovers, and between marriage partners are sometimes so tightly interwoven that no room is left for emotional breathing. At least one of the parties and sometimes both literally have a sense of choking. Panic soon follows. Distance must urgently be created, since the situation is experienced as potentially deadly, and hate often arises automatically then in the service of surviving.

Well-meaning counselors who preach "love" or compromise at such moments make a bad situation much worse. What is needed is an immediate separation, emotional or physical, perhaps only of short duration. But many family "counselors," psychiatrists, psychotherapists, rabbis, ministers, and priests themselves become very anxious at the thought of any separation. Thousands of painful, disruptive, and very expensive hospitalizations could be avoided but for their "help." When no other way of separating is proferred, the hospital becomes the last refuge left for creating distance, short of murder or suicide. Even these are precipitated at times by the shortsighted and self-serving interventions of such "helpers." In extreme despair, without hope, suicide and murder sometimes seem to be the only ways of exit from impossible situations.

Hate is rarely treated successfully or undone, except by chance and by the passage of time. The same is true of romantic "love." Both are psychotic-like states, yet those lost in their midst do not know that they are in any trouble. They are sure that others do not understand them or the depth of their feelings.

To dissolve hate and to change persons afflicted with it require that they first experience the fear underneath it as such; this can only happen in the presence of someone with whom they feel secure. Only then does the frozen hate begin to thaw out slowly, eventually turning into rage. This in turn must be neutralized, not merely talked about or recognized as such. Interpretations about the causes and origins of anger are basically irrelevant in this process, since they have no power: They originate in reason and appeal to reason. The heat of fury and the explosive intensity of rage found at the root of hate must be experienced as such, and expressed verbally or vocally at someone willing and able to stand in as a symbolic target. It requires exquisite skill, inner strength, sensitivity, good timing, and enormous patience on the part of very experienced and courageous therapists. The dangerous task becomes completely safe, and success can be achieved, but only in well-designed and well-constructed therapeutic environments as described in Chapter 6. This is not where people with hate usually end up. Besides, they are generally much too afraid of such intense emotional involvement. They do not trust very much and are more eager to destroy others than to save themselves. Usually they end up in deep trouble: in jails, in electric chairs, and prematurely in cemeteries.

9. Anger

Even mental-health professionals generally do not yet realize that all feelings are natural, necessary, and unavoidable expressions of our physiology. Instead they classify some as "positive" and others as "negative," using these terms not in the neutral mathematical sense but as value connotations. Love and happiness are usually labeled "positive" and considered to be good feelings; hate, anger, hurt, and sadness are customarily spoken of as "negative," undesirable, or bad. Fear is often found on neither list, perhaps out of a naive wish that what is ignored might simply go away and disappear.

Such a moralistic classification is commonly used not only by professionals and the public but in the mass communication media also. It overlooks the fact that feelings are "designed" to help us preserve ourselves, survive, and prosper. Even the "negative" feelings have a positive value, and we are severely handicapped when we cannot experience them.

Anger is often very frightening to the person experiencing it as well as to those against whom it is directed. It looks menacing, and losing control is frequently experienced as a threat. Yet like other feelings, anger is safe in itself. The fear of its uncontrolled force is such however that even the word "anger" is often shunned. People speak of being frustrated, irritated, annoyed, mad, bothered, troubled, miffed, or even vexed, but they often disclaim being angry, furious, or in a rage. Even the milder substitutes come with modifiers; they are often preceded by "a little." We go to great lengths to protect ourselves from that which we perceive as dangerous.

Anger can be either rational and justified or an irrational and pathologic expression of the self. The first kind is a reaction to chronic and repeated negligence of real obligations by others with whom we are involved. It is a reaction to disappointment and hurt that are rooted in current circumstances. Such anger helps us reassert our sense of power and maintain our dignity and self-respect. But it is only rarely understood or used this way.

Much more common is the second kind of anger, which hides fear and replaces hurt; it is prominently associated with depression. Basically, such anger is an impotent, if loud, chronic temper tantrum consisting of much complaining, screaming, and heat, but without real force. It is meant to change the behavior of others, not the self. It guarantees that the complaining person will remain emotionally a pathetic, unhappy, miserable, and hurt child, which is what such a person unconsciously prefers to be. Sadly, the angry complainer knows of no better way to survive, for he or she is emotionally sick.

Such outbursts of anger are meant, at least unconsciously, to demonstrate that it is safer and better for others to accommodate themselves to us; they might get hurt otherwise. The hidden threat of angry explosions might include disapproval or loss of love, desertion, or even some form of physical violence. Animals assert themselves by using primitive threats of force to intimidate, and we humans have not yet totally left our heritage behind us. Such angry threats produce bitterness and counteranger, at least in hidden form. People often believe that they are more powerful when they can run roughshod over others, but this generally proves to be a hollow and short-lived power. Besides, the sense of powerlessness is increased when others are not intimidated by our verbal attacks. Some people try then to escalate their angry expressions, hoping to increase the other person's fear. It is a losing proposition; either way is ruinous to relationships. The one who fails to curb such angry behavior is damaged in the process, at least in the long run.

Even when anger is realistic and justified, it is best never used as a basis for corrective action. Vocal expressions are its only legitimate and safe outlets. Feelings are not well calibrated without a lot of prior work to correct their errors; until then, they are unreliable as a guide to reality. It is much wiser to cool down before any decisions are made and before any new behavior is initiated.

As a rule, threats and acts of violence committed in anger are signs of weakness, not of strength, desperate attempts to prevail by those who feel impotent and vulnerable. The more extreme the outbursts, the greater the hidden sense of defeat. Neither threats nor violence are an integral part of anger but merely dangerous distortions grafted upon it. People who use force or threaten others with it deprive themselves of the benefits that anger can offer as a healing and restorative tool.

Many people hide their anger or suppress it for fear that it might lead to destructive acts. Since they are not sufficiently confident of their ability to distinguish between feelings and actions, they lack an important and needed mechanism to repair the bruised self. Worse yet, anger that is not expressed openly does not just evaporate; its residues are stored within us. Ever-increasing stores of such internalized rage eventually overload the system, leading to explosions that are directed inwardly or outwardly. Volcanoes and people erupt when the inner pressure exceeds the strength of that which contains it. The very situation that people try so desperately to prevent is often precipitated because the efforts at containment are aimed in the wrong direction.

The accumulating inwardly directed anger often produces

symptoms of physical illness. People can literally "eat their guts out." Gastric and duodenal ulcers as well as many other gastrointestinal symptoms are among the most prominent psychosomatic illnesses resulting from chronic inhibition of the physical need for angry self-expression. Other common illnesses are hypertension, arthritis, skin disorders, and cardiac irregularities. But any illness, including cancer, can be triggered by long-standing tension that never finds appropriate channels.

When the direction of an uncontrolled explosion is outward, the results are no less tragic. Even without violent outbursts that kill, maim, or destroy by design, hundreds of thousands die "accidentally" in car accidents and in other mishaps resulting from suppressed anger. Lesser outbursts cause major difficulties in personal and professional relationships. Those with a chip on their shoulder have difficulty maintaining jobs, marriages, and friendships. They constantly irritate those with whom they associate, evoking resentment, disappointment, hurt, and more anger. The price of living this way is exceedingly high.

Even so, a recent rash of books and articles by various psychological popularizers recommend that anger not be expressed. This could have been predicted. We are now in the middle of a reaction to the 1960s and '70s, when "experts" insisted that people should "do their own thing." This was often understood to mean that expressions of rage and actions based upon it were desirable, regardless of time, circumstances, and other people. Remember the film in which a character suggested that we all go to our windows and scream, "I'm mad as hell, and I'm not going to take this anymore"? Unrestrained, irrational, and impersonal expressions of anger were recommended as a sign of liberation from the yoke of reality. It produced a generation of obnoxious, cynical, bitter, and abrasive youths who vented their personal pique on individuals and institutions in the name of freedom. It did not cure them of their inner rage. The pendulum is now swinging to the other side.

Fads come and go. In areas where knowledge is fuzzy and the need is great, new "truths" are frequently trumpeted by the media and others with much excitement and hype. "Stress management" is the latest popular version. Stories of new "discoveries" raise the ratings of television programs and fatten the wallets of their promoters, which is not so bad. But it is unforgivable that they hold out false promises to the already weary and hopeless, only to have them cruelly dashed.

Anger is often not only a cover-up for hidden fear but frequently is mixed with it. It is a little easier and less horrible to be angrily active than to wait passively in dread. This is why many people typically appear to be irritated much of the time and generally impatient; it keeps others at a safe distance. "As-if" anger is so common because fear is so common.

But real or not, a permanently angry demeanor and loud screaming can be very frightening to the young children of such people, even if harmless. Unlike hate, anger is not usually associated with psychosis, and its noise is not necessarily an indication of real danger. The loudness of screams and the primitiveness of profanities are often inversely proportional to their threat. The weak, the scared, and the impotent have no other recourse besides screaming. More often than not, the parent who is screamed at prevails, and besides he or she can appear to be the victim and thus receive the sympathy and support of children, family, and neighbors. This further deflates, hurts, and angers the screamer, increasing his or her sense of impotence, helplessness, and hopelessness.

Real anger has direction and force. When it is not an attempt to intimidate but an act of self-restitution it also has dignity. Such were King Lear's pain-filled roars. No one is ever truly angry without an aim, and no one can ever really be angry at himself. We cannot intimidate ourselves, nor would we ever wish to; and it makes absolutely no sense to protest loudly against ourselves. We can and do blame ourselves sometimes while claiming to be angry, but this is no more than self-recrimination. The effects of self-blame, unlike those of anger, are deflating, not inflating, to our view of ourselves.

The reason so many people claim so often that they are never angry or that they are only angry "in general" is that directing anger at specific others was always forbidden to them. They are too scared to ever do so knowingly and openly. This is also why some claim that they are angry at themselves. People who characteristically live this way have recently been classified as Type A, the ones prone to have strokes and heart attacks. Such stereotyping is undesirable. It is often understood as implying that the tendency to suppress anger is fixed, permanent, and unchangeable, perhaps hereditary through one's genes. Yet such traits are completely changeable with competent professional help, although not all at once.

Conscious control of anger is sometimes temporarily lost for a second in innocent settings such as crowded elevators. Without meaning to do so, we may react to somebody's stepping on our toe as if it were a major assault. The self-righteous protest is so out of proportion, even in the eyes of the protestor, that fear, shame, and embarrassment follow. This aggravates an already bad situation by increasing the old fear of losing control, creating a vicious cycle of more suppressed anger and more worry about it. The residues of anger continue to grow until death intervenes, an illness is precipitated, professional help is sought, or a nervous breakdown occurs. But most psychiatrists and other psychotherapists are unable to help much; they are also afraid of anger and of its full and open expression. They succeed only rarely in truly changing the self-damaging ways by which people cope with their anger, although they are usually able to help a little by ameliorating the acute distress.

Academic learning alone is clearly not sufficient in preparing therapists to do this work properly. Psychiatry residents, psychology students, and budding social workers are usually not less angry than other people; and like others, they too are very scared of losing control. Their anger and their fear of it must first be lessened and essentially eliminated; only then can they help others. Not before they are themselves emotionally ready can they construct safe therapeutic settings in which "non-acting-out" rage finds room for open expression. They must be able not only to tolerate but also to welcome and to encourage forceful expressions of anger directly *at* them, standing in for others in the patient's past. In such settings it soon becomes obvious that anger is not dangerous in itself, since actual harm comes neither to the person who expresses it nor to the one at whom it is directed.

The accumulated anger residues of a lifetime are feared even by professionals who have not undergone such a process. They too approach anger as one would a ticking bomb capable of destroying, burning, and killing. Only relatively few know that it can be discharged safely and defused without causing damage; fewer yet know how to do it. Chapter 6 outlines the setting and conditions that make this task possible.

Many people are so afraid of the hidden monster that lurks within them that they appoint themselves its permanent warden. They want to make sure that it is never released from its internal prison. It is a full-time job, which saps much energy from all waking endeavors and often even interferes with sleep. Life is much easier when this dangerous beast is turned into a domesticated animal that obeys our commands. But since this powerful force exists within us, we cannot harness it alone. A competent outsider is needed to help us do so. It is obviously not enough simply to "control" anger or to "suppress" it, to "channel" or to "manage" it. Above all, it makes no sense to try to "reason" it out of existence.

It is obvious why young children feel threatened when they witness outbursts of rage, even if no violence is ever involved. They cannot understand how the one differs from the other, and they fear both. Parents are not only much bigger than the child, but rational or not, they are in complete charge of the child's life. Even though their angry outbursts may be benign, no child can ever be sure of that, especially if he or she has been physically punished at times. This confusion about anger often lasts throughout life, as if nothing ever changes. Many adults live as if their power is no greater than in early childhood. Having been sensitized to the sounds of angry conflict long ago, they still expect chaos and danger later on.

Young children also fear angry and loud disagreements between father and mother because they sense them as possibly leading to the breakup of the family. They behave as if they consciously worry whether either or both parents will get hurt or disappear, leaving them without protection or care. Even families in which restraint is exercised produce children who are scared of anger, since the least conflict can be misinterpreted and given unrealistically catastrophic meanings. Lasting emotional scars and a profound fear of anger can develop without any history of physical or even emotional abuse. The death of a parent when the children are young or chronic withdrawal, passivity, and other symptoms of depression in a parent also produce individuals who shun the power of anger; children often assume responsibility for acts they did not commit. They often render themselves powerless and humanly impotent for life as a punishment and as a precaution.

Children of violent parents usually appear especially docile and eager to accept the dictates of reality. Fear is a great teacher. But their acceptance of limits normally represents only a yielding to external pressure, not the completion of an internal struggle. Rebellion against external constraints often becomes evident as soon as it becomes safe to rebel. They frequently become violent then, since violence tends to breed more violence and irrationality, just as love or hate, flexibility or rigidity, kindness or cruelty, all tend to produce more of their kind. The behavior of such people is often volatile because it is hate, not anger, that propels them. Disappointment, hurt, and anger all tend to produce hate in the absence of basic trust. Anger finds room only when reality is basically sensible and predictable, even if not always fair.

Parents who do not understand that even the strongest feelings do not provide a license for action often try to protect their children and others by demanding that not only irrational acts but feelings also be suppressed. This is particularly true for anger. The justified concern about the possibility of dangerous violence has thus been converted into a harmful prohibition. Respect for one's elders is often given as the reason. Yet denial of feelings and wishes only forces them out of consciousness, not out of existence. Chronic denial of angry feelings makes it more difficult to keep angry actions under conscious control. Although well-meaning, such parents plug the safety valve that could relieve excessive internal pressure. Much damage is thus inflicted upon the next generation, all without malice. The prohibition against rational anger often breeds psychotic hate.

In reality, it makes sense to be quite angry sometimes at those we love when they repeatedly act in ways that appear damaging or destructive to their own welfare. We may be wrong in our evaluation, but our anger may nonetheless be a pure expression of genuine concern. People led by strong feelings cannot usually be stopped by gentle reminders alone. An expression of anger under such circumstances is not an attempt to intimidate, but to awaken. To observe but remain uninvolved when friends or relatives expose themselves to danger is easiest for most people. Angry expressions are generally resented. Yet friendship imposes certain obligations: Sometimes we must extend ourselves beyond our comfort for the sake of those who are important to us. There are times when only our angry warnings are powerful enough to be heard. By not disturbing those who damage themselves we may condemn them to destroy themselves. We become an accessory to a cruel and needless loss of life if we do not firmly try to stop a blind person from walking into the path of an oncoming truck.

Live-and-let-live attitudes are clearly harmful when used with very young children. Even guidance is often not enough. Impulsivity is easiest to curb early in life, but this requires the use of intrusive and forceful interventions. Yet many people condemn intrusions in general, claiming that they are basically wrong and disrespectful, even more so when they involve adults. For children there may perhaps be no better way to teach self-restraint and self-control, they sometimes finally say, than by the use of a restraining force from the outside. But how can disapproval, impatience, and even anger be justified when used with adults? Yet maturity does not always come with years. "Most adults are physically grown-up children of various emotional ages. They typically act and react on the basis of their . . . feelings." Adults are often thoughtless, and many of their positions are often ill-considered and self-damaging. Their validity must be questioned at times by those who notice and care. "Many intellectually mature adults are . . . emotionally not much older than toddlers." Few people would seriously claim that it makes sense to let a toddler play with a loaded gun.

Still the open expression of anger can endanger relationships between grownups. Adults who resent angry corrections have the power to get up and leave. A willingness to risk losing an important involvement with someone dear to us may be an indication of the deepest love, much more than smiles, hugs, kisses, and unconditional support. These may be no more than tranquilizers that we administer to those who should be awakened, yet we fear to awaken them. True love is not always sweet, and the excessive "ersatz" sweetness of saccharine is never a part of it.

The fear of the horrible consequences of losing control over their anger causes many people to become chronically passive, thus sacrificing their power and ability to act decisively. Such people are typically slow in response, in thought, and in deed; they consider issues fuzzily and behave ineffectually. They become conciliatory at all costs, seek consensus under all circumstances, and promote peace at any price. They always compromise and expect others to do the same, even when uncompromising stands are objectively called for. Their positions and manner are forever flexible and non-controversial. So is their language. They cannot be pinpointed and often not even understood. For them lack of clarity is a clear advantage. Since accommodating attitudes are socially attractive, people who have them often reach important positions in government, the media, and other institutions. Neville Chamberlain and Cyrus Vance are obvious examples.

But parents, political leaders, and psychotherapists who compulsively seek the middle ground under all circumstances become tainted as reliable agents of reality. Enforcing it requires that sometimes we stand firmly for or against something. On many occasions it is best to say things clearly, even angrily. Reality is unpleasant at times, and accepting its unbending rules is usually painful. Those who refuse to yield find it easier to dismiss demands that contain an implied readiness to retreat. Flexible standards and limitless patience are not assets in a process that aims to defeat irrational narcissistic tendencies. Those who fear their anger also have difficulties in properly exercising their personal power in other areas. Yet nothing works well without it. A legitimate strong authority is essential for the orderly and successful functioning of individuals, families, and societies. They falter and eventually fail in its absence.

Blacks, Jews, and other minorities have special difficulties with the appropriate and open expression of anger. Anxious parents who have personally suffered because of their minority status often fear that a child who expresses his or her anger openly at home might also do so in school and elsewhere in public. This would subject the child to dangerous retaliation by a prejudiced majority. Even today some parents and grandparents demand that the young lower their profile, Uncle Tom style, and tolerate abuse without protest. In some groups anger is labeled "evil." Tragically, the frightened but well-meaning elders who insist on such behavior often become the focus of derision and rage. By now everyone but such older parents seems to know that pride and dignity are human, not racial, rights. Those who give them up willingly are often despised. Their fear is no longer understood and the love that motivates them is often not seen. The next generation is less afraid of expressing their justified anger openly.

Man's fear of anger has a very long history. Even in the past anger had few legitimate channels for its safe expression. Actual and symbolic scapegoats have often served as recipients for it, but when no dog was available for kicking, Man usually mistreated his brother, his wife, his children, and strangers. Crazy Captain Ahab piles upon Moby Dick's "white hump the sum of all the general rage and hate felt by his whole race from Adam down . . . all that most maddens and torments . . . all truth with malice in it; all that cracks the sinews and cakes the brain; . . . all evil." Others usually searched for and found other targets than a whale to vent their fury upon so that they themselves would remain safe.

Man slew his brother Abel in anger and his neighbors and many, many others. He alone of all the creatures on earth kills not only for food or in the pursuit of a mate but also to save himself from his internal caldron. Organized wars are one of his unique inventions, helpful in reducing his fear and his anger even though he is also their victim. He always found religious, political, ethnic, or other rationalizations to justify his horrible acts; but even so, most crusades, riots, campaigns, pogroms, and wars have failed to settle anything for long. They were mainly useful as outlets for venting anger and hate. Now that Man has also invented nuclear weapons he must finally find better ways to survive, or he will literally destroy himself. Soon it will no longer be possible to kill others without everyone and everything being destroyed in the process.

10. Hurt

Hurt is emotional pain. Unlike most physical pain, it is not usually localized. People are often very hurt without any apparent cause. Hurt is an ache in the heart, a tear in the eye, a burden on existence. It makes all muscles droop and our spirit as well. Hurt can be acute and sharp, but more often it is dull, persistent, nagging, and gnawing. When severe, it tears us apart, and then even death appears as a welcome release.

But though the cause of hurt may be hidden, it nonetheless exists. Few of us are free of deep disappointments, and everyone has unfulfilled dreams, wishes, and yearnings. Everyone has been overlooked at times, forgotten, slighted, rejected, unheard, unseen, uninvited, unwelcomed, short-changed, and unfairly dealt with. Since the deep roots of hurt often remain unseen by those who bear its heavy burden, they treat their pain like an illegitimate child, having no proper parentage or position. We feel shame that we feel hurt, especially when life has favored us. A tall, handsome, and successful executive poured his heart out in therapy one day, saying; "People envy me, and I too know that I should count my many blessings every day. So I often smile when I want to cry; I don't complain and I act as if all is well. But, there's something inside of me crying all the time: 'Let me out! Let me out!' "

Many grownups, especially males, find few opportunities to say such words. They are too revealing and intimate for most people, even addressed to potentially sympathetic listeners. Most of us carry a heavy load of old and new hurt, and we protect ourselves from its pain by attending to business every day in a matter-of-fact way. Many people try to avoid sensitive encounters for fear that the other person might touch them and pierce their protective shield. This is why they usually are very quick to reassure a person who dares to bare his soul and that all will be better soon, thus maintaining a safe distance between themselves and their yearnings and hurt. Even in professional relationships designed for this purpose there is usually not enough room for such tender expressions.

"That thing that cries out all the time is me," the executive continued, "the inner me, little Joey. It's my bottomless hurt. It distorts the features of my face and saddens my eyes. He was always so shy, so afraid, so nice, this little Joey, even when he wanted to scream in pain. He lived as if he was shut in a cage, unable to speak out for himself with a voice. Only his eyes spoke." Most people resemble this man, except that they never speak of themselves so honestly and perceptively. Hurt is universal, like all other feelings, and it is almost universally dreaded.

Hurt is so painful because its origins are rooted in a time when we could not yet understand why we should be rebuffed at all, and because it was often elicited by the people we most wanted to fulfill our desires. For the baby, hurt is an unjust breaking of a promise, a deprivation of a birthright.

A combination of despair, good timing, safety, and courage is required before anyone dares to speak openly to another. More commonly the hurt is drowned in alcohol or in drugs, in sex or in overwork. It also hides below thick layers of anger. Most children grow up without ever noticing how deeply hurt one or both of their parents have always been; and parents frequently fail to see the deep hurt of their children.

We all had to put up with the whims of those who cared for us, upon whom we were totally dependent early in life. It is impossible to reach adulthood without having been deeply hurt on many occasions, even before we remember. Virgil knew over 2,000 years ago that hurt was to be found everywhere. "Had I a hundred tongues, a hundred lips, a throat of iron and a chest of brass, I could not tell Man's countless suffering."

Hurt results when our expectations from important others are not met, especially if they involve our being accepted, preferred, loved, welcomed, or desired by those in whom we have invested hope, yearnings, lust, or "love." The greater the unmet expectations, the deeper the hurt and the longer it lasts. We can be profoundly hurt, therefore, without anyone hurting us. Yet this is not how most people think of it. The words "I am hurt" are usually understood as meaning "You have hurt me," though the two are obviously not one and the same. Even if a person is deeply hurt by someone's word, gesture, or act, this does not prove that the other caused it. Not only may the first person's expectations have been unrealistic, but his or her threshold for hurt may be so unrealistically low that no amount of caution on the part of the second is ever enough.

Spouses and lovers commonly have major disagreements and difficulties in this area before they give up and withdraw, at least emotionally. Until then they often hurl bitter accusations when they believe they were hurt by the other, as if the unfulfillment of some unspoken expectation proves the insensitivity of the mate and the absence of true love. Why else would anyone forget an anniversary, a birthday, having the right shirt ready and pressed, or even such a minor thing as taking out the garbage? But in fact, most hurt is essentially a self-made product. We are the only ones who can invest emotionally in anything, and we do so even when others do not consent or welcome it.

Hurt is experienced similarly by all, but people treat it very differently. Most brush it aside, minimize its importance, and try to ignore it. Others are even eager to display it. They have discovered in growing up, probably only half consciously, that hurt can be a powerful weapon with which to manipulate others. Eventually they become masters of this technique. They "advertise" their suffering, both real and imagined, in manner, in dress, in speech, in gesture, in posture, in facial expressions, and in a thousand other clues. They find mates, associates, and acquaintances who cannot bear to see a person hurt, so they offer sympathy, pity, solace, and help even while they protest loudly about being manipulated.

But even people who are compulsively driven to help the helpless and the hurt are not always filled with resentment. The prospect of pleasing is sometimes so enticing that solace and help are offered eagerly, as if they were free gifts. A beautiful, desirable, and fragile-looking woman in discomfort and distress finds many willing male rescuers. In a sense, gentlemen still compete for the right to pick up the lady's dropped handkerchief. Some even treat the act as an honor. Her innocent-looking doe-like eyes are like magnets that draw the "rescuers" powerfully toward her. They "feel" so strong when they help her, ignoring the fact they they are themselves needy and desperately wanting to be "loved" in return. Men commonly experience such a woman as very young children perceive their young mother.

Disappointment and hurt usually follow. The woman does not

find a reliable and loving partner, and the man does not find the magical creature that he expected. Both are bitter. He becomes a purveyor of crumbs, and she lives constantly by hurt, getting less than she deserves. We must grow up emotionally and become free of fear to avoid such tragic traps.

Relationships between children and their parents are also often based on the exploitation of hurt. The "quietly" suffering and "self-sacrificing" Jewish mother is merely a prototype of many others. Her "selfless" devotion contains not-so-hidden expectations of a payback from her guilty children. Men are also not free of this tendency, although their style is different. They are the lost boys of all ages who must forever be kept from getting into trouble—nice, innocuous, pathetic, a little boring, and always hurt. Apparent powerlessness sometimes hides an almost calculated use of power.

Such efforts to elicit sympathy are pathetic and desperate attempts to find help for real if hidden needs—relief from fear and from the real hurt underneath. A truly hurting person always exists within the one addicted to false hurt. Such people would sob deeply if they experienced themselves as accepted, safe, and really understood. Their crying actually causes the chest to heave. Deep sighs rise from unknown depths, tears stream in torrents, and the entire body trembles. When it finally stops, some of the old heaviness will have lifted. This obviously is much better than living off the crumbs that can be gained from the addiction to false hurt; they are not very nutritious. Having been extracted by the manipulation of others, such crumbs are not even coated with real love.

Those who live by exaggerating their real or imagined hurt and by displaying it were probably cared for most lovingly as babies when they were in pain. This is how the addiction to hurt becomes ingrained. Such people repeatedly tend to get into all sorts of difficulties, specifically including being sickly. Johnny is such a man, and his story may seem contrived, but it is true. He is a persistent seeker of trouble. As a child he would fall out of trees and regularly bruise himself, and he would always have difficulties at school. As a young man he was laid off from job after job, and sometimes he could find no work for over a year. Unwilling or unable to note that he had never worked steadily in his life, he nonetheless complained endlessly about the economic situation and government policies. Then his wife left him. Finally he was stopped by the police and ticketed for drunk driving while his two very young children were romping in the back seat. He is now fighting in court for his right to have the children stay with him on weekends. And he is only twenty-nine years old.

On the other hand, babies who are not well attended to even when they are sick or needy tend to become stoic if they survive. Even as grownups they typically ignore their hurt, believing it to be a sign of weakness. They take pride in being insensitive to themselves, like fakirs. As parents they raise children who are also anesthetized to their real emotional needs. Such children often become self-indulgent or sickly to compensate for what they never got and still need. The sad history of the Kennedy clan is a near perfect example. In the span of three generations we repeatedly see pain ignored, tenderness downgraded, and toughness exalted. Even great success cannot hide the chain of tragedies and sadness that followed. Children in such families learn not to cry while they are still too small to understand the meaning of words. Instead they withdraw and clam up when injured, sick, or hurt. They develop a stiff upper lip as they grow up, and rarely complain. Eventually they drink, they take drugs, they carouse, they overachieve, and often they die young of a broken heart. When hurt is extinguished, other feelings become numbed also. Such hardened people are unable to love; they are clumsy with tenderness and in general insensitive. Even when they are physically close to another person, they are still distant and never really intimate with anyone.

Allergies, ulcers, asthma, emphysema, skin disorders, slow-growing cancers, and other chronic illnesses are some of the many ways by which such people bring attention to themselves. Yet not having developed the capacity to reach for help, they often do not know how to accept it when offered. Other people soon forget their needs, just as they themselves ignore or minimize them. A vicious cycle is thus set into motion. Less is offered to them than to almost anyone else in the same circumstances.

Young children are often teased good-naturedly, if somewhat insensitively, when their hearts seem to break because of some objectively minor disappointment. Their exaggerated pained innocence appears amusing to those already hardened by experience. Kids are sometimes even laughed at on such occasions because they are so "silly." Since the mocking comes from their parents or older siblings, the most beloved, powerful, and important people in their lives, many children begin to assume that to be sensitive, tender, and hurt is indeed silly. They begin to harden too. The fact that the mocking may have been free of any malice does not alter the subjective experience. To avoid future humiliation and pain, all hurt is tucked away and kept well hidden, even from the one experiencing it.

The tendency to minimize hurt starts even earlier. The baby's delusion of being absolutely powerful is not given up without a drawn-out struggle and much pain, and only against stubborn resistance and with extreme reluctance. To be denied is a humbling experience; each time it adds fresh hurt to previously accumulated stores of old hurt. As a result we have more reasons to swallow our hurt, to hide it and to hold it within. The weight of it rests in the chest, but it burdens one's entire being.

There is no easy escape. Those seemingly lucky children whose delusions of power have not been sufficiently challenged early in life must face the hurt of repeated disappointments and shame later. "Spock babies" often become self-indulgent children and adults, unwilling to postpone the immediate gratification of their many wishes. They often act as if they really could not exist without getting what they want. Victims of grossly underdeveloped self-discipline, such persons may indignantly refuse to try curbing themselves. In many ways they resemble people with special talents, looks, money, position, or other advantages. Unlike the rest of us ordinary mortals, they typically expect the quirks of their behavior to be tolerated, since they are so special. Very beautiful or sexy women, very talented or famous artists, and very rich men or those in positions of great power, like spoiled brats, can maintain the delusion that they will always prevail for longer. They often live as if disregard for all humanity were a natural right bestowed upon them at birth. Since their hurt, obviously, has unique pathos, they fully expect others to immediately change themselves to fit their wishes. When they finally have no choice but to face reality, they fall harder. Usually they wither gracelessly, as the pathetic end of the Duke and Duchess of Windsor amply demonstrates.

Such are the lives of people who as boys and girls were overprotected against being hurt. Talent, wealth, physical beauty, and being privileged in other ways are generally not pure blessings. Only children and others raised by overanxious parents are often similarly overprotected, though they lack these advantages. Like the privileged ones, they too expect exquisite sensitivity as a bare minimum. People with special status or sensitivity are frequently very successful in attracting "friends" and mates, and their relationships usually survive for a while, although they are often pathologic. Multiple marriages and a rapid turnover of "friendships" are the rule. Excitement is always an integral part of such involvements, and hysterical-like ups and downs are common. Such busyness is very distracting and therefore an effective device to banish the fear of abandonment for a while. The continued demands to be protected from hurt usually determine the behavior of the mate until it becomes intolerable. But the need for protection from "unbearable" hurt can serve as a de facto means of enforcement for life, if the mate is very frightened of ending up alone. Almost always the one who uses hurt prevails, and usually his or her will arbitrarily determines the outcome of any situation. Hurt can indeed be a powerful tool with which to manipulate others.

Don was such an overprotected boy and it crippled him too. This is why he finally gasped for help. Because his mother was always so very sensitive to his tender soul, he clung to her practically until adulthood. His father, who tried in vain to break this pathologic bond, always seemed to be humiliating him. He still claimed to be deeply wounded by hurt decades later because that father sometimes called him "dumbwit" in exasperation. Only with much effort did he begin to realize that his father had been right all along. "Hurt was such a good protector to me," Don would say in tears as a middle-aged man. "I hate to say goodbye to it even now. I'm like a Ping-Pong ball these days. One moment I want to destroy, punish, and defeat everyone who is not perfectly sensitive toward me; the next moment I know they're right. What convinces me more and more of my need to change is the pleasure I'm getting from being an adult with and around people. My wife was teaching me to play the piano yesterday. I really enjoyed it, even when she corrected me. I did not stop or withdraw to pout as I used to, nor did I get confused. Even when she was impatient at times I could stay with her and with the task. But I fear that without my hurt to protect me others will take advantage of me. I know better, but only at times." Although Don is finally able to stop using hurt as the coin of his realm, he may nevertheless fear exposure to the deeper layers of his real hurt. The former increases one's control over the environment, the latter one's vulnerability.

The fear of being hurt often causes people to avoid any real intimacy, except with those who have already proven themselves to be trustworthy beyond any shadow of doubt. But since complete trustworthiness can never be fully assured, really close relationships are never formed. Cats, dogs, and other pets are safer. So are collectibles of all sorts. Walls built for protection against hurt also exclude all love and friendship. Shelters become oppressive prisons, their inmates living in solitary confinement. In such cold cells many people perish slowly in loneliness, often in the midst of friendly persons who would be eager to welcome them. But the truth that they are petrified by closeness because they dread being hurt must remain a secret. Revealing it would expose their vulnerability to public view. Superficial relationships in great number sometimes fill the time, which is supposed to prove how eager such shut-ins really are to be involved with someone.

They say that it is better to have loved and lost than never to have loved at all, but most people are not willing to take such chances. To have loved and lost is the source of some of the most profound hurt of all. It is so much simpler and safer to be in love with love, a myth of perfection.

Feelings usually change in rapid succession, and it is sometimes very difficult to know at any one moment which of them is primary. They rarely exist in pure form, except for fear. It is in a class all by itself, dominating the human experience. But hurt often lives together with fear as a twin. Published stories about Tony Curtis suggest that his loneliness was a result of such a combination. He is quoted as saying that he was "battered" by life: three divorces; innumerable affairs; addictions to alcohol, barbiturates, and cocaine; the near disintegration of his career; and the collapse of most of his relationships. He looks like a man running for his life. His children are said to be essentially strangers, since he apparently could not be there as their father when they needed him the most. Now they are not there when he needs them. Was he more hurt or more scared? Like a true figure of tragedy, he appears to be alternately pulled and pushed by fear and by hurt, stretched on the rack every day by these two tormentors. One or the other always seems to have its heavy hand on him, never letting go.

Perpetual victims who use hurt and stoics who appear not to be touched by it represent two extremes. Both have serious difficulties with mature mutual relationships, but to change they must obviously be approached from opposite ends. Unfortunately this is not what usually happens when they seek professional help. Medical and non-medical psychotherapists frequently gravitate toward their profession because they half knowingly seek help for their own unresolved personal problems. They are therefore often compulsively pushed to help oth-

ers in the same manner in which they would want to be helped
—with endless compassion, much caring, and infinite patience.
These qualities might help stoics get involved; but "as-if" victims, the users of hurt, need something else. They stand a chance
only with kind and committed therapists who take firm stands,
never compromise with reality, and never yield simply because
the patient claims to hurt too much. Such therapists are extremely hard to find.

Confirmed sufferers commonly seethe with anger just below
the surface, believing that they have always been treated unfairly. Though they generally try to hide their anger, it must be
teased out, aroused, and given repeated opportunities for powerful expression. Sympathizing with the hurt merely gratifies their
pathologic wishes and condemns them to never change. Sympathy and limitless tolerance are outright poison here. Such people
must cease seeing themselves as victims. Stoics, on the other
hand, must be patiently helped to take real risks in human relationships, beginning with the one that they may have with a
truly loving and deeply involved therapist.

Residues of unexpressed hurt, like those of anger, also accumulate. Weeping into one's pillow is less damaging than total
denial; but lonely crying adds insult to previous injury, since
hurt originates in our expectations from others. The very freedom to shed tears of hurt openly in the presence of someone who
can be trusted with our pain has an altogether different effect. It
confirms that somebody cares and that our vulnerability and
hurt at least deserve a respectful hearing. Such an experience
reduces the hurt and it helps in the efforts to regain a more
realistic perspective.

Hurt that is not stored but expressed openly and properly can
also be helpful in repairing relationships. Speaking of one's hurt
to the one who supposedly caused it provides room for correcting
inaccurate impressions and opportunities for making amends.
Apparent or real insensitivity can be replaced with friendly attentiveness, provided that the person addressed is receptive and
willing to be involved in such efforts.

Breathing actually becomes easier and deeper once an episode
of real hurt is resolved this way. The deep sobbing that is part of
and follows such a resolution often makes a crack in the thick
walls of self-protection whose construction usually begins in
early infancy and continues throughout life. Such crying only
happens when a person senses that long-overlooked grievances
have finally been heard. It is a sure sign of relief. Difficult as

such open expressions of hurt usually are, they lessen pain, add stability to relationships, and reduce bitterness, withdrawal, and anger.

But most people never have such opportunities, and they must carry enormous burdens of old and new hurt. Frozen tears that needed shedding become ever more weighty with time, and lacrimal ducts that are chronically congested also cause other organs and systems of the body to malfunction. In general, men consider it particularly unbecoming to be seen as hurt. They are taught while still very small that "big boys don't cry," even when they are hurt. Virgil was said to have been the wisest man of his day, but even he wrote only of "a mother's tears." The tears of fathers were overlooked even then. Hurt is the one feeling where gender makes a difference and a sex bias exists: Men hurt no less than women, but they have to hide it more. By tradition a man is seen as the hunter and provider, and he is supposed to be always strong and tough. Robbed of their right to feel and to express their hurt openly, men have no other choice but to die younger. They usually do.

11. Sadness

Sadness is also painful; but unlike hurt it has a tinge of sweetness, since it is only experienced in the relative absence of irrational fear and turmoil. Sadness comes from emotional understanding, from having made peace with the passage of time, and from having acquired good vision. With it we can see that reality is and always was imperfect, and that so it shall always be. Seeing distant consequences, we are often sad because we must sometimes decide to forgo pursuing things that are both desirable and attainable; the cost is too high. While hurt is associated with powerlessness, sadness does not render a person vulnerable. It is neither troublesome nor dangerous. In fact most people are able to experience sadness and to acknowledge openly that sometimes they do. To be sad is not considered a weakness, and shame is not generally involved.

Sadness leaves no residues and therefore it never weighs a person down, unlike suppressed fear, hurt, and anger. It can even uplift, because wisdom often arrives in its company. It represents the mature acceptance of some aspect of existence, the calm realization that some dreams can never be realized, that the real world is unlike a fairy tale, and that there is no free lunch to be had. Sadness is a sign of our knowledge that easy solutions and happy endings are very rare, that all relationships, like life itself, invariably come to an end, and that nobody has enough time or money, and often not enough of either. No matter how fortunate and careful we have been and how hard we have tried, sadness is our lot because everyone makes errors in life and nobody takes advantage of every opportunity.

What makes the great classical tragedies tragic is that their main characters have no choice but to follow the inevitable dictates of fate, as determined by their personalities. The bitter and painful endings are both unavoidable and expected. We are gripped by tension because we participate emotionally in the unfolding drama, almost straining to halt the coming disaster that we anticipate. Why do we subject ourselves to such sorrow and torment? Because we are enhanced by bearing witness to such heroic struggles. The grandeur and courage of the human spirit are best revealed in the painful attempts to escape truly tragic webs. Thus we too are helped to extricate ourselves from the warp and woof of childish notions and unrealistic hopes. We are willing to share in the agony of defeats because the glory of victories comes only to those who neither turn back nor run away from that which life presents. Such people are more sad, but they hurt less deeply and less often than others.

Only reasonably mature individuals make room for tragedy in their lives. They know that even with pain a thoughtful life is easier and much more enjoyable than a mindless existence. Such people react to losses with sadness, and the more profound the loss the sadder they are. Sadness is associated with life and with death, with growing up and with growing old, with the hardships of trying to reach a peak and with the triumph of having reached it. Since life is so impermanent and so imperfect, sadness is what we experience much of the time as we grow older, after irrational fear has been lessened. It is a normal reaction to our human limitations and to the unavoidable pain and suffering of others.

Children and immature adults try to avoid discomfort and pain at all costs, which requires that they live much of the time in fantasy. They are not commonly sad, only hurt. They often depend on the easy laughs of a situation comedy to distract them. Johnny Carson's late evening show is so popular because it succeeds in doing this so well. By poking good-natured fun at the ridiculous and silly in others who are very much like us, we accept the pathetic in ourselves somewhat more easily. Although "having fun" cannot eliminate fear and hurt, it often can direct our attention away from them for a little while. Sadness, unlike having fun, permits us to remain aware of things as they are, and thus it increases our real power to contend with them.

Those who do not avoid sadness are fortunate enough to also know true happiness. Being opposites, they often alternately replace each other, and on occasion they even make an appearance together.

12. Happiness, "Happiness," and Contentment

Happiness, like real love, is self-produced and results from being self-contained. Yet people normally think that others "make" them happy or unhappy, that happiness can be lost and found, that it can be pursued, and that we can hold on to it as if it were an object. Many still believe that material success is synonymous with happiness, that power over others helps us find it, and that it is best assured by having what one wants or needs. But such a yearned-for happiness is really no more than the temporary absence of anxiety and fear. To distinguish it from true contentment we shall refer to it from now on as "happiness."

Real happiness, like love, fills the person with a sense of well-being that requires nothing else. What is, is enough. "Who is rich?" asks the wise old Rabbi Hillel, and his answer is simple: "He who is content with his lot." Such contentment does not imply a lack of striving for excellence or for a better world or a withdrawal from all competition. It means that one has no further interest in chasing; since one's heart and mind are at ease, more is not just superfluous, it is meaningless.

As in real love, those who are content sometimes overflow with joy; it is almost painful then not to share it. So they frequently offer of themselves to others, as if they wished to embrace the whole universe. Since conflict, pain, loss, struggles, and disappointments do not suddenly vanish even with happiness, there is room in it for much sadness. It lives with joy comfortably, taking over for a short while and then receding again. Happiness occasionally has peaks, but they rise from a bedrock of basic contentment, an awareness of the beauty, harmony, and marvel of life and of nature.

The biblical ideal of contentment is one of peace and plenty, where Man lives undisturbed "under his vine and his fig tree." These were the components of happiness when security, food, and shelter were not assured. But in affluence we define it differently. Comfortable houses, condominiums, and country clubs are filled with happiness only after they have been cleared of the demons that often haunt their inhabitants. These usually block the way to contentment. Being loved, accepted, and even popular is obviously not enough, nor is being invited into the homes, parties, or even beds of others. The "happiness" that these bring is mostly a momentary relief from acute unhappiness. To be taken in merely diminishes the horror of being left out in the cold. This has a lot to do with fear but nothing to do with real happiness, which is never based on delusions. Happiness co-exists with anger or with hurt only poorly, and it is totally and immediately banished by fear.

The pursuit of happiness by those who lack it is a never-ending preoccupation, since moments of joy do not leave permanent imprints. For such people the promise of wealth, new relationships, or travel to faraway places is a constant enticement. Perpetually busy, they have no leisure to take a deep breath, to look out of their window, to notice a little bird, or to look someone in the eye. They become very anxious at rest, unable to delight in living each moment; busyness helps them survive. Some people are so devoted to photographing important events, beautiful settings, or special moments that they never have time to enjoy or even to see any of them. Trying to preserve past happiness for future use, they buy souvenirs, collect photographs, and keep mementos of special occasions. Yet nostalgia cannot match actual experience any more than the thought of eating can nourish. What we really need are fresh supplies of happiness every day. In the absence of fear these are abundant and found very easily. Joy falls into our laps all day long if we are not too busy pursuing it.

Yet happiness evades pursuers. So why was the right to pursue it declared to be unalienable by the U.S. Declaration of Independence? Because even Thomas Jefferson and Benjamin Franklin were not infallible. Poverty combined with religious persecution and political repression produced misery and great misfortune in many of the European countries from which the American settlers had come. It must have been obvious even then that no one can promise happiness to all men, but they believed that at least the right to pursue it was endowed by the Creator. Yet in reality, happiness can be achieved only when we are no longer busy with the pursuit of anything. No matter how fast we run, as long as we run, happiness will always exist just beyond the next horizon.

Enjoyment itself commonly gives rise to much anxiety in people who come from families bound together by suffering, with strict prohibitions against being happy and content. They see happiness as one of the devil's many tricks. The desirable goal of discouraging self-indulgence may have been distorted, or else a bitter reality was idealized. Either way, such people cling to suffering and to hurt and they avoid joy almost automatically. They experience happy moments in life as dangerous and seductive traps to be shunned, a betrayal of their roots. Somehow they succeed in tarnishing even pure gold.

Reasons for happiness, contentment, and joy exist everywhere. Health, life, the marvels of nature, and our own existence provide an endless flow of reasons to count our blessings. People whose personal boundaries are essentially intact not only have good receptors for happiness, but for a short while they can also hold it. Such people often experience an embarrassment of riches, since frequently they literally overflow. Tears of joy may fill their eyes when they see a perfect gymnastic performance or a truly beautiful flower, when others triumph over their weaknesses and doubts, and simply because they are alive and well.

Happiness is found in discovering, not in having discovered; in the search, not in having found truth. It is unexpectedly in us and everywhere around us when we no longer run after, or away from, anything. In this sense the preachers and gurus down the ages were right. They were only wrong in believing that anyone can map out the way to happiness for someone else. Happy people often have a real sense of oneness with the universe, an almost physical bond with everything, yet without losing themselves. No frivolous waste of anything is therefore possible; all inert and living things are a part of ourselves then. Such wondrous moments are only fleeting, but they are real nonetheless.

FIVE

Healthier Children
in a Saner World

Fear of parents and of social institutions can bring about behavioral conformity, but usually not internal change.
CHAPTER 8, SECTION 84

Learning to really think requires first that we make room for it by diminishing the domain of feelings.
CHAPTER 8, SECTION 80

A well-meaning and seemingly humane new regulation went into effect on March 22, 1983. The U.S. Department of Health and Human Services required maternity and obstetric wards as well as nurseries in federally funded hospitals to post a conspicuous warning that "failure to feed and care for handicapped infants in this facility is prohibited by federal law." The rule allows federal investigators twenty-four-hour access to such facilities, if necessary, to protect the life or health of a handicapped newborn. It also establishes a hot line for reporting violations by anyone who suspects "or has reasons to believe" that the life of a handicapped newborn is in danger.

This makes sense on the surface. Who among us is not in favor of life, and who would not want to protect helpless babies from abuse? But the regulation may not have been in anyone's best interest, least of all that of the handicapped infants. In our attempt to do good we may have helped multiply the torture of innocents, and we may have increased needless pain and suffering.

All sensitive humans identify emotionally with others; this is what makes them sensitive. Even the less sensitive tend to "feel for" helpless babies and children, especially those existing in

194

precarious situations. This is why the new policy enjoyed such immediate and widespread support. But overidentification, when we actually see ourselves in others, is generally self-serving, and it always distorts our judgment. Those responsible for issuing the new regulation were probably also swayed by feelings, and neither reason nor thoughtfulness seems to have been involved very much. Feelings often masquerade as thoughts, and as we have seen in Chapter 3 they are commonly the basis of private decisions and public policies. The H.H.S. regulation is by no means an isolated or unusual exception. Our own lives and our families' are often in serious trouble as a result, and our societal priorities are often confused.

1. A Personal Word to the Reader

In my days in medical school and soon afterward I was repeatedly forced to make important decisions concerning the lives of others. But since nobody carries such a heavy responsibility lightly or eagerly, I too wished to avoid it. One day during my internship in a very busy emergency room of a large city hospital, a police squad car came speeding in, lights flashing and siren wailing, with a badly bleeding young man, an ice pick stuck in his heart. I almost ran with the others to call the doctor, forgetting it was me and wishing that someone with much more experience would have been there. The man's life was eventually saved by a large team of dedicated physicians, of which I was but a junior helper. But at the very first moment it was all my responsibility, and I could not evade it.

Likewise, parents are often forced by circumstances to make the most weighty decisions about the life and welfare of another. Those expecting their first child are usually very young, very scared, and very inexperienced, even more than I was in that emergency room. But even so, they must make extremely difficult determinations involving the unborn child to whom they may already have an intense emotional attachment. Not only must they decide whether and when to have a child and how to protect the fetus in utero, but sometimes also whether an extremely damaged fetus should be aborted. Severe overpopulation also forces us into difficult choices affecting the lives of born and unborn others. Our positions on birth control and our individual decisions about bearing children, and their number, have a direct effect on the welfare of all. The way we raise our children ob-

viously has a lot to do with their future welfare and health. Are
we doing it right? Will they become strong, stable, and sensitive
adults?

Most people are ill-prepared for such situations, but ready or
not they are cast into roles that leave them no choice but to do
something. We try to be thoughtful or else we avoid the issues,
but either way we determine the outcome. We cannot escape
reality, whether or not we are aware of the consequences of our
actions.

Our responsibility in these areas is so enormous and our decisions so difficult that people are often overwhelmed by confusion, guilt, and fear. Yet we must maintain our capacity to think
clearly and find a way to guard ourselves against the pull of
emotions to minimize our failures and pain. This is particularly
true when the decisions are momentous.

To help themselves out of confusion, many people try to hide
their nakedness behind a mantle of some hallowed values, hoping that these will guide them out of the dark. Strong feelings
can often be found beneath such "values." But once concepts of
"right" and "wrong," and perhaps even "God," have been en-
listed into service, thoughtful consideration of what is involved
becomes almost impossible. We stick to our positions vehemently to avoid being overwhelmed by confusion again. Yet our
own integrity and the avoidable suffering of many other people
dictate that we try again. With effort we can set our confusions
and feelings aside and maintain our continuing ability to think
clearly. This is the only way to do things better. The confusion
that results from mixing thinking with feelings can be lessened
by pausing briefly from time to time, especially when we are
heatedly engaged and sure that the other's position is wrong.
Although difficult at first, people can eventually learn to do this.

We cherish some positions and refuse to question their validity because they bring us a sense of safety and coherence to our
view of the world. Understanding the universe confirms our sanity. Even so, we serve ourselves better if all our "convictions"
remain open for consideration. Reality is not a function of our
comfort. If finally we are to succeed in avoiding even a few of
the many tragedies that we humans reproduce so regularly, then
we really have no choice but to continue examining everything
that we stand for, or against. People can often resolve even their
most persistent disagreements if they remain thoughtful. This, I
hope, will be possible here as we consider several emotionally
charged issues that affect us all.

2. How Far Must We Go in Saving the Lives of the Seriously
   Handicapped?

Our *automatic* wish to defend and to protect all helpless newborns strongly suggests that we overidentify with them. In an
emotional sense we are fighting for our own survival, always the
most just of all causes. But we can be less hesitant, less embarrassed, and much more self-righteous if we take extreme positions on behalf of others rather than ourselves. Fighting for any
cause pushes our sense of powerlessness aside; when the cause
is also just, we can even overlook the fact that it is an attempt
to lessen our own fear. Even though no decent person would ever
knowingly impose suffering on others to make him- or herself
feel better, with the new regulations we are doing just that, albeit
unknowingly. We comfort ourselves at the expense of vulnerable
and defenseless little creatures. Consider the following true
case.

After a five-month pregnancy a premature baby was born
weighing 450 grams (approximately one pound). It had a brain
hemorrhage which caused a hydrocephalus to develop, requiring
neurosurgical placement of a permanent shunt to drain fluid
from the head to the abdomen. If the shunt had been withheld,
the baby would have died. She was so small and weak that she
also needed an intravenous feeding catheter that could only be
placed surgically. She was too debilitated to drink normally. The
emaciated tiny creature soon developed a bowel obstruction.
This was initially treated successfully, but it progressed to gangrene of the entire intestine, beyond surgical cure. Like a newly
placed little plant, she simply withered.

But the patient languished in the newborn intensive care unit
on a respirator for over five months. Her agonies are not recorded
in any chart, and the many efforts required of doctors and nurses
to keep her alive, day in and day out, morning, evening, and
night, month after month, must also be left to the reader's imagination. But the size of the hosptial bill is known: It was for
$151,000, not including any fees for medical or surgical services.

Here is another true case. This premature baby was the unwanted eighth child of an indigent alcoholic mother. The child
had fetal alcoholic syndrome, which causes a peculiar appearance, retards physical growth, and results in moderate to severe
mental retardation. He also had a systemic infection and jaun-
dice. Very extensive gangrene of his intestine was discovered
soon thereafter, requiring removal of the bowel and leaving so

little intestine that the baby would at best be a gastrointestinal cripple for life.

Yet heroic efforts to save his life continued. He was surgically given an intravenous feeding catheter and a respirator. His veins eventually clotted in the upper chest, sending blood clots to the lungs. So the feeding catheter, the apparent cause, had to be removed. Fluid then repeatedly collected in both lungs and eventually perforated them several times, requiring the placement of eight different chest tubes over a period of several weeks. He also required six other fluid drainage procedures. At no time did the mother keep any of her appointments with either doctor or the social worker. Nor did she or any other relative ever call or visit.

Life soon became even more precarious. No doctor and no technician could replace the feeding catheter, because the baby had so many clotted veins. But he could not be fed orally either, since so much of his intestine was gone. The child became infected with abscesses at every little skin abrasion because of his poor condition. At five months of age, after multiple cardiac arrests from which he was always resuscitated, he died of malnutrition, congestive heart failure, and infection.

The end could have been hastened many times, simply by not treating or by not resuscitating—but this would go counter to the moral obligation to save every life. It was now also illegal. And beyond the ethical and legal responsibility of physicians to prolong life, the doctors and nurses treating this young organism had also become emotionally involved with it. They could no longer let it die.

The hospital bill alone was $134,000. The emotional cost has no price tag. Since the mother who never came to visit also had no resources, the public—everyone who pays taxes or health insurance premiums—paid, as it always does in similar cases.

3. One More Personal Note to the Reader

The cost in money is only the smallest and the least important part of the picture. Chapter 2 has graphic descriptions that begin to convey the enormity of the fears that even healthy full-term normal infants experience in the first few minutes, hours, days, and weeks of life. Section 12 in that chapter on "Life from the Infant's Perspective" deserves to be reread here. The experiences of the two premature babies who died are obviously much more horrible.

I assume that you, like me, found the details of the struggles of the two little newborns very disturbing. Yet I know of no other way to illustrate the gravity of the issues that we are considering here. Public policies involve real lives of real human beings, not disembodied ethical problems. We can do no less than put our comfort aside for a few minutes to see the issues realistically. The goal of public regulations is to advance the common good and to minimize suffering. At least in design they are not meant to make us, the public, less guilty.

You too, like most sensitive people, may have been in favor of the new regulation, and you may still be. But seeing the agony in detail forces us to look again. Now we are legally required to extend such needless suffering for as long as possible. This is happening right now in major hospitals all over the U.S. Do we have the moral right to impose suffering on others, even in the name of whatever high-sounding principle we believe in? This in effect is what we are doing.

Even physicians and nurses have to agonize with such tragic choices; non-professionals are less well prepared. Such cases illustrate the urgent need to think rather than to be led by feelings, at least when life-and-death issues are involved. More so now than ever, our future as a species and as free men and women may well depend on the ability of individuals to make hard and painful choices, following a rational course in spite of human inclinations and feelings.

The pursuit of reason is at least as difficult as the pursuit of happiness, and much more likely to bear fruit.

4. The Tragic Results of Overidentification

Medical progress may soon permit us to save the lives of damaged little creatures such as these two. But how deep and how wide would their emotional scars be? Surely not any less crippling than the gross anatomical alterations that have been described. No one has ever survived for long without an intenstine, but maybe someone soon will, perhaps by being permanently attached to some new machine. What kind of life will this be? A human being who will never be able to eat, drink, or engage in most other activities, just as some people in a coma can never breathe without a machine. Without any concern for his human rights we will have forced that person to exist like that until he dies. The two immature newborns might not have given us their consent to be treated the way they were had they had the ability to understand. Other people are often forced to pay an enormous price in suffering for our good but self-serving intentions. We seem interested only in prolonging lives, not in their quality.

Many other examples can be cited of the horrors created by decisions based on feelings without thinking. Bleeding-heart psychiatrists, legislators, and civil rights defenders with diffuse personal boundaries overidentified with the pain and suffering of the chronically ill in mental hospitals in the 1960s. The Community Mental Health movement, born with great fanfare, soon declared that since patients did not get much therapy in those hospitals they should not be institutionalized at all. It cost billions of dollars but they were returned to live in their communities, where nobody wanted them. The reformers felt better.

The tragic results are seen everywhere: abandoned castoffs huddling in doorways, wandering pathetically and aimlessly, dirty, hungry, cold, and sometimes drunk. Hundreds of thousands of scared and sad creatures with empty eyes and with nowhere to go pay the price for this brutal hoax. In the name of patients' rights, they all bear the crushing burden of the "freedom" that the do-gooders have imposed upon them.

Severely handicapped newborns like those described are even worse off. Existing in total isolation, they are subjected to the most extreme intrusions upon their physical being, knowing absolutely nothing but experiencing everything. Unlike the mentally ill, they cannot comfort themselves even with a crumpled old cigarette butt or with a colorful piece of garbage. They must remain connected to machines and to tubes at all times. If such babies survived they would generally grow up to be barely reachable, uncommunicating autistic emotional monsters, as much a burden on themselves as they would be on their families and society. All they would know is pain, loneliness, darkness, and almost complete isolation.

The same is generally true of very young infants who undergo organ transplantation. Jamie Fiske was pathetic-looking but alive when she was finally discharged from the hospital with a transplanted liver. Television reporters and radio announcers fell all over themselves with excitement in describing this miracle that medicine had wrought. The baby that would have died before Thanksgiving was heading home to Massachusetts in time for Christmas. It was the main feature on evening television news programs for several nights running because we are all eager to hear of miracles. They assuage the fear of non-being for a little while. But it was a blessing mixed with much sadness. Even if she makes it physically, what price will she pay emotionally? She could surely use a second miracle to help her live a full life.

A surgeon near Chicago, driven by scientific zeal and human compassion, and perhaps also by overidentification, has perfected procedures that allow him to save infants previously destined to die, born with spina bifida. Some eight hundred of them have now reached their teens, all having repeatedly required surgical procedures to correct their deformed limbs and internal organs. Many have undergone major surgery every six months since they were born. Their whole existence, and that of their entire families, is centered around the struggle for survival. We rejoice so much *that* they live that we completely ignore the question of *how* they live. We also forget to wonder about the emotional cost to siblings and to parents. How much life have they lost? How many future tragedies are we creating in repairing past ones?

Asking such questions is impossible for the people who are directly involved with those who have been saved. Each has a name, a face, personal characteristics, a life history, and hopes. Those who know them as real people are emotionally attached to them, and they cannot and should not treat them as unborn statistics. We recoil from the thought that everyone might have been better off if they had not been saved. We are so disgusted by such an idea that even our freedom to wonder about this possibility is painfully limited. Yet we have no choice but to wonder anyway. Physicians are supposed to prolong life and to minimize suffering. What should they—and we—do when the two oppose each other?

Our ability to live just below the angels is tested in horrible and painful contexts such as this. We humans are capable of rationality, but can we reach for it even when our feelings are so strong? Are we "heartless" if we do? We are all susceptible to the pull of emotions; it becomes almost impossible to resist this pull when even the most respectable newspapers appeal to them. This explains why we are where are are.

Yet how dare anyone set himself up to question the value of someone else's life? Still, how dare we avoid it? Once we start to interfere with God's ways of determining "who shall live and who shall die," the questions are ours whether we like it or not. The laws of Man are different from the laws of nature. They include compassion. This is what gives us the right to question whether some children should be born. Many newborns would naturally die without our compassionate interventions, since no one would help them survive.

Both "life" and "death" are no longer as easily definable as they once were. Our obligations and responsibilities in such matters were clear and unambiguous for most of our history on earth. But then we changed the rules. We started to interfere with the laws of nature, prolonging lives that it meant to destroy. Not only do we do this routinely now, but a government regulation requires us to do no less. We only wanted to insure that helpless newborns would not be abused, but in doing so we have unlocked a monster that now tortures us daily. We have been catapulted into God's position and place, even though we remained limited by our human capacities and understanding.

What believers think about the qualities of their God determines how much or how little freedom they have to make human choices on earth. Expanding this freedom to evaluate issues objectively is our only concern here, not speculating about God's will. People who live together must make rational decisions about their existence, or perish together. For the believers this is God's commandment, yet the same is also dictated to non-believers by humane considerations and by self-interest.

5. Natural Selection vs. Human Selection

People who have special difficulties with trust get frightened by the possibility that someone could make life-and-death decisions about others. When such fear is excessive, it is a good indication that the boundaries of the self are not whole. "Open . . . boundaries of states or of people are perceived as dangerous to the existence and the integrity of those involved. Invasions from the outside are believed to be an ever-present possibility, and so are takeovers and annexations by more powerful neighbors." Such people panic at the thought that physicians would be allowed to terminate hopeless lives, even though physicians are the ones who made the prolongation of life possible in the first place. When someone's objections to the death penalty are especially persistent, they may well reflect a personal concern for oneself more than pure moral outrage. In a sense such people are engaged in defending their own right to life. Overidentifiers actually feel the panic of those suddenly about to die. Such panic is highly contagious, and this is why fear is such a powerful factor in determining public policy. "Unrecognized overidentification with others poses extreme dangers to democratic societies in the age of mass communication."

The U.S. government was mobilized to the rescue of little helpless creatures in hospitals not because they were in actual danger of being abused but because some people overidentified with them. Bureaucrats are not immune to overidentification. "Protective" policies that were not needed became the law of the land, thus suspending the ethical judgments of competent professionals in favor of rigid regulations. Scared and suspicious people often prevail when they succeed in spreading their fear. Extreme and unreasonable caution can paralyze both reason and action. Harm to all is often the result.

Medical science has now provided us with the means to modify the harsh and unforgiving reality of natural selection. Using more compassionate standards, we are now able to substitute human selection for it, but some selection is unavoidable. A line will be drawn somewhere, by us or by nature. We may soon be able to save all its freaks, creating horrible suffering in the process, weakening our genetic reserve, and depleting our resources to boot. Societies that do so, even in the name of humane considerations, may well hasten their demise and the disappearance of their worthy values. We do not have all the answers yet, but we cannot safely avoid asking the questions, even though doing so turns our stomachs.

Copernicus understood that the little planet on which we live was of no great account in the general scheme of nature. We are not the center of the universe. This enabled him to unravel the hidden scheme, thus helping Man to live more securely in the real world. But the basic distortion that skewed all the astronomical observations of the day had to be given up first. Although everyone could see that the sun and the stars were shining on *them*, this was not factually accurate. The local point of view had to be surrendered.

The same here. We really cannot impose human ethics on nature, no matter how hard we try. Natural selection is a very cruel way of deciding who shall live and who shall die, but it is nature's way. Its laws are totally unaffected by our wishes or by human emotions. We can alter it a little, but like it or not we must bow before it. We really cannot substitute our judgment and preferences for God's without destroying ourselves. This was the basic lesson that the biblical builders of the tower of Babel refused to accept. Apparently we must learn it all over again.

6. The Urgent Need for a Dictatorship of Reason

Western civilization is not likely to survive for long unless the majority of the population in democratic societies becomes aware soon of the corrupting influence of feelings on the political process. In the current political climate it is practically impossible to pass any laws or to initiate any policies that go counter to the emotions of most people, even if they are clearly in their best interest. We often lack consistency in foreign and in domestic affairs because feelings swing rapidly. "Totalitarian regimes have a built-in advantage by suppressing mass expression of preverbal hunger and rage and by treating public behavior based on fear as treason." There is no free press or commercial television to fan irrational fears in a dictatorship. Personal preferences based on feelings can be safely ignored; neither ideas nor products compete in the marketplace. Totalitarian functionaries survive by demonstrating their loyalty to the political apparatus, not by catering to the wishes of the people. In the absences of free elections, they are safe.

The "dictatorship of the proletariat" insulates totalitarian regimes on the left from the crippling influence of mass feelings; autocratic military dictatorships protect those on the right. Only democracies remain wide open and unprotected. To survive they need a "dictatorship" too—of reason. Without it we often vacillate under pressure, and one day we will collapse and be devoured. The idea of such a "dictatorship" must at first sound preposterous to people accustomed to living largely according to their feelings, almost everyone. People who are at liberty to do so normally try to maximize their comfort and pleasure, even when these interfere with the pursuit of more pressing and more important needs and interests. Affluence, peace, and political freedom make room for this tendency; the advent of television has intensified it. Television has the power to evoke strong feelings in millions of viewers simultaneously and instantaneously. The graphic display in dramatic detail of close and distant horrors tugs on our most primitive fears and sympathies. Popular demands for action based on such feelings often follow, and policies that satisfy such wishes are often instituted.

Yet if a "dictatorship" of reason could somehow really come into being, it would surely be experienced by many as oppressive and unjust and also as undemocratic; it would prevent people from living thoughtlessly in self-preoccupied and self-coupled ways. But there is no other viable basis for a civilized existence according to democratic principles. Feelings would still be experienced and openly expressed in such a sane society, but all action would be expected to result from careful consideration of all the alternatives. Spontaneity would be welcomed but not impulsivity.

In such a society reason would dictate that in general severely handicapped newborns be left to die naturally. It makes sense even now for us. Such an emotionless approach cannot be shared by deeply involved and grieving parents, but it can be advanced by coolly objective and rational physicians acting as the agents of nature in spite of our arrogant wish to override it. Wishful "thinking" only prolongs everyone's agony. Birth defects and other "natural disasters" are not disastrous at all from nature's point of view. They are not necessarily the result of neglect and surely not of corruption, but even so they often evoke righteous indignation rather than sadness. This is how overindulged people typically react to their tragedies. The Health and Human Services regulation about handicapped newborns sprouted from this kind of soil.

Emotionally charged issues such as the prevention of child abuse need no lobbyists; masses jump on the bandwagon in support. But building up hope with false promises and enticing voters with regulations that make no sense are dangerous. "Powerful storms of hurt and rage are unleashed when personal or political promises remain repeatedly unfulfilled." Emotions that are repeatedly stirred up give rise to expectations that are not easily relinquished. Democracies "are therefore always exposed to the possibility of breaking up from within."

We cannot survive for long as free men and women except on the basis of rationality. The course dictated by reality cannot be changed just because traversing it is emotionally difficult. Constitutional and legal changes to counter the temptation "to follow the path of least resistance" will eventually have to be enacted by democratic societies that wish to remain both free and viable. The suggestion later in this chapter to license childbearing is but one example.

7. The Consequences to Humanity of Overpopulation

President Reagan was obviously appealing to the *emotions* of his listeners when at a convention of religious broadcasters he attacked abortions and spoke of the "50 million children who will never laugh, never sing, never know the joy of human love." Most people respond with compassion to such words, especially when spoken by a likable man who is also sincere.

But, "politicians . . . are human too, and . . . they often tend, therefore to overidentify . . . Help is frequently offered [as a result] at the wrong time to the wrong people, in the wrong form and in the wrong amount." President Reagan is known to strongly uphold the values of self-sufficiency and self-reliance. He is generally opposed to more than minimal governmental intervention, even in defense of disadvantaged industries or people, believing that it condemns them to never finding power within themselves. So his great eagerness to protect the unborn fetus appears out of character, although nothing ever is.

As a rule, what fits poorly in the present often reflects fixed attitudes from the past, and what is not consistent with thinking usually fits with our feelings. People often take uncompromising stands for or against birth control or abortion not because of real convictions based on thoughtfulness. Reason is not usually characterized by rigidity; feelings are. When they determine public policy, misery and suffering are often multiplied.

Pediatricians, teachers, and counselors in low-income neighborhoods in the U.S. report that the situation there is infinitely worse than most people know. Several hundred thousand babies are born every year to unmarried teenage girls who keep their infants in circumstances that are grossly unfit. They are usually unwilling to let anyone adopt these newborns, although they are totally incapable of raising them, because the babies allow such disturbed girls to leave their own disturbed homes. The mothers are paid by society to care for them. The children are normally subjected to chronic neglect, abuse, and impulsivity. Drugs and crime, prostitution, venereal disease, and AIDS all find a fertile ground among such lost mothers. If their babies live, they soon grow up to give birth to another generation very much like themselves.

Even if it were true that a twelve-week-old fetus can experience some primitive pre-pain, this would hardly be reason enough to oppose abortion under all circumstances. The very wish to minimize pain would often dictate that a fetal cluster of cells not be allowed to develop. The agony of poorly cared for children is infinitely greater and lasts much longer than any possible momentary discomfort of any fetus. A lifelong existence

in perpetual pain, fear, and rage at the margin of society is obviously much worse. As voters, each of us will ultimately determine whether or not some fetuses will be condemned to live,
perhaps as children who are grossly deformed physically or as
cripples who are hopelessly deprived and retarded emotionally.
Although we must continue to value life as sacred and inviolate,
a pro-life stance is not necessarily always morally superior.

The situation is infinitely more horrible in poorer countries.
The world population is exploding: from three billion in 1960, to
4.75 billion in 1984, with projections of as many as 8.3 billion in
the year 2025. Eighty-five percent of these 8.3 billion people will
exist somehow in undercapitalized, underdeveloped, and under-
nourished Third World countries where chronic hunger, disease,
cyclones, wars, riots, and other natural and man-made disasters
are rampant even now. Millions of emaciated children in Ethiopia, Bangladesh, India, and many other countries "never laugh
and never sing" even now. They also never eat enough. They
usually have no sanitary facilities, no clean water, hardly any
medical care, and practically no education. They just try to survive, but from time to time gale winds rip off the tin roofs over
their heads, or the sea just washes them and their families away,
as if they were ants.

The fertility rate in Bangladesh is 6.3 per woman. By the year
2025, 266 million people are likely to be squeezed into an area
the size of Wisconsin. A typhoon in 1970 simply washed one
million people into the sea. A cyclone in 1985 was more merci-
ful; only 10,000 people were lost.

We in the developed and rich countries usually send them
a few planeloads of food and medical supplies, we give well-
publicized concerts to "mobilize help," we make phonograph
records to raise a little money for them, and we feel more righteous and a little less guilty as a result. This obviously never
solves any problem. Our well-intentioned help is never more
than first aid. What happens afterward when the media are no
longer interested? We sleep better and remain undisturbed then,
until a new disaster is brought to our attention. But out there
where real people actually die of hunger, disease, and exposure,
the situation is getting worse.

The consequences of our failure to act rationally in bringing
world population under control are truly appalling. The cost of
existing according to the dictates of feelings is almost incompre-
hensibly enormous. Chronic joblessness, environmental devas-

tation, political instability, economic erosion, and endless apathy, helplessness, sickness, and despair are all permanent features of *most* living humans. Hundreds of millions will never live differently.

The average number of children born to a woman in Kenya is now eight. With a declining infant mortality rate, the country's population is likely to swell from 20 to 85 million by the year 2025. Food, medical facilities, and schools are already in short supply, and neither human nor financial resources exist anywhere to close the widening gap.

In greater Mexico City, the largest city in the world, over 18 million people crowd into facilities built for three million. More than two million people have no running water in their homes, more than three million residents have no sewage facilities. "If fecal matter were fluorescent," said one Mexican newspaper, "the city wouldn't need lights." Tourists only see the other sights. Millions of cars, buses, and factories spew so much contamination into the air that just breathing it is the equivalent of smoking two packs of cigarettes a day. *Time* reports that a caged bird placed in a central downtown square usually dies within two hours. A mixture of overcrowding, poverty, pollution, and corruption is about to literally choke its inhabitants to death. Over 100,000 people a year are estimated to die as a result of air pollution. Yet Mexico City continues to grow.

Cairo was built for one to two million people, but 13 million crowd into its dusty streets and hovels. "The population density in some areas runs as high as 300,000 per square mile (more than four times the density of Manhattan)," reports *Time*, and they do not live in skyscrapers. Close to one million people now live permanently in the City of the Dead, a huge cemetery that has become home for three generations of Egyptians. Four million residents live in dwellings not connected to any sewage system; human waste regularly overflows the existing sewers and the stench fills the streets. Toxic fumes cover the ever-present traffic jams. Overloaded ancient buses compete with swarms of old cars, animal carts, beggars, baksheesh seekers, and blind peddlers. The meat for sale hangs in open air markets and is often covered with hundreds of flies.

The fertility rate in India is 4.7 per woman, and by the year 2045 its population will exceed that of China. One and a half billion people will be clamoring in squalor for food, water, and sometimes merely for breathable air. The story is the same everywhere: Medical facilities and supplies are already grossly inadequate. The situation is bound to get much worse. It will never get better.

There is only one water faucet for each twenty-five slum dwellings in Calcutta. The last main sewer was built in 1896, and about half of the city's houses have no indoor toilets. The city's only garbage incinerator has broken down daily for the last forty years, and tons of trash litter the streets at all times. Six hundred thousand of Calcutta's poor live permanently in these streets, and they die there. The population is expected to more than double in the next forty years. Improvements in food production and housing are always outpaced by even faster increases in the population.

Things are a little better in Shanghai, but not much. Many families must share a single room that is too small to hold enough beds for all of them. They sleep in shifts. China is more successful than most other countries in checking the exploding birthrate because more regimentation is possible in this totalitarian state. But with a population of over one billion, China's problems are immense.

Yet many people still fail to see the obvious connection between such a harsh existence and the prohibitions against abortion and birth control. Pro-life and pro-abortion activists share the same basic ethical principles of civilization. Why do they oppose each other with so much heat and venom? Because they *feel* differently. Most are emotionally overloaded and therefore vehement and irrational. The pro-life people overidentify with the fetus, which supposedly pleads, "Don't kill me." The pro-abortion group overidentifies with the babies already born who supposedly beg, "Give me space," fearing the possibility of being pushed off the face of the earth.

Everyone agrees that in general life is sacred and that it should be cherished, but as long as people are led by feelings they cannot define "life" in a sensible and coherent way. This is why the two camps cannot agree on a course that would minimize suffering the most. Good people populate both camps, yet in following their hearts they fail to defuse this time bomb that threatens to destroy us all. It is at least as dangerous and probably more immediate than the threat of a nuclear holocaust.

The two grossly handicapped newborns described at the beginning of this chapter were surely no less alive than any unborn fetus. Did we do right by them? Without birth control and at least occasional abortions many others would be similarly destined to exist in constant fear and pain. People would reject such a cruel solution in moments of clarity. We mean well, whether propelled by religious commandments or by humane considerations. The confusion results from our desperate wish to escape the panic that is evoked in us by overidentification. "The push away from fear or dread supersedes everything." Nobody wants to perpetuate misery, but "fear is often responsible for major errors in judgment since it greatly interferes with the capacity to evaluate what one sees."

Malthus wrote in 1789 that "population, when unchecked, increases in a geometrical ratio. Subsistence increases only in an arithmetical ratio." He was wrong. He did not know of the Green Revolution. He could not have foreseen the development of modern agriculture, highly mechanized, attending to crop rotation, creating new hybrid grains, using regular fertilization and highly economic methods of irrigation. He did not know that new crops would feed many more mouths than anyone ever imagined possible. But he was right in principle.

Civilizations in which Man had the opportunity to develop his human potential with dignity only developed when both the weather and the size of the population were free of extremes. This is how nature willed it. We humans can bend its rules a little and we can expand its constrictions a lot, but basically we really cannot change nature. Thomas Henry Huxley may have been prejudiced but he was not altogether wrong: "It is futile to expect a hungry and squalid population to be anything but violent and gross."

We humans have committed ourselves to be our brothers' keepers. We organize airlifts to feed the hungry, send relief missions to aid victims of disasters, help underdeveloped countries industrialize and mechanize their agriculture, distribute food stamps, Medicaid and Medicare payments, and aid to poor families with dependent children. We support good education, nutrition, housing, and hospitals. We have rejected the mores of the jungle and do not allow the young and the weak simply to die. Once it is born, we have some obligation to help the ex-fetus survive. So we have a responsibility to think first and to decide carefully what we are able to do, and what not.

To let emotions lead us is irresponsible and destructive to ourselves and to others. Now that societies assume an increasing responsibility for the financial, emotional, social, legal, and educational welfare of all their citizens, it makes good sense that they protect themselves against an excessive drain on their resources.

"Be fruitful and multiply and fill the Earth" was God's commandment to Man long ago; and we have fulfilled it faithfully ever since, much more so than we have attended to many of the other commandments. By now the earth is already more than full. God's will is done. Clearly, to the extent that God is more than nature, He must be life-affirming, as we must also be. We cannot therefore condone overpopulation, which diminishes life, causes death, and may even endanger the very survival of our species.

A PERSONAL NOTE OF SELF-DISCLOSURE

As a child, my God had a long beard and stern eyes, and He sat there on His huge throne watching everything and seeing that nothing went wrong. His features and qualities have changed over the years. His eyes have softened, and He has become more compassionate. And like the man that he has fashioned, He too appears to be very sad. His world is so imperfect, and His man so ungodly.

With the years I have slowly learned that men who see God do so differently. Some see Him as suffering, unconditionally forgiving those who believe in Him, and always loving, like a perfectly accepting mother. Others fear Him even now as bloodthirsty, wielding an angry crescent sword with which to slay all infidels. Was God really so jealous, vengeful, and fearsome as Moses described him to the Hebrew slaves, or was He just painted this way because primitive people are often best civilized by fear?

My God always was the unbendable standard of justice, His love only conditional. I had to measure up. Nevertheless He always watched over me from a great distance, as a benign and wise old father would. But their God and mine, I was told, were one and the same. For many years it was a very confusing picture, and I continued to wonder. In any event, I knew that only good deeds would redeem me.

I finally began to realize that the one God was all these things, and perhaps none of them. I was real, and if I believed in His existence then He existed, at least in me. Since I was the creator of my God's features, they always fit *me* exactly, and they were always just right for my understanding of His nature. The one unknowable God must have as many different features as there are different people. Even the Pope and anyone else who speaks in God's name could only know their own personal God, not mine.

8. The Golem of Prague

Man alone was given the opportunity to choose between good and bad, between a blessing and a curse, and between life and death. Those who might have thought that God was merely a disinterested observer in such a choice were told specifically "and thou shalt choose life." But, as every gardener knows, a row of seeded plants must often be thinned. Weeding maximizes the chances of the remaining ones to thrive. The same with Man.

The Maharal of Prague, Rabbi Judah Löw, is said to have been a very holy man, shepherding his little Jewish congregation in God's ways during the Middle Ages. His virtue was so great, we are told, that he was given the power once to breathe life into a clay model of a huge man that he had shaped with his hands. This Golem would defend the Jews against their enemies and against the vandals that were in the habit of attacking them from time to time.

In the meantime, the Golem lived in the rabbi's courtyard and performed various chores around the house. Once on a Sabbath afternoon, just as the holy Maharal was about to take his afternoon nap, he commanded the Golem to go and fetch him some water. Then he promptly fell asleep. Half the city was submerged when he awoke. Being brainless, the Golem continued to perform as he was commanded. Having no judgment, he was unable to evaluate the meaning of what he was told, or the consequences of what he was doing.

To interpret God's commandments to fill the earth and to choose life in the literal and narrow-minded way of the Golem is to completely abdicate our unique human abilities to evaluate and to judge. We become thoughtless and blind servants of the master then. Surely this is not the way God meant Man to be.

9. Should Childbearing Be Licensed?

At a time when cohabitation by young unmarried adults is common, getting a marriage license is a meaningless act, consisting merely of taking a blood test and paying a small fee. The original intent of licensing marriages was to minimize gross health hazards in the next generation. It made sense when first introduced, but it is hardly sufficient now. Yet the concept is still basically correct. One of the most important responsibilities of any society is to insure that its future is not threatened by major health or other problems.

Society's concern for its overall welfare always limited the freedom of individuals to act as they wished. For reasons of national defense young men were often obligated to give up a few years for service in the army, and some were even called upon to lay down their lives. Extreme sacrifices are sometimes needed for the common good. Limiting the right to have children is based on the same rationale. Many young parents are totally unprepared emotionally, intellectually, financially, and socially for the difficult tasks of parenting. Even with the best of intentions they severely damage their young. But worse yet, there is often a complete absence of good intentions. Being children themselves, such parents are usually very angry that any demands are being made upon them, even by their own offspring. Emotional and sometimes physical abuse commonly follow, along with more children. Society must often step in to protect its next generation. Yet no one has the right to repeatedly place the fruit of their womb on our collective doorstep. The time may be ripe even in the West for licensing childbearing.

"The raising of children by adults who are still emotionally in childhood is responsible for societies with childish mores. . . . The self-indulgence that typifies much public and private behavior in such societies could not have been so prominent before the age of waste and affluence, when self-restraint and individual responsibility were needed for survival." People who conduct their affairs minute by minute and who live haphazardly are always in trouble; societies that do not plan ahead well are also headed in the same direction.

But modern man lives on credit, having abandoned the old-fashioned view that one buys only what one can afford. Many people and societies are deficit-financed. We commit ourselves to desirable programs and worry only later how to pay for them. People often live nowadays as if they fully expected all their wishes to be satisfied. Deep disappointment, apathy, bitterness, and widespread rudeness are the inevitable result. Was "the good life" not repeatedly promised to them? We have more but enjoy it much less. Many people can see only what they are missing. It is a very hard and thankless job to "rule" in modern free societies. The electorate, like an unhappy child, is almost always dissatisfied and complaining about something.

Having children that one is ill-prepared to care for and to raise properly is part of the "living on credit" mind-set. The burden falls on the rest of society. The cost of Aid to Families with Dependent Children is a tolerable burden, even if some people complain about it. But the presence of a large population of emotionally immature, bitter, disturbed, impulse-ridden, and marginal people affects the security of everyone's home and the quality of our schools, the physical safety of our children in their classrooms and our own safety everywhere, the levels of suspicion and trust, the quality of public transportation, how we are served in restaurants and elsewhere, how well and how speedily our cars and homes are repaired, how helpful people are, how much graffiti mars our subways, how littered our streets, how rude our manners, the productivity of labor, the standards of justice—in short, the quality of everyone's life.

The environment we live in can be improved only if a larger segment of our population is emotionally healthier. This cannot be achieved without somehow reducing the number of children born to grossly immature or emotionally disturbed mothers and fathers, and without insisting that all parents attend to their parental tasks more competently. "The young usually receive insufficient as well as incorrect guidance or help in the difficult task of maturation." "Only the chronologic age matters before the law, in the marketplace, and in the electoral booth. Ignoring the emotional age of individuals . . . explains most of the gross distortions in all societies."

Improving the quality of parenting is not a goal that can be achieved easily, and it may never be reached at all unless we alter some of our basic attitudes about human rights and individual responsibilities. Do societies, like individuals, also have the right to protect themselves from being abused and possibly destroyed by an onslaught of irresponsibility? This, at the bottom, was the rationale and the justification used by free democratic societies for requiring a license to marry.

Yet many people are likely to react instantly and strongly against the suggestion that all young women be required to obtain a license to make children. Even policies that make good sense often prove to be impossible politically, at least for a while. The specter of Big Brother abrogating one of our basic and natural rights is quickly evoked. Fear, showing itself as anger, may immediately surface. Who would decide on the prospective mother's qualifications? Who will play God? Do we know what to test for and how to do it properly? How can we insure that such a regulation would be fairly enforced? There are no ready or easy answers. The carrot or the stick may be used to induce prospective mothers not to have children before they are ready. How do we insure that those holding the stick would not abuse it? And so on, and on and on.

The fear stimulated by such a proposition is that of engulfment. Some powerful authority will surely do us in. The Bill of Rights in the U.S. and similar documents in other countries have all been adopted because of bad experiences with and deep suspicion of autocratic authority. It has abused citizens throughout history. Man wanted to make sure that this would never happen again. By now most people side automatically with the rights of individuals whenever they compete with those of society at large, ignoring the overall picture.

But the idea of licensing the right to have children must nevertheless be considered seriously on its merits. Unpleasant as this task is, it fell to us by our interference with the laws of nature. By determining to support every child born in our society and also to maintain high levels of medical care we already decided, in effect, who shall live and who shall die. Who shall be born and who shall not is merely an extension of this principle. It lessens our need to play God later. If we wish to minimize abortions, then we must practice stricter birth control. Only the severely deformed will have to be aborted then.

Like capital punishment, abortions are best minimized, because performing them may eventually condition us to regard life itself as expendable. But one way or another we must limit the size of our population and keep it down. Limiting the right to have children may be the most humane and the least dangerous way to control births. The moral and ethical dilemmas involved are not ours by choice. Religious people who welcome medical advances that save and extend life cannot reasonably oppose decisions that limit it. The Pope who allows a heart to be transplanted into his chest is a party to a system in which someone must decide when not to transplant a heart into another chest. The available resources and space on earth were determined by nature or by God, not by us.

Ours is the first generation that is haunted by these painful issues, and we have no precedents to learn from. It should not be surprising therefore that so many inconsistencies beset us and that they are not always immediately resolvable.

The potbellied and wide-eyed children of Ethiopia whose heads always appear too large because their bodies are too small look at us longingly from our television screens and they leave an indelible mark on our conscience. It is hard to forget their quietly sad and deep eyes and their non-complaining faces. We discharge some of our guilt by helping them a little, but still *we* are deeply damaged in the process: Our joy is contaminated each time we partake of our overflowing plenty, or else we have to sacrifice some of our capacity for empathy and for compassion. How else can we block their real misery out of our consciousness? We can live with less shame in the same world together with them only if we consistently oppose unchecked population growth. Not only those who are starving and dying are affected by overpopulation. We all are.

No easy escape routes exist, especially if we are honest enough to admit that we enjoy our relative affluence and our high standards of living and that we wish to keep them. If the poor in Calcutta or in Cairo are truly our brothers, then we must do much more than piously sympathize with their plight, and even more than send an occasional check to the Red Cross. We must open our homes to them and welcome them in. This we are not generally ready to do. On the other hand, we sacrifice some of our humanness if we disown them as human brothers. We cannot avoid this horrible dilemma. But our burden is heavier yet if we stand in the way of possible solutions. Rationality dictates that we support measures to reduce births, especially by emotionally irresponsible mothers. Harlem and the Hamptons, Kenya and Grosse Pointe, are all included. All those whom we welcome into the world must be cared for properly. Not only must they receive sufficient protein not to contract kwashiorkor, but they must also grow up in sufficiently healthy homes so that they do not drift into prostitution, drug addiction, and crime.

Mentally retarded people have often been prevented from reproducing, and it would not be so out of the ordinary to eventually place limits upon us all. The burden that unfortunate emotional cripples impose upon their societies lasts for many years, just like their pain. They usually live longer than physically deformed children. Even though "affluence and relative security enable individuals and societies to exist in the feeling mode for a while and therefore unrealistically, [it] is a luxury of questionable merit, since it encourages delusional living." The tender-hearted sometimes claim that our society is rich enough to take care of everyone, and that it is our humane duty to do so, without realizing how cruel are the consequences of their well-intentioned self-indulgence.

The moral strength, the common will, the economic vitality, and the courage to make difficult political decisions are all weakened when a large segment of a population consists of crippled people. Physical and emotional health is an urgent need of nations, not only of individuals. When we finally recognize "actions based on emotions" as an extreme danger, we will have a unique chance to save our institutions, our values, and our way of life. Other civilizations without this understanding simply vanished.

A policy of licensing the birth of children is already in effect in some countries. The stick is used in China, where it is not permissible to have more than one child per family. Offenders are often punished. The carrot is used in Singapore, where women unfit for mothering are given free houses in exchange for sterilization. The U.S. and most of Western Europe are too affluent to face such difficult choices at this time. But a political impossibility today may well become an urgent necessity tomorrow, when the consequences of living according to feelings begin to damage us more severely.

10. A Brief Guide to Good Parenting

In general, parents raise the best children that they are capable of raising. The well-being of the child is largely determined by the emotional maturity of the mothering figure, a role that is usually, but not always, filled by the biologic mother. Even a father can fill it. His job of fathering, although crucial later on, is unimportant in the first few months of life, when the essentials of character are established. If Mother is emotionally unstable, scared, too young, too needy, perhaps unmarried, perhaps destitute, not much can be done except to try repairing the damage later on.

But for those who can use it, here is a short list of recommendations to help parents raise healthier children. Following these principles will help the young become emotionally more stable, but only if the parents are able to remain consistent, firm, and loving most of the time. This obviously means that they are themselves reasonably mature and emotionally comfortable. These principles are based on the observations and conclusions about Man's nature found throughout this book. As we shall see in the next chapter, the same principles apply and are used in effective psychotherapy. Raising healthy children and healing emotional illnesses are parallel in many ways.

1. *Attend to the newborn's physical being.* Through her body the mother conveys all that the child can "know" about the universe. It is most impressionable at the earliest moments of life, when the physiologic basis of character is determined. The baby begins to sense that all is well with it and with the world if Mother can be calm, consistent, attentive, sensitive, loving, not overprotective but available within reasonable limits. Indulging and overprotecting newborns or older children is not the same as loving them.

2. *Attend to their feelings.* Children should be allowed to express all their feelings in any intensity that they are capable of, in the presence of and directly at either parent. This includes senseless anger, exaggerated hurt, crying and sobbing, loving and hating, sadness and happiness, and above all fear. The fact that these feelings may not make rational sense should not matter. They are not necessarily supposed to. But room is made for the expression of feelings only if the time and the circumstances are right. Opportunities for expressing feelings must always be made available, however, if not now then later.

3. *Attend to reality.* No matter what feelings the child experiences and expresses, they cannot and should not be the basis of any action. Reality is. It comes before feelings, even when they are most powerful. No compromise is ever allowed on this score. Parents similarly must not act on the basis of their feelings, although they too need not always hide them. The open expression of feelings by a parent in front of the children is only acceptable if the young can tolerate it without getting confused and without experiencing such expressions as demands. Cool judgment must guide decision-making and action at all times. Punishment should not be meted out on any other basis; it is never justified to relieve the exasperation of a parent. There is no insanity defense: The child and the parents are always responsible for all their actions, provided, however, that the demands never exceed the child's real capacity. Partial efforts are not usually acceptable.

4. *Attend to thinking.* Children do not know how to think, and they generally do not want to learn how to. The new human organism is at first all feelings and no thinking. It is easier and more natural to express and to live by feelings. We must be

patient with the children's inability to think but not give in to their unwillingness to be thoughtful. "Learning to really think requires first that we make room for it by diminishing the domain of feelings." The task of forcing the child to think requires patient efforts over a period of many years. Many children never learn to think and as grownups they cannot teach their own children to do so. Others must then try to do it, if it is to be done at all.

Children who are treated along these lines do not necessarily turn out well. Many influences shape a person's life. Even though we try to follow reasonable principles cognitively, our actions and behavior may contradict what we try to do. Principles such as these nevertheless provide a good basis for relationships of mutual respect and concern.

Blood really is thicker than water. Families that are based not only on the accident of birth but also on a set of principles such as these often produce good people and real friendships. Such blessings are so worthy that they deserve any efforts required to achieve them.

SIX

The Treatment of Emotional Disorders

Reality . . . comes before feelings.
CHAPTER 5

A master of himself is stronger than a conquerer of a city.
PROVERBS 16:32

*Individuation is the active process of mourning
for dreams that cannot be.*
CHAPTER 1

1. Objectives and Basic Principles

Approximately 10 percent of the population in any advanced society is in acute distress at any one time because of overt or hidden depression. Not only is it the basic and most important component of all psychiatric syndromes and the commonest of all illnesses, but it also masquerades as most others. As we have seen in Chapter 2, many of the symptoms of depression are disguised and therefore remain generally unrecognized. So millions of people who urgently need treatment go without proper or sufficient help. William Holden, Marilyn Monroe, and many others are obvious examples. Depressed people normally find no more than amelioration of their acute distress.

The system of therapy outlined here has an objective that is easy to describe but not so easy to achieve: to actually cure depression. Even now many experts do not consider this possible, but we finally have most of the knowledge needed to reverse the pathologic process and also adequate techniques to heal people afflicted with it.

This type of psychotherapy is basically different from psychoanalysis and from all other types of psychotherapy in its view of Man and in its methods. (The first is the subject of this book; the second will be detailed in a later work.) Here are the eight basic principles upon which the system stands:

i. *The surgical model.* As described in Chapter 3, what needs to be done is to change the pathways established in the visceral brain. This alters the typical physiologic reaction patterns that cause the depressed person to react automatically in self-damaging or self-destructive ways. Since such brain pathways are merely preferred connections between adjacent nerve cells, no anatomic change occurs in the process. But "surgery" is nonetheless the best analogy for this work. The surgeon cuts into the live body of the patient, following strict clinical procedures, in order to repair or remove pathologic structures that interfere with health or endanger life. Psychotherapists must likewise intrude upon the patient's habitual ways of response to affect the personality. Outer layers must be disturbed in both cases to reach and to alter inner structures. Both procedures involve pain, both disrupt one's normal life-style, both are dangerous to some degree, and both are often lifesaving. Obviously all intrusions in surgery and in psychotherapy must be based on the free and informed consent of the conscious patient. A person should not be involved in either unless it is clearly indicated; but neither should be avoided or postponed merely because of fear.

The surgical model often evokes apprehension and anxiety, since it conjures up images of losing control; in addition psychotherapy is sometimes experienced as threatening to one's identity. Many people do not really know who they are and what they stand for, or against. They are always concerned about being used or manipulated by others. Everyone was once a child, and we and our bodies "remember" the humiliation of powerlessness and the associated panic. Relatively few people have fully competent and firm personal boundaries. They fear the surgical model less. Though they will get cut and bruised as a result of surgery, and may even die, they do not also have to fear the disintegration of their personality.

Psychotherapists are often themselves repulsed by the idea of surgery; they normally share the fears of other humans. They usually prefer to see themselves as humane helpers and as loving healers. This is one reason why their sincere efforts frequently yield only poor results. Too much empathy with the fears, pain, and anger of patients is often present, a consequence of overidentification. This sharply curtails the ability to operate on others. Surgeons generally refer their close relatives to other surgeons who are not limited by emotional entanglements. Therapists who are too sympathetic can lessen their patients' pain for a while, but they can do little else.

Unlike surgeons, psychotherapists cannot protect themselves from overidentification by draping the patient and looking only at the area that requires their immediate attention. They must be deeply involved, but without losing sight of themselves as distinct and separate individuals. This strong involvement with their patients makes it possible for therapists to intervene intrusively, thus eliciting the hidden old fears and bringing them up to the surface. Visceral brain pathways and established physiologic patterns do not yield easily, and they do not give way at all without such pressure.

ii. *Establishing a strong real relationship between therapist and patient.* Surgery is brief in duration, but psychotherapy that heals depression requires several years of hard work. During this time a powerful and close relationship normally develops between the therapist and his or her patient. The strength and quality of this relationship enable the therapist's personality to impact upon the wholly conscious patient. This is how the intrusions are achieved. The therapist is, in effect, the equivalent of the scalpel.

In a sense, two parallel relationships must develop and remain in existence between therapist and patient—a real one and a therapeutic one. The basis of the real relationship is complete honesty and mutual respect, combined with a two-sided commitment to remain involved even in the presence of powerful expressions of hurt, anger, or irrational fear by the patient. (Therapists are expected to be essentially free of these, at least in relation to their patients.) But in the therapeutic relationship room is made for the expression of any thoughts and all of the patient's feelings, without limiting their intensity and with no need to hold back or hide anything. What is unpleasant, painful, or embarrassing to the patient finds room here, and so does any criticism, disappointment, and anger at the therapist.

The existence of two such parallel relationships is unique. Psychoanalysts and most conservative psychotherapists relate to their patients essentially in a cordial but formal manner. They are usually somewhat aloof, cool, and distant, believing such qualities necessary to the development of the "transference."

Such therapists not only hide biographic data, they also remain essentially unknown as real human beings. Since patients cannot really know them as people, they are usually not willing or able to risk being involved with them emotionally beyond a certain point. On the other hand, "humanistic" and "open" psychotherapists tend to "encounter" their patients with limitless "love" and compassion. They often side with them uncritically, and sometimes they even get sexually or socially involved with them. This, some claim earnestly, is a useful way to undo loneliness, pain, and fear. But endless sympathizing with unrealistic wishes infantilizes the patient, and gratifying primitive yearnings causes harm by encouraging impulsivity in the name of freedom. Such therapists do not realize that some separation and distance are needed to accomplish the therapeutic task.

Powerful confrontations must occur during the process of therapy between the patient's health and his or her illness, between thoughtfulness and feelings, between rationality and irrational impulsivity, between mature living and infantile tendencies. All these inner struggles are expressed between patient and therapist. The latter steadfastly supports the healthy part of the patient (the first half of each preceding pair), adding the weight of his or her personality to it. This is how the emotional scales are repeatedly tipped in the desired direction. In this sense the therapist is not neutral. When properly confined to the therapeutic relationship, these confrontations often shake but only rarely destroy the real-relationship. (Since it has a special meaning here, this term will be hyphenated from now on.) This relationship is continuously being cemented by consistent support for the patient's self-sufficiency and by the therapist's unyielding intolerance of any actions based on pathologic needs.

Developing relationships of trust in people who fear trust is in itself a formidable first step, yet an unavoidable part of the process. Even those whose main trouble stems from the fear of engulfment must become closely involved. We have already observed in earlier chapters that most people, patients and nonpatients alike, are burdened with at least some hidden fear. To avoid it, people are eager to trust even blindly; but much patience and persistence are required to increase the capacity for realistic trust. Therapists must usually pass a long series of overt and covert tests before they are regarded as truly trustworthy. Irrational fears can be challenged by the therapist effectively only after the patient reaches this point. Patients often feel a little better even without such challenges, simply because they associate with sympathetic therapists who are decent human beings—but they never get well.

Establishing a genuine relationship within a "surgical" framework is the beginning of the long effort leading to individuation, the process of becoming self-enclosed and whole. "The attainment of well-defined ego boundaries is the ultimate goal of maturation, and it is not achievable through formal learning or by gaining insight."

iii. *Working with feelings.* Feelings, yearnings, and forbidden wishes are not generally recognized as having their roots in the distant past. Since they often make so little sense in the present, people commonly hide them from others, and even from themselves. As a result, feelings often remain consciously unknown, and even exploring them is frequently difficult. Emotions are widely feared, since they make people more vulnerable to hurt and thus open to the possibility of ridicule. Blushing is a common automatic reaction to being "caught" in an unwanted self-revelation. Even in therapy, shame commonly prevents people from experiencing and expressing their feelings openly. Yet crippling residues of blocked and hidden anger, hurt, love, and fear cannot be neutralized before they are fully accessible. They must be teased out of their hiding places, repeatedly stimulated, and experienced with sufficient force to activate new physiologic reaction patterns. Emotions must be calibrated to fit the present.

Reaching this goal is time-consuming, since lifelong habits of response are not easily given up. Therapists who are themselves scared of emotions for fear of being overwhelmed by their own strong feelings send subliminal and insidious messages to their patients to refrain from such "irrational" expressions. This dooms the process, and the patient.

iv. *Working with thinking.* Since "learning to . . . think requires first that we make room for it by diminishing the domain of feelings," chronic confusion is much more common than most people realize. Emotional health allows people to maintain coherent and clear thinking as a guide to their actions even in the presence of very strong feelings, which always try to take over. By nature, feelings are much more powerful than thinking, a relationship that must be reversed if we are to conduct our affairs rationally. This is slowly achieved by regularly exercising the capacity to reason and think while the patient is in the grip of powerful emotions. Learning to think is the goal of every educational effort, but it is reached only rarely. It ought to be a central ingredient of child rearing and of psychotherapy. It normally is ignored in both.

v. *Working with the body.* The pressure of feelings is experienced in the body. No work with feelings or with thinking is possible via the cortex alone. The failure to realize this is one of the basic flaws of psychoanalysis and of most psychotherapy. Emotional illnesses are not merely disturbances in thinking, but this is how they are treated almost universally. They are real illnesses, like all others, and they reside in the body and affect it. The jaw that locks itself when a strong emotion is felt condemns the diaphragm to move only slightly. Breathing then remains shallow, and feelings as well as thinking remain locked within their accustomed patterns.

Yet working mainly with the body is not sufficient either. Physical touching and other similar techniques can evoke strong emotions, but these must be brought into solid, sane relationships and put into proper perspective there. It is not enough to release strong feelings in a vacuum. Catharsis can be addictive because it temporarily lowers tension—it also is useless or even harmful in the real world.

vi. *Combined individual and group therapy.* Like human interactions before and immediately after birth, most therapy and counseling are based on a relationship between two people. So most patients find some solace in such exclusive relationships; they lower anxiety for short periods of time. But such contacts do not cure, because "personal independence and self-sufficiency . . . only develop in the crucible of no-choice."

Group settings can also lower anxiety and ameliorate loneliness because emotional support is also obtainable from the nonexclusive company of other human beings. A healthy group environment can in addition inculcate habits that are less pathologic than the patient's own. But socialization does not cure depression. Support groups that prohibit drinking, excessive eating, or other self-destructive habits are often very helpful, even lifesaving, but they do not alter the basic emotional needs, nor do they change the physiologic modes of response.

In the therapy system described here, individual sessions help in bonding and in supporting the patient, while group sessions serve as the "crucible of no-choice." "The group" is never used as a yardstick for anything. It merely serves as a setting in which the internal distortions of its individual members are reflected and repeatedly confronted.

vii. *The presence of multiple therapists.* Two therapists are ideally present in any one group session. It is enough to have a good mother to feel reasonably safe. A good father is also needed, however, to enforce reality, which often is unpleasant and painful. The support of one provides some of the strength to tolerate the constrictions of the other. The same is true in all "crucible[s] of no-choice," personal and political. Neither surgery nor psychotherapy can be performed successfully in any other way.

viii. *Developing emotional dependency.* Character is shaped in early infancy because the newborn has no choice but to adjust to its external reality, or die. The personality is further molded in early childhood because parents can force the young organism to remain in positions and in places that it wishes to avoid. It has no choice but to adapt. This power that parents have over their young children is often abused, at least in minor ways, but even then it shapes character. Most adults are understandably eager therefore to avoid being powerless again. This is why most patients and even most psychotherapists reject the idea of emotional dependency. They prefer to talk about things, even though it is essentially useless in the process of altering lifelong habits and physiology.

To alter these, patients must be kept from escaping what is subjectively "felt" as dangerous but actually is completely safe. Free grown-up men and women would agree to submit to such a situation only when they are deeply involved in a relationship. Some degree of emotional dependency is therefore a necessity, and it is basically different from real dependency. Only in the latter does abandonment result in real danger, as in the case of the newborn with its mother. Not so for grownups. When a therapist suddenly dies or must stop practicing for other reasons, his or her patients sustain a real loss; but they generally continue to live as before, and their existence is not endangered. Unlike young children, adults can be aware of their reactions and observe, examine, and assess their feelings. And they have the option of leaving situations in which actual abuses occur, a choice not available to the baby.

But the obvious differences are repeatedly blurred, since those experiencing either form of dependency *feel* a subjective diminution of their freedom, which always evokes fear. To keep it from overwhelming the patient, therapists must repeatedly highlight the fact that the dependency is not real. Holding patients responsible for all their acts and decisions serves as a useful reminder.

Because we need conditions that resemble the setting of early childhood, when character was first shaped, therapists must help foster emotional dependency in their patients. Together with the real-relationship it is meant to hold the patient during crises in therapy in the same way that a young child is held in the arms of a sensitive parent in moments of great fear. The emotional dependency provides the necessary lever to "force" change, although never without the informed and free consent of the fully conscious patient.

The "pull of regression" and the "push against progressing" as well as the fears of abandonment and of engulfment are eliminated as powerful forces once individuation is achieved. When the boundaries of the self are made whole, emotional self-sufficiency and a sense of mastery naturally follow in time. The ability to think clearly, to concentrate, and to handle difficult situations improves, often leading to a greater capacity for efficient work and for earning a living. Anxiety no longer interferes then with relaxation, and joy is often found even in the most mundane aspects of daily existence.

2. The Growing Value of Patients' Consent

In surgery we obtain the patient's consent only once, before a procedure is started. The task in long-term psychotherapy is infinitely more difficult. Patients are always free to withdraw their consent during the process, and they repeatedly want to do so in moments of fear and pain. Here no anesthesia is available to lessen the fear and the real agony that patients experience from time to time. Since some of the most profound fears of the fully conscious patient must be challenged in almost every session, a powerful push away from such experiences is often present. What then keeps patients from withdrawing their consent? The relationship with the therapist. When his or her concern is authentic and true and the involvement strong enough, it provides the necessary margin of safety.

Cordial, correct, but somewhat distant relationships do not have the power to hold patients in moments of intense fear, yet this is the nature of most therapeutic involvements. The basic fears of abandonment and engulfment remain therefore generally hidden, untreated and unresolved. Even lesser and more superficial expressions of fear are usually only interpreted or explained, or merely numbed with drugs. Psychoanalysts and other psychotherapists who recognize the need to address the fears of patients usually depend on the "positive transference," an idealization that assigns them magical powers, to keep patients from withdrawing emotionally or from leaving therapy in tired disappointment. But this works only for a while. The process of properly conducted long-term psychotherapy is painfully tedious and difficult, but those who use shortcuts discover quickly that their relief is only temporary and superficial.

The informed consent in psychotherapy, much more so than in surgery, should not be based on blind faith and cannot be for long. It must reflect realistic trust. But desperate people in panic give their consent to almost anyone for almost anything, since "the push away from fear or dread supersedes everything." Such initial consent must therefore be regarded as having only limited and tentative validity. It is neither really informed nor really free. The "yes" of people who are unable to say "no" is meaningless, and for ethical and practical reasons it should never be accepted at face value.

The questionable validity of the initial consent to intrude must be repeatedly and patiently re-examined, and its value must slowly be enhanced with time. Even very scared and suspicious people can thus begin to develop a relationship of real trust. Without it, patients tend to leave therapy as soon as they can, once the panic is replaced by lesser fears.

Irrational fear, bottomless hurt, and explosive anger are all remnants of the distant past. The therapist is the spokesman of the present. As such he or she helps the patient take steps toward reality in spite of, and beyond, these feelings. Much push and pull are often involved, yet every step in this direction involves a sense of discovery. What seemed to be mortifyingly dangerous minutes before turns out to be totally safe just a little bit later. The patient's body must repeatedly be slowed and stayed from acting willfully according to the dictates of the visceral brain, a tedious but exciting process that constantly expands one's freedom to be. Over time, the established subcortical pathways change in favor of newer and more adaptive ones, and the person begins to react differently to the sense of danger. Even its outlines and scope are no longer the same. The tolerance thresholds of fear, hurt, and anger rise steadily in the process till they essentially reflect reality as it is.

3. The Real- vs. the Therapeutic Relationship

Only within the real-relationship of properly conducted therapy is there enough room for a parallel therapeutic relationship in which the patient is free to express every thought and feeling and which requires no mutuality except for the payment of a fee. No other lasting relationship allows such complete freedom, unless it is based on fear. Vanquished partners are often forced to accept such terms because of their fear of abandonment.

Therapists with reasonably intact personal boundaries can practice in such a setting because they do not need emotional support, admiration, or love from their patients. These they obtain mainly from within themselves and to a lesser extent from their personal relationships with others. Their involvement with patients is deep and genuine, even though therapists do not eat, drink, sleep, or live with them. They also do not socialize with their patients, except on rare and special occasions.

Therapists must be able to "be there" under conditions that are much more trying and difficult than those existing anywhere else. Patients often address them venom-mouthed, expressing murderous rage. At other times they become the focus of their patients' profound yearnings, and of love that has the purity and innocence of little children. Patients are often deeply hurt by even the simplest words of therapists, or emotionally wounded because some of their actions did not fit the patients' wishes or expectations. A sensitive and ethical therapist with well-defined personal boundaries has no need to shy away from such intense involvements, nor is he or she likely to lose perspective, patience, objectivity, fairness, or tolerance, even under such stressful conditions. Usually the limits of tolerance are much lower. People often pay a high non-monetary price in dignity and in self-respect elsewhere, much higher than any fee paid to any therapist.

The reason biographical details of therapists, as well as their tastes and values, are best kept out of their patients' direct line of vision is that it gives them enough latitude to imagine anything. The specific content of such fantasies helps patients see themselves. Yet many therapists have used this as an excuse to keep all their contacts with patients stiff and sterile, since they are uncomfortable with real closeness. Such therapists are not emotionally ready for this work, regardless of their credentials. Their own fear of engulfment causes them to create distance.

The human qualities of the therapist do not remain altogether secret if the relationship is long enough, nor should they. The therapist's capacity to empathize, and the degree of his or her true concern, compassion, and sensitivity (or the lack of them) eventually show through. Patients can thus assess the therapist as a human being and slowly determine to what extent realistic trust is justified. Those who never have a chance to know their therapist as a real person can only have blind trust, something of little value. Only in extreme despair and fear do we trust that which we do not know. Besides, patients of a therapist who remains basically anonymous can never become equals; the inequality is artificially maintained without hope of resolution. But when genuinely involved, therapists convey rather clearly what they are as human beings by their facial expressions, tonal quality, manners, and general demeanor and also by their dress and the way they furnish and maintain their offices. Even some biographical details become known eventually in real-relationships of long duration.

The therapy setting, like an operating room, should be designed to maximize the opportunities for healing the patient. The therapist's comfort comes second. Yet many therapists use their relative position of power to arbitrarily dictate terms that fit their personal preferences and needs, ignoring those of their patients. The freedom of patients to experience and express strong feelings is commonly interfered with, and their real concerns are often brushed aside with smart explanations and with interpretations that fit old preconceptions. Therapists often refuse to inconvenience themselves even when patients are in great distress; they behave and bedeck themselves to fit whatever their life-style is; they see patients only individually or only in groups; and in general they do only whatever they "are comfortable with." To justify such positions, therapists can easily find some theoretical rationalization from among the many that are so readily available. Neither a real-relationship nor a therapeutic one can exist under such circumstances, and not much good comes from such efforts. In general such therapists cannot repair the defective and incomplete personal boundaries of others because theirs are not whole. They cannot cure depression in their patients because they are themselves still depressed. But the sick people who happen upon them discover this only years later.

What makes the real-relationship real is the absence of anything unreal in it. The patient is free of any need to compromise dignity or integrity, since the relationship is based solely on mutual respect and responsible action. What makes the therapeutic relationship therapeutic is the unique freedom that the patient has in it to feel and to say anything, to hide nothing, to express any thought openly as a reflection, and all feelings as true products of the self, not as intentions. Room thus exists in it for real experimentation without fear of reality consequences.

4. The Therapeutic Setting and Contract

The nature of any workshop is dictated by the task that must be accomplished in it. A large enough drydock is needed to repair the bottom of a seagoing ship. Damage below the waterline cannot be efficiently repaired otherwise. The same with Man. The first step in healing depression is to construct a setting in which the patient feels safe enough. Those fearing abandonment cling a little less then, and those who fear engulfment allow the therapist to come a little closer, enough to make real emotional contact.

The patient's fear can sometimes be enormous, resembling that of a man from a primitive and distant tribe about to undergo a surgical procedure by a visiting team of doctors. How is he to understand that the strangers only mean to remove the large cancer that grows on his nose? The sight of the approaching surgeon, masked and gloved with knife in hand, would elicit powerful resistance, regardless of any prior consent. Surely the patient is to be seriously harmed, even murdered. Eyes riveted on the sharp edge of the scalpel, the body of such a man would tense, fight, and try to escape. All he can feel is panic and the strong arms that restrain him. Butchery is all he can associate with such circumstances. *He* is the lamb! Although meant to save his life, he would surely resist the procedure and any attempt to touch him. He does not know surgeons as competent and ethical professionals, careful not to cause harm. The subjective experience counts. The first spurt of blood proves the validity of his suspicions. The fear of the unknown is worse than the fear of death.

Patients who undergo good psychotherapy often feel similar fear when the therapist intrudes upon them beyond the point of subjective safety. We tend to push away instinctively that which we do not know to be safe. The established pathways of the visceral brain "protect" us, even when we do not need or want such protection.

Many people automatically push away not only the therapist but also everyone else who is experienced as coming too close. They cannot satisfy their real needs for adult closeness. This is why such a symptom must be eliminated, not ignored or chemically overridden. Temporarily lessening the fear by charm or reassurance is also harmful. But when the therapeutic relationship is free enough, patients increasingly begin to experience such fears in relation to their therapist and less so with others. The real-relationship holds the patient in place.

Constructing a safe setting begins by making real contact with the patient. This is much more than saying hello. The therapist must touch and welcome the patient's "soul." The hidden and denied fears and hurt must be recognized, verbalized, and sensitively addressed. The patient's confusion and silence must be listened to, and heard. An immediate sense of relief follows when this is properly done, and contact is thus established. This is a solid base for the beginning of a solid real-relationship.

It is soon necessary, however, to diffuse the magical expectations that such an exquisite understanding often gives rise to. Everyone has had lifelong yearnings to be perfectly heard, even without uttering a sound. Not only are gifted ethical healers and physicians attuned to such yearnings, but so too are charlatans, gurus, and charismatic political leaders. The false hope that is evoked by such perfect understanding must be actively discouraged in non-exploitative relationships based on real trust. People normally tend to idealize those who relieve their fear.

Even in the absence of great secrets, few people bare their souls to another unless anonymity or confidentiality is assured and maintained. This is why people can sometimes talk most intimately to total strangers, as long as they expect never to meet again. Such strangers have no opportunity to reject us or laugh at us. Family therapy sessions do not usually deal in depth with sensitive, shame-filled, and conflictual material of individual family members, in part because the sessions are almost universally experienced as too public an arena. This is generally also true for psychotherapy in groups, unless special precautions and procedures are meticulously followed.

The therapeutic contract stipulates in addition that no weapon of any kind is ever permitted on the premises and no spontaneous physical contact is ever allowed. Non-spontaneous and strictly non-sexual physical touching may occasionally be initiated by therapists, but only after obtaining anew the patient's explicit consent on every occasion. Otherwise all expressions must only be verbal or vocal. The defense that holds that someone was temporarily overcome by strong feelings is never acceptable. A firm commitment to avoid impulsive acting of any kind is the basic condition that governs all interactions, in and out of the therapeutic setting. Difficulties with this standard and minor deviations from it are the bread and butter of the therapeutic work, but major breaks in this regard are sufficient cause at least for the immediate termination of a patient's involvement in therapy.

Even anger of the greatest intensity can be expressed in such a setting without danger of anyone getting hurt. Because the therapeutic setting is free enough and safe enough, intense yearnings and love are also revealed without shame and without leading to any change in the real-life arrangements of either patient or therapist. Infantile yearnings to be loved and held are often expressed elsewhere in terms of adult sexuality. It is much less embarrassing for an adult who wishes to appear rational to speak of his or her strong and strange urges this way rather than give voice to the seemingly irrational demands of the infant within. But no therapist is ever an ideal mate or sex partner for a yearning patient, even if they might fit under different circumstances. Sex has no place in the therapeutic setting.

Unblocked old anger and hurt are usually experienced and expressed in this system as disappointment in the therapist or in therapy in general. Feelings of old can be experienced more easily once they are anchored to something real in the here and now. The human imperfections of the therapist and of the setting, as well as the fact that patients pay for their therapy, are commonly used to trigger such expressions. Even intense anger or hurt is not necessarily a good enough reason for terminating the process. Such feelings must be examined seriously and discussed openly, but not before they are expressed fully enough. Action is called for only if the hurt and anger reflect reality, whose outlines are often blurred for a few stormy days. Therapy should be stopped only if the therapist really has serious and persistent shortcomings.

Feelings are relatively short-lived, sometimes only fleeting in duration. They result from the totality of a person's past experiences and do not usually reflect current reality accurately. It is best therefore not to connect them automatically with any action whatsoever, and they are not in themselves an acceptable reason for any real-life decisions. Acting on the basis of emotions alone is as valid as conducting one's affairs according to astrologic or tea-leaf readings. Once in a while it may work out well by chance, but in general it is a sure prescription for real trouble.

New patients are often reluctant to express feelings such as anger or hurt *at* the therapist or *at* another patient, since such expressions do not usually produce an actual change in behavior, and are not meant to do so. They have said it once, twice, or three times already, they claim. What's the point in doing it again? People do not want to do what appears to make no rational sense. Yet it is essential to reverse the lifelong sense of resignation and futility and the tendencies to withhold, to withdraw, and to close up that were firmly established many years before. These cannot simply be reasoned away. The specific content of any one expression is usually of secondary value only; the process itself is primary. Activated feelings become increasingly more intensified as the lungs and throat open up and as the fear of one's own power diminishes. The dormant wish for meaningful human contact is slowly rekindled. Such invigoration must occur in the body, not merely in thought; the muscles must become more vibrant and more responsive.

The changes that eventually occur are apparent in facial expression, in stance, in the quality of one's voice and speech, in manners, habits, and dress. They affect personal involvements, intellectual aspirations, and professional competence. Others usually see such changes long before the patient does, and they normally begin to respond differently even before he or she is consciously aware of the differences. The therapeutic workshop is constructed properly when it provides enough room to reverse the pathologic tendencies and trends that are the hallmark of the illness.

5. Mothering and "Holding" as Part of Healing

The involvement of therapists with their patients as described here must be based on real love. But is it really possible for anyone to experience so much love toward so many people, and strangers at that? As we have seen in Chapter 4, those with essentially intact personal boundaries, "like a well-constructed vessel in good repair," can easily replenish themselves with self-love and with occasional praise from others. "It is really true that the more real love one 'gives' to others the more one has." Such therapists usually cannot help responding empathically, with concern and true compassion, to the agonizing child within the struggling and sometimes unpleasant adult who comes to them for help. Their love is neither unlimited nor unconditional but quite real at many moments. Those essentially free of old fear, hurt, or anger cannot remain aloof in the presence of someone experiencing acute anguish. Very few people remain totally indifferent to a little child lost in a crowd. We are usually more cautious with adult humans, probably because we are more scared of the consequences of our involvement with them.

On the other hand, therapists and non-therapists who are very needy cannot really love themselves or others. They may pretend that they do, but all they have to offer are platitudes and phony interest. They usually mean well, but they try too hard, they make insufficient room for their patients, they are too busy with "helping," and they often miss the point. What the therapist is as a person is paramount.

No therapist should ever be "in love" with a patient, but no patient can be healed by a therapist who is not genuinely and lovingly involved. This alone gives one human being the right to cause pain to another, as psychotherapists and physicians must at times do to their patients. The quality of a therapist's love for a patient essentially parallels that of an emotionally healthy mother for her child. Not needing the child to sustain herself emotionally, she is consistently supportive, kind, warm, and loving. But not unconditionally. This may not even exist in utero.

The love of individuated therapists for a patient is in fact usually more genuine than the love of parents for a child, and much more reliable than what lovers feel for each other. Therapists do not normally get scared, angry, or hurt by direct verbal attacks upon them, and they can usually maintain a loving attitude even in such situations. Their sense of "self-worth . . . is safely anchored within the self." They also do not get seduced, manipulated, or otherwise confused by expressions of love toward them. Such a range of reactions can only exist fully in therapeutic relationships. Few mothers or fathers allow their children such freedom. Within the family, feelings are generally confused with judgments and often misunderstood as permanent attitudes. The open expression of feelings is therefore often completely prohibited or at least sharply curtailed there, although necessary for the raising of emotionally healthy children. Because the love is less contaminated in therapeutic relationships of the type described, the freedom that exists in them is generally much greater than that found anywhere else.

The payment of money cleanses the relationship with the therapist of all other permissible expectations. Therapists normally expect to be compensated for their time, but this (and adherence to the non-acting-out contract) is all that they have the right to expect in properly conducted therapy. Although their efforts are designed to help patients improve or change, and this is their personal wish for them, they cannot legitimately expect even that. Patients sometimes need to exercise their human right to remain stubbornly stuck and emotionally unwell for long periods of time. Their inner struggle for independence is against unseen others who wished to influence them; they are often unconsciously determined not to budge till they are ready to steer their own life's course. Such struggles are common in therapeutic relationships, the stage upon which old and unresolved conflicts are replayed. Here the charged confrontations of early childhood are finally re-enacted with immense hurt and ferocious anger in saner relationships with therapists. Resolution occurs when the patient is finally ready to let bygones be bygones, not when the therapist believes he or she should. Only therapists capable of truly loving their patients can stay the course and not become impatient with them, or burned out.

Even good parents are not so patient. They expect more, as they should. Raising children properly requires that increasingly more difficult standards be set, and adhered to. But in addition, parents normally see their children as extensions of themselves and as reflections of their worth. They want to be proud of them. Their love is often very conditional, depending on the children's performance, or absent altogether.

But therapists have freely chosen to commit their energies to this work, and they have no legitimate right to complain about the tedious and painfully long struggles that are so common. The therapist who conditions his or her commitment to patients on their getting well is distorting the real-relationship and condemning all efforts to certain failure. On the surface patients may improve as long as they wish to please the therapist, but no real or permanent change occurs at the point of a gun.

The therapeutic relationship is often extremely stormy, but as long as it occurs within a real-relationship that holds the patient lovingly, firmly, and consistently, all the storms eventually subside. Patients who experience extreme fear or intense dissatisfaction, hurt, and anger at the therapist would simply leave without the mothering that the real-relationship provides. This is how most other relationships end under similar circumstances. But divorces make sense only when real, basic incompatibilities exist and, like all other decisions, should not be based on feelings alone. But the push to avoid pain and fear is extremely powerful; when the going gets rough, leaving therapy often seems almost irresistibly attractive, and sensible to boot. We humans have a special gullibility for believing our own rationalizations. Such a move would obviously represent impulsive acting-out of feelings, and it must be strongly discouraged.

No child at home, and no patient in therapy, dares express fear, love, hate, anger, or hurt unless he or she feels really safe in these settings. Such safety must be physiologically sensed, and it cannot be achieved merely by verbal assurances. The newborn "knows" when it is properly held and whether Mother is content. Adults also sense this about others, including therapists. When patients acquire a sense of true safety and inner security, they risk expressing their wishes and feelings as they never did before. With time, this relative freedom to be as one really is also begins to exist outside the therapeutic setting.

The mothering in therapy does not usually involve physical holding, but to be useful it must be just as real and just as steady as it would have been for the well-held newborn. Physical contact as a form of mothering is relatively uncommon in work with adults. It sometimes is the only way, however, to reach beyond wide chasms of primitive fear that are not bridgeable otherwise. But unless the therapists are mature and emotionally whole, the indications clear, and the limits unambiguous and strictly adhered to, it is best avoided.

Mothering and "holding" are merely prerequisites. Not too much will happen in the relationship with the patient unless the therapist is emotionally healthy and basically free of inner conflicts and irrational fear. The therapist's fears always influence the quality of the relationship, and they determine the limits of safety. They cannot be hidden from patients for very long, even when they are denied by the self. In general, patients are not "held" or mothered well in relationships that are emotionally distant, formal, excessively proper, cool, or rigid. It also cannot happen if the mothering therapist becomes a friend, a playmate, or a buddy. But when a sane framework exists, the difficult work can be pursued further.

6. The Need for Fathering and for Limit Setting

People who have already given up hope generally hold on stubbornly to their hopelessness because it too can be used as a mechanism with which to survive. Those who love them tend to worry about them, they encourage them, and they don't easily forget about them. Those who have folded up and folded in do not easily open themselves up again. It often takes years of hard work and of building trust before they reach out toward anyone. The yearnings of the infant that have been squelched do not suddenly blossom, even when room is made for them to do so. Feelings that have remained underdeveloped must be actively stimulated and repeatedly exercised before they become functional. The sense of futility often hangs on like a dark winter cloud. Many interventions are necessary to activate that which was dormant to the point of appearing dead. It is a task of major proportions to awaken the preverbal hunger and rage of people who have been used to living in the depths of hopelessness.

One reader of the preceding sentences made the following comment:

> This paragraph is the most important one to me personally because it gives meaning to the many, too many, years of living with the wish that my mother, my god, or some benevolent guru would relieve my hurt. It never happened. As I became less comforted by this false hope, I experienced increasing panic as a constant reminder that I was moving toward the fringes of sanity. I held on with the help of proctoscopes, cystoscopes, upper GI's [gastrointestinal], lower GI's, daily injections of dust and mold, and a laparotomy to check for Hodgkin's. No cancer, only fear, leaking from every orifice. It often saddens me to know that I did it to myself. There are no free rides to healthy living. This paragraph points out a reality that I have gradually discovered over the past few years namely that those "who have already given up hope generally hold on stubbornly to their hopelessness because it too can be used as a mechanism with which to survive." I am grateful to discover that better ways exist than to offer up one's belly to the scalpel.

This, however, is merely the beginning. The primitive demands of old must be repeatedly and powerfully expressed once the unfulfillable dreams have been awakened. Storms of rage and hurt erupt, and they begin to sweep the scene one after another as the silent disappointment of decades finds a clear and strong voice. Fisted roaring and sobbing from the depths of pain are common. Now patients finally dare to ask for more, then to demand it, and finally to froth at the mouth for not getting it. They "want . . . what . . . [they] want . . . now, without delay."

If the psychotherapy workshop is set up properly, it provides room for repeated opportunities to make such "unreasonable" demands in a totally unrestrained fashion. Such "outbursts" seem "crazy." Why demand again what was already shown many times before not to be available? Why awaken old hurt, anger, and yearnings that are unfulfillable? Because to give up without a heroic struggle is to live with a sense of powerlessness. This is what happens in infancy and in psychoanalysis. We "realize"that we can't prevail, and we painfully accept the futility of our human position. Anomie, resignation, and at least subclinical depression are the inevitable results. Not so if we walk away from our infantile notions reluctantly but proudly, without a sense of defeat. We must exercise our strength to experience our competence. We may not get what we want, but the struggle itself proves us powerful. Although no one can get from life all that can be wished for, much is available to those who reach for it.

Even at the height of demanding, a patient really knows that the therapist is unable to fulfill the wishes that are so powerful emotionally. The feelings can be titanic even when we fully understand cognitively that their content makes no sense. The judgment of the cortex can be temporarily suspended with effort during such moments, once embarrassment is set aside. The new mammalian brain does not approve, but new pathways in the visceral brain are being established anyway. Most psychotherapists have never gone through such powerful experiences; they do not understand their rationale; and they find it difficult to accept the need for it. Being prisoners of rationality, they normally dismiss such primitive and unreasonable demanding as silly at best and undesirable. In reality, such episodes are necessary experiences of controlled regression in the service of repairing defective boundaries of the self.

Patients are not only reluctant to engage in such exercises but at first they are also rather clumsy. Like everyone else, they are used to trying to be rational. Such experiments with new ways of being are at first artificial and often ineffective. They become a little less strange and more useful with time. Patients reaching this phase have already changed in some major ways: They are less scared. They dare to demand. They are no longer so ashamed of having irrational wishes. Like healthy infants, they sometimes make very loud and unreasonable demands.

Such powerful wishes and demands must, however, be frustrated in reality, because they are unrealistic. Yet people who are less scared are also less willing to accept the limits of reality. They sometimes really want what they want just the way they want it and just because they want it. Finally they can afford to enjoy being impudent and unruly brats. They want to make up for all the lost time in which they demanded nothing. Now they sometimes challenge the therapist by not adhering so strictly to the non-acting-out contract to which they have agreed freely.

Open defiance is new to many people, and they relish small opportunities to exercise it. They miss sessions; they are late; they "forget" to pay their fees on time; and they sometimes insist on quitting therapy even though it is not finished. Therapy is time consuming and costly, they suddenly remember. The drive to the sessions in the snow now causes more hardships than before, or else sailing in the summer suddenly becomes much more attractive.

Almost anyone who has ever been in any form of psychotherapy for a while becomes at least a little bit less frightened and a little freer to say no. For many this is the cure, and they leave. Being bitter, angry, or obnoxious becomes their typical mode of existing. But patients are still depressed at this point, although less acutely than they used to be, and less deeply than many people "out there" who have never been in therapy. They "feel" better, and often they live a little better. Although patients have greater freedom now, it is the freedom of infants and of healthy young children. It is not governed often enough by good sense. To leave therapy now means to court disaster. It is analogous to leaving the hospital soon after the fever breaks but while the patient's severe pneumonia is still raging, the lungs are still congested, and life itself still hangs in the balance.

The fathering abilities of the therapist now begin to be tested. In general, psychotherapists have proven themselves to be almost totally inept in this area, with grave consequences to millions of patients. Many female patients have suddenly deserted their families and children at this point to seek their fortunes. They "felt" free and no longer "under the yoke" of their husbands or society's mores. They "felt" invincible. Male patients have suddenly divorced, given up their careers, chased women or other dreams that caught their fancies, and thrown all responsibility to the wind. Freedom is a strongly intoxicating substance with which individuals as well as societies often abuse themselves. They get intoxicated and then harm themselves seriously. This is what happened to many newly formed states such as Angola and Mozambique once they gained political independence.

Those who leave therapy abruptly and prematurely often find themselves at a loss, facing a new world without new tools. Despair soon sets in, but they often have an overwhelming wish to save face and cannot easily admit their serious error. So they commonly seek out the supernatural, the spiritual, the strange, the holy, or the "healthy" as their refuge. They need something urgently. They spurned the values of the establishment. What else is left?

Patients often claim at this point that their rebelliousness represents thinking and that they are not acting out. This is not only because they are less scared but also because an internal shift often occurs around this time. The patient's fear of abandonment is lessened to the point that the fear of engulfment now becomes paramount. It is always necessary at this difficult juncture to insist that patients check and double-check the face of reality. "Feelings commonly camouflage themselves as thoughts," especially at times like this.

The therapist must exercise the fathering role of limit setting with great care at all times, but it is critical to do so properly at this point. The task of fathering is always very difficult and often grossly misunderstood. People do not like to be curbed; and the fact that real fathers, rulers, and therapists have often abused the powers invested in their roles is commonly used to justify impulsive living. Anarchy and irresponsibility are often the result. Many of the ills of our families and of our societies are directly traceable to failings in this area.

A therapist has no right to direct a patient in any way except one: to continue adhering to the non-acting-out contract. A contract should not be broken unilaterally, and the patient must be held to its terms. This is easier said than done. The rationality, sanity, and responsibility of the patient must be called upon, as well as the real-relationship and the emotional dependency upon the therapist. Even so, success is not guaranteed. This is the moment of truth. It must sometimes be faced several times before the crisis is over.

Therapists who themselves have difficulties with authority

figures, and many people do, cannot exercise this limit-setting function very well. Many of them even claim that such a role is inappropriate or unnecessary, and they construct ideologies and theories to justify such a position. They often speak of the "need to have a flexible approach based on the patient's level of motivation," as one author did recently. Here is an actual quote from a promotional blurb for a major textbook on psychotherapy that was published recently:

> The author believes that a person's therapy experiences should be tailored to fit his psychological set. Thus, persons who conceive of their problems in terms of symptoms can be given direct means to relieve their discomfort, usually through advice, suggestions and other forms of support. Those who relate their difficulties to interpersonal issues can be treated with a focus on interpersonal relationships, and people who conceive of their problems as intrapsychic can be encouraged to introspect.

Because of their inability to father, such therapists accept the patient's own diagnostic impression as the basis of their "expert" opinion. A patient with a swelling who claims that it is an infection is thus given an antibiotic, when in fact it is a cancerous growth. Basically, such theories are excuses to mask a therapist's deep distrust of all authority, and his or her resultant inability to serve in this capacity. Patients' feelings, and especially their fears, thus become the limiting factor of the therapeutic process. No wonder that it commonly fails to cure.

The non-acting-out contract requires that all decisions be based on true *deciding,* the cool consideration of all the relevant facts and choices. This obviously applies also to the current dilemma, the push out of therapy. People in free societies generally think of freedom merely as a function of political organization. Not sufficiently aware of the powerful inner forces that hold us prisoner, they often become self-righteously insulted when anyone dares to suggest that some of their "decisions" or statements may be expressions of hidden feelings, not thoughtfulness. It strongly suggests that such people have never been fathered properly. They are spoiled infants, now physically grown up, able to live thoughtlessly because their societies do not publicly condemn self-indulgence. Patients at this juncture often forget what they seemed to have known before, and they try to join the ranks of other "liberated" people.

But even if the people who live this way prevail with their mates, their children, and their subordinates, they and those whom they affect are condemned to remain depressed until they free themselves from this slavery to impulse. Acting out is no less damaging than the previous acting in, which resulted in a withdrawal into the self. To be healed of depression, people must go beyond this phase of rebelliousness, anger, and self-indulgence. They must inwardly accept the fact that it is not possible to always prevail, except in the short run. The unrealistic expectation that one can get his or her way at all times inevitably leads to much bitterness and anger, and to repeated disappointments. Emotional maturity and contentment are incompatible with such living, which is widely known as narcissistic.

Some people are more depressed than others, either because their biologic heritage predisposed them to it (a small minority of all cases) or because their earliest life experiences have subjectively been more panic-filled (the majority). Sooner or later we have no choice but to face these personal ghosts from the past. To overcome their power we must discover that they cannot really harm us, which requires that we enter the haunted house we fear so much, their alleged dwelling place, and find it empty. Being intelligent and sophisticated, we understand that there are no ghosts, but we nonetheless break into a cold sweat and tremble as we come near them. Every next step is experienced as our last. We can reassure others when they find themselves in similar fear-filled situations, as they assure us now, but we still refuse or are unable to take the next step.

Most psychotherapy consists of discussions between a well-meaning therapist and a frightened patient in front of the haunted house. The therapist helps the patient see that the fear is a remnant from early childhood, that it really makes no sense for an adult to still have it. If all goes well, the patient is eventually convinced that all is safe. There obviously are no ghosts. The therapist's presence is reassuring, and after a while the patient may no longer feel so much anxiety. But as soon as he or she must again walk by that house, the patient's heart starts pumping more rapidly, the muscles tense up, eyes widen in terror, a cold sweat reappears, and the walker stops cold. The house is still haunted.

This is life, we finally tell ourselves. We tried to overcome this nonsensical fear, but we nonetheless cannot go forward. We are stuck wherever we are. We adjust our entire existence so that we always take a large detour around that haunted house and all the others in every neighborhood that look so much the same. Soon our entire existence is devoted to taking detours everywhere. In severe cases we become altogether immobile. We just sit there, wherever we are, frozen in panic. As many readers know, this is not an exaggerated picture. In a less severe form it is true for practically everyone.

To live without the fear and pain of depression we must physically experience the haunted house as empty. We must repeatedly enter every one of its rooms till our body "knows" it is safe. No one, ever, can muster enough courage and strength to enter it alone. A therapist who is really not afraid must first be found, and the patient must then slowly discover by repeated testing that the therapist is truly trustworthy. If so, the two stand together as if hand in hand and slowly proceed toward the entrance. The therapist must often nudge the patient and help him or her along, patiently but persistently, one small step at a time. At other times the therapist must encourage, coax, demand, insist, or call upon the patient's competence and pride as the basis for taking the next step. Sometimes a crisis must be mobilized to move the patient ahead: Continue or quit. But somehow the patient must be helped to overcome the understandable reluctance to taking further steps. The alternative is often literally life threatening.

In the process, fear will cause patients not only to break out in a cold sweat and to tremble but sometimes also to shake violently, to vomit, and even to become quite confused for a few moments. Patients want to run away and to terminate therapy many times before victory is won. At times the cure seems worse than the illness, and at such moments patients jerk their hand out of the therapist's and begin running in the opposite direction. But if the relationship between the two is real enough, if it is based on integrity and mutual respect, not on blind trust, and if the emotional dependency upon the therapist is strong enough, then the patient usually stops running when called upon to do so.

Using his or her fathering authority, the therapist must frequently pull a patient beyond the point where he or she normally would go, even risking the relationship. "Follow me" is the message to the discouraged struggler who wants to give up. But therapists must never push patients. Even a friendly push is often experienced as an impatient act tainted by anger.

Beyond any shadow of doubt the patient must know that the

therapist is committed to the task, that he or she is really dependable, that no tricks are involved, that no sudden letdowns or desertions will occur in the zone of danger. Tearfully, fearfully, and carefully the two must continue their difficult journey till they enter the empty house, staying in each room long enough for the patient to calm down physically. They must often even revisit the same areas before fear-free living is possible.

The system of therapy described here is called "Crisis Mobilization Therapy." Paradoxically, the process of change is similar in some ways to behavior therapy, and yet the two are totally different from each other, both in the degree of involvement and the goals. Patients are desensitized—not to any phobic object but to irrational fear itself. As new and more appropriate reaction patterns become established, the patient increasingly fails to respond when the old neural pathways are triggered. Old and maladaptive modes of behavior and response slowly but steadily fall away and disappear.

With the therapist's firm support, patients are increasingly willing to experience the fear involved in willfully "disobeying" some of the dictates of the visceral brain. They learn to control their tendencies to escape, to close up, to breathe in a shallow manner, to discharge anxiety by compulsive smiling or laughing or by repetitive "nervous" movements of hands and fingers, feet and legs. At first this increases their overt anxiety, but the automatic bodily expressions of anxiety also change sooner or later. The previously established visceral brain pathways become weakened by disuse, just as they were established by frequent use. Eventually they yield to competing pathways used over and over again by the conscious patient. Feelings change last, and only after the patient has been repeatedly willing and able to resist yielding to their pressure.

This monumental task extends over a period of several years, because each step must be repeated many times before a person's physiology responds automatically in ways that are more suitable to the present, and therefore less costly. The focus of patients' attention shifts in the process, and much of their fear and anger becomes directed at the therapist, the one who does not relent. Sometimes the therapist is experienced as having no pity, no compassion, and no moderation. Yet through the heroic and long struggles with the therapist the patient discovers his or her strength. Profound hurt is often present. Is there no respite, no end to the pain and to the struggle? But eventually patients also experience gratitude and deep love toward the one who never left the scene and who never deserted them during their long ordeal. The patient's physiologic perception of human relationships and commitments changes in the process. Resignation and hopelessness cannot co-exist with this new perception for long. The lifelong depression begins to lift.

7. The Yearnings for Dependency and the Fear of It

Most of psychotherapy, including psychoanalysis, essentially follows educational principles. Patients do not learn a subject; they learn about themselves. They begin to understand their motives and those of others; they gain insight that helps them explain and comprehend events more clearly; they learn to become more objective in their outlook. The assumption underlying all these efforts is that understanding has the power to heal. This is also the rationale of the various types of brief psychotherapy. In five to ten sessions, patients can be "shown," communications "opened," decisions made by reasoning and by will. In all these, people are assumed to be rational beings who will stop reacting in self-damaging and self-destructive ways once they understand what they are doing. Yet in general, we humans do not act rationally and thoughtfully; we follow our feelings. When the basic assumptions about Man's nature—how he got to be depressed and how he might get well—are in error, all the attempts to cure him are condemned to certain failure.

The correct model for a healing psychotherapy is the child-parent relationship. The main task is not "educating" the mammalian brain but forcing changes upon the visceral one. This can only be accomplished in a relationship that duplicates in an emotional sense that of early mothering and of later fathering, when the child had no choice but to adapt to whatever conditions were set down by its parents. These rather obvious explanations of the need for emotional dependency upon the therapist are not yet generally recognized; the prospect of dependency evokes too much fear, as we have seen earlier. As a rule, the general public still pins its hopes for a depression-free and "happy" life on invalid approaches, and most "experts" earn their livelihood by following wishful-thinking fallacies. The many tragic results speak for themselves.

Some emotional dependency inevitably develops in all long-term relationships, because the yearnings to hold on to someone reliable are so strong. Even though people fear emotional dependency and want to avoid it, they take to it when the conditions are right, like a fish takes to water. "Unlike tortoises, we know our mothers and we . . . hold on to them tenaciously and refuse to let go."

Yet emotional dependency is the source of many of the difficulties that develop in love affairs, in marriages, and in therapy when the therapist is ill-prepared to manage the dependency properly. Many therapists are repelled and claim that they are being "put upon" and "sucked" dry by their endlessly demanding, complaining, and dependent patients, who are often unwelcome and discharged too soon. And their therapists are often quick to point out that such behavior is inappropriate for adults and that it makes "absolutely" no sense, thus shaming the patient into a retreat. Like other people, many therapists also yearn to have someone they can emotionally depend on; and like others, they are less eager to be depended upon, unless this provides them with a sense of importance and power. They often try to retard the development of dependency, and when successful in suppressing its open expressions, they deny that it exists.

Such denials are welcomed by people who are scared of becoming dependent. So denying the existence of dependency is also good for "business," as is the custom of referring to patients as "clients." This camouflages the issues enough and sometimes lures patients. But pleasing sick people by helping them deny their crippling illness is a cruel hoax, even if done without malice. Besides, it makes it more difficult for many people to seek help, since it perpetuates the old stigma associated with emotional disorders.

The sense of dependency activates the dormant fear of abandonment, thus making it possible to begin eliminating it. This is yet another reason why some people want to avoid dependency at almost any cost. The ultimate goal and result of therapy that heals depression is personal independence. But to achieve it we must actually win the battle against the pull of emotional dependency, not just deny its existence.

What happens in therapy is merely a replay, not a new play— a re-experience, under new and safe conditions, of terror-filled experiences of long ago. The danger of abandonment experienced by emotionally dependent patients is obviously not real, but the cortex repeatedly forgets this. They must often be reminded of what would otherwise be obvious and self-evident. Many husbands and wives are practically enslaved for many years in intolerable marriages because they do not realize fully enough that their dependency is only emotional.

Emotional dependency plays an important role in the earlier phases of therapy, when the real-relationship and the non-acting-out contract are not yet strong enough to protect the patient from his or her impulse to run. "The push away from fear or dread supersedes everything," including the contract with a therapist. But even extreme fear can magically and delusionally be reduced for a little while by emotional dependency. The patient "feels" protected by the one upon whom he or she has come to depend, almost as if they had become physically attached and one. For a little while these delusions have the power of reality. Fear has to be lessened before adult commitments and contracts can hold, which happens with time; the real-relationship then becomes the primary tool for holding the patient. Similarly, the mothering function is more prominent at the beginning, the fathering one later on, when the major crises begin to occur. This obviously is an exact replication of the real importance of mother and father in the lives of young children.

Powerful storms of fear, anger, hurt, and love belong only in the therapeutic relationship; the real-relationship is meant to remain always supportive, respectful, and rooted in reality. But cyclones of primitive feelings that sometimes erupt in the former occasionally threaten to overwhelm the latter also. Too powerful to be contained within the therapeutic relationship alone, they spill over on occasion and contaminate the real-relationship. At such moments even relatively sane patients can lose their perspective, and they may be totally unable to see the therapist as a real person. The entire process would be in danger then were it not for the presence of a powerful emotional dependency.

While emotional dependency is fostered in good therapy, actual dependency is not allowed to develop. Patients are expected to attend to all aspects of reality meticulously. The responsibilities and obligations of patients as non-dependent adults are never compromised. This is why therapists do not usually give advice; adults are capable of discovering what is best for them. Because emotionally dependent people are often eager to imitate, as children tend to imitate their elders, it is not only undesirable but also ethically unacceptable for therapists to try to mold their patients in their own image or to inculcate values. It also goes counter to the goal of helping patients become whole and self-dependent.

Patients who are "held" carefully, firmly, tenderly, and lovingly enough eventually experience an inner security and a sense of being at home, often for the first time. Such a sense of safety is not given up easily by anyone at any time. It is normally cherished for as long as possible, unless the closeness itself activates too much of the fear of engulfment. Toward the end of therapy it is often necessary to insist firmly that patients give up this home, commonly the best one they have ever had, so that they can spend more time and energy making a real home for themselves in the world outside. By that time the emotional dependency upon the therapist has been essentially dissolved and replaced by a mutual relationship of equals.

8. Individual, Group, and Marathon Sessions

The relationship between a single patient and a therapist in many ways resembles the one that existed between the young child and its mother, and it is the basis for anything that ever happens in therapy. But the company of other humans in similar struggles has been found to be extremely useful in temporarily lessening irrational fear. Group members have repeated opportunities to observe others take emotionally frightening risks and survive. The real terror of the one who is taking another step is usually clearly evident to other group members present, and so is the profound relief and the sense of triumph at overcoming it. Proceeding in a similar path still remains exceedingly difficult but a little bit less terrifying than before.

Prospective patients do not know this and they commonly fear the possibility of being "exposed" in the group; they often wish to avoid or to delay their participation. Shame, a particular variant of the fear of abandonment, usually hovers about at such times, not as a remote possibility but as an immediate certainty of dread. This is usually dissipated soon after the patient enters the first group session. Even so, the group continues to be the setting that exerts the necessary pressure to experience what is subjectively known to be unsafe.

Strong emotional reactions are evoked by the existence, behavior, and words of group members and their therapists. Competition for the attention of the other members and the help of the therapists elicits preverbal hunger and its accompanying rage. Fear, envy and jealousy, hurt and anger, compassion and empathy, joy, sadness, and love are all unavoidable as personalities and situations bump into each other and reflect off each other. Even the differing requirements for distance and for closeness create ongoing tension and powerful mutual interactions. This is the setting in which emotional crises can be safely mobilized, powerfully experienced in the body, and consistently worked through. The one-to-one relationship with a therapist is almost totally ineffective for this purpose, since by nature it is supportive and mothering. But during group sessions, even real panic is repeatedly re-experienced and patiently resolved.

The specifications for the psychotherapy workshop are best met therefore by alternating individual and group therapy sessions. This combination repeatedly evokes irrational fears and other feelings very intensely in an environment which is known to be safe. Patients often flinch, but only rarely do they give up and leave.

Marathon sessions lasting for twenty-four hours or even longer, with only brief pauses for eating and resting, having twenty to twenty-five participating patients, and conducted by several therapists, are even more useful for challenging profound fears successfully. Although frightening at first, they are eventually experienced as even safer than the other two settings. (Such long sessions can only be held from time to time because of the great physical demands made upon those who must conduct them.) Patients often need a little time in each individual or group session to adjust before they are emotionally ready to proceed. They usually leave jobs and families to come for their sessions, and it is not always easy to suddenly switch tracks. Irrational and powerful yearnings—to be taken care of, for instance—are normally well hidden, since they obviously do not fit with adult living. They do not suddenly surface merely because one walks into a room where experiencing and expressing them is no longer regarded as taboo. The usual individual and group sessions are often too short.

Marathons are the only setting in which it is possible to undergo major episodes of controlled emotional regression, and also to experience new levels of competence and mastery over periods of many hours. Patients go further, deeper, and faster here in reliving and resolving some of their old pathologic distortions.

Ideally, the repair of defective personal boundaries could probably be achieved most effectively when attended to continuously without interruption till the job was done. The pressure could thus be kept up. But this is neither practical nor possible. The realities of existence require that relatively short sessions follow one another, with long non-therapy intervals in between. At least two to three days pass between sessions. The marathon is as close as one can come to meeting the ideal conditions for the necessary therapeutic work.

9. Cost Considerations

Outpatient psychotherapy that aims at curing the serious and lifelong illness of depression requires years of very hard work. The process will perhaps be shortened somewhat as our theoretical understanding and our technical skills improve, but it will never be something to be undertaken lightly. As it is, patients are usually expected to participate in individual and group sessions three times a week. Even so, it takes five to seven years, and occasionally longer, for the task to be essentially completed.

Nobody obtains a certificate of good health even then. The work of monitoring one's feelings and of attending to reality must continue throughout life, although the task becomes easier with time. Practically no effort is eventually required, and it happens almost automatically. The need to observe all of one's reactions constantly does not necessarily diminish spontaneity. On the contrary, the need for caution is lessened when the real pitfalls of living are seen quickly and with clarity. Continuous thoughtfulness and self-observation are the opposite of rumination and endless hesitation, with which they are sometimes confused. The dark clouds of worry disappear and life is really brighter and much easier when we fear only that which is real.

The monetary cost of therapy is always considerable because so much time is involved. It often appears as an impossible hurdle, especially to those too afraid of the task anyway. But the cost is a genuine hardship for most people, even if insurance companies or other third parties defray part of it. Yet giving up the chance to live without the crippling effects of panic just because the goal requires financial sacrifices is itself a hidden symptom of the illness that needs healing. People directly involved rarely see this connection.

Preposterous and unbelievable as it sounds at first, chronic financial hardship in the midst of reasonably affluent societies is one of the most prominent signs of depression. One's earning capacity often doubles and even triples when depression's heavy weight is finally lifted. Those who have the get-up-and-go to start therapy in spite of the real monetary strain usually discover that the difficulties lessen with time; their ability to care for themselves, financially and otherwise, almost always improves before long. They commonly increase their skills, change their employment, get promoted, and otherwise exercise their competence much more than before.

People who still believe in the power of the intellect to rescue them from their emotional turmoil may hear such statements as a shrill and self-serving promotion of a therapist. But life and health are indeed worth any monetary sacrifice, and these are really at stake, even if physical death is not imminent. Relatively poor students and young people without advanced training sometimes hold two and three jobs to pay for therapy. They consider the effort hard but not excessive, considering what is involved. They may not know why Hemingway killed himself or why the Duke of Windsor lived the way he did, but everyone has seen many others in deep trouble, and most people know their own pain and torture. Those who chance upon a therapist able to help them generally hold on, even when it requires extreme personal sacrifices. What is a reasonable price tag for enjoying "a sense of personal mastery . . . [and] real power . . . [that comes from being] self-sufficient, psychologically and otherwise"?

Ideally, health should have no price tag at all. We should enjoy its blessings for free. But in practice someone must always pay for anything, not only in capitalist but also in socialist and communist societies. Although a cliché by now, there really is no free lunch. Workers expect to be paid for their efforts, or the work does not get done. Individuals naturally prefer to shift the burden away from themselves, but at best this will probably be possible only in part.

No society anywhere is rich enough to provide each of its citizens who needs it with the kind of intensive therapy that is described here. Some financial contribution and personal effort will probably always be required from everyone seeking it. This is also clinically desirable. Shouldering at least some of the financial burden involved is an important aspect of becoming self-sufficient. Nobody "outside the self can forever provide warmth, comforting, assurance, and nutrition." Weaning is really inevitable and unavoidable. "Like it or not, . . . [Man] was commanded to eat his bread by the sweat of his brow." Since almost everyone has a need for competent help at one time or another, not enough well-qualified therapists are ever likely to exist, even if the financial resources were available.

10. The Urgent Need for More Competent Therapists and What Limits Their Number

The work of individuated therapists is hard and the hours long, but their lives are much more than merely interesting. Because their days are full of that which most people seek and never have enough of, meaningful human contact, they are richly rewarded for their efforts. Nothing in the cocktail or dinner-party circuit is comparable to it; no theater play comes close in drama to what happens routinely in therapy rooms in which this type of work is done. Here is a continual chance to be deeply involved in the heroic struggles of many good people , to witness dead eyes being rekindled, and to help awaken a vitality that seemed already extinguished. There will always be more patients in need of good therapy than competent therapists able to offer it. The field is wide open, and the opportunities for earning a good living practically unlimited. Why is there yet no rush into it?

Because potential therapists, like other people, are also crippled by fear. It must be overcome before this work is possible. But no one is eager to rush into surgery, especially of the psychological kind. Psychiatrists and psychotherapists can earn a decent living even without facing themselves and their emotional limitations. Like other people, students of psychiatry, psychology, and social work also try to avoid frightening situations. They too fear entering the haunted house. Most have never been in any therapy, but even if they have, only very few are free of irrational fear. They usually are sincere, dedicated, and well-meaning young men and women who probably studied with teachers who tried to evade fear by denying its existence.

Sophisticated people usually "manage" their fear and handle its horrors by the use of denial and intellectualization. Like their teachers, these students will eventually become experts, they will "see" patients, write articles, and publish books; and they will deliver learned lectures explaining the behavior of people and their motivation. But for most, the physiologic reactions to anxiety will continue to be exactly like those of anyone else. As therapists they will quickly burn out. They will become teachers and administrators as soon as they can. To become healers, those entering this field must be healed first.

Many established psychiatrists and non-medical psychotherapists admit openly that they are disappointed and emotionally very tired after a few short years of unrewarding work, "bored," discouraged, and drained by their professional efforts. Their lives are strained with self-doubt. Even their most sincere efforts being them very little satisfaction or enjoyment. They sense that something is not right, but they cannot correct it. This would require a complete overhaul of their personal lives and of their professional practices. Their status, self-esteem, and income might all be threatened by such a radical change. An unusual measure of courage and integrity is required to objectively assess the value of new ideas that might affect them adversely. Most have no choice but to continue living and practicing as before.

Graduates of medical and other professional schools just entering this field are more fortunate. It is much easier for them to change personally in preparation for this exciting work. They have less at stake in things as they are. As in the biblical days of Moses, only the next generation, the one not accustomed to the slavery of Egypt and not addicted to its dubious blessings, has a chance to really become free.

What a therapist is as a person, not only what he or she does, is of the utmost importance. The equivalent of the scalpel in surgery, therapists cannot be defective without harming their patients. They are the instrument that largely determines the outcome. No therapist can ever challenge fears in a patient that have not already been resolved within the challenger.

Besides the reluctance to risk facing one's fear, a real obstacle must be surmounted on the way to becoming personally individuated and professionally competent. Relatively few therapists are available to help others go through this process. This shortage is a very narrow bottleneck that both regular patients and future therapists will have to squeeze through, if they can.

11. Using This Chapter as a Guide to Therapy

Seriously depressed individuals with disturbed marriages and suicidal children, alcoholics, drug addicts, pathologic gamblers, insomniacs, and those suffering from phobias and a variety of disabling psychosomatic complaints or sexual difficulties are regularly being treated now by non-licensed and often non-qualified professionals and non-professionals. So are people who are a little less seriously troubled. Without anyone looking over their shoulders to insure that the patient does not get hurt, even students and bachelor degree holders in psychology and in social work are plowing the marketplace. Over 450 different forms of so-called psychotherapy are now available in the U.S., and their practitioners eagerly hawk their wares. The distressed and "perplexed seeker of help" mentioned in the Introduction faces a plethora of helpers, usually without knowing whether their many claims make any sense, and without any tools to find out which do. How does one choose? It is really much easier to find a good physician for even the rarest of physical illnesses than competent help for the serious emotional difficulties that are so common. It makes no sense, but unfortunately it is true.

Most states, including New York, have no minimum legal requirements and no standards for the practice of psychotherapy. Anyone can call himself a psychotherapist, advertise, and solicit patients. Many sincere housewives, nurses, counselors, ministers, rabbis, salesmen, even masseuses and other "free-lancers" who took a psychology course or two, as well as many psychotherapy ex-patients, simply imitate what they saw or try what they read about. Recent graduates from schools of social work without any additional clinical experience often just fix up their basement and begin "treating" some of those who need help. Since such "therapists" do not charge too much and sometimes even collect their fees from insurance carriers, they find people interested in their services. Those with a master's degree are already beyond question; they consider themselves experts and look for "clients."

Worse yet, the majority of psychiatrists, psychologists, and family physicians who counsel patients are also not competent to administer more than psychologic first aid. But this hardly deters anyone. While some do commendable work, many have not much more to offer than kindness, reassurance, and a pill. But since a much larger army of barely trained incompetents is also operating out there, feeding off the despair of others, the help of such professionals is understandably most welcome.

The reason for the enormous growth in the number of "therapists" is obvious: Millions seek help, and the government and insurance companies are willing to pay for much if it. The number of therapists has therefore more than doubled in the last few years, and in the U.S. it now stands at over 140,000. Some are attracted by the chance to make an easy dollar, but most are hardworking, honest, and well-meaning. Too much in fact; they often overidentify with their "clients." Basically, many have only their goodwill and their good intentions to offer. In acute despair, even these can help, but not much. A recent *New York Times Magazine* article ("Navigating the Therapy Maze," August 30, 1987) states that "one American in three has been in psychotherapy, and in 1987, 15 million of us will make roughly 120 million visits to mental health professionals—nearly twice as many visits as to internists." The problem is immense, and so is the confusion.

Most people do not know what they need, and they do not know how to check the quality of what they are about to receive. The all-important choices about therapy are usually made blindly, almost totally by chance. Psychoanalysis and weekend retreats, drugs and prayer, brief and longer therapies, all lower the anxiety for a while. So do work therapy and weaving baskets, dance therapy, music therapy, climbing mountains or riding horses, meditation, medications, screaming, and silent introspection. These are all being offered as cures. The confusion and despair are such that they all find some willing takers. The *New York Times* article mentions the Yellow Pages as a possible source for finding a therapist, but this obviously is not a good solution. A therapist must be trusted not only with one's secrets and health but often with life itself.

This chapter is usable as a yardstick and as a guide. The general requirements of a therapeutic system that works have been outlined. To the extent that these principles make sense to the reader, they can be used to assess the claims of others. Understanding the basic illness and the essentials of a therapeutic approach to overcome it allows the reader to ask at least some of the right questions. Less time, money, hope, and life might be wasted as a result.

Here are a few practical suggestions that might be helpful in choosing a therapist.

WHAT TO OBSERVE

1. What is the therapist's demeanor? Is he or she self-respectful? How are you addressed as a human being? How does the office look, and what is the therapist's personal appearance and dress? Is the therapist careful with your time, and is he or she comfortable or uncomfortable and apologetic in discussing compensation for his or her time?

2. Does the therapist make eye contact and human contact?

Is the therapist too formal, too rigid, too aloof, or too cool, or on the other hand, too loose, too friendly, too eager to please, or too much of a buddy? Either way is bad.

3. How sensitive is the therapist? Can he or she really hear you, see you, understand you beyond your words?

4. How emotionally healthy is the therapist? Is he or she more or less of normal weight? Does he or she seem comfortable in general, and specifically in the body? Does the therapist seem preoccupied or present, well- or ill-kempt? Does he or she convey an air of inner peace, or is he or she jumpy and fidgety? Does the therapist smoke? This usually is a sure sign of much anxiety. Is he or she talking too much, or too little?

5. Depending on the age and sex of the therapist, does he or she seem comfortable with his or her position in life and with his or her sexual orientation, as evidenced in behavior and in manner? Especially if you are of the opposite sex, is the therapist too friendly, or hostile? Male chauvinists and women's liberationists are driven by their own agendas. Both males and females are likely to be confused by them, each in a different way.

WHAT TO ASK

1. What are the therapist's formal credentials? Should all therapists have had therapy? Has he or she?

2. What does the therapist believe is wrong with you?

3. What is the plan for your therapy, and what is his or her goal? How does he or she normally go about getting there? How long does therapy usually last?

4. Does the therapist see patients only briefly, only individually, only in groups, only on the couch, or only face-to-face? Is one preferred over the others? If so, why? If not, why not?

5. What is the therapist's position about your getting angry in sessions, or hurt, or feeling and expressing love?

Listen not only to what they say, but also to how they say it, and how they react. How clear is their thinking? How well do they understand what they are doing? How anxious or impatient do they get because you wish to know so much?

For valid reasons, many therapists will not talk about themselves and prefer not to reveal some personal details. They may wish to leave room for your fantasies about them. But you are fully entitled to have answers to most questions of this nature, at least the five above. See how they handle your questioning attitude, even if they believe that some of your questions should not be answered. Do they seem too eager to answer every question, or do they stubbornly refuse to address practically all of them? Neither is a good sign.

WHAT TO WATCH FOR

Everything that is happening in therapy should be under your continued observation. What therapists say is less important than what they are and what they do over time. Young and relatively inexperienced therapists may be ill at ease at the very beginning but may turn out to be solid human beings able to help you. The real characteristics of people show better with time. Sometimes two or three sessions are needed for you to know, but in any event most answers to all these questions ought to become clear after a few weeks. Continue only if the relationship makes sense.

Do not trust the therapist blindly, never accept his or her words on faith, but never discard them out of hand. Feelings often interfere. With time, some things that at first make no sense become easier to see and easier to accept.

You do not necessarily have to like the therapist, either at first or later on, but you must respect him or her. Liking or disliking a therapist is not a good basis for making a choice. Therapists must sometimes say or do things that are frightening, unpleasant, or painful. Occasionally they may seem out-and-out wrong. Take time to evaluate such situations. Do not trust your quick responses; they usually reflect emotional reactions. Fear of not finding a better therapist should not be a reason for staying, and resentment should not in itself be a cause for leaving. Consider the real qualities of the therapist as a person, his or her competence, and the degree of commitment to the task.

Finally, you may wish to refer back to the earlier sections of this chapter from time to time. Once in therapy, they may appear to have new meanings, giving you an even greater ability to evaluate what you find.

SEVEN

Notes on the Future
of the West

Never has a man who has bent himself been able to make others stand straight.

MENCIUS

For barbarism is always around civilization, amid it and beneath it, ready to engulf it by arms, or mass migration, or unchecked fertility. Barbarism is like the jungle; it never admits its defeat; it waits patiently for centuries to recover the territory it has lost.

WILL DURANT
The Story of Civilization, I

Excessive fat and feasting without exercise and with an insistence upon remaining comfortable and always at rest cause occlusion of life-sustaining blood vessels not only in individuals. Societies that regularly shun taking necessary risks also stagnate and become calcified. They lose their agility and their capacity to respond to disease as well as to danger, and they die.

CHAPTER 8, SECTION 96

The future welfare of our Western civilization, like that of each individual, is also dependent upon our success in breaking the oppressive hold that hidden feelings have on us. So far we are only politically free. In many other ways, our hands are tied. This is dangerous, since the West is under attack both from within and without. Our success is unparalleled in the history of Man, and our way of life is therefore the envy of many, but this hardly guarantees it a long and secure existence.

259

We in the West have the highest standard of living ever, our spirit has room to soar and our creativity to flourish. We have developed a rich variety of life-styles. Moreover, our abundance is not merely the lot of a few chosen people but of a large majority of the population in our societies. But Man's nature is such that he takes his blessings for granted and always wants more. So promises for more are regularly made in democracies at election time, thus forever raising the level of expectations. These have become so high by now that they are not usually fulfillable. "Powerful storms of hurt and rage are [then] unleashed. . . . Throughout history they have sparked revolutions and wars and caused the disappearance of the most advanced societies. . . . Cynicism about the political process . . . represents only a small part of the damage that is inevitable when such promises are made and then violated."

As a result, many young Americans, Germans, Scandinavians, and others live in perpetual disappointment with a sense that they have been cheated and wronged, and they are ever ready to protest, demand, and strike. The roots of such disappointment are really personal, but most people are not aware of this and express it in the political process. They often feel no gratitude for their affluence and for their many freedoms—to be, to do, to believe, and to express themselves. They regard their many opportunities to pursue a higher education and a career as a birthright and are bitter about having to contribute anything in effort or money. Hostile and self-righteous, they are often disloyal, disruptive, and disrespectful of the rights and property of others.

Such attitudes are rather common these days, and not only among the young. Just about everybody, rich as well as poor, has persistent wishes for a better, fuller, easier, happier, and more satisfying life. This is how the hidden and relatively unknown "preverbal hunger" shows itself. "Having more . . . does not satisfy the yearnings for more, which are irrational." These yearnings have such deep roots within us that their power is awesome. They take over, once legitimized by social acceptance, and then they blind people to their real blessings and good fortune.

Affluence and relative security have always been effective sedatives for societies that have reached the blissful state of maturity. We wake up then only at times of crisis, when international flights are hijacked, when hostages are taken or murdered, when car bombs explode, wars erupt, or widespread rioting occurs. Even at such times people act according to type. Editorial writers and commentators rebuke; policymakers point out the complexities of the situation; we bury the dead and sympathize with their families; we help the survivors express their disgust, anger, or fear; we discuss the merits of alternate policies—and go on with our business as usual. As soon as a crisis passes and we no longer react emotionally, we forget it and return to our comfortable existence. Usually nothing changes.

The danger from within is even greater than that posed by outside enemies. They just exploit our tendencies to delude ourselves, to live according to how we feel, and to "follow the path of least resistance." We tend to deny the existence of unpleasant and dangerous realities, expecting them simply to pass with time, as they often do. Still very powerful and very rich, the West has enough reserves to survive this way for a while, but not for very long. The next century will look altogether different if we continue to be the way we are.

Terrorists and totalitarian regimes already give us clear indications of the kind of life to expect once our traditional Western values are lost. Genocide is not only permissible but common. They even practice it against "undesirable elements" of their own people, such as intellectuals who are more difficult to tame, teachers, political activists, ethnic minorities, and "infidels." The Khmer Rouge systematically exterminated one to two million of their own Cambodian people after the U.S. left Indochina, almost a third of the population of what is now known as Kampuchea. Men were grotesquely hanging from trees everywhere. Suffocation in plastic bags was standard punishment for breaking the work rules. And all this supposedly to "educate" the Cambodians, for their own good.

The Ethiopian Marxist-Leninists killed and imprisoned tens of thousands of their skilled workers and students, the potential resistance. Their "Armed Forces Coordinating Committee" denied relief to the 500,000 starving people in Eritrea, and convoys trying to bring help to the dying were attacked from the air. Fearing moves by the Ethiopian government that would jeopardize other relief operations, the U.S. abandoned as "impractical" a plan to provide 200,000 tons of supplies that were to feed as many as three million famine victims.

Mass starvation is an established policy of the Soviet Union in Afghanistan. So is deliberate trickery that causes whole villages to suddenly abandon their houses and fields and flee in panic. The Chinese "emptied" entire regions of their Tibetan inhabitants. But even now, several decades after occupation, the push for independence and freedom persists and hundreds of Buddhist monks and others are beaten and jailed.

Iranian revolutionary guards have shot 50,000 people in the dark of night after summary trials since June 1981. Most of Khomeini's estimated 140,000 prisoners were and are reportedly being subjected to torture and to cruelties normally beyond the human imagination. In 323 official and secret prisons, men, women, and even children are flogged, burned, electrically shocked, and mutilated. People have been kept blindfolded for many months in tiny isolated cages or coffins and otherwise tormented by over 4,000 professional torturers who compete with each other in bestiality. Teachers were taken out of classrooms and shot in front of their pupils. Many of the condemned, unable to stand or walk, are carried to their place of execution on stretchers. The Baha'i religion and its believers were altogether eliminated. What the Iranians are already doing to their own people they will surely do to their number-one enemy, the U.S., and other Western countries if they ever get the chance.

We live in the same world with all these regimes, and with others not much better. Most people here do not yet realize that the direct and indirect attacks upon Western societies and values are not independent occurrences but links in a chain of destruction. An undeclared state of war has already been imposed upon us, and it slowly but steadily bleeds us and weakens our strength and our resolve to fight back. Western economies and institutions are not in any immediate danger, but the decline has begun. It stops, or we and all our values fall, soon to disappear.

This war is not only undeclared but also fought by proxy, by terror, by arming gangs of confused youths, by inciting and training local armies, and by helping religious fanatics to avenge real and imaginary grievances. The more of those the better. Third World juntas are recruited by giving them arms on credit and political protection. Moral scruples are ignored. A cooperating Idi Amin or Qaddafi is a desirable bedfellow. The West is subjected to consistent military harassment, systematic thievery of industrial secrets and military technologies, deceit, disinformation, and distribution of hard drugs. The Soviets regularly ignore copyright laws and other international agreements such as the Helsinki conventions, and by now we have even stopped protesting. What's the point, some say, since we have no power to control these outlaws anyway. Besides, more urgent issues, such as nuclear disarmament, need our attention.

Fear, confusion, and internal discord render us vulnerable, and they are all fomented by design. Nothing is sacred or forbidden. Even the fact that a total war is being waged must be concealed and denied for as long as possible. The slumbering and naive giant is best left undisturbed until he is too weak to resist. Conciliatory gestures and words often help to confuse the decent but innocent populations of the West. We tend to believe others; even the idea of purposely designing national policies to deceive is foreign to most of us. Cunning, trickery, and lies are all successfully used to chip away at our sense of morality and decency. The Soviet propaganda machine regularly magnifies our self-criticisms and takes them out of proportion, inundating us with them till we seem like true villains to ourselves. Totalitarian regimes and terrorists know that the greater our disorder, our bewilderment, our distrust, our uncertainty, and our self-doubt, the better for them.

Because we are so much the prisoners of our feelings we are often quite ineffective in dealing with chronic internal lawlessness and with international terror. None of the Western societies has a chance of winning in the long run, unless we change course. We have sufficient understanding now to enable us to do so while there is still time. International terror is the focus of much of our attention in this chapter, but the same principles also apply to the war that must be waged against the internal disrespect for and disregard of the rule of law.

1. The Root Problem: The Dictatorship of Feelings

The West's political and economic establishment is full of internal contradictions, which its outside enemies and the discontented inside focus on and try to exploit. The fact that justice is not yet equally available to all is a pet complaint used to condemn the system as a whole. They deliberately ignore the wisdom that Winston Churchill summarized so well: "The inherent vice of capitalism is the unequal sharing of blessings; the inherent virtue of socialism is the equal sharing of miseries." They also disregard Aristotle's wise observation that the shortcomings of democracy arise out of the mistaken notion that "those who are equal in any respect are equal in all respects, [or] because men are equally free they claim to be absolutely equal."

Structurally weak, flawed by its very nature, battered by the self-indulgence of its citizens and by their incessant demands, the West is nonetheless the envy of the Third World and totalitarian regimes. Not just a geographic concept (the western half of the earth as distinguished from the Orient) but a point of view, the West stands for a system of government in which the individual, not the state, is supreme. It consists of the technologically advanced societies of Western Europe and the Americas that are run according to democratic principles, with a constitutional form of government based on the consent of the governed, and with economies that make substantial room for at least a modified form of free enterprise.

NATO narrowly overlaps the political nucleus of the West. To it should be added other states in Europe and the Middle and Far East, such as Switzerland, Israel, Japan, Taiwan, South Korea, and others that normally align themselves politically, economically, and morally with these principles.

The term "free societies" is used here synonymously with "the West," but the freedom of the individual in such free societies is not absolute. This would be anarchy. No orderly society can function without some limitations on freedom, though many immature, innocent, ignorant, or indulgent individuals experience even the most reasonable limitations as a gross injustice.

The freedom of free societies consists of Man's right to believe or not to believe in any value system, to move, to emigrate, to be safe from harassment by the authorities, to associate with others, to speak his or her mind, and to elect his government. The supreme power rests with the people. They elect and they can remove those who rule them. But even this freedom is limited, for elections only take place at guaranteed intervals or under certain specific conditions. Although legally guaranteed, many of these freedoms are routinely abused, misused, or simply not used. Even in free societies, Man's freedom is usually severely limited by inner shackles that constrain him and never let go.

A full-blown nuclear war is not likely to break out, because it would not bring victory to anyone. But the patient and clever seeding of self-doubt can paralyze the West and eventually destroy it. This is why the Soviet Union is actively and systematically spreading disinformation and outright lies about us, and why Iran, Libya, Cuba, and others are financing and training terrorists. They regularly try to embarrass us politically and to damage us economically as well as militarily. The aim is to rob us of pride and to break our spirit. They have long-term goals.

Even if it takes several decades, or longer, the West should eventually collapse from within. Both Islam and Marxism think in terms of centuries, and both explicitly state that their victories are historically inevitable. Everything, including the occasional warming up of relations or the goodwill created by *glasnost*, is meant to serve this long-term goal.

The totalitarian regimes on the left and on the right are not always equally virulent; at times they share common interests with us and are eager to cooperate. But neither fundamentalist Islam nor Marxist Communism can co-exist with a system in which the individual is free to choose. Although they basically have opposing points of view, the two are often tactically allied. Potentially enemies of each other, the anti-West activity of one in practice advances the interests of the other. Such regimes *must* attempt to destablize us and to highlight our shortcomings because we are a glaring alternative that is generally much more attractive to their populations. As long as they must co-exist with free societies in which the lot of the average citizen is so much better, their own continued existence is always in doubt.

Every defector to the West from behind the Iron Curtain or from the Islamic gulag is a reminder to totalitarian rulers of the need to destroy us. Very few people defect to them. The outcome of the current war against us is yet unclear, but in the past mature societies have usually failed in confrontations with young and muscular regimes. These are not bound by civilized codes and have no scruples about using brute force and cruel methods to achieve their goals. Civilized people call such methods "inhuman," but since humans perpetrate them, we cannot easily think of the perpetrators as vermin to be destroyed in self-defense.

We are free from the Marxist dictatorship of the proletariat, from the dictatorship of mullahs, and from the dictatorship of poverty and starvation that chokes most of Africa and much of the Third World. But the dictatorship of feelings is as real and at least as oppressive and destructive as the others. Fear limits our freedom to think clearly, to act rationally, and to choose what is best for us. It forces us to speak lines that often make no sense and to live lives that are full of self-deception, loneliness, and hurt. Worse yet, fear often forces us to take political positions that are likely to lead to the eventual destruction of our civilization and our way of life.

Only now are we beginning to recognize the existence of this dictatorship of feelings, and this explains why we have not yet mounted a reasonable defense against it. We must think and consider what we do, yet the ability to think cannot simply be learned. It only grows slowly when sufficiently exercised as we continue to wrestle with our feelings. We can enjoy the freedoms that are potentially ours in free societies only after we are able to be thoughtful.

Democracies would never be in serious danger if their citizens stood tall, each a free man and woman. But as it is, they at least need political leaders who steadily point them in the right direction. These are very rare, which puts our free societies in great jeopardy. An unreasonable and unchecked drive for self-advancement all too often determines how our leaders conduct our affairs. They frequently take ludicrous positions that make sense only in the realm of feelings, but still they find some support for them. A coalition of powerful interest groups sometimes coalesces around some such emotionally charged issue, and like a cancer it then burrows into the marrow of Western vitality. Many controversies that sap the strength of our societies exist mainly because they relieve personal fear, anger, or pain.

Man makes very few choices independent of his wish to "avoid re-experiencing the panic he had to endure early in life." This is why "without courageous leadership, majorities will always be shaped by fear and policies determined by caution." The situation is even worse now because "the primitive and immature nature of individuals finds wider expression . . . in the West['s] . . . more permissive societies. In such settings, the concept of democracy" is often distorted, making room for irresponsible action. Diogenes the Cynic said it well, over 2,300 years ago. When asked what the proper time was for supper he said, "If you are a rich man, whenever you please; and if you are a poor man, whenever you can."

Difficult decisions must often be postponed in democracies, and when irrational fear has been fanned they cannot be made at all. But even under normal conditions it is extremely difficult to reach consensus in a free society when the goals require sacrifice, involve hardships, or evoke fear. Every citizen has the right to object, and the lowest common denominator usually prevails, unless wise and bold leadership changes the course. "Self-indulgence . . . typifies much public and private behavior . . . [since] self-restraint and individual responsibility" are needed less now for survival. Thomas Carlyle claimed long ago that "Democracy is, by the nature of it, a self-cancelling business."

The opposite holds true in highly structured totalitarian societies. Here the population is forced "to act in maturelike modes that . . . limit irresponsible action . . . at least in public." Law and order can be enforced much more easily, since nobody has the right to legally challenge measures that they object to. This happens routinely in the West, and efficient law enforcement is often crippled.

Bureaucratic rigidity, populist politcal rhetoric, consumerism, corruption, and the fight for racial and sex equality have all combined to produce angry individuals who believe they have been taken advantage of. Seeing themselves as powerless, they also feel much fear, like so many others who experience their old vulnerability and dread when law and order seem to be breaking down. Everyone was helpless once, early in life, and that was more than enough. The orderliness that is part of the strictness of oppression suddenly looks more attractive. Totalitarian regimes claim to have achieved perfect justice and they have indeed "markedly reduced street crime," so a few confused people are drawn to them. "One way to preserve oneself is to trade independence for protection." To justify their position and to make it more honorable they use the slogan "Red is better than dead." The attraction of "a clever and determined 'Big Brother' who offers protection in return for obedience usually meets little resistance" when fear is great, and he "has wide appeal, at least for a while."

Since "irrational fear is given no room to influence public policy" in totalitarian regimes, some naive Western idealizers do not see their real weaknesses and claim that fear has been eliminated in their imaginary paradise. Such innocents are often happy to serve as spies who cause severe damage to their societies, sometimes even without an internal struggle. The Walker family spy ring in the U.S. and the many high-ranking officials in Great Britain and in West Germany are good examples. Greed is hardly ever a sufficient explanation for such deeds; one must first be blinded to the real blessings of a life in freedom.

2. The Basis of Civilized Existence

Civilization is based upon the principle that the life, space, rights, and property of every person must not be arbitrarily violated. If this simple rule were adhered to strictly, peace and the absense of crime and friction would result, and no need would exist for either police or courts of law. Such an idyllic situation has never existed in the past, nor is it likely in the future, because the personal boundaries of most people are ill-defined. A person is frequently unable to sense "clearly where he begins and where he ends, what is internal and what is external." As a result, people frequently make claims on rights, property, and life space that others also claim. Overlapping expectations breed conflict and dispute, sometimes resulting in criminal acts. But even if the cause is confusion about one's rights, crimes must still be curbed and the offenders penalized. Yet such people pose no danger to the civilized order. They live within the law in principle, even when they break it in practice.

But others in society are not willing or able to live by any law that limits them and interferes with their impulsive wishes. They break the laws of civilized existence without compunction or guilt, whenever they "feel like it" and can. They are known as psychopaths, but more normal people who are extremely narcissistic also act this way at times, although to a much lesser extent. Basically, all these people live by the law of the jungle. Might alone, not right, limits them. When they commit crimes they are against humanity and against the civilized order itself, even if only one person gets hurt. Genocide begins as a point of view. The rest of society cannot live in a civilized manner unless it finds ways to restrain them.

A major reason why our judicial and penal systems are failing is that the basic differences that exist between people committing similar offenses are not understood, and therefore are completely overlooked. An effective system for one group is often insufficient for the other, yet we have only one code that applies to all. Everyone is equal under the law, which makes sense, since we assume that all people are created equal. We allow for mitigating circumstances but have never made provisions for the fact that people make themselves unequal, once created. Some err, others become habitually destructive. Inconsistencies and tragedies abound, and justice is very often poorly served. The issue is even clearer internationally; not all disputes can be settled peacefully on the basis of fairness. An incorrect and delusional view of Man has gotten in our way, and it leads us repeatedly into trouble.

Civilized societies do not yet have satisfactory guidelines to protect themselves from those who repeatedly challenge the rule of law, often violently. This is at the bottom of our vulnerability. The social contract that Jean-Jacques Rousseau believed to be the basis of civilization has been weakened because we increasingly tolerate non-adherence to it when the excuse is good enough. Some who are especially bitter for not having whatever they wish use this sense of having been cheated as a reason to disavow the rule of law altogether. For such people we need a second and separate system of compliance with the basic tenets of civilization, to protect our lives, our institutions, and our values. They refuse to be bound by any contract, social or otherwise. We must obviously be extremely careful and thoughtful so that in correcting our system we do not destroy it. No one must be abused. We can begin by recognizing the need for change.

Banding together for the protection of the civilized order demands that we submit to a unified command. This is extremely frightening to those who sense power mostly as a potential for abuse, perhaps the majority of all people. "The most dreadful sense of danger [is often associated] with the experience of powerlessness . . . [since] everyone's earliest experience consisted of being subjected to the will of others, more powerful than oneself." Quite naturally, people are reluctant to hand over any of their individual rights to anyone, even to the society of which they are part, insisting instead on maintaining as much individual control over power as possible. The need for a common defense is often minimized as a result, or even ignored altogether. The fear of being abused individually is sometimes responsible for people being destroyed together.

Overidentification with lawbreakers stems from the same fear of being abused. If orderly societies are to survive, those who violate their laws must be apprehended, held responsible, and penalized. But when we see ourselves in the offenders, the mere idea touches our sense of powerlessness. Many people have this experience, and as societies we have therefore been overly sensitive to protect the rights of the accused, and not sensitive enough to those of the victims. Having already been victimized, we know the damage done to them, and this limits our fantasies and lessens our anxiety.

3. The Law of the Jungle

Disputes are resolved simply in the jungle, by the use of brute force. Large animals eat smaller and weaker ones if they can catch them. Physical strength, speed, agility, and cunning are all forms of power in nature; but with the special abilities developed with the help of our new mammalian brain we overcame our shortcomings and learned to dominate them all. Natural selection insures that only the fittest survive, those who learn quickly how to do so. The others perish. Since nature does not abide by Man's morality and does not provide special protection to those who are superior by our standards, some of the surviving species eat their young and many of the others are among the most cruel to their prey. Moral man would have ordered the universe differently, but he had no power to enforce a more humane system on anyone. So he merely observed the unjustified suffering and wondered about God's ways.

Like all creatures, we humans exist in nature, which follows the law of the jungle. From it we have diligently tried ever since the dawn of human history to carve out a small part for our civilized existence, and we have succeeded marvelously in our efforts. But barbarism and the jungle remain all around us and they quickly take over when we relax our vigilance even for a little while. All the achievements of our Western civilization can quickly disappear and become no more than interesting relics from a forgotten past, like Mayan ruins. This is exactly what happened to many other societies, also very successful in their day.

Those living among us but outside the laws of civilization quickly take over any space they can dominate, just as cancer cells push other cells aside and take their place. This happens in interpersonal and international relationships. Khomeini's Iran is the most obvious current example of the latter. We must protect ourselves from such humans exactly as we do from a cancer, an invading bacterial attack, or locusts. We cannot, and obviously should not, simply exterminate all humans who threaten the civilized order; we must find less radical ways to control and to contain them. But in the last analysis, any and all means must be used to overcome them if we want to insure not being overcome by them.

Yet how can society coerce, isolate, or neutralize those who violate its laws without becoming uncivilized? How can it limit the rights of some without threatening the human rights of all? How can civilized people execute even outlaws, terrorists, and murderers without condoning murder itself? All flourishing societies of the past, not having understood these issues and Man's nature well enough, failed to answer these questions effectively. They have been either too lenient and permissive or too harsh and repressive. Either way, they soon found themselves more vulnerable. Before long they were destroyed.

We are in a position to do better because we see more clearly into Man than others before us; we can predict more accurately how people will act, and therefore can at least try to change that which is not compatible with our survival. Much change is needed. In the relative comfort of life far removed from the jungle we have forgotten many of our survival skills. Our need to remain constantly alert was sharply reduced, and we lost our acuity; we live by more forgiving standards, wishing to be less like the beasts around us; we take much pride in our refinement, our compassion, and our sensitivity. We even taught our young that conscious self-sacrifice may sometimes be preferable to a life of dishonor, and that some principles have a value greater than life. This wish to ennoble ourselves beyond our animalistic nature distinguishes us, in fact, as unique. We have learned the value of compromise and of finding merit even in the positions of those with whom we disagree.

This preference for living on a higher moral ground has become such an important feature of modern Western man, and so important a source of his pride, that he is usually unable to separate himself from it. He finds it very difficult to give it up even when it seriously threatens his continued existence. Immobilized in the jungle by our moral nobility, we cite the laws of the civilized order to those who tear at us like packs of mad dogs, wishing our demise. It is not only naive but also very dangerous; they become more vicious when they see us without a stick.

We are poor fighters against beasts. We value every life highly; they do not. We wish to save our humanity and refuse to become brutal; they use our refinement against us. Most police departments advise law-abiding citizens against arming themselves. They are said to be better off without a gun. In a confrontation with an armed intruder such people usually hesitate just a bit too long and get killed. But as the guardians of our civilization we cannot afford to take such a risk. Lying down, belly up, is hardly a good recommendation for survival in the jungle. Those who do so usually get eaten up very quickly.

We in the West must change and accept the need to fight the war that was imposed on us, or recognize that soon we will have to surrender unconditionally and give up everything that is dear to us. Sadly we must adjust ourselves to living in a world in which it is necessary at times to relinquish some of our most cherished qualities. We do not want to fight like animals in the wild. We want peace. We believe in decency and in justice. These have been our convictions for so long that by now many of us are no longer willing to take up arms to uphold even what we always valued the most: living by the rule of law. We yield quickly to fear, compromise too easily, and too much. Socially as individuals, and politically at home and abroad, we rarely stand up for what we believe is right. Doing so raises our anxiety. We have even begun to pick and choose our values and to adjust our behavior to minimize confrontations. Beating a retreat is no longer so shameful.

Even though we renounced the law of the jungle long ago, others still live by it. We can blind ourselves to this fact and become their prey, or we must learn to fight them off. This may require that we use the same cruel and inhuman tactics that they do, for nothing less is effective in the jungle. Only a quick response with a pitchfork might save us from a poisonous snake that is about to strike. We wish it were not necessary for us to kill, but it is. Even if we win the battle against barbarism, we lose something: some of our human refinement, our greatest achievement. But if we refuse to fight, we no doubt will loose everything. We cannot clean up an infestation without at least dirtying our hands. For a while we will not be as pure as we would prefer to be.

Man usually tries to evade the pain and fear involved in making such difficult decisions by avoiding the issues for as long as possible, usually making things worse. Obviously, no problem ever disappears just because we look the other way. We must try to preserve our humanity even as we reluctantly sacrifice our commitment to the sixth commandment and sponsor selective murder and assassination. If we fail in either, both civilization and the rule of law are lost. This is the unavoidable danger that wars and barbarism impose on civilized men and women.

Cunning, treachery, trickery, and big lies are being used to humiliate, weaken, and eventually destroy the West. We cannot successfully fight such enemies while scrupulously adhering to our legal and moral constrictions. Even though cunning is not free of deception, we too must use it in self-defense, internationally no less than domestically. We too may want to lull the enemy by false assurances before we attack him. We will hopefully react with a sense of angry revulsion against the idea, but do it anyway, since it is necessary.

Cunning always was and still is Man's tool for mastering others in nature. All hunting and fishing, by Man as well as by other species, is essentially based upon it. Even in the civilized order we sometimes use cunning when we look for a mate or jockey for position, although we like to pretend otherwise. But intellectually sophisticated and affluent Western man has lost much of his raw ability to be cunning. He has become soft and naive, and his ability to assess reality has been impaired. Seeing the world through idealizing eyes, he even ascribes the good qualities he admires in himself to confirmed murderers, terrorists, and thieves. He insists on being "fair" to them. He paroles and pardons them even after they have repeatedly proved themselves to be unworthy of forgiveness, living outside the civilized order. Like a good child, he believes every sweet-talking stranger.

A convicted mass murderer known for cruelly torturing and then executing his victims was interviewed recently and spoke softly to a national television audience, just before he was put to death; a storm of support immediately erupted. Close to a hundred people stood vigil in protest in front of the prison gate all night. This is the power of feelings! Any superficial human gesture is accepted as solid proof of basic human decency and of adherence to the civilized order. But even ayatollahs love their children. If an Andropov liked jazz, then he must have been like one of us, a "good guy" to be trusted. Since Raisa Gorbachev dresses elegantly in Western style, how dangerous can the Soviets still be? We in the West no longer sense or smell danger, as all animals do. The U.S. had early information that the Japanese planned to attack its naval forces, that the attack would probably occur on December 7, and even that it was likely to be in Pearl Harbor. But most posts were unmanned, 350 planes were on the ground, clumped together to "protect" them from sabotage, and most men were asleep. We do not learn well. The same thing happened again in Beirut just a few years ago, and several hundred Marines died. Our intuition and feelings are most unreliable as guides, but we use them for that nonetheless.

Those plotting against the West lay their traps, confidently expecting that self-delusion will cause us to walk straight into them without caution. Based upon the experience of the last few decades, they have good reason for their confidence. The more rigidity, stubbornness, and extremism on their part, the more has the West doubted the rightness of its positions. They were abandoned one after the other in a long and steady series of retreats.

4. Fighting Domestic and International Terror Successfully

Forty American tourists were hijacked by Shiite Muslim terrorists on a TWA flight from Athens in June 1985. The plane was flown back and forth twice between Algiers and Beirut before it finally landed. Robert Stethem, a twenty-four-year-old U.S. Navy petty officer, was tortured and savagely beaten till every one of his ribs was broken. He was then shot and his mutilated body dumped on the tarmac, as if he were a dog. His only crime was carrying a U.S. military passport. Hostages with Jewish-sounding names were separated from the rest and immediately taken away. The highly trained anti-terrorist Delta team, specifically established to combat such incidents, was never used. Excessive caution is always the easiest course to follow, since the high price that it extracts is not immediately visible. President Reagan was outspoken in his televised condemnation of the abductors: "The U.S. gives terrorists no rewards and no guarantees. We make no concessions. We make no deals. Terrorists be on notice! We will fight back against you in Lebanon and elsewhere." Off camera, he referred to the movie *Rambo*, suggesting that he was seriously considering retaliation.

But the hijackers were not frightened and even insisted in one of their many interviews with the West's television and press that all threats of retaliation be withdrawn before any hostages were released. So the threats were muffled, and a legalistic point of view was adopted instead. We soon read that "the U.S. would use every available legal procedure to extradite the hijackers." It also considered offering a reward of $500,000 for information leading to the arrest of the two original hijackers. That it was humiliating for the greatest power on earth to offer such a reward apparently escaped the attention of Washington policymakers. Could anyone imagine the Soviet Union offering a reward under similar circumstances?

The gang of Islamic jihad youths continued to hold seven Americans after releasing the others. Their blackmail continued, and again they were effective in outsmarting and outmaneuvering their powerful enemy. Rationalizations to justify further retreat came in quickly. Newspapers reported that "U.S. officials worry that American reprisals might result in the deaths of these seven hostages . . . ruling out our relatiation." A senior administration official claimed that "vengeance isn't a satisfactory basis for policy. . . . Members of the group live in urban areas, and it is manifestly unfeasible . . . to conduct violent raids against them."

Live television coverage of the hijacking reached millions, and many people all over the world unwittingly allowed the criminals to become their guides in matters of right and wrong. While the murdering outlaws succeeded in appearing as underdogs, exempt from all guilt, many Americans began to blame those identified by the abductors as responsible for all the trouble. A significant shift in U.S. public "opinion" polls against Israel occurred. Though the public here was not under the gun, it behaved as if it were. Fear can cause major errors in the judgment of all adults and gross distortions in their perception. This is one example of how people often arrive at their "point of view," especially in democracies where the press is free. Policy is frequently modified to fit such pressures from the public.

We need and must adopt a set of basic principles to help us act rationally, often contrary to our natural irrational tendencies, if we wish to protect our way of life. It is unwise to just do what comes naturally, and not only in foreign affairs. In times of war it is disastrous. Such principles might have to be changed and refined from time to time as circumstances dictate, but never under pressure. It is then that we most urgently need to fortify ourselves. This we can do by adhering to principle in spite of our wishes to do otherwise.

PRINCIPLE I. *The goal of every decision and policy should always be to maximize justice and freedom and to minimize death and suffering.*

Western democracies have or have sprung from a long history of religious, racial, and ethnic persecution by autocratic rulers. The French and American revolutions happened only yesterday, and guaranteed individual human rights did not exist in most countries until less than two hundred years ago. A few privileges had sometimes been granted by benign kings and princes before, but they knew that they could always reclaim their power and often did. So it is understandable why the individual in the West guards his hard-won human rights so jealously, and why he always worries about individual freedom being very fragile. He is not yet emotionally adjusted to the new realities of his existence, and still has pre-emancipation attitudes. He has installed his rulers and he can recall them, but he still suspects all authority as likely to have evil intentions. The more powerful it is, the more it is suspected. This applies to a policeman and a president alike.

The public needs for safety and for maintaining the civilized order are thus sometimes jeopardized. Western societies are reluctant to exercise authority, confusing it with authoritarianism. The legislative branch is often very suspicious of the executive branch, consistently denying it many powers needed to impose the rule of law on recalcitrant citizens within, and on international outlaws outside. Judges are not above fear and other human emotions, and the courts of law generally share in this suspicion of the power vested in authority. Many people still react as if they lived in the eighteenth and not the twentieth century.

The supreme power in democracies rests with "the people." Their general welfare must also be supreme. This is the legal and moral rationale for taxation, compulsory education, conscription, and health and safety regulations. Whether we like it or not, we must abide by the law even if it causes us hardship and occasionally even death. The general good requires some sacrifices from individuals. This has always been true in principle, but in practice it is increasingly being rejected now. In our jealous pursuit of individual rights we often forget that freedom in democracies is neither total nor absolute.

It has been claimed that "power corrupts and absolute power corrupts absolutely." Kings and popes, big corporations, organized labor, and impersonal bureaucracies are known to have been insensitive to the people's wishes and needs. But could this also be true of "the people" themselves? We are almost totally unaccustomed to considering this possibility. But "the people" are individuals. In the voting booth each acts as a sovereign, able to abuse his or her power at will, even at the expense of the common good. Witness the repeated failures to approve taxation even for very worthy projects.

When elected officials are denied the power they need and the judiciary does not exercise the power it has, repeated breakdowns of law and the civil order multiply and fear increases. We know that the executive branch of government is in a position to abuse power, but so can legislators and judges. This is what they actually do when they fail to legislate or refuse to enforce laws that maximize justice, freedom, and welfare for all, such as when they slant any decision in favor of the underdog just because of his relative powerlessness. It is an abuse of power, whether the result of overidentification or of seeking political advantage. Politicians who are always running for office and who are therefore always eager to appear as if they please everyone usually have no interest in remembering that their job is to lead, not follow, their constituencies. They contribute to the disintegration of society.

The subway cars in New York City covered by ugly graffiti are a clear example. Millions of New Yorkers must spend hours every day against their will either looking at this offensive unsightliness or else blinding themselves to their surroundings. The unruly and irresponsible few have been allowed to limit the freedom of the many. Although minor in the scheme of things, it represents a major breakdown in respect for the civilized order, and it sends a clear message that private and public property and rights can be violated with impunity.

After years of wrangling and inaction, the mayor finally signed into law a prohibition against selling spray paint and broad Magic Markers to minors. But this obviously was not enough to maximize order and to minimize the problem. We cannot magically construct healthy families in which acting-out youngsters would be properly supervised, but society must at least be uncompromising in punishing those who break its codes. Even though those who violate the rights of others are emotional orphans, they must be held strictly accountable. Society can understand their pain; it can empathize with their anger at their meaningless lives; it should help them to the extent possible. But it must not excuse their actions.

In the absence of internal control, fear of authority can limit most anti-social behavior. This is the situation in totalitarian states. It is by far more desirable to build civil yardsticks within each person, which must be the primary ongoing goal of democracies. But in the meantime, doing nothing in the face of civil disorder is extremely dangerous. Irresponsible forces come into play in the absence of a just, strong, and firm authority. Witness Beirut.

At the international level, maximizing freedom and minimizing death and suffering require us to retaliate in force against those who try to destroy our civilization, when, where, and how we choose, without hesitation. This may consist merely of strong economic measures; military force is called for only when lesser measures fail. Whatever we do is dictated neither by pique nor personal preference nor by any wish to advance our political interests or philosophies but only by the goal of enforcing the civilized order. Its continued existence and strength are so critically important to us that to defend it we may sometimes have to sacrifice more lives than the number of hostages that we wish to save. We aim to minimize death and suffering even among our enemies. The least punishment that will achieve our goal is enough, but nothing less will do.

Revenge is a primitive form of response that does little more than discharge anger. Many people fail to see that powerful military initiatives may not have been designed to avenge but to achieve necessary political ends. In reality, the stick is the only effective tool for restraining wild animals. Carrots do not tempt them, because this is not what they eat. Officials who dismiss military strikes out of hand mostly because brute force offends them, shirk their duty and violate their oath of office. Our aim is to force pirates and outlaws to pay such a high price that they would have no choice but to yield to the civilized order. This cannot be done by strengthening our passive defenses. Improving the safety of airports, airplanes, and embassies, important as it is, leaves the initiative to the enemy. We must hit him actively till he knows the taste of terror. In the jungle, this usually is the only thing that is effective.

We must never talk tough unless we follow with the big stick. Our credibility is an important weapon which may save us from the need to actually use force. Paper tigers embolden the enemy, once he discovers what they are made of. If the U.S. carrier *Nimitz*, loaded with swift warplanes and escorted by several highly sophisticated destroyers, is speedily dispatched to a crisis zone, as it was in Lebanon, it should only be because we want to use it. We may, or we may not actually attack the enemy, but with such backing we do not beg, we threaten and demand. Our carriers and planes are indeed "silly and expensive toys," as the Shiites ridiculed them, if we allow terrorists to dictate terms to us while these weapon systems are pointed at them. Negotiations that do not take such power into account are merely posturing to hide our lack of nerve. They maximize death and suffering in the future, even if they happen to save a few lives now.

A main function of any responsible political leadership in the West must be educational. In a political reality in which feelings and not thinking predominate, a frightened electorate spurred on by shortsighted pundits would normally rise to stop any military intervention. It is relatively easy to "activate Man's barely dormant fears and doubts." Wave after wave of courageous political leaders of great moral stature are needed to challenge the non-thinking, non-rational attitudes of the public, risking political defeat. It is a difficult, thankless, and perhaps an impossible mission, but one that the West's future rests upon.

PRINCIPLE II. *The West is already under siege. A total war has been imposed upon us. The front is everywhere; every citizen is a soldier.*

Those who are out to destroy the West do not want to acknowledge that they are waging a war, and surely they do not want us to know where and when they are lying in ambush, waiting for us. This is why the war is undeclared and why it has no front lines; any Western interest or institution can suddenly and without warning become a target. Also there are no uniformed armies; the enemy's stormtroopers usually wear ski masks or stockings to hide their features. Because they are hard to identify we cannot easily retaliate against them. They want to blend into the general population as soon as possible after they have massacred, mutilated, and destroyed. This not only protects them but it also sows uncertainty and panic among us. This is an important feature of their tactics. Terrorists succeed in spreading terror by shooting into a crowd, blowing up civilian planes in midair, and threatening entire populations by blackmail. Unlike freedom fighters, who also throw bombs, the hands of terrorists are never stayed because innocent children may get hurt. On the contrary, the more pointless death, cruelty, and destruction they leave behind the better.

Freedom fighters who also use violence must be fought off with equal ferocity by the societies they aim to destroy. The civilized order must be defended against anyone living by the rule of the jungle. Such fighters live by the sword and they must be ready to die by it. But freedom fighters generally understand and accept this necessity, although they obviously hope to win and not die. Unlike terrorists, they often struggle inwardly with the moral question of whether they have the right to kill, and they consciously accept the possible consequences of their deeds. In principle, freedom fighters are committed to the existence of the civilized order, even though they choose to live by the rules of the jungle to achieve some goal more important to them than even life itself. Believing in the "propaganda of the deed" and "the philosophy of the bomb," they continue to fight anyway.

But terrorists observe no civilized conventions of warfare, and they use any means to kill innocent travelers and bystanders, schoolchildren, women, and the aged. The war is total. They bomb hopsitals, slaughter hostages like sheep, and use chemical weapons; they systematically murder or exile writers, thinkers, and others with a greater than usual potential for human independence; they attempt to assassinate a pope. Confusing the gullible West is one of their tactics. The Lebanese Berri and the Syrian Assad claimed publicly that they were "against hijacking," as did Qaddafi, even as they negotiated the hijackers' demands and benefited from their acts. The Soviet Union invaded, occupied, and subdued the Baltic States, Hungary, Poland, and Afghanistan—all in the name of socialism, justice, and freedom. The most repressive regimes in the world call themselves Peoples' Democratic Republics. Between attacks, the terrorists and those who train, finance, and "run" them are very eager to appear as humane peace lovers. This will soon lull the enemy to sleep again.

The reason that some of our own citizens sometimes pick up the propaganda of our enemies and echo it is not only that it jars their decency and touches their guilt about being so fortunate, but it also comes from the general lack of understanding that we are already at war, and a very cruel one at that. The American who acted as spokesman for the hostages of the hijacked TWA plane expressed publicly in front of TV cameras a "profound sympathy" for the cause of the murderers who had just killed a countryman of his in cold blood. But captured soldiers are only supposed to give their name, rank, and serial number; and in this war every citizen is a soldier, even the one held hostage. It is perhaps excusable to speak the lines of an enemy when a crazed killer actually holds a cocked gun to one's head, but this was not the situation here. Most people in the West simply do not realize yet that the front is everywhere. Even politically naive adults must not lose their self-respect by praising murderers with bloodstains still on their clothes. It is an act of cowardice and disloyalty to one's country and to the civilized order itself.

PRINCIPLE III. *We remain committed to the sanctity of life, yet realize that no war can be waged without casualties.*

To assure the survival of free societies and the civilized order we must painfully accept the need to sometimes sacrifice innocent citizens of both sexes, young and old. Such a decision must often be made quickly but never frivolously.

Our choice is terrible. Either we have to lower ourselves to using the tactics of terrorists or accept that we have no effectifve defense against them. They are trying to take advantage of our respect for ourselves, for the rule of law, and for every living person. These, they hope, will tie our hands and prevent us from hitting them. Since political murderers are seldom extradited, we either let the killers of a Robert Stethem roam free or we tarnish ourselves by having them assassinated or kidnapped, to be brought to quick justice here. Letting the killers get away invites more killings, so it is the worse of the two alternatives. We are therefore forced to bloody our hands. Man realized long ago that to remain civilized he had to protect his achievements from being reclaimed by the jungle. "He who comes to kill you should be killed first" is a very old rabbinic saying. To allow murderers to go unpunished returns us to barbarism.

Only with time did it become clear how pathetic, incompetent, and naive it was to try solving the problem by an attempt to extradite the terrorists. Two years after the hijacking, one Mohammed Ali Hamadi who was wanted by the U.S. in connection with it was arrested in Bonn. The crew members of the TWA plane traveled to Germany especially to view him, and identified him positively as one of the terrorists. But then two West Germans were kidnapped in Beirut. The same group to which the arrested terrorist belonged claimed responsibility. Naturally the Germans wanted to win their release, so they looked for and found the right address. In Teheran they met with high-ranking Iranian officials to negotiate a deal, and following the West's usual custom, they yielded. Bonn agreed to reject the U.S. extradition demand, breaking its legal obligation. Attorney General Edwin Meese then went to Bonn to "discuss air piracy and the murder of hostages." He and others pressured and probably pleaded, but failed. "Bonn said it will decide next week," reported the *Wall Street Journal.* Finally, on June 24, 1987, the U.S. was informed that Hamadi would not be extradited. Perhaps trying to save face, the White House was quoted as saying that "it is satisfied that Hamadi will be prosecuted to the full measure of the law" in Germany. More probably, before long he will quietly be released under additional pressure.

The Reagan administration officials who "insisted that their thoughts were riveted entirely on the lives of the passengers" (*Time,* June 24, 1985) may only have wanted to conceal other plans from public view. But if they told the truth they failed to understand their responsibilities, revealing gross incompetence and a yielding to fear. A commander of an army at war whose thoughts are "riveted entirely" on saving the lives of a platoon of soldiers would be court-martialed.

Fear often causes the West to be woefully shortsighted and ineffective. Without clear principles for rational response we blunder from trouble into greater trouble. In the same issue of

Time we find one expert claiming that "if we hit Iran there is certain to be terrorism in the the the U.S. . . . There are thousands of Iranians in the U.S. and the Ayatollah Khomeini has among them a network in place which could respond almost immediately." If true, why has the U.S. allowed such a network to exist in the first place? Walter Cronkite reported in 1980 that the FBI was instructed not to check too closely on Iranians admitted into the U.S., so as "not to alienate Khomeini." They were admitted even when they were known to be "ex"-terrorists. How does one renounce this status?

The U.S. might have had its own network in place in Iran, Syria, Libya, and elsewhere, so that it, and not the carrier *Nimitz*, would have been the instrument of our retaliation. We must defend the civilized order in any way that is effective. If terrorists use civilians as a shield, or if they live in urban areas, we still must bomb them. This was Truman's rationale for dropping the atom bombs on Hiroshima and Nagasaki, and this is the rationale for any aerial bombing of any target at any time. Civilians and non-combatants always get killed and non-military property always get destroyed. If Western hostages are killed by our attacks, we grieve for the lost lives and we doubly punish those who put them there. Vengeance that is not blind but tempered by reason is often the only satisfactory course that will turn the tide.

We must sometimes engage in subversion and cunning, since frontal attacks are not always possible. Surgical precision and the complete excision of a cancer are preferable when possible, but we use less precise methods when we have no choice. Chemotherapy and radiation cause much damage to healthy tissues, but we do not reject them on this basis alone. We never compromise with the basic goal of minimizing death and suffering. The same here. We either go with our feelings of repugnance at exterminating human outlaws as if they were cancer cells and remain civilized till they kill us, or else we ignore our preferences and follow a distasteful, dangerous, but rational course, weapon in hand.

Unfortunately, life is cheaper for our enemies than it is for us. Ho Chi Minh said in 1946, "Kill ten of our men and we will kill one of yours. In the end it is you who will tire." He was right, and we must change. Saving the civilized order from the law of the jungle requires that we occasionally violate some of the same principles of civility that we are out to preserve. We must never pursue safety for a few if it undermines it for the many. The cost of appeasement is always greater appeasement.

Our dilemma is so horrible because in following a rational course we sometimes have no choice but to become morally tainted. In terrorizing the home bases of terrorists we too become part-time terrorists. In an ideal world there would never be a need to compromise with absolute virtues, no moral relativism ever. But here on this earth we must on occasion reluctantly accept less than perfect justice. If it advances the course of civility and saves lives in the short and long run, we swallow our pride and even thank a Berri, an Assad, or the devil himself, the ones who controlled Lebanon in 1985 and who were ultimately responsible for what happened there. But we never thank anyone out of gratitude that they have killed only one and not forty hostages. And we should never be a party to internal power struggles among murderers. Those who kill fewer people are not "moderates" and they should not be described as such.

The crazed Shiites in Beirut had reason to believe that they had brought the mighty U.S. to its knees, and they were understandably jubilant. But what really held the U.S. hostage was its own excessive concern with saving every single life. President Reagan promised "swift and effective retribution," but even after 241 U.S. Marines were killed in their sleep nothing was done. Why not? Because in societies such as ours, where feelings predominate, the political cost of any military act is always extremely high; no casualties are tolerated. The public can always be quickly and easily mobilized against a military operation when some of the carnage is shown on television accompanied by interviews with widows and orphans in grief. Congress in the U.S., like the Greens in Germany and others elsewhere, is often not of much help either. Extreme anti-action posturing and thoughtless vilification are common. Some will ridicule any decision to take action, and the verbal attacks become vicious if something goes wrong. But even the best planned and most carefully executed operation normally involves some losses. Not a single battle can be fought unless we change such unrealistic expectations, and the war is already lost. To be paralyzed in the company of a demented killer is not only life-threatening, but it also invites extreme cruelty. This basically is our situation.

Tragedies that are dramatic enough sometimes wake us from our dangerous delusions. The explosion of the space shuttle *Challenger* in January 1986, in which Sharon Christa McAuliffe and six others lost their lives was a painful horror experienced as a personal loss by many. So much hope, collective effort, courage, and dedication had been riding in that little capsule before it simply vanished in a sudden puff. The harsh reality that seven lives and a billion-dollar spaceship could vanish in a second was watched by millions of schoolchildren because McAuliffe was the first teacher to go on such a mission. She was to teach two lessons from space. They too were horrified, but it was not "a lesson gone tragically awry" as one commentator claimed. On the contrary. Judd Allen, a sixth-grader, expressed it well: "At first I didn't know what was happening. I thought it was supposed to smoke like that. Then our guide told us that this was no movie like Steven Spielberg's. This was the real thing." The children reportedly were quiet, sad, shocked, in pain—like the rest of us. Christa McAuliffe taught only one lesson from space, but she taught it very well: Lives are sometimes lost in Man's worthwhile efforts to expand his horizons and to advance civilization. It cannot be any other way.

The political atmosphere now prevailing in the West leaves leaders pitifully little room to maneuver. The popular demand is for an easy life without pain or sacrifices in which everything will always go well and be well. Such "unrealistic wishes are . . . [especially] dangerous when they relate to justice, equality, and fairness, which are never perfect." The Shah of Iran is a good example.

Mohammed Riza Pahlavi sat long enough on his throne to have known better, but even so he did not fit our prescription for either an effective or a just ruler. He lived lavishly in the midst of poverty and did not do enough to increase his middle-class power base. He grossly abused basic human rights with his cruel SAVAK units, but he also hesitated to use them to crush his fundamentalist opposition. He raised the standard of living and introduced compulsory education even for girls, but he was autocratic, haughty, and pompous. Yet Khomeini is clearly much worse. His theocracy is a dangerous cancer in the body of the Iranian people and the entire Middle East. Generations of Iranians will have to repair the damage that is being done to their self-image, economy, and society. The global balance of power, the West's strategic interests, and the welfare of most Iranians and others all demanded that we support the Shah as the lesser of two evils. But since he was responsible for the killing of people, President Carter did so only hesitantly, too little and too late. Feelings took precedence over a very unpleasant reality.

Defeats will continue to follow one another unless the back of this dictatorship of feelings is finally broken.

PRINCIPLE IV. *Feelings must be ignored and their public expression forbidden in crises.*

By nature, humans are sensitive and they have all known fear. Its residues are semi-dormant in us much of the time but can easily be reawakened, causing us to hesitate when decisive and immediate action is called for. Fear can totally paralyze us when the pressure is especially great, when lives are at stake, cars collide, natural disasters suddenly occur, or planes are hijacked. People are sometimes rattled even when only the delivery of basic supplies, say water or electricity, is interfered with. Fanning fear and defeatism in the midst of war has therefore always been considered an act of treason. Quislings and stool pigeons were despised and shot not only because they helped the enemy but also because their example might weaken the resolve to fight. Nobody is eager to get killed. The reluctance to undertake a necessary but dangerous mission can easily become contagious. This is why the public expression of feelings must often be tightly controlled during crises.

Our right to exist and our wish to stay alive obviously have a much higher priority than our right for information and our freedoms of speech and of the press. The zeal that is commonly shown by the news media in defense of these latter rights is tainted by self-interest and not always pure. At least in part their bias reflects their position.

The cursed ethic of war demands that we repress our natural tendency to be compassionate. Anonymity makes it easier to consider others merely as statistics. Once we get to know the faces, qualities, and personal histories of our hostages, it becomes much more difficult not to do everything to save them. But some things should not be done, such as sending sophisticated arms to the ayatollahs. The reason President Reagan failed in the Iran-contra affair was directly the result of his emotional involvement in the fate of the hostages. His human weakness overcame his strong convictions about not yielding to blackmail. He did not remember that we must sometimes sacrifice a few to save many more lives. Televised interviews with hostages and with members of their families increase the pressure to save them now, even if the cost is much higher later. Such reporting is against the public interest, because it increases the leverage that terrorists can use to blackmail us.

Yet human interest stories are popular with editors and with broadcasters: they capture the emotions of viewers, thus increasing circulation and ratings. But since the ability to think and to reason is reduced when feelings become engaged, when to air such stories and when not to ought to be responsibly considered. At times of crisis, they must sometimes be curtailed altogether. We may even have to endure the ugly and dangerous beast called censorship if it alone can guard us, but effective self-censorship by the media is much preferred. Thoughtful professionals are almost always more trustworthy, more responsive, and more responsible than entrenched bureaucrats.

The choking hold of emotions can be loosened in the short run by reducing the number and intensity of the stimuli that evoke both irrational fear and compassion for others. Because of this, no effective defense against domestic or international terror can be mounted in a free society without the cooperation of the news media, the political leadership, and the political opposition. Any one of these three can easily torpedo an attempt to fight the enemy. No civilized society should learn to live with a picture of itself as the cause of death and destruction. Those who live in the jungle, our targets, are human too, our brothers. They look like us, bleed like us, and hurt like us. We may have to play havoc with them anyway, but our politicians and media must spare us the additional pain of knowing and seeing every last detail. We might otherwise soon be forced into inaction again. For both young and old, it is much more damaging to watch our own armed forces engage in violence than to see criminals do so. But sensationalism still determines the selection of news, which is understandable but not excusable. Although they operate mostly as commercial enterprises, the media's freedom is constitutionally guaranteed because it was expected that they would advance the general welfare, not harm it.

The media play a crucial role in cultivating the West's self-image as the upholder of the civilized order, even when innocents are killed and mass destruction results from our war against terrorism. Commentators, reporters, and editors usually fail to see the profound damage they often help create, though without malice and without meaning to. They often serve the cause of those who actively seek our demise. It is not a mindless pursuit of ratings, they claim. They sometimes rationalize that we become ennobled by the disgust that is evoked whenever destruction and death are depicted graphically. But we have already noted that our goal must sadly be the opposite. We must become a little less noble to survive. We must prepare ourselves to tolerate acts of war that civilized people would naturally shrink from.

Those who sponsor international terrorists are eager to sow discord in the West by highlighting the human suffering that results from our retaliation. They wish to weaken us by appealing to our compassion and decency and by evoking guilt about the compromises that we reluctantly must make in order to fight them. The Germans in 1943 would also have liked the American people to see the effects of the mass nightly sorties by heavy Allied bombers. Thousands of innocent German citizens were killed and burned each time. But innocents die in every war. The needs of the war effort demand that Western newsmen and newswomen not cover the human side of such carnage. It is hard enough for a civilized society to perform such primitive and cruel deeds in the first place; it is nigh unto impossible to do so when the horrors are repeatedly displayed.

The news media in the West, and in the U.S. especially, are generally not sophisticated enough on these issues, and they regularly intimidate the political leadership and evoke fear in the people. They apparently believe that their hostility toward military action serves the cause of peace. But chronic criticism paralyzes our ability to act, therefore endangering the survival of societies in which action is needed. The peace that is thus promoted is that of graveyards.

Although self-restraint and self-discipline are essential for the survival of free societies, these are becoming less common as the powerful yearnings of individuals become politicized. Once aroused, preverbal hunger and rage are not easily put aside, especially when regularly and repeatedly restimulated. By definition, one-issue voters forget the overall good. They push for what is dear to them at the expense of everything else. But highly organized small groups nonetheless succeed in the pursuit of their narrow goals because they form alliances with others who also ignore the common good. The political process is thus squeezed out of shape, often grinding to a complete halt. The efforts to combat domestic crime and international terror are often hampered as a result.

An atmosphere has thus been created in the affluent and permissive West in which many young people grow up without having any sympathy or even respect for anyone's position but their own. They "judge" mostly by feelings. Such self-centered people cannot usually think of the safety of others. In the name of the Freedom of Information Act, they sometimes legally demand to know highly sensitive data useful to our enemies, and in the name of free speech they spit upon our most cherished values. Some are openly disdainful of such terms as "loyalty" and "patriotism," seeing them as tainted catchwords of the extreme right. As "emancipated" citizens of the world they owe loyalty to no one, least of all to those who sustained them and gave them the freedom to become what they are. Giving up personal comfort for higher societal goals is looked upon as old-fashioned and silly. What have we done to raise such ingrates?

The highly pressured and usually thoughtless comments and questions of reporters are among several contributing factors. Reporters often imply in their frenzy that government in a democracy has but one duty, to help everyone and to do whatever the population wants. All other considerations are overlooked. Sensation-seeking reporters rushed to ask people immediately after the *Challenger* explosion whether they "felt" that the space program should be discontinued, thus making room for pain, disappointment, bewilderment, and fear to influence public opinion and perhaps policy. Such bias and thoughtlessness are common.

We must never give terrorists an opportunity to use our television and press to air their propaganda. Otherwise we provide them with the means to achieve what they want, stirring our fears and gaining our sympathies. The incentive for taking hostages would be sharply reduced if it did not attract so much attention. Domestically and internationally, exposure multiplies the pathologic satisfaction of those who experience themselves personally or politically as small, insignificant, and powerless; and it often prolongs the torture of their victims. The Russians wisely keep such affairs out of public view, and we too should never reprint in our magazines the belligerent nonsense of our enemies. A few angry Amal youngsters brandishing Russian Kalishnikovs are not a "giant [that] has been let out of the bottle . . . never [to] be bottled up again," as one of our important newsmagazines suggested. It is similarly unwise and undignified for us to print photographs that show such bearded thugs and goons grinning widely and laughing at the West's naivete and helplessness. These reward our enemies and play into their hands while damaging our self-image, our pride, and the way others see us.

Standing firm under fire always requires the ability to keep one's emotions under control. Soldiers, physicians, nurses, and others are specifically trained not to be distracted by the sight of blood, destruction, and death. They must continue functioning effectively even in the midst of carnage. Since everyone is a soldier in this war, everyone's tolerance for such horrors must be increased, undesirable as it is ideally. Cultivating a true respect for life under such conditions is painfully difficult yet exceedingly important. Otherwise we too begin to live in the jungle.

Military commanders can make decisions that are likely to result in death only by setting all their emotions aside while attending to the task. Sadly, each of us must learn to do the same. It is not easy to keep strong feelings out of the way, but easy or not, this is what we must often do. Even in the fight against inflation somebody suffers as a result of any one move; determination and courage are needed to stay the course. Only a James Bond never gets rattled by anything. He is a caricature, an unreal fantasy figure, and a good example of inhuman behavior. Even tough old generals sometimes break down and shed a few tears after an especially costly battle.

"I shall tell you a great secret, my friend," said Camus many years ago. "Do not wait for the last judgment. It takes place every day." This is even more true now. In this long war of attrition against the West we are constantly in crisis; every day is judgment day. Public expressions that awaken unreasonable expectations or fan fear must therefore be forbidden, so they find no room to weaken us.

PRINCIPLE V. *Those living outside the law are not entitled to expect treatment according to the laws that they violate.*

Apprehended terrorists, killers, and other violent criminals at home and abroad brazenly demand and routinely receive treatment according to the laws that they have just broken. We in the West never question their right to benefit from the orderly existence that the rest of us have imposed upon ourselves. But humans living by the law of the jungle have knowingly excluded themselves from our midst; they do not recognize our rights and trample on them, and on us. They do not deserve to benefit from the civilized order and should be denied its protection.

When the human rights of international terrorists or domestic outlaws are occasionally violated by outraged victims or others, we regard it as a serious failing of our system of justice. And yet such an attitude may not be the sign of strength we always believed it was but a weakness that invites further violence. Such murderers count on the fact that they will not only be safe but also very well taken care of if caught. The Geneva Convention of 1864 provides for the neutrality of ambulances and hospitals in time of war; Shiites in Lebanon slaughtered hundreds of wounded Palestinians in their hospital beds, but then complained bitterly about being transferred to prisons beyond the international border. (The Israelis who had thus violated the Convention were officially condemned by the U.S. and others.) The same Convention also requires that medics in the field not be personally attacked; Iranians booby-trapped Iraqi corpses, but were indignant because some of their captured were held in excessively cramped quarters. They kill hostages deliberately, cruelly, and in cold blood, but demand Red Cross and due-process protection.

We in the West usually reprimand or punish offenders, and we apologize publicly whenever international conventions are not observed meticulously, thus upholding our standards and guarding our self-image. We regard fair treatment of prisoners as their right, not their privilege. But we do not insist often enough that rights be packaged together with responsibilities. The same on the domestic front. Clever lawyers easily manipulate the legal system so that habitual criminals are punished leniently, with a good chance for early release. Prisons for serious offenders, the ones who live by the rule of the jungle, are usually comfortable as befits civilized societies. Lawbreakers who serve time for lesser offenses are more common and their quarters are often much more crowded.

The civilized order is the real victim when we accord civil treatment to outlaws who have not earned it. They laugh at our naivete and great concern for fairness. From their perspective it is a sign of weakness and it proves their superiority. It hardens their resolve, their indentification as outlaws, and their behavior as criminals. They often come back to bleed us again. Those who engage in systematic genocide, who car-bomb schoolchildren and sleeping Marines on a peace mission, who use infants and their mothers as a protective shield, starve millions, flaunt international conventions, and try to destroy the civil order itself must be treated as agents of barbarism. They deserve no better than martial law. The legal standards of civilized man do not apply to them, although they try to use these too as a shield.

Former U.S. Secretary of Defense Caspar Weinberger insisted

on having satisfactory legal proof of culpability before he approved retaliatory actions against the TWA hijackers who had already killed one American and who were still holding many others. The wrong criteria were used. The West was and is regularly being raped and humiliated. It is legally and morally praiseworthy but practically naive and stupid to demand that the raped party assemble incontrovertible legal proof of guilt. The "rapists" were known and the facts were not in question, only the legal validity of the evidence. It is foolhardy to let criminals continue their pillage while long and tedious legal procedures are being exhausted. We remain virtuous but also dangerously exposed if we refuse to compromise our strict adherence to the rule of law even when its very existence is endangered by a direct attack upon it. Some say that we must set an example, but those who have chosen to remain ethically pure even in confrontations with barbarians have usually been discovered very dead soon thereafter.

The reason that mature and well-off societies have always succumbed to hungrier, leaner, and meaner ones is that civilized and refined people are usually more choosy; they are more careful in protecting themselves, more hesitant, more delicate, and less vicious when they fight. More primitive people are generally more cruel, less self-protective, and less pampered. They normally have had the advantage. But noting this in time provides us with an advantage also, for we can prepare by toughening ourselves and by not yielding to our more compassionate and softer nature. Other civilizations without this advantage followed their feelings; enjoyed wine, women, and song; and kept denying the dangerous reality that faced them until it was too late. They vanished as political entities. If we wish to at least postpone going their way we must reluctantly but decisively lay aside the rules of the civilized order that restrain us, and meet the wild and crazed beasts with everything we have. Either they are forced to abide by the rule of law or we too get swallowed by the jungle.

To use more force than is necessary is inexcusable; it is an expression of our feelings. To use less force than is necessary is also inexcusable for the same reason. Brute force, especially if administered decisively, should always remain loathsome to us; but whether politically liberal or conservative, we must follow the course that rational considerations dictate. Striking out at Westerners and Western interests has become a mark of honor and a symbol of manhood for fanatic Iranians and excitable young Lebanese Shiites, but even wild animals can be restrained if the alternative is too painful. This is how we have all become civilized. Moses had to insist on such harsh measures as an eye for an eye and a tooth for a tooth.

We do what we must, or the West and its civilized order disappear. As individuals, many of us even prefer to die rather than kill. But as the defenders of civilization we cannot afford this luxury. Man's general welfare and his long and slow progress toward rationality and the rule of law command us not to abandon the cause even though it is both loathsome and frightening.

5. A Personal Note

I am no killer. The inevitable conclusions about our choices do not sit well with my view of myself as a compassionate and kind man. As a youth in summer camp, I was very clumsy when it was my turn to kill a chicken. Even now I am somewhat embarrassed to recall that I struggled with the bird for a few seemingly endless minutes, razor in hand, but it finally escaped squawking loudly but unharmed, not even bleeding. Even now I prefer to let a fly escape. But if the choice were to be wantonly killed or to kill an attacker, I am certain that I would force myself to do what I must to save my life.

President Harry Truman actually was in this predicament when he ordered the two atomic bombs dropped, sparing Japan at least ten to fifteen times the 200,000 casualties the bombs caused. Japan still had 2.3 million regular soldiers and 5,000 kamikaze pilots. It reportedly had trained children to strap themselves with explosives and to roll under tanks. Okinawa and Iwo Jima are only two examples of the bloodbaths that would have followed an invasion. Truman's choice was horrible, but it appears to have been right. It is conservatively estimated that it saved at least a million American lives. The war with Japan ended with its unconditional surrender very soon after the second bomb was dropped on Nagasaki.

Truman was known as a sensitive family man, a good father, a loyal friend, and a devoted husband—not a power-hungry Machiavellian schemer. So no one accused him of having had secret fascist tendencies. He struggled with his difficult choices but slept well once he made up his mind.

Whether or not I hide my head in the sand and refuse to consider these issues, they nevertheless affect me personally. But even as I know all this, I note how fidgety, tired, and physically uncomfortable I have become as I consider these issues, and how much longer than expected it took to work on this chapter. Feelings tug on us all. But there is no escape from the problems of this world except into insanity or suicide. Neither of these are acceptable to me or, I hope, to you, the reader.

6. The Expertise of Experts

The West clearly possesses the resources, the power, and even the wisdom to defend itself economically, politically, and militarily against its enemies. What it lacks is resolve. Feelings intervene. Confusion often results from inner contradictions, but people usually think that it comes from a lack of understanding. So they urgently seek advice at such times, turning to experts. But experts are also human, and their expertise too is often colored by their emotions. Even their thinking can be "circular . . . and leads to conclusions already arrived at by [their] feelings. . . . Notions from our infantile past in the form of feelings commonly persist as guideposts in adult living." This is why the expertise of experts is not always of much help.

How to fight vicious terrorists effectively is hardly a subject that is free of emotions. Experts agree on one point: that terrorists are also subject to the pull of feelings. This Achilles' heel is what terrorists try to overcome in their training; it is their weakness as fighters. Keep them negotiating and soon they will become emotionally involved with their intended victims, who stand a better chance not to be killed once their human characteristics are known. Beyond this point the experts usually disagree, even though they have studied similar subjects, read the same books, earned university degrees in the same or adjacent fields, and acquired reputations as experts in the same area. But since even intellectually mature adults are often emotionally quite immature, they too cannot necessarily "envision distant consequences."

What experts advise about power and its use often reflects no more than personal confusion, a leftover from childhood. The use of power is not a neutral or conflict-free subject. "The political push toward isolation from world affairs is usually couched in high-sounding and thoughtful phrases, but it generally represents a summation of hidden individual fears."

Experts are very often quoted by the media without being

named. Not only can we not evalutate their credentials without an identity, but we also must ignore the all-important question regarding the degree of their fear. Do such experts really exist? Reporters are often eager to flesh out their stories and give them credence, and sometimes they snap up offerings of people who claim that status to impress others. The opinions of experts should therefore not be given any special weight until you know how much weight they deserve.

One expert has been reported in a news story to "vehemently disagree" with the desirability of any covert action, specifically the assassination of terrorist leaders. "We have no business hiring our version of a Carlos, or matching terrorists car bomb for car bomb," said he. "Any retaliation ought to be done by legitimately constituted armed forces." But if the goal is to let terrorists and the governments that sponsor them know that justice will reach them one way or another, why limit our capacity to strike them unexpectedly? Why give them any advantage? An unambiguous message as to who did what and why it was done should always follow. This is enough to convey the message. Some "experts" obviously do not understand the basics of the situation. Their counsel is misleading. Intellectual credentials are not enough.

7. Liberty in New Hands: The Media

To a large extent, the fate of the West rests in the hands of its television executives, anchormen, and reporters. None of them have been elected by the public, and none are accountable to it, but by accident of timing and place they find themselves holding this precious trust, barely knowing that they do, or what to do with it. Harry Truman and Lyndon Johnson were each in a similar position when the mantle of the presidency suddenly fell upon their shoulders. But unlike these two situations, the power of television has not yet been formally recognized, the duties and responsibilities of those operating the networks were never spelled out, and no precedent exists. Especially in the U.S., liberty is at risk.

Advertising was recognized years ago as the "hidden persuader" of Western populations, but the power of television is a thousandfold greater. Long before the press had the wide circulation it enjoys today, journalism's great influence was acknowledged when it became known as the Fourth Estate, assigning it a status equal to that of the Lords Spiritual, the Lords Temporal, and the Commons—the clergy, and nobility, and the bourgeoisie. But the printed word only affects the reading public, and it must be sifted through the brain. Responsible newspapers have always shaped public mores and policy by influencing a slowly expanding intelligentsia, an all-important but relatively small group. But the effect of television is direct and immediate, and its audiences are enormous.

Toddlers, senile people, and almost everybody in between reach for television at times, and some are practically addicted and watch it nearly all the time. In a sense these people are consumed by it, this being their central involvement. Television is directly absorbed, it reaches the heart immediately, and much of the time it strongly affects the physiology. Viewers often become glued even to average presentations and to commercials, not only when their powers of discrimination are poor. It does not require that the brain also become engaged. Television does not shape character, and it probably does not increase violence, but by numbing its viewers for hours on end it powerfully changes the way people behave and live. Like opium, the effect of television depends on the dose, and its power to lull the brain and to push thoughtfulness aside is similar in potency. Religion was never as powerful an agent for young and impressionable populations, even when Marx likened it to the narcotic.

Access to television and the successful use of it are coveted because of the tremendous results that can be obtained. Fifty or even a hundred million people can be simultaneously reached and physiologically affected at least for a moment. This is why a few seconds of exposure on national television in the U.S. can cost millions. Yet it sells not only products but also modes of being, styles of behavior, values, fashions, and loyalties. It defines what is humorous, clever, proper, and wise. In many little and big ways, people tend to unknowingly mimic what they see on television, and it thus sets standards for public and private relationships. This is how Bill Cosby has come to be considered such an expert on fatherhood and on growing old.

By its very nature, television promotes passivity and non-striving. Like an intravenous tube, it feeds automatically and nullifies the need to make the effort of sitting at a table and eating a nutritious meal. Without malice and without intention, it lowers the attentiveness and the alertness to everything else, and it sharply lessens the ability to think independently, to reason, to discriminate, and to judge. But it has a silver lining:

Television vastly expands the pool of facts, especially among the young.

In the U.S., where television is mostly in private hands and profit-motivated, programming and personalities are especially chosen to avoid anything that might annoy, offend, frighten, or otherwise displease the average viewer. No strong colors or opinions please; bland is in. Distraction and entertainment are the only goals. The common denominator is generally low, since the medium wants to cater to the largest possible audience. This is its weakness and what has made it so very powerful. Directly or at least indirectly, we are all affected by its dominant presence.

Even heads of government, senators, congressmen, industrialists, and others with considerable economic or political power are often clumsy in front of the camera, knowing that they are being seen and judged by a huge unknown audience whose reactions cannot be immediately gauged. Nonetheless they generally are very eager to have so much exposure. But in front of this audience it is even more difficult for most people to stand up for what is right. They cannot see how they come across. So in general politicians say mostly what is already acceptable, easy, popular, and pleasing. This is definitely not the place to try out new ideas, unless a leader has great human stature, much wisdom, and a great vision. The readiness to lead and the ability to inspire are often woefully inadequate in the first place, and the medium makes this bad situation even worse. Besides, the attention span of most viewers for serious talk has become rather short and is getting shorter. In the relative absence of political and moral leadership, television sets the country's tone.

Although especially true in the U.S., the future of the West as a whole is involved. As its leader and most powerful member, what happens to it affects all. Few people in or out of government have begun to comprehend the magnitude of the burden that rests on the shoulders of those who manage, produce, and report for television. They probably have much more to say about our common fate than the commanders of our armies. The Fourth Estate, and especially television, is increasingly subsuming the power of the other three branches of government, although as yet grossly unprepared to discharge this awesome responsibility.

The family used to be the guardian of the West's values. Here they were slowly inculcated. Schools can help consolidate such gains, but they cannot in themselves do the job, as we can see from the results. With the weakening of the ties that held families together and the complete breakdown of many others, large numbers of the young have never been held long enough, or at all, in a consistent "crucible of no-choice." They have not learned to discipline themselves and are impulsive and irresponsible; they have not had enough of a home, and they live with the loyalties of vagabonds; they had no one to really talk to, and nobody to learn from—so they turned to television. This is where feelings can be felt, a little thinking imitated, teaching occurs, life is being lived. This is home. This is the new instiller of values. In a sense, television is the unwitting trustee of liberty. If it is to survive, television must become its guardian.

But even people who are much less dependent on television are influenced by it, sometimes greatly. We are all regularly being subjected to a continuous and not-so-subtle brainwashing. The exaggerated hysterical behavior in many commercials is supposed to be funny, but many young children imitate it anyway. They learn by watching. And what is normal human conversation like? Is it the way people talk about their new detergent with enthusiastic delight, or more like the extra happy chatter of the anchor teams on the morning shows, always smiling, overly familiar and folksy, so cute and so trivial?

Most reporters seem totally oblivious to the long-term effects of what they do, or what is at stake. Above all, they try to become more popular personally. Their reporting is sensational because it jolts the viewers, causing them momentary excitement, a proven if short-lived antidote to depression. But what happens to the thoughtfulness and humanity of people who constantly see others being asked questions like "How did you feel when your wife was kidnapped and your house burned down?" There are not requests for information but a manipulation of both the interviewee and the viewers. Yet such things are routinely shown as "news." Even some of TV's "analysis" is on that level.

For example, the U.S. government is the unhappy owner of literally mountains of nutritious and high-grade honey and cheese, stored in huge caverns and warehouses across the continent. Long-standing price supports for agricultural products cause endless overproduction. The program continues because of well-placed political pressure. Many farmers got rich from this wasteful giveaway. The government, which really is us, continues to buy vast quantities of these and other products at prices that are more than double what the consumer pays at retail outlets for imported products of the same quality. Consumers obviously prefer to buy the much cheaper products that are equally good.

When price supports were finally about to be discontinued, farmers brought their trucks and tractors to Washington, clogged the streets, lobbied Congress, and aired their personal pain on national television. Eager reporters, delighted to find "live" human interest stories, rushed to interview them. Their faces and voices were understandably sad, angry, and really worried. Some wives cried in true anguish. A television crew was set up at a forced sale of a family farm, where good, honest, hardworking people were shown in trouble. This was definitely good copy, sure to elicit wide interest and sympathy.

TV viewers naturally respond to such pictures. Most people "feel for" those in hard times, and once their sympathy is engaged they forget to think and tend to overlook the merits of whatever issue is at stake. They will continue to buy imported cheese and honey as before, but many will nonetheless write to their congressmen urging them not to allow such heartless policies to become law. They forget that they are the ones who pay for the subsidies, even though indirectly, and they also forget that thousands of other such claims exist. Congressmen are usually eager to respond when the public is mobilized this way, not only because they are supposed to represent the people but also because they are concerned about getting re-elected. Yielding to the pressure of powerful lobbies becomes more respectable when grass-roots support is present. Even programs that are clearly irrational, expensive, harmful, and contrary to the public good are often continued.

Presidential addresses, like comments on the editorial page and unlike news, are consciously addressed to the viewer's thinking. Even people who are not very confident about evaluating opinions at least try to judge the merits of ideas that are presented to them as such. But they often swallow "news" uncritically as fact. This is how sentimental and politically unsophisticated reporters do so much insidious damage. They often have more influence than a president.

More responsible selection and editing of the news is obviously needed. Sometimes only money appears to be involved, but lives and the future of our civilization are directly at stake on other occasions, and yet the carelessness is the same. One of the three major U.S. television networks broke the news about the widening Walker spy scandal by quoting denials of guilt by the indignant-looking lawyer of Jerry A. Whitworth. How dare they indict an innocent man? The FBI was wrong! The accused was eventually found guilty of passing key lists that allowed the Soviets to decode virtually all of the U.S. Navy's most sensitive messages over a period of many years, but none of the accusations were even mentioned that morning. Room was made only for the lawyer to besmirch the FBI. Is it not obvious to those who report and edit that what they do weakens their own societies?

News leaks of confidential information about the movements of the anti-terrorist Delta Force spoiled the chances of a possible rescue attempt of the TWA hostages in 1985. Pentagon officials complained at the time that the U.S. "is going to need an Official Secrets Act," but the making of policy was hampered in the meantime, and lives remained needlessly in jeopardy.

Did the U.S. television networks ask themselves what the likely effect would be of showing angry Iranian mobs repeatedly vilifying the hapless and helpless U.S. every evening for 444 consecutive days? The proclaimed intention was to not forget the hostages, but were terrorists everywhere encouraged or discouraged by such programming? Did the West's prestige and influence increase or decrease by playing up this event in such a fashion? What did it do to the self-image and sense of pride of U.S. citizens? Was it not all a thoughtless and self-serving exploitation of a national tragedy?

Why have no Iranian citizens ever been held hostage? Why have no Soviet planes ever been hijacked? Why can Cubans and Cambodians, Bulgarians and Russians, travel without fear but not Americans, West Europeans, or Japanese? Because the latter all live in democracies which subscribe to the civilized order; the others are part of the jungle and need not defend themselves from its agents. But in addition, free societies cannot now assure their citizens of personal safety. Their own public "opinion" prevents them from doing so effectively.

The power of television and films is such that even the most repressive totalitarian regimes have failed to completely shut out behavior and attitudes shaped by Western magazines, movies, and television. Border guards routinely confiscate copies of *Playboy* and other Western magazines from tourists entering the Soviet Union by train, but to no avail. Russian children are so eager to have chewing gum, blue jeans, and other popular Western items that they offer tourists fancy Red Army medals for them. In spite of the extreme brutalities of the Islamic revolution, youngsters in Teheran are still willing to risk public humiliation by revolutionary guards for wearing Western T-shirts and sneakers. Rock music and punk hairdos have the power to penetrate even the barbed wire and the minefields of the Iron Curtain.

For the better educated, the press and radio play a relatively more important role. But even here the appeal to emotions is stronger than generally realized, and sometimes dangerous. A single photograph of a bleeding, burning, or panicky child in agony printed on the front page of a leading newspaper can have such a profound effect on so many readers that it eventually affects our political stances, even when it should not. One such picture helped turn the U.S. public sharply against the war in Vietnam. Many people have a few such images etched permanently in their mind.

Here is another example. National Public Radio (NPR) some time ago presented a nine-minute, forty-five-second segment on its popular "All Things Considered" program about the "out of control" U.S. border with Mexico. Over 1.5 million illegal immigrants are arrested yearly, but this is only a small fraction of those crossing the border. Most make it. The U.S. Immigration and Naturalization Service arrests no more than one in three. The program described a carnival atmosphere on the Mexican side at dusk, with vendors selling beer and people joking, waiting for the illegal journey north to start. The in-depth analysis soon becomes an emotion-packed story strongly slanted against the INS. Many people are interviewed. The complaints of so-called immigrants' rights groups are the centerpiece of the presentations.

Illegal immigrants spoke with voices full of hurt and anger; it was difficult not to overidentify with them, especially since the reporter did so, and very blatantly. How dare "they" treat people this way? The arrested illegals did not get food and water quickly enough. Some complained bitterly about the harsh treatment administered by a few officers. Some were pushed, others rudely spoken to. The regional head of the INS admitted that such things do indeed occasionally happen when hundreds of thousands of desperate and sometimes angry human beings must be turned back against their will. Officers often have no choice but to act in self-defense. The most blatant incident was thoroughly investigated by six separate legal agencies, and no fault was found. "What do they want, a lynching?" asks an exasperated officer. The eager reporter was not mollified. Here is another case, and one more. "The border patrol is not accountable to local residents," she complained angrily and very righteously, "it is part of the Justice Department instead, and one congressman is already introducing legislation imposing criminal penalties for any violations."

No one pointed out during the long program that these complaints about possible violations of the law were all made by lawbreakers. Some INS officers may have lost their cool under the continual stress of an impossible job, but they were nonetheless our agents trying to enforce our laws. They were not the enemy. The radio program showed a lot of compassion for the illegals but none for the exhausted officers who were jeered daily, harassed and stoned on their jobs, and occasionally shot at. The INS men and women were made to look like villains.

The listeners were not reminded even once that all these "immigrants' rights" groups are organized to defy the law of the land, and that their sole purpose is to help lawbreakers. Such groups may be composed of very compassionate men and women, but they promote the law of the jungle and thus threaten the civilized order. Since their efforts are on behalf of human beings, they are automatically termed humanitarian, and hardly anyone notes that it is a form of organized crime.

Such gross and indiscriminate siding with everyone who suffers is typical of this and other programs. Almost automatically they are against those who exercise judgment or use the power inherent in their positions. And it is all publicly financed, part of an educational network with supposedly higher standards, and meaning to promote thoughtfulness, fairness, and justice.

The high value we assign to anything called "rights" is such that groups of this kind are commonly treated with great leniency and enjoy widespread support, even though their challenge to the civilized order is more serious than that of the Ku Klux Klan, the American Nazi, or the U.S. Communist Party. These three are dangerous and often vicious but insignificant in their numbers and influence; they do not have educators and ministers as their spokesmen; they are clearly part of the lunatic fringe. Not so the people who help others to break our laws.

Does such "reporting" not undermine the rule of law itself? Does it not promote the principle that anyone's "morality" has a superior claim on loyalty higher than the basic tenets that hold civilized societies together? What happens to societies that are subjected to such "reporting" day in and day out, year after year?

The reporting and editing of news must not remain the haphazard and thoughtless business that is now. Those helping to shape public opinion must always remember that feelings are extremely powerful, and that free societies are rather fragile. So is thoughtfulness. But in general, any attempt in the U.S. to focus on the dangerous flaws in the use of our mass communications media is quickly thwarted by somebody citing the First Amendment. Yet regarding the Constitution as Holy Writ, never in need of review, was probably not how anyone envisioned it two hundred years ago. Basic laws should not normally be tampered with, unless the conditions of existence have basically changed, which they have. The old separation of powers equation has been grossly thrown out of balance by the very heavy weight of the media. Some Constitutional scholars might even argue that the guarantee of freedom of speech and of the press does not include the offshoot called television. But with or without a Constitutional amendment, something must quickly be done to limit the ongoing damage. Self-policing may be enough, but we may also have to modify some of the West's basic assumptions about freedom if we are to keep any of it.

8. Idealism and Naivete: From William Jennings Bryan to Cyrus Vance

President Woodrow Wilson and William Jennings Bryan, his Secretary of State, personified the idealistic and moralistic attitudes of their age. They governed by feelings and were largely governed by them. Neither would have been able to attain power except on the crest of this unreality. Even though they tried and succeeded in attaining political power and in controlling it, using it made them uneasy. Their public image probably reflects their self-image as highly principled human beings committed to the sanctity of life and to decency in personal and international relations. Too much so. Both were practically allergic to the use of force, almost displaying an open revulsion at the idea that civilized beings would have to settle any dispute in such a primitive way. They refused to look and were unable to see the jungle all around them. Neither understood the realities of the conflicting interests that led to World War I. The treaties that settled it were greatly influenced by Wilson's vision, and in large part they were responsible for the outbreak of World War II.

Unreality reigned supreme in the paradise of fools from which the U.S., and with it the West, are only beginning to emerge. Wilson claimed that World War I was "the war to make the world safe for Democracy," and many believed that the millennium was really about to arrive. Western man is unwilling to give up this very tempting dream even now, although the price paid in lives is already enormous.

Wilson and Bryan were both visionaries imbued with humanistic and religious principles, and both preached on behalf of international cooperation and world peace. Who can disagree with anything like that? The imagination of the American people, and to a lesser extent of Western man in general, was caught. We all like to see ourselves as morally superior and righteous. Young children are taught that being fair and saying "please" and "thank you" is the right way to be, and in the comfort of the West many well-meaning adults hold on to such innocent and charming notions throughout life, believing them to fit all situations and all people. They even assess political candidates for high office on this basis, giving much weight to how wholesome they look. Although pleasant, such people are obviously misfits in the jungle. So was Wilson.

Barbara Tuchman writes that "a phenomenon noticeable throughout history is the pursuit by governments of policy contrary to the welfare or advantage of the body being governed." Above all, those in power usually want to remain where they are and will therefore follow even the wildest dreams and wishes of the electorate, injurious or not. Unlike them, Wilson pursued his own harmful fantasy, as exemplified by his behavior in connection with the sinking of the British passenger liner *Lusitania* on May 7, 1915. The U.S. was still uninvolved, and Wilson urged all Americans in a formal proclamation to "remain neutral in thought as well as in behavior." He repeatedly offered to mediate between the warring nations, really believing that his neutrality, his fairness, and his good intentions would impress them enough to settle all disputes amicably. Surely all were civilized people of goodwill.

Wilson's naivete was also charming but disastrous. He could not emotionally comprehend the long-standing enmity that existed between the Germans and the British. Irreconcilable economic and political differences made worse by psychotic hate did not fit into his fairy-tale world.

On February 4, 1915, the government in Berlin announced that it would use its U-boats to sink without warning all ships in the war zone. This caused Wilson to warn Germany in a formal note dated February 10 that it would be held to "strict accountability" for the lawless actions of its submarine commanders. Destruction of an American vessel or of American lives, Wilson said, would be an "indefensible violation of neutral rights." The

Germans were not deterred. They knew Wilson's nature and counted on it. Threats by such a man were meaningless, they believed, and they were right.

More than 1,000 persons drowned, among them 128 Americans, when a German submarine sank the *Lusitania* without warning. Wilson and the American public were enraged, but their anger was short-lived. Fear is often hidden under anger. In any event, feelings are never a good reason for action, and neither Wilson nor most Americans wanted to see the truth about the Germans. Above all, they did not want to go to war. Wilson ascribed to Prussian militarists qualities typical of God-fearing Quakers, a feat that stretches even normal overidentification. Underneath the intellectual facade of competence he appears to have been a man driven to avoid confrontations almost at any cost, and needing to be conciliatory beyond all reason. Standing firm is experienced by many people as an invitation to disaster. Wilson was surely among them, but being bright he constructed a Weltanschauung that allowed him to accommodate to his fear without shame. He was described as being "determined" not to become beastly like the Europeans.

His brave warnings to Germany notwithstanding, Wilson knew that above all he had to avoid war. Like the U.S. in 1985, he tried to obtain justice in the jungle by moralistic preaching and legalistic maneuvering. Historians tell us that Wilson "displayed long-suffering patience," and in spite of the events unfolding before him he continued to believe that his sincerity would "compel" the Germans to at least abide by the conventions of war. We are told that his faith in his mission was "unshakable."

When action could no longer be avoided, Wilson finally decided to send a strongly worded protest to Germany, to shame them into civility. But even strong words were too much for Bryan, who refused to sign the protest and resigned. The Germans cleverly stopped using their submarine weapon against unprotected vessels for the following seven months, figuring that this would help the weak Wilson get re-elected. The American people were duped again. "He has kept us out of war" was the slogan that determined the outcome of the election. The pacifists rejoiced while Wilson outlined some of his idealistic concepts for peace, the harmful and confusing effects of which haunt us even now. Peace must exist without victory; no nation should ever extend its policy over another or dominate the land or the sea; secret diplomacy is not to be permitted; and all these will be assured by a League of Nations that will "protect the territorial integrity and independence of its members." The West has essentially lived by the spirit of these unrealistic principles while totalitarian outlaws regularly extended and consolidated their holdings. Then, on January 9, 1917, the Germans simply announced that they were renewing their unrestricted submarine campaign. The *Laconia* was sunk. Even Wilson no longer had any choice but to wake up.

President Truman, by contrast, was not so brilliant or articulate, but his personal boundaries must have been much better defined; he was not so inclined to overidentify. This enabled him to make very difficult decisions realistically and in the common interest. The hindsight of history proves that essentially he calculated cost-benefit ratios without the encumbrance of feelings. From personal experience he knew the real struggles of real people, and he did what he could to minimize their suffering. Not idealistic like Wilson, he was realistic like any other small-town haberdasher worrying about paying his bills on time. Respected even by those who did not admire him, a "small man" of the people, Truman was not tainted by high-sounding sentimentality. This was his strength.

The bankruptcy of idealism and of moralism as guiding principles in international relations has been obvious to all for some time. But Man's feelings overwhelm his reason even when he knows better. The science of international relations has become more realistic theoretically since the teachings of Hans Morgenthau replaced those of Wilson, but in practice not enough has changed.

Naivete continues to be an important component of the West's dealing with its adversaries and foes, and it typifies the way Americans personally relate to strangers. We trust cordiality too much and lower our guard too quickly; we expect honesty and fairness to override real interests; we are mostly pleasant, though ugly and pushy on occasion. The same qualities show in our international relations. Here all too often we still reject any use of military force. Endless accommodation and retreat have been familiar traits of the U.S. State Department ever since Bryan. Cyrus Vance also resigned because he rejected the idea of using armed forces, this time to try saving the American hostages in Iran. Such a man can still be appointed Secretary of State even now.

9. The Dangerous Fiction of International Law

Wilson's idealistic view of the world, a product of his feelings and wishes, became the foundation of what is known as international law. Its basic assumptions are simple: that the world consists of a family of nations; that the relationships among them must be conducted in an orderly fashion according to the rules of civilized existence; and above all that the use of force by one family member against another, termed "aggression," is a crime.

But there never was an international "policeman" strong enough to enforce this law, and it is unlikely that there ever will be. Aggressors such as the Soviet Union simply ignore such a code with impunity. Only the West accepted it and only the West is limited by it. The U.S., having been a prisoner of Wilson's fantasy for so long, often tried to act unilaterally and righteously as the world's policeman, only to be rebuffed and lose prestige. The West and the cause of civilization have not been served well by Wilson's dream.

Because it is rooted in wishful "thinking," this international "law" fails almost completely to reflect reality. Yet Wilson's stature and political influence were such that his fictional view of the world became the new theoretical standard of political behavior. It formed the basis of the U.N. Charter and its treaty of Universal Human Rights, hence their weaknesses. Most Western foreign policy decisions in the last seventy years or so have been guided by this "law," causing many issues to be ignored and major trends to be underrated. Chamberlain's appeasement of Hitler was justified by these delusional assumptions, and like a sedative they caused the West to overlook the rise of German and Japanese militarism. Nothing was done to stop them early.

The damage done by this belief in a nonexistent law continued near the end of World War II, at Yalta. FDR was already dying, Churchill was tired and eager to trust at least his allies, but Stalin, shrewd and scheming, was busy carving out the Baltic States and Eastern Europe for the Russians. He encouraged the other two to believe in the existence of an international law that would establish order after the hostilities ended, but he was not taken in by this idealistic nonsense. He lulled them with it. He did not tell them that the freedom that they were all supposedly fighting for would be immediately withdrawn in any area assigned to Soviet domination, and they did not want to know.

The people of Czechoslovakia, Hungary, and Poland are still paying the price. They have tried several times since 1945 to throw off this yoke, but like others in the Soviet empire they have failed. The iron fist of Russian imperialism has repeatedly expanded the borders of its empire while the West protested, piously citing this "law." Some are taken in even now by the catchwords and slogans of Communism.

Innocent young people are often unrealistically idealistic before they learn what life is really all about. Historically, the U.S. is still such a youngster, born to riches and, unlike the Russians, without powerful foes on its borders. It was even more true in Wilson's day. He represented a delusional trend that could develop only in a secure, affluent, and immature republic, still filled with the hope of easy solutions for everything. We are not yet far enough beyond that phase even now. We throw a lot of money into cancer research or anything else, and are almost surprised that the answers do not come out neatly at the end of the production line. Wilson's dream was expressed even more poetically a very long time ago:

> The wolf lives with the lamb, the panther lies down with the kid, calf and lion cub feed together with a little boy to lead them.
> The cow and the bear make friends, their young lie down together.
> The lion eats straw like the ox.
> The infant plays over the cobra's hole; into the viper's nest the young child puts his hand.
> They shall not hurt, nor shall they be harmed.
>
> [Isaiah 11:6–9]

But unlike Wilson, Isaiah was very realistic. He timed his fantasy for the "end of days." Nobody ever claimed for it the force of law in the present.

10. On the Need for Truth and the Current Necessity for Lies in Democracies

Why did the Reagan administration claim that the invasion into Grenada was only meant to save the lives of medical students? It was, in fact, to secure the island against a Marxist regime feared by all its Caribbean neighbors. Why did the British government forbid all press and television coverage of the war for the Falkland Islands, and why did it try to deceive the British public about the cost in lives and matériel? Why did Israel similarly exclude the international press from the front lines when it invaded Lebanon, and why did Ariel Sharon claim repeatedly that it was a much more limited operation than it turned out to be?

Because decades of sentimental moralizing and idealistic posturing have conditioned public opinion in Western societies to automatically reject such actions. Confused by the legal fiction of international "law," the public has come to expect the impossible as a matter of course: no fighting except to push back those trying to force themselves into our backyard. Grenada, the Falklands, and Lebanon all involved military attacks against political entities outside the international border of the attackers.

In each case, governments deliberated, considered, calculated, and finally acted in what they believed was self-defense. They did what they were elected to do—use good judgment and lead. But according to Wilson's simplistic "law," actions such as these three are defined as a crime called "aggression." No outward thrust is ever recognized as defensive. The Israelis counterattacked those who came to annihilate them; but they were reprimanded in the U.N. for crossing the international border while giving chase. The real aggressors who were pushed back did not consider it fair. Even the Strategic Defense Initiative, "Star Wars," would probably not pass the test of this strange "law." Incoming nuclear missiles would be destroyed in space before they hit us on the ground. Although grossly flawed, the yardsticks of this "law" are still being used by many in the West to judge the merits and worth of their societies. The massive protest movements of the last few decades all rose from this source. Pacifism makes no sense, but it dies hard.

International "law" became a more complex system with the passage of years, but the basic principles and attitudes remained the same. A powerless World Court has been stacked with biased representatives from underdeveloped countries, and they regularly render predictable opinions against the West. But like individuals, states reserve the right of self-defense even when others wish to deprive them of it. Besides, governments are sworn to protect the interests of their peoples.

Even if they had been wrong on the issues, the leaders in each of the countries involved acted openly according to their oath of office as they understood and interpreted it. Yet none of these three wars would have been tolerated by the people in whose interests they were waged had the truth been known early. The leaders had to shield themselves from emotional storms of indignation coming from a hostile electorate that was duped into believing in the fallacy of international "law." Western populations often condemn their governments for not following rules that no nation should or could follow in the first place.

The roots of Wilson's, and our, confusion are found in the false assumption that sovereign states follow the same rules of behavior that apply to individuals within a civilized order. But political entities exist in the jungle, and there things are different, and will continue to be. Nobody is powerful enough to enforce the rule of law on all others; and in historical periods when one superpower was hegemonic the power to police was always abused. Policemen without control usually become bullies.

As things stand, it is often necessary for leaders in free societies to lie, even when they perform their duties faithfully. Important segments of the Western press and television have appointed themselves special guardians of the idealistic fiction that states are never to defend themselves by initiating an attack, and they display much zeal in performing this task. They generally hold their governments to the standards of civilized individual behavior, as if this makes sense. Sometimes they actually delight in their power to catch a leader in a lie, as if they were young children seeing a parent fumble.

But lying must really be avoided, because it weakens the basic fiber of democracy. A failure of will after Vietnam, the result of such a breakdown of trust, rendered the U.S. ineffective for many years. The Vietnam war was never declared properly; perhaps no war, justified or not, can get the support of the people now. The resolve of the Israelis was similarly lost for a while after their controversial invasion of Lebanon. They wavered afterward even with regard to the basic principle of never yielding to terrorists. Both the U.S. and Israel are only beginning to recover from the damage done to them by the necessary duplicity.

Although truth must not be bent or distorted, the power of emotions is such that it must sometimes remain hidden for a while and out of public view. This used to be self-evident in earlier days, when life was much harder. Bad news was not always spread immediately, to avoid discouraging people who were discouraged already. But the explosive expansion of individual rights that resulted from the wild pursuit of self-fulfillment by the "me" generation has changed this situation.

Now many insist on knowing everything immediately, and journalists show little restraint in revealing whatever they can. Who can trust those in power anyway? Some want "participatory" democracy because they lack trust in their leaders, everything is to be decided by referendum. It never worked. Even very small democratic units need rulers, those chosen to make rules between elections. Someone better have the power to veto impulsivity and irresponsibility desired by an inflamed majority, or else chaos is sure to follow. But the idea of democracy is often misunderstood. Many fail to see that even in a free society citizens cannot always be privy to everything as soon as it happens, without endangering their own survival and that of their society. They also cannot always do or refuse to do whatever they wish. Yet both have become common expectations.

The orderly business of government in democracies is in danger, and paralysis eventually sets in when politicians begin to be chronically distrusted. Anarchy and barbarism then stake out ever larger claims. This is already true in parts of the West. Suspicion of the executive branch has become rather common, since it must repeatedly act in contradiction to what the people have come to expect. A sharp split often exists now between the two, as if they were antagonists. Even President Reagan, often popular and beloved, was not usually described in print or on television as a respected head of state. His programs were usually portrayed by the media as if they represented his personal agenda and interests, not those of the country. When he sustained a defeat in a battle with Congress, it was often reported gleefully as a victory for the common man. In the absence of truth the common interest is commonly forgotten.

Practically every opposition party in Western democracies has occasionally been very critical of those in power for not adhering more closely to moralistic, idealistic, and legalistic stances, only to disregard them once they come into power themselves. Real issues must be faced in a real way. Liberals and conservatives usually act in surprisingly similar ways under such circumstances. The responsibility of power is a great equalizer.

At best it is very difficult to rule in democracies, since even under ideal conditions Man submits to rules only reluctantly. He refuses to submit at all to those who lie to him. So governing becomes almost impossible when officials cannot always be truthful. With difficulty people understand the need for military secrecy and are usually willing to accept it for a while, but not the fact that basic policies are portrayed differently then they really are.

President Carter's naivete was so great that he believed the fiction of international "law" almost as much as Cyrus Vance did, and he had no choice therefore but to sacrifice the morally corrupt Shah. He did not have a legal way to intervene, and as an honest man could not invent one. Ronald Reagan and Margaret Thatcher never accepted these principles and did not adhere to them, yet they had to lie anyway. The people whose wars they waged still believed that such a "law" existed, and *they* lived by it.

This is why it is essential to renounce the principles of international "law" openly and consistently, and to make clear that we do not consider ourselves bound by it. Governments will then no longer need to cover up their legitimate activities, and they will not have to perform them furtively and sneakily, in the manner of the thief stealing in the dark of night. The truth that international "law" itself is a fiction and that its basic principles are lies must become widely known. Discarding it is not a matter of concern for legal experts only or for sophisticates interested in world affairs. Every citizen in the West has a direct personal stake in this issue, since everyone's safety and welfare are dependent upon the government's ability to govern.

11. A Sensible Code of Conduct for International Relations

The following is one possible alternative to Wilson's ideas, providing a basis for conducting international relations realistically. In many ways, this reflects the situation as it already exists.

1. Although we pretend otherwise, the world's affairs are essentially determined by the law of the jungle, not according to the rules of any civilized order. No world "community" or "family" of nations exists, and no general agreement to abide by any one law. So it is delusional and utopian for the West to act as if they existed, and it is naive to expect that anyone but believers would follow a nonexistent code.

2. Every country claims moral superiority for its rights, values, and system of government; no agreement exists about which, if any, have universal validity. No one can rationally expect its own yardsticks of morality to be used by everyone else.

3. In the jungle, might alone determines what is right. No one has sufficient power to dictate moral and political principles to all others. Even if the West had such power it would still not have the *moral* right to demand that those who follow practices that are abhorrent to its tastes and values should change. Our repugnance for man's inhumanity to man causes some of us to promote efforts to overthrow the regimes of South Africa, Nicaragua, Iran, or even those of Poland, Czechoslovakia, or Bulgaria. Whatever our claims, our only right is our power. Whether and to what extent we use this power are separate questions.

4. Justice is irrelevant in the jungle. We do not even agree on its content. Those without it often enforce their will on others anyway, if they have the power and the will to pay the required price. Since everyone in the jungle resorts to the use of force to advance and protect themselves, the West must also be strong enough, or disappear.

5. The most stable order that the world can hope for is based on the principle of living according to one's own preferences and letting others live according to theirs. This does not maximize justice by our standards, but it helps the chances for peace.

Non-aggression is however not always acceptable to everyone, including us. Not always can we force others to abide by this or by any other principle, and we should only try if we stand a good chance and are determined to succeed. Decency as defined by us and commitment to our truth do *not* give the West a superior right to become the world's policeman.

6. History has repeatedly affirmed that relative stability in the jungle is obtained only from a balance of power, so no one benefits from a hostile confrontation. This has again been proven true in global affairs since 1945.

7. Economic, political, and military power determine each nation's spheres of influence; and they alone validate international treaties and agreements. Honesty, truth, fairness, and justice, while highly desirable as civilized human qualities, have no force in international relations. Moral stature can sometimes be converted into political power, and everyone always tries to do so. There is no international law separate from these principles.

8. It is in the interest of the states committed to the civilized order to reduce the domain of the jungle. This is why they often join together in an alliance lasting as long as their separate interests mesh. In all economic, political, and military matters member states favor one another and no one else. This sometimes is an incentive for those in the jungle to also become civilized.

Membership is conditional upon continued adherence to the civilized order, and non-adherence is a sufficient reason for exclusion.

Although internal differences will sometimes limit their effectiveness, members of the alliance ideally should act as one, since barbarism threatens the security and existence of them all. But any member may retaliate alone against outlaws without protest from the others. Although honesty and truth do not generally apply in relations between sovereign states, members of the alliance may find it advantageous to deal with each other mostly on this basis.

9. Member states are expected to respond to any challenge from the jungle according to the five principles of rational response described earlier. This becomes especially important when a legally constituted state engages in terror or tries to indirectly blackmail by surrogates with nuclear weapons. Free societies would be wise to prepare themselves for such an eventuality now, before it becomes a reality.

10. Some legally constituted states not only engage in acts of terror against outsiders but also terrorize, repress, murder, and commit genocide against groups within their own borders. Empathy and concern for the victims is not a legitimate basis for action by another state, according to these principles. But gross violations against the civilized order anywhere threaten its existence everywhere. Those who possess enough force and the will to do so may wish to destabilize such states and eventually intervene directly, provided that failure is highly unlikely. Only success in such interventions would enhance the power of the one who intervenes, expand the civilized order, and save lives.

Aristotle observed that "law is order" and that "a good law is good order." The best order achievable in the jungle is based on the existence of clear boundaries and a stable balance between adjacent powers. No one can interfere then with the life, space, and property of others, even if they have no respect for their rights. This in fact turns the jungle into a de facto civilized order.

But how are we to define clear boundaries? It is not always easy or possible to do, and it can be done only as far as one can reach. No matter how strongly we disapprove of what happens outside our sphere of influence, we cannot usually do anything about it. Although we wish it were otherwise, we also have no moral rights, if point 3 above is valid. Besides, such efforts are bound to fail. Peaceful protests on our safe streets and demonstrations in front of an embassy may raise consciousness and make us "feel" a little less guilty, but they do not topple regimes. This may require leaving civilian jobs, joining the armed forces, mobilizing the economy, doing without the natural resources of the country we attack, sacrificing lives, and risking the civilized order. The real price is higher than what it appears to be at first. Sometimes it ought to be paid, but such a course should not even be advocated in the heat of passion.

If we insist on changing the policies of those outside our sphere, we must first weaken them economically, sow political discord, foment internal unrest and insurgencies, and eventually accept the possible need for direct military action. This is exactly what the agents of the Soviet Union, Libya, and Iran are trying to do in the West.

Decisions to intervene with force must be made on the basis of several simple factors:

A.   Power in various gradations is only used overtly and covertly to defend vital interests that lie within one's reach.

B.   We destabilize only those who live by the law of the jungle.

C.   We consider whether the civilized order is advanced with the existing, if imperfect, regime, or with its most likely alternative, with our intervention or without it. The welfare of the local population must also be carefully considered, but it does not in itself determine our course.

D.   We decide whether or not we are willing and able to pay the price required in blood, toil, tears, and other resources. Can we afford not to pay it?

What then should the West do in relation to South Africa and Libya? Decent people, white as well as black, cannot but be revolted by apartheid and by Qaddafi, but this turns out to be irrelevant if we are guided by the above principles. We may decide to destabilize the two if their international behavior is governed by the law of the jungle or if a gross violation against the civilized order takes place within their borders. These are relatively easy to determine when we are dispassionate. Our legislative bodies must then decide whether we are willing and able to pay the necessary price. Talk is cheap. Ruling out intervention in either case, we have no other option but the emotionally frustrating one of trying to persuade them without threats.

What about the likely outcome of our intervention? Will the

civilized order and South African blacks be better off if we succeed in destroying the current regime? Will the Libyans be ahead
without Qaddafi? Some claim that poverty and death would increase dramatically without the well-functioning economy of
the morally inferior white regime in South Africa, and that a
Lebanon-style civil war without end would pit black tribes
against one another, and fully armed whites against all those
who threaten them.

Surely no set of principles will fit all circumstances. Subjective
evaluations based on what we think we see will cause each of
each of us to give any principle a somewhat different meaning.
But even a crude and imperfect code is by far better than none. It
will lessen the chances that impulsivity in the guise of reason
will mislead us.

12. Three Practical Suggestions

It would probably make good sense for the U.S., as the leader of
the West, to seriously consider adopting one or all of the following:

1. Strive to somehow change the proclamation of Man's rights
in the Declaration of Independence to "life, liberty, and the pursuit of excellence." We have already seen that happiness is not
achievable by pursuing it. It may be found only when we no
longer pursue anything. But excellence is reachable if pursued
diligently enough, long enough, and consistently enough. Since
both the idea and the legal form of such a basic change would
require much discussion, this proposal will help focus attention
on the need to redirect our national efforts.

2. Redefine the legal guarantees of the First Amendment. A
wise and moderate formula will have to be devised that continues to guarantee Man's basic right to speak freely and to have a
free press, even when *public* expressions by the media are sometimes curtailed. The survival of the West and its rule of law may
not be possible without a change.

3. Free all elected federal officials from the need to follow
every whim of their constituents, thus making room for them to
lead and to be thoughtful. Political survival now demands that
representatives of the people attend to even the narrowest interests of their supporters, ignoring the overall welfare. This will be
lessened once no elected federal officeholder is ever allowed to
succeed him- or herself. It would still make no sense to become

insensitive to the needs and wishes of the electorate, since re-election for non-consecutive terms always remains a possibility.

Since everyone will be a lame duck equally, this status will no longer be a hindrance. Such representatives will be forced to actually live within the communities they wish to represent again, thus maintaining stronger local ties and independent careers as sources of income. Being a professional politician will come to be seen as a disadvantage.

Such a system is not only likely to improve the general quality of government, but it may also be essential for attaining fiscal responsibility, balancing the budget, and eliminating the U.S. federal deficit. Those with integrity will find it easier to pursue unpopular but necessary policies. Staggered terms will insure continuity.

The West is not made of one cloth. In general, those countries whose currencies are stronger attend to reality more faithfully than others. Self-interest as reflected in the financial markets is often more realistic than public policy. The Japanese yen and the Swiss franc have been reasonably firm for a long time, with the German mark following them on the list. The corrupting influences are everywhere, but they are not present equally in all free societies.

13. A Concluding Personal Note

The vision of a basically just, peaceful, and prosperous society has been Man's dream for thousands of years, and we in the West have come closer than anyone to achieving it. By now, many take Man's liberties, affluence, and dignity for granted, and they are no longer willing to sacrifice much for their preservation.

But the majority of people in the world can only dream of what we already have. The billions degraded by poverty and by hopelessness as well as those imprisoned behind the Iron Curtain or hidden by the black veil of fundamentalist Islam would give or do just about anything to trade places with us.

I vaguely remember from childhood the reluctance of good but naive Westerners to believe that the evils of Hitler and Stalin existed. Luckily I did not have the personal experiences of an Elie Wiesel or an Aleksandr Solzhenitsyn. But I will never forget the many white sheets, all stained with big blotches of bright-red blood, draping the bodies of those killed by terrorists, one truckload after another. Maybe eighty, or even a hundred bodies. It is perhaps necessary to have such experiences personally before impossible dreams about a perfect world finally die. Innocence is not given up easily.

As a young man I used to speak and write of the need to "preserve the purity of our weapons," only half understanding the difference between freedom fighters and terrorists. Painful realities have slowly taught me the difference. My own family, other families, and civilization itself have all paid a heavy price for our ignorance and self-delusion. We must never repeat such mistakes again, for we may not make it the next time around. The West's future must be insured by our vigilance and by our strict attention to reality in preference to all our wishes and feelings.

The sanctity of life and the rule of law are our moral armor, but such armor can remain shiny and always spotless only in museums. It is bound to get sullied in real battles in which it sometimes must be used.

EIGHT

A Unified Theory of General Human Motivation and Behavior

When we are born, we cry that we are come
To this great stage of fools—
SHAKESPEARE
King Lear

A vague but powerful sense of impending doom in the face of the unknown that was us and everything about us is every person's first experience after birth . . .
SECTION 1, THIS CHAPTER

. . . personal independence and self-sufficiency . . . only develop in the crucible of no-choice.
SECTION 99, THIS CHAPTER

Introduction

Early man survived despite a more or less constant sense of dread and impending doom. He existed within a terrifying unknown. What did he do to help himself? He invented a rich variety of belief systems to feel somewhat less vulnerable. By arbitrarily assigning some characteristics to the unknown features of his environment he felt more secure. In many ways primitive man was almost like a newborn infant, unable to comprehend or to control most of his environment. But unlike the newborn he was

318

at least conscious of externality and able to manipulate his body at will.

Fear would have become unbearable without his delusions. Man would have had no choice but to tune out his awareness much of the time, the least efficient way of coping with reality. Living by erroneous beliefs based on fabricated "knowledge" of the universe was not ideal, but it cost less. He had to find some way to survive in a world densely populated by dangerous ghosts without faces.

"In the beginning . . . the earth was without form, and void; and darkness was upon the face of the deep. And the Spirit of God moved upon the face of the waters. And God said, Let there be light: and there was light." Now we know that these words from Genesis reflect people's birth experiences more accurately than they mirror the creation of the world, but for a very long time we claimed that our own personal experiences provided the key to understanding the universe. This egocentric and simple-minded view pervaded our theories, including those of physics. The Ptolemaic system was based on Man's belief that he was favorably situated at the hub of the universe, and that from this grandstand the scheme of nature would simply unfold itself to him.

Even now most people see themselves, their relationships, and the universe from a naive perspective. We still derive much reassurance and solace from those whom we proclaim deities or personal saviors. Widespread mental depression, interpersonal conflict, and premature death by suicide, homicide, wars, and avoidable illnesses are the result.

Man was unable until recently to explain the nature of things on the basis of factual knowledge. He was capable of verifying only his most immediate physical experiences, acquiring bits and pieces of knowledge only slowly. Even so, throughout history he had to discard some of his primitive beliefs as his understanding of reality has constantly expanded.

Copernicus, Galileo, Newton, and Einstein elucidated the basic laws of the physical universe in the relatively short span of several hundred years. They have enabled us to look out ever further into space. It was relatively simple to verify hypotheses about gravity by dropping objects from the Leaning Tower of Pisa, but a revolution in thinking had to precede this development: Facts had to be verified.

Nonexistent tools and novel procedures are often needed to check the validity of new hypotheses and theories; these must first be developed. Though proof may not be immediately obtainable, it must eventually be found. Einstein's general theory of relativity has not been conclusively confirmed in all its details even today, since our knowledge and instruments are not quite sophisticated enough even now. So the process of verification continues. In spite of such difficulties we have been rather successful in uncovering the secrets of the physical world. With the big bang theory we have even made a serious attempt to explain creation itself, 10,000 million years ago.

We have not done nearly as well in the psychologic realm. Here we must look inside ourselves, and we are simultaneously the observers and the subjects of the observation. Whatever we see affects us directly. We naturally tend to shy away from looking into areas that cause us pain, embarrassment, or fear. So we know less of what happens in our inner space than of what happens far away in outer space. We are only beginning to grope in this dimly lit internal universe.

It was only yesterday that we learned to correct many of the physiologic and anatomic malfunctionings of our internal environment. Until recently medicine was almost completely nonscientific. Before the introduction of anesthesia, surgery was woefully primitive; antibiotics, organ transplantation, and the many technologic marvels that we now take for granted simply did not exist. And we are even further behind in knowing how to treat the ailments affecting Man's mind, which has not been mapped out as well as his anatomy. Even now these conditions are considered to be of interest mostly to priests, social workers, and gurus; or else they are regarded as chemical disturbances treatable by medications alone. Ignorance abounds.

The Cartesian view holds that nature is composed of two independent realms, matter and mind. This separation enabled science to develop, since it overcame the powerful Aristotelian model upheld by the Catholic Church. God's nature and the human soul were no longer the main subjects of interest to the seekers of new knowledge. Contemplation and speculation were henceforth regarded as less valuable than observation and experimentation. "Inert" substances and mechanistic relationships became legitimate subjects for scientific study once they were separated from the spiritual.

It is becoming increasingly clear, however, that compartmentalizing and dividing the universe was a mixed blessing. We have achieved technologic success but with it came human alienation and greater despair. In spite of our unique brain, which allows us to understand so much, we failed to see that all phenomena were still bound together, as always. Although Man could neatly categorize the physical universe, he remained a complex being full of contradictions between thinking and feelings. *He* was not inert and could not be packaged so neatly. He, the observer, was wrong in believing that his powers of observation made him as easy to define as the other things he observed. Even though he could explain so many of the phenomena around him, he did not become explainable; many of his acts were not rational.

Because of the miraculous abilities of his mind, Man began to think of himself as essentially different from all the other living creatures. Having eaten of the tree of knowledge, he began to behave as if he were becoming a god. His ability to make judgments and to choose filled him with so much pride and with such a sense of power that he was blind to his continuing fragility and error. Perhaps he could banish powerlessness forever by the use of his rationality! In the flush of discovery Man forgot that in spite of all his achievements he remained not only mortal but also subject to the sway of his emotions, those irrational forces that delude him again and again.

Man can indeed become more powerful and exist just below the angels, but not easily and not while he clings to his delusions. Like the Patriarch Jacob, every person must first wrestle with and conquer the basic tendency to avoid the frightening and the difficult. It is easier and much more natural to dream and to evade fear by repeatedly escaping into unreality, even if this condemns us to remain smaller and weaker than we potentially are.

Our wishful thinking has led us to believe that we have become powerful already. But Man is destined to continue groveling in depression unless he finds the courage to look at and into himself realistically. Descartes and Freud took us a few important steps forward in the dark abyss, but we must now detour around them if we wish to proceed further, just as Einstein did with Newtonian concepts.

The Eastern mind sees the universe in terms of unity. All opposites are regarded as parts of the same, all comparisons recognized as belittling and confusing. This integral view is closer to modern physics, which explains the universe as an internally consistent system, an ever-expanding and contracting whole. Nothing is inert. Even our mind is part of the physical universe.

Man is not basically different from all the other physical phenomena. In spite of his unique potential, he remains part of the animal kingdom.

According to Einstein's general theory of relativity, space is not three-dimensional and time is not a separate entity; both form a four-dimensional "space-time." Mass is nothing but a form of energy stored in the resting object. Gravity curves both time and space. Such difficult concepts stretch our imagination. Ordinary language and knowledge derived from direct personal experiences had to be transcended. This caused an unsettling revolution in our understanding not only of the universe but of ourselves. We had to give up Euclidean geometry and mechanistic Newtonian physics, and with them some of our smugness that we had a "solid" understanding of everything. The same is even more true as we consider a new theory of human motivation and functioning.

Is it not likely that in the psychological realm, as in the physical one, a single key exists that can unlock the mysteries of all the strange and divergent behavioral phenomena of our species? It is, in fact, much easier to imagine one basic motive uniting the seemingly unrelated and complex behaviors of Man than it was to conceptualize the unity envisioned by Einstein.

This chapter is an attempt to elucidate such a theory. In its light, every human act should make sense. It will have to be modified, or its claim to be a general theory will have to be dropped, until it is capable of explaining all aspects of Man's behavior. The fact that full verification may not be immediately possible does not invalidate it, however. Acceptable proof must be marshaled, but this may require some time if the instruments needed for validation do not yet exist. Careful scrutiny by many independent and objective observers will determine the eventual worth of this effort.

The Theory

MAN'S EARLIEST BEGINNINGS

1. A vague but powerful sense of impending doom in the face of the unknown that was us and everything about us is every person's first experience after birth, always completely out of consciousness. Since we exist in that situation before we have any comprehension of anything, including time, it is a timeless

experience. It is felt as eternal. The entire experience has absolutely no meaning for us, no direction, no framework, only dread.

2. The sense of dread is the direct and unavoidable result of the newborn's suddenly being thrust into an altogether new environment. After many months of living in a relatively constant and finely regulated setting, it abruptly finds itself under radically new conditions, without any time for transition. It must suddenly adjust to a gaseous environment, totally different from the liquid one in which it existed before. Its physiology must suddenly function in a totally new way.

3. Dread or irrational fear is therefore the earliest and often the most persistent companion of every living person. This was not obvious in the past because realistic dangers were much more prominent. Only in modern affluent societies living in peace has Man's physical survival not been constantly under threat. Large and powerful animals do not devour humans anymore, death from hunger or exposure is less common, the Black Plague and other scourges have been wiped out, and lesser illnesses are being treated better than ever. Dread is much more evident these days, since it is no longer so obscured by real danger.

4. Nothing is lost in the universe. Even though we have no conscious memory of our early experiences, our body remembers. We adapt to them or perish. The sudden infant death syndrome may well be a respiratory expression of such a failure to adapt. Every person's physiologic reaction patterns are residues of these earliest experiences. Our automatic bodily reactions are usually fixed for life, although they can be altered by persistent therapeutic efforts. These early adaptations are the most central ones of the personality, and they limit and color all future adaptations and learning by the organism.

5. In the absence of prior knowledge about how to adjust, any stimulus that exceeds the threshold of sensation shakes the entire body and affects it in a generalized and non-specific way. Differentiated and partial reactions occur after a while, but the original reactions are generally total and out of proportion to the strength of the stimulus. Such all-or-none reactions exhaust the organism. Further stimulation during regressive periods used for regrouping may cause only a faint reaction or none at all. Such periods are the prototypes of the resignation and the deep sense

of futility often associated with disappointments and defeats later in life.

6. The fear of non-being is the earliest and the most profound fear of all. It is generally unconscious and unknown as such, although every living person experienced it and fears its re-emergence. It is not the same as the fear of dying, which is less intense.

7. Above all, Man wants to avoid re-experiencing the panic he had to endure early in life. Any knowledge or memory of it is usually blotted out of consciousness. Gaining power, real or imaginary, in order to undo the sense of vulnerability is the single, basic force at the root of all human behavior. The push away from fear or dread supersedes everything. All the otherwise unexplainable phenomena of human behavior begin to make sense in the light of man's omnipresent push to gain real or even imaginary power and thus to avoid re-experiencing unfathomable panic.

By nature Man is neither good nor bad, he just is. Capable of compassion when he feels safe and content, he can also be extremely cruel when in the grip of fear. At such times he may totally lack any consideration of anyone besides himself.

8. Whatever anyone does is *subjectively* experienced at that moment as the best one is capable of doing. Even the most dastardly, stupid, and self-destructive deeds must be regarded as such. This does not imply that illegal or immoral acts should therefore be tolerated or excused by others. Deeds that may be objectively damaging or even destructive to the doer are often not recognized as such until much later. Everyone would surely act more wisely if only they could. Why does anyone ever do anything that is not really in his best interest? Because the urgent push to avoid fear commonly distorts perception, often in a surprisingly gross fashion.

9. Character change and even lasting behavioral change require a prior shift in one's perception of all relationships to oneself and to others. Improved insight and greater understanding do not, however, in themselves bring about much change of any kind. Feelings usually continue to exert a powerful influence, forcing a person to remain the same for as long as possible.

10. The newborn is constantly alert for as long as it has the strength, as anyone would be who suddenly finds himself in a

totally incomprehensible environment. Even the most terrifying science-fiction films present only mild examples of such a fear-filled situation. A viewer can separate himself from the experience; the newborn cannot. The only escape the newborn has is to withdraw emotionally into itself.

11. The newborn is best understood not as a person but as a developing complex of physiologic reaction patterns. A person has at least some conscious awareness; the newborn has none. Subjectively it exists in a precarious state, at the mercy of powerful and strange stimuli that rob it of its tranquility without rhyme or reason. Even objectively the newborn may be subject to much abuse. René Spitz observed, for instance, "that surgeons in leading hospitals routinely perform mastoidectomy without any anesthesia on defenseless infants."

The sense of dread is greatest during the earliest moments after birth when the extrauterine reactions of the physiology are first being tested and before the organism "knows" that they can sustain its life. Although we can ameliorate the shock slightly by improving the external conditions of the birthing room, no one can escape this experience.

12. Every person reading these lines, rich or poor, king or servant, is therefore truly a survivor. A sense of impending danger and at least traces of irrational fear are imbedded in everyone's body. People generally try to deny the experience of such fear, partly because they know of no good reason for its existence; its dimensions are much larger, however, and its roots deeper than ever described before. The fear is often responsible for major errors in judgment since it greatly interferes with the capacity to evaluate what one sees.

13. Being consciously frightened makes people aware of their vulnerability, so they deny and hide their fears, both from themselves and from others. Fear that is successfully repressed or suppressed is not experienced as such, but it nevertheless continues to be a powerful force. All other feelings are experienced and expressed only in the space that fear does not occupy. Anger, hate, and romantic "love" often serve to keep fear out of sight.

14. The attempts to hold fear and the accompanying sense of powerlessness at bay command much of Man's time and resources. All conscious choices, including life-style and value

system, are limited to and determined by these attempts. Thoughtful and fear-free living is possible, but it is achievable only with much work over time, never spontaneously.

15. Most newborns are not ordinarily in real danger. The sense of dread that carries over into adulthood is therefore not only unrealistic but usually also incomprehensible to most adults. This further fuels the pump of anxiety. People are generally sustained by their belief that they at least know what to expect in reality. Powerful subjective experiences that make no rational sense threaten this belief. A correct theory of human behavior cannot eliminate dread, but it can help preserve some of Man's rational self-image.

THE "PULL OF REGRESSION" AND THE "PUSH AGAINST PROGRESSING"

16. No mothering is ever perfect. Everyone experienced at least brief moments of panic when the mothering person did not respond properly or fast enough to some physiologic need. The absence of, or delay in, response at such moments causes a generalized tensing within the organism, which then uses its entire force to undo what it experiences as danger. Its crying, screaming, and shaking appear to observers as powerful efforts to summon help, but more accurately they are merely attempts to re-establish equilibrium.

17. Such powerful early experiences leave traces in the body. The wish to live without fear is synonymous with the wish to be mothered perfectly by oneself or by others, and it continues to be every person's basic goal throughout life. In adulthood it has many of the same forms it had in infancy (as listed in Section 65): to be touched, to be held and seen, to be given to, and to be unconditionally loved, welcomed, and accepted.

18. The generalized wish to be mothered by others rather than by oneself is the "pull of regression." It normally exists at least as a minor force in everyone, and it commonly interferes with intimate, mature relationships. It is responsible for much interpersonal friction and conflict, especially but not exclusively within the family. This "pull of regression" is universally an important part of Man before he matures psychologically, and it remains a central expectation till death, unless the process of individuation is essentially completed.

19. Mammals know the engulfing warmth of Mother's body, and their young are not weaned easily. Even some birds have to be pushed out of the nest before they attempt flying. In Greek mythology, tortoises were evil demons, perhaps because humans could not otherwise explain why those creatures buried their eggs in the sand and let their newborns fend motherlessly for themselves.

Unlike tortoises, we know our mothers and we understandably hold on to them tenaciously and refuse to let go. In some primitive cultures mothers paint their nipples with a black and bitter substance when their babies are old enough, to force them off the breast. This must also be done psychologically. The growing human organism does not assume responsibility for its own care automatically. It wants freedom to have its own way and to make its own decisions, but it also expects others (mothers) to do whatever it does not wish to do for itself.

20. The continued wish to be mothered is not always recognized easily. It is often expressed in the form of chronic helplessness, with the obvious aim for getting attention and help. In order to be cared for, people sometimes become sickly, chronically ill, financially dependent, or professionally incompetent. Criminal and other socially unacceptable behavior that forces society to take the offender into custody and thus care for him and chronic poverty in the midst of affluence can also be disguised forms of this hidden wish. Chronic forgetfulness, inattention, confusion, and functional learning disabilities sometimes serve the same purpose. Such pathologic expressions may remain totally unconscious, but they nevertheless keep some people helpless in spite of all the help that others repeatedly offer them.

21. Mothers who were themselves not mothered properly or not enough find it difficult to mother their children or to wean them appropriately and on time. They are often impatient with the clinging and scared baby, or else they overidentify with its needs and overlook its increasing competence. Babies who are not weaned properly—too early, too late, or too abruptly—tend to remain dependent and to become addicted to helplessness in its many forms. They unconsciously expect that helplessness will assure Mother's presence forever. Weaning in the broadest sense refers to the giving up not only of Mother's breast but also of the possibility that anyone outside the self can forever provide warmth, comforting, assurance, and nutrition.

22. The "push against progressing" is the persistent refusal to grow up and to acquire mastery, and it may be conscious or unconscious. It is also the persistent refusal to mother oneself appropriately and lovingly. The "push against progressing" is based on the delusion that infantile wishes are fulfillable, and it ignores the basic changes in circumstances that occur with time. Normally, both the wish for mothering by others and the refusal to become self-sufficient are given up only after protracted struggles, when it finally becomes obvious that no other choice exists but to adhere to the unyielding demands of reality. (See also Sections 9 and 99.)

23. Unlike the "pull of regression," which is normal and universal, the "push against progressing" is pathologic. Both the pull and the push are powerful forces that affect the personality profoundly and often determine a person's entire life-style and level of competence.

24. The "push against progressing" blossoms fully only in the absence of an effective father and in the presence of an immature mother who approves at least tacitly of the child's refusal to progress. No child dares to reject self-sufficiency for long without a powerful ally. Very early in life this is always the person who provides the mothering.

Mothers who are frightened and ill-prepared are most likely to be insensitive as they wean their babies, and they are likley to do so clumsily and at the wrong time. They commonly misjudge both the real helplessness and the growing competence of the infant, thus withholding help it really needs or overprotecting and pushing help that it does not. The child's "push against progressing" is often tolerated as an unconscious compensation for inadequate mothering. Besides, the mother may herself be addicted to it.

25. The pathologic "push against progressing" commonly masquerades as the non-pathologic "pull of regression," because the wish to be taken care of forever has less legitimacy. Although people in general do not consciously know the difference between the two, they tend to be much less tolerant of those who refuse to grow up than they are of the others who are truly afraid to proceed.

In the last analysis, the resources of society are called upon to provide for all those not producing what they consume, whatever the cause. One of the basic requirements of all past civilizations was therefore that Man not yield either to the "pull of regression" or to the "push against progressing." Like it or not, he was commanded to eat his bread by the sweat of his brow. In leaner days this was also a necessity for survival.

26. In highly developed and affluent democratic societies the "push against progressing" is often accepted as legitimate. Those living by this push are also voters. Self-indulgence, which consists of thoughtless acts that provide regressive gratification in an area already freed from fear, is thus encouraged.

Legislation that legitimizes the pathologic refusal to mature and that supports those living by it sabotages their chances ever to become self-sufficient, and condemns them to living without maturity, mastery or a sense of pride.

27. Politicians, journalists, and reformers are human too and not exempt from the "pull of regression" or even from the "push against progressing." They often tend therefore to overidentify with both the truly disadvantaged and those who merely claim to be helpless. So help is frequently offered at the wrong time to the wrong people, in the wrong form and in the wrong amount. Such "help" tends to perpetuate the "push against progressing," since it diverts the normal "pull of regression" into pathologic channels.

28. Healthy maturation consists of overcoming both the regressive pull and the associated push. The satisfaction and pride obtainable from mastery are soon recognized as having far greater value than receiving any handouts. Emotionally mature individuals can mother themselves whenever they need support, although they can also accept solace and help from others. Such "self-mothering" consists of settling down while in the midst of anxiety, without regressing. It requires taking appropriate time away from adult responsibilities and duties for resting, relaxation, and recreation.

29. Adulthood is correctly defined by age and body size. It does not necessarily signify intellectual or emotional maturity (as the terms "adult education" or "adult movies" prove). The chronologic, intellectual, and emotional ages can be and often are totally unrelated.

Most adults are physically grown-up children of various emotional ages. They typically act and react on the basis of their earliest life adaptations as reflected in their feelings and physiologic reaction patterns. They often keep their feelings hidden from public view, however, because of the fear of social disapproval. Shame and embarrassment cause people to hide and to deny their infantile connections for as long as possible.

30. Hidden or not, feelings always yield reliable clues about a person's emotional age. Behavior and body language reveal the nature of hidden feelings. Many intellectually mature adults are often emotionally not much older than toddlers. Intellectual, political, financial, and other achievements tend to confuse and to conceal the marked discrepancy that often exists between the emotional and the chronologic age.

THE BOUNDARIES OF THE SELF

31. The boundaries of the self (or ego) are not as clearly demarcated as those of the physical body. Once the umbilical cord is cut we become a separate physical entity, but our dependency on Mother continues for many years, and so does our wish to be taken care of. For a very long time humans are really incapable of caring for themselves, and their extensive need for others becomes addictive to many. In a sense, we are all born prematurely. Becoming psychologically separate is not as automatic as physical separation, which is abrupt and about which we have absolutely no say.

32. The boundaries of the self are only symbolic concepts, existing psychologically without physical representation. They cannot be observed directly, but their nature can easily be deduced from the ways a person typically relates to other people and things. Such external attributes as educational achievements, financial status, political position and power, and physical attractiveness are all irrelevant in judging the integrity of personal boundaries.

33. A person must individuate to become a separated individual, and this is achieved by clarifying and firming the boundaries of the self. An individuated person senses clearly where he begins and where he ends, what is internal and what is external. Such clarity about one's boundaries is quite uncommon, and it is hardly ever fully achieved automatically. Anxiety in varying degrees is everyone's occasional companion before individuation is achieved. Panic is commonly evoked when a non-individuated person suddenly senses his or her aloneness. A desperate need to be psychologically attached to another person, a cause, or an

activity generally drives people at such times without respite or mercy.

34. The wish to remain psychologically attached always co-exists with an opposite wish for self-sufficiency and separate-ness. But since all children encounter situations that they are unable to master, fear often overrides the wish for independence. Really letting go of all mothering figures is therefore a very scary prospect, analogous to, but much more frightening than, letting go of the side of a deep swimming pool for the first time and daring to venture into its middle. (See also Section 22.)

35. Those with fuzzy or imperfect boundaries tend to hold on to mothering figures longer and more tenaciously. The more clearly defined one's boundaries are, the less the fear of self-sufficiency and personal independence. Paradoxically, reason-ably intact boundaries also allow a person to become somewhat emotionally dependent, since fusion is not perceived then as a real danger.

36. No real intimacy or closeness is possible without a sense of clear boundaries. Close contacts without tension are best maintained between individuals or states that are stable and se-cure within their boundaries and more or less equally matched in terms of power. Disturbances in the balance of power typi-cally precipitate turmoil and unrest. When the psychologic or geographic borders are not clearly demarcated, the person or state is in constant uncertainty and flux, and closeness is com-monly experienced as a dangerous encroachment.

37. Open or indefensible boundaries of states or of people are perceived as dangerous to the existence and the integrity of those involved. Invasions from the ouside are believed to be an ever-present possibility, and so are takeovers and annexations by more powerful neighbors. One way to preserve oneself is to trade independence for protection; another is to arm oneself heavily and let no one come close. The first is taken by those who expe-rience themselves as having no better choice, since their sense of vulnerability is extreme. The second way is open to those who experience their fears as less extreme or less immediate. With sufficient armor and while on constant guard they can perhaps maintain their independence and separateness.

38. Open borders of states or people are often sensed as open-ings through which one's "life substance" might ooze out. To-

talitarian regimes cannot prevent their populations from escaping except by coercive barriers, as the Berlin Wall and the Iron Curtain illustrate well. People lacking an intact psychologic skin also put up barriers to keep others from coming too close, lest they be sucked dry by them. The fear of losing all of one's strength, vitality, and even identity causes many people to continually maintain great distances from others. Intimacy can only be achieved after the boundary defect of the self is repaired.

39. People with ill-defined boundaries therefore shun real love and friendship; their predominant fear is of engulfment. They usually seek romantic "love," the security pact of the non-individuated, while rejecting the gifts of true love. Conflicts, divorce, and even violence are common in romantic "love," because the closeness eventually exceeds the tolerance for it by one of the partners while insufficient for the other. Discord often results for no other reason than one partner's wish to maintain a safe distance.

40. The earliest conscious fear is that of abandonment, and clinging is the typical way by which infants and adults defend themselves against it. Infants never feel really safe before they attain an internalized sense that Mother can be counted upon to be present. Without it, the developing organism exists essentially in a state of intermittent panic.

But all clinging must eventually come to an end, even if the boundaries between the self as a separate being and Mother have not yet been clearly demarcated. The inevitable separations intensify the panic. The greatest boundary defects result from premature or abrupt separations from Mother, since they activate the fear of abandonment.

The fear of engulfment originates from a somewhat later stage of development, and pushing away is the typical way of defending against it.

41. Both the fear of abandonment and the fear of engulfment normally co-exist in every person, along with the tendency to cling and the urge to push away. But the proportional strength of each changes from time to time, depending on later life experiences. More intense anxiety is usually associated with the earlier fear of abandonment than with the fear of engulfment, so clingers are generally at the mercy of pushers-away and are often exploited and used by them.

42. Clingers typically camouflage their panic about being abandoned by offering romantic "love," which is how they trade independence for protection. Those fearing engulfment sooner or later become suspicious of such "offers," which they eventually experience as choking. The stronger their sense of choking, the more powerfully they push away, usually using the power of anger. Pathologic relationships often persist for long periods, however, even when they are destructive to both partners, if the fears of those involved are complementary and essentially in balance.

43. Pushers-away are generally too fearful to experience their yearnings to be held or to cling, but such wishes always exist underneath. Although clingers experience much more overt anxiety and appear more fragile, they actually face a more primitive fear and are therefore usually somewhat ahead in the struggle to become whole.

44. Those basically afraid of abandonment cling to causes as well as to people. Political and religious movements and even places of steady employment serve as attachment points, as do real mothers, marriage partners, lovers, and gurus. Clingers always become followers. The anxiety and dread are held in check as long as the psychologic attachment remains essentially undisturbed.

45. Those basically afraid of engulfment and of being taken over tend to withdraw from others and into themselves, even when they appear to be socially involved. Psychologic isolation is often hidden by excessive physical mingling.

46. A person's predominant fears yield reliable clues about his or her earliest life experiences. Major alterations in later life circumstances sometimes modify a person's way of being in the world, but these are usually only temporary changes. The type and magnitude of a person's typical fears also convey useful information about the state of his or her boundaries.

Those with unclear personal boundaries tend to develop a rigid character structure which helps them define themselves. Rigidity is not an indication of strength, as flexibility and softness are not necessarily signs of weakness.

47. Those with unclear personal boundaries also tend to overidentify with others with whom they have an emotional affinity, even when they do not see that similarities exist.

The more extensive the boundary defect, the greater the confusion that results from overidentification. The fears, hurt, and rage of others are experienced by those who overidentify as if they were their own. Such overidentification always interferes with the ability to assess the real interests of those with whom one overidentifies. This is a common difficulty among those who enter the so-called helping and teaching professions.

Overidentification generally remains unrecognized, and its very existence is commonly denied because it is self-serving. Veiled or not, overidentification is a common source of much harm. For instance, decent people normally empathize and identify with the powerless and the sexually abused child, not with the abusers. But overidentification interferes with understanding the problem and it reduces the chances of containing the damage.

In general, unrecognized overidentification with others poses extreme dangers to democratic societies in the age of mass communication. Public opinion is very malleable, and the feelings of viewers can now be influenced most powerfully, and even changed directly and instantaneously. Widespread confusion and doubt are often the result, even though generally no malice is involved. Personal relationships are regularly damaged by overidentification, and it often paralyzes the ability of free societies to pursue policies of reason in their best interest (See Sections, 89, 90, and 92.)

48. People with well-defined boundaries also identify with others, but they do not overidentify. Since their psychologic skin is more intact, they are generally less fearful, and they tend to identify with those who are perceived as more powerful. They often espouse conservative positions even if they are economically not so well off, since their subjective experience is one of greater safety in the world. They are not so eager to change things as to conserve and preserve them.

49. Those with diffuse personal boundaries, on the other hand, usually experience themselves subjectively as powerless, and this colors their "choice" of values. Such people commonly identify with the have-nots, and they tend to become liberal or even revolutionary in their politics or economics, even if very wealthy. The paradox of the Kennedys or Patty Hearst is often described in terms of guilt, but it probably is better explained in terms of diffuse boundaries. Although such people usually insist on holding on to the many objective advantages that they have,

they often support those who wish to destroy the existing order. In spite of their riches, they are looking for a better world in which they too would feel safer. Wealth obviously does not insure safety, and it is not the key to real power.

50. Ill-defined personal boundaries are often shored up and strengthened by pushing against something outside the self, usually another human being. Seemingly senseless angry attacks upon objects or people often serve an important, if socially unacceptable, purpose: to define for the attacker what is not part of the self and indirectly what is.

51. People with ill-defined boundaries tend to be "other-directed." The greater their boundary confusion, the more they are dependent upon outside influences to define who they are, what they stand for or against, and what they must do. Their antennae are always acutely attuned to the outside to make sure that they either please or displease others, depending on which of their fears is predominant. Such a state of unrest and agitation eventually leads to premature physical or emotional collapse.

52. Those with reasonably well defined boundaries, on the other hand, tend to be "inner-directed." Both the sense of self-esteem and the basic understanding of right and wrong are well rooted within. They comfort and discipline themselves more competently than others. They fear less, they get hurt less frequently and less severely, and they become bitter and angry only with greater provocation. In general, fewer pressures from the outside threaten self-worth when its measurement is safely anchored within the self.

53. The attainment of well-defined ego boundaries is the ultimate goal of maturation, and it is not achievable through formal learning or by gaining insight. The self is only defined by repeated testing of one's size and strength in relation to other humans and things. This yields reliable and useful lessons only if those with whom the testing is done are predictable, consistent, and emotionally stable.

Damaged or incomplete boundaries of the self can be repaired provided that the same conditions exist; the work can be done only in long-term relationships that are deeply involving and truly reliable. They must be sturdy enough to withstand even repeated tests under the most intense stresses that can occur between people. Formal, superficial, or essentially intellectual relationships do not provide the setting needed for reaching this difficult goal. Most current attempts to repair boundaries in psychotherapy fail because the relationship is not real enough and the mutual involvement only tenuous and insubstantial. Character change is at least as difficult a process and almost as time consuming as character formation was in the first place.

54. Only the chronologic age matters before the law, in the marketplace, and in the electoral booth. Ignoring the emotional age of individuals is unavoidable, especially in democracies, but it explains most of the gross distortions in all societies.

55. The primitive and immature nature of individuals finds wider expression today because affluence and relative national security in the West have combined to form more permissive societies. In such settings the concept of democracy is often incorrectly understood, which sometimes encourages irresponsible action. Democracy does not mean that everyone is entitled to "do his thing," but only that everyone has the right to have a say and to expect his vote to be counted.

Highly structured totalitarian societies force their populations to act in mature-like modes that obscure but do not change the underlying emotional immaturity. This limits irresponsible action, however, at least in public, and it has markedly reduced street crime. (See Section 89.)

OBSERVATIONS ON PERSONAL POWER AND ON POWERLESSNESS

56. Long before we gain consciousness we associate the most dreadful sense of danger with the experience of powerlessness. The push to gain power has such a tremendous force because it is the only hope Man has had of overcoming his sense of precariousness.

Max Weber, like many others, defined power as "the possibility of imposing one's will upon the behavior of other persons." Everyone's earliest experiences consisted of being subjected to the will of others more powerful than onself, so Man reasoned in adulthood that power must consist of the ability to control rather than be controlled. But such definitions cannot be correct. Men and women with much political, financial, sexual, and other power to control others are not free of dread. It affects high military and governmental officials and millionaires no less than poverty-stricken and marginal people.

57. Like desperate alcoholics or drug addicts, those who experience themselves as powerless always frantically grab at any

straw, any idol to believe in, anything offering momentary relief, regardless of the cost.

58. Powerlessness and dependence are what we dread the most. All excessive pursuits of wealth, pleasure, political influence, and territorial dominance—even the pursuit of happiness itself—are attempts to minimize vulnerability and the possibility of being hurt by others. Yet happiness is not achievable by pursuing it, only by not pursuing anything.

Most people spend most of their resources throughout most of their lives to attain power in whatever form they believe it exists. But if the goal is ever reached, unexpected disappointment and despair often follow. The pursuit itself keeps hope alive. Joy and peace of mind are findable only in the absence of irrational fear, which commonly rises to the surface just as one reaches the goal of retirement, riches, or fame. This may well be the secret meaning of the biblical dictum that one cannot see God and live, for having found a god outside of the self condemns Man to never discover power within himself.

59. Confusion about the correct definition of power has always kept Man busily pursuing pleasure, distraction, wealth— or anything else he thought or felt power to be—without finding peace of mind. The push was always so intense that neither the prophets of old nor the preachers of today have ever dissuaded him from the pursuit.

Man has understandably equated finding "pleasure," which lessened his panic, with attaining real power. He felt less vulnerable for a while in the embrace of an accepting mate or in the grip of some cause, under the influence of alcohol or in the numbness of drugs—even though many of these pursuits were labeled "morally inferior." Like a drowning person, he knew that his urgent need was immediate relief, not a promise of rewards in a world to come.

60. As suggested in Sections 48 and 53, real power is a function of individuation, the attainment of well-defined ego boundaries. Then neither the fear of abandonment nor the fear of engulfment play any significant role, although the fear of nonbeing may continue to lurk in the background. This most horrible of fears may still haunt us in extreme or life-threatening situations.

Real power is derived from control over one's own life. Rather than being at the mercy of emotions or constantly having to please or displease others, those with personal power face adversity as well as joy with their whole beings. Little energy is wasted on attending to unreal concerns or to unresolved conflicts from the past.

61. First religion and then science claimed to have the power to free Man of panic and dread. As long as he faithfully believed in either system the promise was kept, at least in the short run. Since death often arrived before disillusionment, the short run was all that mattered. But we no longer die quickly enough today to escape anxiety or disillusionment, and this is why they appear to be more common.

62. All delusions have the power of reality for those who live by them, because they temporarily dispel the sense of powerlessness. This is why so many deranged individuals claim that they are Christ or Napoleon.

63. True believers exist by their beliefs, even if these are objectively fallacious. Their fanaticism is derived from their semiconscious sense that their feeling of relative security depends upon the validity of their belief system. This is why they commonly display so much zeal in proselytizing non-believers: Every convert firms up their own shakiness.

64. We have already observed in Section 15 that newborns are not ordinarily in real danger; panic is mostly a subjective experience. The newborn's physiology nevertheless adjusts to such non-objective experiences, since they are perceived as real. In general, most of our knowledge about the universe is subjective, and subjectivity contaminates practically all objective observations. The way we are is the way we survived, so we tend to hold on to our basic convictions and views about reality with the greatest tenacity. It is often obvious that what we claim as rational is no more than a poor rationalization, but we are usually the last to notice it.

Achieving objectivity requires the courage to critically examine cherished positions and to abandon those that no longer make sense, even though they may have been important sources of our security in the past.

THE BASIC WANTS OF INFANTS AND OF ADULTS

65. All the newborn "wants" is to feel safe. This is primitive pre-knowledge, obviously physiologic and not cognitive. Obser-

right way, even when she wishes to do so. The panic that results from the subjective sense of having been forgotten or perhaps even abandoned forever is always followed by resignation to one's inevitable fate, as already suggested in Section 5.

A deep sense of helplessness and hopelessness eventually emanates from such early experiences. They sensitize the organism to expect pain and panic as unavoidable. These are the progenitors of the expectation that life is full of disappointment and despair; they are the foundation of all distrust and at the root of all depression.

73. Profound physical exhaustion is associated with the sense of resignation each time the infant emerges from an episode of panic and rage. The "realization" of its powerlessness over the environment soon brings the panic back, but not before it expresses its fighting spirit again in explosions of preverbal rage. Yet psychologic acceptance of relative powerlessness gradually becomes an integral part of everyone's personality, as the physiology eventually tires of the repeated efforts to reach out and fight back. Narcissism is a delusional attempt to deny this painful reality.

A deep sense of futility eventually becomes an important feature at the core of most people's character structure, and it forms a matrix for their future expectations. It is referred to as "subclinical depression." This is the basis of the common sense of foreboding which holds that it is ultimately impossible to prevail. Losses later in life often activate this dormant matrix and add to it, to form the clinical syndrome of depression.

74. Months later, when the young infant learns to express itself at will, it will notice that other people seem to respond to its command. It is understandable therefore that humans tend to idealize their capacities to demand and to speak. We hold these to be almost all-powerful, since they appear to have helped us to reverse and to undo the terrible sense of helplessness.

The tenacity with which adults hold on to the delusion that they have real power when they can command others is directly proportional to their sense of panic early in life. "Difficult" and colicky babies typically become complaining, pushy, or compulsively rebellious adults. The fear they experienced early in life must have been so overwhelming that above all they dare not become vulnerable again. Commanding others is their way of appearing invincible and powerful.

FEELINGS VS. THINKING

75. Man used to believe that the earth was the center of the universe and that he was not only the crown of creation but its purpose. A major breakthrough occurred when he reluctantly accepted his less exalted position in the scheme of things and realized that the earth was merely one of the lesser planets around the sun, which itself was a minor speck in the cosmos. Giving up his egocentric point of view required Man to realize that he could no longer trust his senses as the source of knowledge. In spite of what he saw, the world was not flat. A similar revolution has yet to take place in our understanding of the nature of Man.

76. Thinking does not exist at the beginnings of life; everything the infant experiences is processed through its feelings. This tendency often persists in adulthood. Consequently, central aspects of most personality theories reflect the fears and wishes of the powerless infant within the adult. This specifically includes the various definitions of power, as noted for instance in Section 56. Such theories are therefore essentially unrealistic.

Many of our political, economic, social, and personal conflicts have remained forever without solution because our basic assumptions about Man were wrong. Inflated and pompous language as well as unnecessarily complex conceptualization are often used to hide the infantile roots of erroneous assumptions.

77. All feelings, conscious or suppressed, are the residues of a person's total previous life experience, at least from birth on. Many of the most profound influences that shape character and determine lifelong reactions occur before consciousness and memory exist. Quite often we all react very powerfully in ways that do not make conscious sense even to ourselves. This threatens our self-image of rationality, so we commonly invent rationalizations to explain and justify our reactions to ourselves and to others. This occurs automatically and usually without awareness, which explains why we also believe that our inventions are true.

Shame and humiliation are commonly associated with panic or hurt, since we frequently cannot find any reasonable explanation for their existence. We therefore often deny that they exist within us, to avoid the experience of shame, but others can clearly see them by observing our behavior and bodily expressions.

78. We hold on to our rationalizations tenaciously, since our view of ourselves as rational beings depends on their validity. Specifically this includes the rationalization that we are rational beings.

79. Modern man never knew a better way to hold irrational fear at a safe distance than to guard his self-image as a rational being. This helped him maintain the delusion that the idealized intellect was the seat of real power. At one point rationalism was progress. Man still tends to hide even from himself the fact that many of his life's most important choices and decisions are made on the basis of feelings, not rationally.

Daily speech confirms this. We are routinely told, for instance, that "the president feels that the situation is well in hand" or that "the financial analysts feel that the dollar will rise (or fall)." Even so, the suggestion that Man is essentially guided not by rational thinking but by irrational feelings is often unwelcome, since it endangers our sense of power. We have the potential to live thoughtfully, just below the angels, but too seldom do we do so. Most people still hold on to the delusion that they are more in control than they really are.

80. Feelings commonly camouflage themselves as thoughts. It is more acceptable and easier to yield to our impulses when we believe that they result from consideration and thinking. Thus we save face and maintain the delusion that we are rational beings. But much thinking is circular and ruminative and leads to conclusions already arrived at by our feelings.

Learning to really think requires first that we make room for it by diminishing the domain of feelings. It is not merely, or even essentially, achievable through academic learning alone. Notions from our infantile past in the form of feelings commonly persist as guideposts in adult living.

81. The residues of fear, hurt, or anger generally accumulate in the body over many years, from birth on. The energy required to keep these stored residues from breaking out and from overwhelming the person is directly proportional to their sum and intensity. Withdrawal into the self, various chemical crutches, and overt behavior that supports the denial are all used to maintain control for as long as possible.

The more that fear, hurt, and anger have been suppressed, the greater the damage if and when the dike finally crumbles under the internal pressure. Such uncontrolled floods of strong feelings are universally feared, with good reason. They can, however, be discharged safely if titrated gradually in well-controlled therapeutic settings. All feelings can be expressed with the greatest intensity yet without causing any damage when they are totally divorced from any other form of physical action.

82. A mature person's satisfactions are altogether different in quality from those of newborns and childlike adults. Essentially they are based on a sense of personal mastery. A person enjoys real power when he or she is self-sufficient, psychologically and otherwise, and free from actual or emotional domination by others or by one's own impulses.

The civilizing efforts of non-totalitarian societies are directed toward this goal. They usually fail, however. Most modern philosophies of education are based on the delusional idealization of the brain as the ultimate seat of power, as if knowledge would make us the masters of our irrational nature. When the efforts succeed, they mainly develop the intellect, and little else. The young usually receive insufficient as well as incorrect guidance or help in the difficult task of maturation.

The central role of feelings, and especially of irrational fear, is usually ignored. Sometimes it is even actively denied. Yet feelings obviously do not simply disappear when their existence is not acknowledged, nor is their powerful influence thus diminished. On the contrary, lack of preparation decreases the ability of people to cope with emotionally stressful situations. This is but one example of the widespread damage wrought by the idealization of the intellect.

83. One of the basic assumptions in free societies is that truth will eventually prevail in the marketplace of ideas. This well-meaning but naive assumption is based on the false belief that societies are made up of mature individuals who reach their decisions through the exercise of reason. The quick up-and-down movements of the stock market and of popularity ratings suggest that this is as untrue in democracies as it is in totalitarian regimes.

Individuals have little freedom to express themselves independently in totalitarian societies, but many opportunities exist in democracies to act out infantile and primitive wishes. By giving a voice to normal anxieties and dissatisfactions, a free press and uncensored television make greater room for them. This exposes the decision-making process in free societies to tremendous irrational pressures. Here people can associate with each other freely on the basis of shared concerns, yet preverbal hunger and rage are often the forces that drive them. Feelings thus often determine public policy.

DANGERS AND OPPORTUNITIES FOR FREE SOCIETIES

84. Fear of parents and of social institutions can bring about behavioral conformity but usually not internal change. Preverbal hunger and rage continue to exert their powerful influences even as we admire mature ways of being and strive to acquire them. Since striving requires much self-control, those not mature enough can at best strive only intermittently.

It is easy to identify with accomplished athletes and to admire their tenacity. Such identification often gives us a vicarious but short-lived sense of mastery and self-sufficiency, but this also does not change us internally. Even athletes do not always live by these standards in their non-athletic lives. They often train hard and perform well in order to fulfill their infantile wish to be recognized and served, to be loved, and to be taken care of.

85. The basic nature of Man does not change just because he is under the rule of one form of government rather than another. Everywhere he tends to act and to react in ways that would decrease his fear and maximize his sense of security. Since Man is easiest to manipulate when he is immature, dependent, and afraid, it is in the interest of totalitarian leaderships to maintain their populations ("the masses") in this state. This is also their fundamental weakness.

86. Man's nature clearly favors the success of totalitarian dictatorships. Since fear is so rampant, a clever and determined "Big Brother" who offers protection in return for obedience usually meets little resistance and has wide appeal, at least for a while. Conscious and fear-free living is only achievable through very hard work, and this goes counter to Man's natural tendency to follow the path of least resistance.

87. The opposite is true in democracies. Freedom is not a free gift, and its maintenance requires thoughtfulness, courage, and the taking of risks. Only in the relative absence of fear can long-range goals be pursued and difficult decisions made. A majority of the population in a democracy determines its course, so it is in the best interest of such a society to have citizens as free of irrational fear as possible. This ultimately is the fundamental strength of free societies. Freedom from fear maximizes the

chances to evaluate risks realistically and to arrive at conclusions rationally.

88. The basic fears of Man must therefore be overcome if affluent free societies are to survive. But even in the past, before almost-instant mass communication existed as a powerful force, they have never survived for very long. Man's hidden irrational fears can be exploited by the enemies of free societies, and they actually are, more so now than in any previous age. Television and other forms of mass media are frequently naive if innocent partners in the spread of disinformation and other "news" items that activate Man's barely dormant fears and doubts.

89. Totalitarian regimes have a built-in advantage by suppressing mass expression of preverbal hunger and rage and by treating public behavior based on fear as treason. Democracies, on the other hand, have been immobilized from time to time when the irrational fears of their citizens paralyzed the ability to govern. These situations are usually characterized as a "failure of will." (See Section 47.)

90. Democratic societies are therefore always exposed to the possibility of breaking up from within. They can only be saved by leaders who understand that their prime responsibility is to dissuade a majority of the population from acting on the basis of feelings. Winston Churchill is the best example in modern times. Even immature adults can act responsibly for short periods of time if mobilized by deft leadership. The personal maturity or immaturity of the leadership determines to a large extent the eventual fate of a democracy. Ancient Rome demonstrates well the consequences of inadequate leadership in a free society.

91. Affluence and relative security enable individuals and societies to exist in the feeling mode for a while and therefore unrealistically. This is a luxury of questionable merit, since it encourages delusional living. Self-indulgence in the pursuit of "more" is possible only when actual survival is not an immediate concern. Having more obviously does not satisfy the yearnings for more, which are irrational. (See Section 26.)

92. Public opinion polls are a feature of political life only in democracies. Politicians who wish to get elected routinely make promises based on them, and they often influence public policy. In spite of their name and claim, such polls reflect not opinions

but feelings, the most powerful of which is irrational fear. The quick swings of such polls confirm that they reflect feelings, whose nature it is to change rapidly.

We have already noted in Section 83 that fear, anger, and hurt are fanned and intensified by media exposure. Public policies and political promises based on polls that reflect emotional storms are therefore inconsistent. They are often not even in the best interest of those whose momentary preferences they reflect. By giving wide exposure to irrational fears and other feelings, the media give them credence which they lacked before the age of mass and instant communication. (See Section 47.)

93. The political push toward isolation from world affairs is usually couched in high-sounding and thoughtful phrases, but it generally represents a summation of hidden individual fears. Without courageous leadership, majorities will always be shaped by fear and policies determined by caution. History has shown, however, that minimizing risk in the short run often maximizes danger thereafter.

But children and immature adults cannot envision distant consequences, so they succeed only rarely in making long-range plans on their own. Normally they prefer junk food now over a nutritious and balanced meal a little later. In poor and rich societies alike the majority of the population tends to live much of the time by impulse and to "choose" on the basis of feelings, provided that they have the freedom to do so.

94. Powerful storms of hurt and rage are unleashed when personal or political promises remain repeatedly unfulfilled. Throughout history they have sparked revolutions and wars and caused the disappearance of the most advanced societies. Those in the West who wish to get elected often fail to understand that promises awaken and activate preverbal hunger and its accompanying preverbal rage, both of which are unsatisfiable in reality.

An explosion of unrealistic expectations is often kindled by new hope that powerful yearnings to be cared for can be perfectly satisfied after all. Cynicism about the political process in democracies represents only a small part of the damage that is inevitable when such promises are made and then violated.

95. Totalitarian regimes are not safe from self-destructive decisions either, as Hitler and Stalin demonstrated well. Here too the maturity or immaturity of the leadership and the quality of their judgments determine the fate of these societies. But the

mettle of dictators is not tested by powerful irrational pressures from below. The push by individuals for more at the expense of society's overall interest has few if any opportunities to express itself. Irrational fear is given no room to influence public policy. Totalitarian regimes can pursue unpopular long-range goals, sometimes for very long periods of time, before collapsing as a result of their inherent weaknesses.

96. The mistaken notion that adulthood is related to maturity has had disastrous consequences in modern permissive societies. The raising of children by adults who are still emotionally in childhood is responsible for societies with childish mores. Having fun and seeking thrills or distractions are not solid bases for building character. The self-indulgence that typifies much public and private behavior in such societies could not have been so prominent before the age of waste and affluence, when self-restraint and individual responsibility were needed for survival.

Nations arise from geographic and historical factors merging with the aspirations of a dynamic population in need of an identity and a home. Like individuals, nations evolve slowly and continuously. Historical forces continue to exert their influence, and from time to time they break up nations no less than they form them.

Excessive fat and feasting without exercise and with an insistence upon remaining comfortable and always at rest cause occlusion of life-sustaining blood vessels not only in individuals. Societies that regularly shun taking necessary risks also stagnate and become calcified. They lose their agility and their capacity to respond to disease as well as to danger, and they die.

97. The family is among the first victims of self-indulgent living. Proper parenting is especially crucial when children are raised in nuclear families without grandparents, uncles, aunts, and other family members. Many such children have only one parent to help them accept the constraints of reality. An increasing percentage of the population in many advanced societies lives under the delusion that such constraints can be avoided, with tragic consequences both to the individual and to society.

98. The mature satisfaction from work and from a job well done is also giving way to a sense that it is almost unfair to make a person work to make a living. From the perspective of the young and perplexed infant, any demands to do anything difficult are indeed unfair, unjust, and harsh, arbitrarily made by

unknown and unreasonable outside forces. From this perspective, all authority is a necessary evil, since it insists that some standards be met. Many adults live this way also, and they are always preoccupied with opposing every authority. Still seeing themselves as small, they experience everyone in a position of power as high-handed, merely because their tendencies to live impulsively may be challenged.

Labor unions were originally established to gain dignity and a fair wage for honest work. They were supported not only by their members but also by many others. But under constant pressure to get "more," some unions have deteriorated into mouthpieces for the preverbal hunger of their members. (This was even somewhat true of the "Solidarity" movement in Poland.)

Expressions of preverbal hunger regularly give rise to outbursts of preverbal rage. These are safe and necessary in therapeutic settings, but otherwise they lower morale and sabotage the productivity of workers and the quality of their output.

99. The survival of free societies, in which Man can speak his mind and determine his governance, requires that both preverbal hunger and its accompanying rage be recognized for what they are, and that fanning such feelings not be allowed. Expectations based on unrealistic wishes are even more dangerous when they relate to justice, equality, and fairness, which are never perfect. When public "opinion" demands absolute justice as a condition for self-acceptance and for the acceptance of others, free societies are condemned to let themselves be enslaved, or die.

Historically, affluent free societies have always failed to repel the onslaughts of barbarism. They have not lost every battle, but eventually they weakened and disappeared. Their peoples usually followed their feelings and lacked both understanding and determination to defend themselves. They are often unable to mobilize the moral strength, the stamina, and the will needed to survive.

If a free society is to be more than a passing historical episode, its public policies must insist that each individual be responsible for all his or her deeds. In must actively shape the characters of free men and women capable of governing themselves, since no one ever is born free, nor is anyone free of fear before he or she is freed from it. This very difficult task is made easier when the laws of the land reward personal independence and self-sufficiency, which only develop in the crucible of no-choice.

Acknowledgments

I wish to thank my teachers, my patients, my students, my associates, and members of my family for what I have learned from them and for their having tolerated so patiently my absences during the time of writing, rewriting, and editing this book. The complaints were few, the good wishes many, and their patience almost limitless. I never took it for granted, regardless of how it seemed. Of my teachers, I must mention Yehuda Burla, the deceased Israeli writer who imbued me with a love for writing, and the late Dr. John Dorsey, my professor of psychiatry who helped develop in me a greater tolerance for unusual views, situations, and people. My patients must remain nameless here for obvious reasons, but not their courage and suffering. Much of what I know about pain, endurance, tolerance, and the greatness of the human spirit comes from being with them. Their long and difficult struggles and victories have often touched me deeply and given me strength. Most of my students will also remain nameless because of their number, but I wish to acknowledge their help. Many concepts in this book have been sharpened and clarified by the need to address their questions and doubts.

But Natan HarPaz, Ronald J. Hook, Joseph Froslie, Paul Shultz, David Baker, Richard A. Seid, Esq., Doron Bar-Levav, Esq., Leah Tuchman, David Fogel, M.D., Ilana Bar-Levav, M.D., Leora Bar-Levav, M.D., and Pamela Torraco—all close friends, associates, and family members—must be mentioned by name. They have helped create this book. The last has been especially helpful in repeatedly reviewing the manuscript, generously giving of her time and counsel. She deserves special thanks.

Thanks also to my diligent editor at Simon and Schuster, Mr. Robert Asahina, for repeatedly helping to sharpen the focus of the final version of this book, and to Denise Boisvert for tending to the manuscript during the years of its growth and development, and for typing and retyping it. Her devoted help has truly been invaluable.

REUVEN BAR-LEVAV, M.D.

Index

Abandonment, fear of, 23–40, 94
  acceptance versus denial of, 28–29
  attachments and, 26–27
  Duke of Windsor's life as illustration of, 32–35
  escalation of, 29
  fear of engulfment and, 41–46
  fear of non-being and, 50
  individuation and, 29–30, 32, 37
  losses and, 26–27
  mothers and, 35–36, 38–40, 44–45
  nature of, 25–26
  Ravel, Maurice, 39, 40
  romantic love and, 26, 31, 149, 150, 152
  sex and, 156
  in therapy, 241, 247
  in unified theory, 332–33
Abortion, 195, 206–7, 209, 215
Accommodating attitudes, 178
Addiction to hurt, 183–84
Adulthood, defined, 329
Adults, as grown-up children, 176, 178, 180–81, 186
  in unified theory, 329–30, 339, 348
Advertising, 137, 294. See also Commercials
  sex in, 155–56
Affluence, 191–92
  in society, 260
  in unified theory, 323, 329, 346, 349
Afghanistan, 261
Age of Anxiety, 91
Aggression, 136
Allergies, 184
"All Things Considered" program (National Public Radio), 300–301

Aloneness, acceptance of, 78, 79
Altman, Leon L., 145
Amal militia, 288
Amin, Idi, 262
Anger, 133, 135–36, 170–80
  against authority, 114
  boundary definition and, 335
  depression and, 171
  expressing versus suppressing, 172, 173, 177
  expression of, 174, 175, 178–79
  fear of, 136, 178–79
  hate versus, 166
  inwardly directed, 172–73
  irrational, 171
  loss of conscious control of, 174–175
  as "negative" feeling, 171
  outbursts of, 171–72
  perceived as dangerous, 171
  physiological manifestations of, 173
  rational and justified, 171–72, 174
  real, 174
  suppressing or denying, 171–73, 177
  therapy and, 175, 233
  violence and, 172, 176
  vocal expressions of, 172
Angst, 65
Animals, 37
  in heat, 157
  humans as part of animal kingdom, 86–88, 122–24, 321
Anomie, 72–74
Anti-anxiety drugs, 106
Anti-depressant drug therapy, 105
Anti-Semitism, 165
Anxiety. See also Fear(s); Panic attacks
  bodily sensations of, 65–66, 83

Anxiety (*cont.*)
    causes of, 68–69
    depression and, 69
    drugs for lowering, 90
    free-floating, 108
    Kierkegaard on, 68
    masks of, 65–72
    physiological effects of, 134
    struggle for survival and, 70
    Time magazine article on, 66–
        68
    in unified theory, 329–30
Aristotle, 263, 313
Armenians, 168
Arthritis, 173
Asthma, 184
Atomic bombing of Japan, 282, 292
Authority, 179
    anger against, 114
    reluctance to exercise, 276–77
    therapists' difficulty with, 241–
        242
Autism, normal, of infants, 55, 58
Autistic living, 58–60
Autonomic nervous system, 124
Axons, 130

Baha'i religion, 262
Baldwin, Stanley, 33
Bangladesh, 207
Barbarism, hate and, 167, 168
Beirut, killing of U.S. Marines in
    (1985), 283
Berlin Wall, 332
Biases, 62
Birth, experience of, 74–75, 96, 325
Birth control, 209–10, 215
Birth trauma, 74
Blacks, anger and, 179
Blondes, 158
Blushing, 224
Body. *See also* Physiology
    therapy and the, 225
Boundaries of the self
    happiness and, 193
    importance of, in the therapist,
        229, 234–37
    real love and, 158–59
    repair of defective, 239
    romantic love and, 150
    in unified theory of human
        motivation and behavior, 330–
        336

Brain, human, 124–28
    development of, in first two years
        of life, 130–33
    evolution of, 127
    fear of non-being and, 57–58
    limbic system, 124
    myelination in, 130–32
    new mammalian (neocortex),
        125, 131
    old mammalian, 124–25
    reptilian, 124, 127
    triune or tripartite model of,
        124–25
    visceral, 125, 126, 131, 132
Brain stem, 124
Breastfeeding, 44
Breasts, 156, 157
Bridal shower, 163–64
Bryan, William Jennings, 302, 303
Buber, Martin, 21

Cairo, 208
Cambodia, 261
Camus, Albert, 289
Cancer, 173, 184
Car accidents, 173
Carlyle, Thomas, 266
Carson, Johnny, 190
Carter, Jimmy, 284, 311
Cartesian view, 320
Castro, Fidel, 47
Catharsis, 225
Catholic Church, 320
Cerebral cortex. *See* Cortex
Challenger (space shuttle), 283–84,
    288
Chamberlain, Neville, 178
Character
    change, 128, 324
    physiologic basis of, 88–93, 125,
        218
Childbearing, licensing of, 212–17
Child rearing, 195–96
Children, 194–219. *See also*
        Parents (parenting)
    anger and, 174, 176–78
    attending to feelings of, 218
    handicapped, 194–98
    inattention to hurt in, 184
    licensing the right to have, 212–
        217
    love and, 147–48
    manipulation of hurt and, 183

overprotected, 185, 193
self-control and, 177–78
self-discipline of, 185
sickly, 184
teasing or mocking, 184–85
thinking and, 218–19
China, 209, 217
Choices. *See* Decision making
Christianity, 86
Christmas, 162
Churchill, Winston, 263, 346
Civilization, 140, 141
basis of, 267–69
Clinging versus pushing away, in
unified theory, 332–33
Clinical data, 62
Closeness. *See* Intimacy
Commercials, 134, 297
Commitment, love and, 146
Community Mental Health
movement, 200
Compassion, 201–2, 285
Complaining, anger and, 171
Compromise, 121
anger and, 178
Concentration, difficulties in, 141
Confusion in thinking, 140–43
Conley, Frances, 109–11
Consent, therapy and, 227–28
Contentment, 191–92
Contract, in therapy, 232–34, 240–
242
Control, loss of. *See* Losing control
Controversy (controversial issues),
113–14, 119
Copernicus, 203
Cortex, 126–28, 132. *See also*
Neocortex
delusional idealization of, 128–
130
parental prohibitions and, 139
Criminal justice system, 268
Crisis, forbidding public expression
of feelings in, 285–89
Crisis Mobilization Therapy, 245
eight principles of, 220–27
Cronkite, Walter, 282
"Crucible of no choice"
in the family, 297
in psychotherapy, 140, 225
in unified theory, 349
Crying, 183
expressing hurt and, 188–89

Cuba, 264
Cults, 54
Cunning, 272–73
free societies' need to use, 282
Curtis, Tony, 187

Daydreams, fear of non-being and,
56
Day's residue, 139
Death
fear of non-being distinguished
from, 50
life after, 52
minimization in public policy
decisions, 275–78
Decision making
feelings and, 115, 289
in therapy, 242
Declaration of Independence, 192,
315
Defiance, in therapy, 240
Demagogues, hate and, 168
Demands, in therapy, 238–40
Democracy (democratic societies).
See also Western civilization
code of conduct for international
relations and, 311–15
corrupting influence of feelings
in, 204
dangers and opportunities for,
345–49
dictatorship of reason needed in,
204–5
the media in, 293–302
necessity for lies in, 307–11
in unified theory, 336, 345–49
Dendrites, 130
Dependency
actual (real), 103, 104, 226
emotional, 103–5
physical, 37–38
Depression, 69–112
anger and, 171
cure of, 220
definition of, 69, 341
diagnosis of, 106
economic costs of, 107
financial hardship and, 251–52
happiness and, 137
job-related, 134
love and, 137
physical illness and, 73–74,
220

Depression (*cont.*)
  symptomatic treatment of, 106–
    109
  treatments of, 105–12
Depressive position, 91–93
Descartes (Cartesian), 320–21
Dictators, 49. *See also* Totalitarian
    regimes
Dictatorship of feelings, 263–67,
    273, 285
Dictatorship of reason, 204–5
Dictatorship of the proletariat, 204
Dictatorships. *See* Totalitarian
    regimes
Dignity, anger and, 171, 174
Diogenes the Cynic, 266
Disappointment
  inevitability of, 98–103
  of young people, 260
Distance in relationships, 93–95
  fear of abandonment and, 31
Distrust, 95
Doom, sense of impending, 322–23
Dread
  inevitability of, 98–103
  in newborns, 79, 131
  in unified theory, 323–24, 326
Dreams, 138–39
  fear of non-being and, 51, 53–54
Drugs
  anti-anxiety, 106
  anti-depressant, 105
  for lowering anxiety, 90
Dryden, John, 153

Eastern Europe, 306–7
Eastern mind, 321–22
Education, of feelings, 123
Ego boundaries. *See* Boundaries of
    the self
Egypt, ancient, 51
Einstein, Albert, 50, 320, 322
Embarrassment, 133, 320, 330
  about feelings, 122
Emotional dependency, 103–5
  therapy and, 226–27, 246–49
Emotions. *See* Feelings
Emphysema, 184
Empty-nest syndrome, 148
Engulfment, fear of, 23, 40–49
  fear of abandonment and, 41–46
  fear of trust and, 223
  hate and, 48–49

homosexuality and, 47
isolation and, 40–41
marriages and other long-term
    relationships and, 46–47
power and, 44–45, 48
romantic love and, 151
sado-masochistic relationships
    and, 47–48
in therapy, 241
in unified theory, 332–33
Enjoyment, 192–93
Envy, 133
Eritrea, 261
Ethiopia, 215–16, 261
Etiquette, 95
Evolution of human brain, 127
Excellence, 315
Existentialism, 72
Expectations
  feelings as expression of, 116
  hurt and, 181–82
  of newborns and infants, 339
Experts, 63, 103, 105, 107, 132, 173,
    220, 246, 255, 293–94

Facial expressions, 19
  in newborns, 75
Falkland Islands war, 308
Family, the, 296–97, 348
Famine, 261
Fanaticism, 338
Fathering, in therapy, 238–46
Fathers, 102, 328. *See also* Parents.
  fights between mothers and, 176
Fear(s), 17, 20–21, 23–63, 116–17.
    See also Abandonment, fear of;
    Anxiety; Engulfment, fear of;
    Non-being, fear of
  of anger, 136, 178
  of emotional dependency, 103–5
  of flying, 108
  happiness and, 137
  hate and, 165–66
  of intimacy, 150
  irrational nature of, 20, 23
  love and, 137
  masks of, 65–72
  of physical closeness, 85
  of realistic dangers, 24
  totalitarian regimes and, 267,
    345–348
  in unified theory, 323–26, 345–
    346

Feelings, 113–22, 133
  animals and, 122–24
  basic qualities of, 133–38, 224
  changing, 127
  choices and, 115
  compromise and, 121
  crisis facing the West and, 285–289
  denial of, 119–22, 135–37, 325
  distorting effects of, 114–15
  downgrading of, 119–22
  dreams and, 138–39
  "education" of, 123
  expectations expressed by, 116
  inattention to, 142
  masquerading as thoughts, 63, 113, 117–18, 195, 343
  moralistic classification of, 171
  nature of, 116–18, 142
  need to separate thinking from, 142
  nervous system and, 124
  as our guardians, 138–40
  parenting and, 218
  physiologic manifestations of, 142
  politics and, 113–14, 345–49
  self-protective habit of hiding, 133
  subcortical pathways and, 127
  in therapy, 224, 232–34
  underground, 117
  unified theory on thinking versus, 342–49
  Zen Buddhism and, 143
Fetal alcoholic syndrome, 197
Fishing, 122–23, 272–73
Fiske, Jamie, 200
Flying, fear of, 108
Freedom
  of speech, 315–16
  in unified theory, 345–46, 349
  in the West, 264
Freedom fighters, 279
Freedom of Information Act, 288
Freud, Sigmund, 15, 20, 59, 129, 139
Fun, sadness and, 190–91

Garden of Eden, 101
Gastrointestinal symptoms, 173
Generosity, in real love, 159
Genesis, Book of, 319

Genetics, panic attacks and, 106–7
Geneva Convention of 1864, 290
Genocide, 261, 268
Germany, in World War I, 303–5
Gifts
  bridal shower, 163–64
  false giving of, 163
  free, 161–64
  ritual of receiving, 163
God, 211, 212, 319–22, 337
Goldwater, Barry, 113–14
Golem of Prague, the, 212
Graffiti, 277
Grasping, 127
Green Revolution, 210
Grenada, 307, 308
Group therapy, 249–50
  combined individual and, 225
Guilt, 133–35

Hallucinations, 59
  fear of non-being and, 56
Hamadi, Mohammed Ali, 281
Handicapped children, 194–95
Happiness, 133, 191–93
  endless pursuit of, 93, 137–38, 192, 315
  expression of, 137
  real, 191
  sadness and, 191
"Happiness," 190, 191
Hartmann, Heinz, 59
Hate, 133, 135, 164–70
  anger versus, 166
  as antidote for panic, 168
  as contagious, 167, 168
  fear and, 165–66
  fear of engulfment and, 48–49
  institutionalized, 165–68
  intensity of, 165
  as separating and disengaging, 169–70
  treatment of, 170
  violence and, 165, 167, 168
Haunted House, 243–45, 253
Health and Human Services, U.S. Department of, 194, 205
Heart attacks, 134
Heart disease, 173
Helplessness. See also Power (powerlessness)
  of newborns, 96–98
  unified theory on, 327, 341

Hermits, 151
Hijackings, 274–75, 280, 281
Hillel, Rabbi, 191, 192
Hiroshima, atomic bombing of, 282, 292
Hitler, Adolf, 48, 49, 165, 166
Ho Chi Minh, 282
Holden, William, 40, 220
"Holding," therapy and, 234–37, 249
Homosexuality, fear of engulfment and, 47
Honeymoon of relationships, fear of abandonment and, 31
Hopelessness, 238, 245–46
Hughes, Howard, 40
Human rights, 275
Humiliation, 342
Hunger, preverbal, 238
  in unified theory, 340, 345–47, 349
Hunting, 122–23, 272–73
Hurt, feeling of, 117, 133, 135, 180–189
  addiction to, 183–84
  causes and origins of, 180, 181, 185
  children and, 183
  crying as way of expressing, 188–189
  expectations and, 181–82
  expression of, 180–81, 188–189
  fear of, 186–87
  hiding, 181
  manipulating others with, 182–183, 185, 186
  physiological manifestations of, 184, 188–89
  residues of unexpressed, 188
  as self-made, 182
  therapy and, 188, 233
  in unified theory, 334–35, 337, 343, 347
Huxley, Thomas Henry, 210
Hypertension, 173

Id, 140
Illegal immigrants, 300–301
Immigration and Naturalization Service (INS), 300–301
India, 208, 209

Individuation
  fear of abandonment and, 29–30, 32, 37
  importance of in the therapist, 254
  in unified theory, 326, 330–31, 337–38
Infants. See also Newborns
  adults as grown-up infants, 78–80
  basic wants of, 97, 338–41
  brain development in, 130–33
  breastfeeding, 44
  expectations of, 339
  handicapped, 194–95
  hurt in, 181
  life from perspective of, 95–98
  organ transplantation for, 200–201
  physical closeness and, 85–86
  real love and, 159–60
  with spina bifida, 201
Informed consent, in therapy, 227–228
Injustice, 99
  fights against, 92
"In love." See Romantic love
"Inner directed" people, 335
Insanity. See Psychosis
Insensitivity, 79–80, 104–5, 138
Insight, 139
Intellect. See also Rationality; Thinking
  delusional idealization of, 128–130
Intelligence, anxiety and, 89
International law, as dangerous fiction, 306–7
International relations, code of conduct for, 311–13
Intervention, military, 314–15
Intimacy, emotional (closeness; close relationships). See also Love
  boundaries of the self and, 331
  caution toward, 95
  crisis precipitated by the breakup of, 94
  distance in, 31, 93–95
  emotional dependency in, 103–5
  fear of, 150
  fear of being hurt and avoidance of, 186–87

romantic love and, 150–51
sado-masochistic relationships
    and, 47–48
I.Q., 89
Iran, 262, 264, 270, 281, 282, 284
Iran-contra affair, 285
Iron Curtain, 332
Irrational feelings. *See* Feelings
Irrationality, acceptance of, 42,
    119–22, 344
Isaiah, 307
Islam, 265
Isolation
    fear of engulfment and, 40–
    41
    from world affairs, 347
Israel, 308, 309

Jacob, 66, 321
Japan, 292
    atomic bombing of, 292
Jealousy, 133
Jews, 48, 122, 165, 166
    anger and, 179
    ultra-orthodox, 51–52
Job-related illnesses, 134
Johnson, Lyndon, 294
Judeo-Christian tradition, 86, 91
Judicial system, 268
Justice, as irrelevant in the jungle,
    311–13

Kafka, Franz, 101
Kennedy family, 184
Kenya, 208
Khmer Rouge, 49, 261
Khomeini, Ayatollah, 48, 49, 168,
    262, 270, 282, 284
Kierkegaard, Søren, 68
Knowledge, expulsion from Garden
    of Eden and, 101

Labor unions, 349
Law
    in civilized societies, 268–69
    international, as dangerous
    fiction, 306–7
    of the jungle, 268–73, 311–13
    in totalitarian regimes, 267
    and treatment of outlaws, 289–
    290
Leaks, news, 299

Learning
    cortical, 139–40
    difficulties in, 141
    to think, 142, 224–25, 342–45
Lebanon, 278, 283, 290, 308, 309
Lesbians, 156–57
Libya, 264, 314
Lies, current necessity for, 307–11
Life after death, 52
Limbic system, 124–25
Live-and-let-live attitudes, 177
Loneliness
    fear of abandonment and, 24–25
    protection against hurt and, 187
Lorenz, Konrad, 124
Losing control, 120, 121
    anger and, 171, 175, 178
Loss(es)
    depression precipitated by, 92–93
    fear of abandonment and, 26–27
Love, 133, 136–38, 144–64. *See
    also* Romantic love; Self-love
    children and, 147–48
    commitment and, 146
    free gifts as expressions of, 161–
    162, 332
    hate and, 164–66
    nature of, 145–46
    promise of eternal, 146
    real, 158–60, 161–64
    of self, 160–61
    sexual aspects of, 155–58
    therapy and, 234–37
    trust and, 145
Löw, Rabbi Judah, 212
Lusitania, 303–4

McAuliffe, Sharon Christa, 283–
    284
McCarthy, Joseph, 48
McGovern, George, 113–14
MacLean, Paul, 124–25
Malthus, 210
Manipulation with hurt, 182–83,
    186
Mann, Thomas, 101
Marathon sessions, 250–51
Marriage
    crisis precipitated by the breakup
    of, 94
    difficulties commonly
    encountered in, 94

Marriage (*cont.*)
  fear of abandonment and, 94
  fear of engulfment and, 46–47
Marxism, 265
Masochism. *See* Sado-masochistic
  relationships
Maturation, 329, 335, 344
May, Rollo, 69
Media, the, 293–302
  fight against terrorism and, 285–
    288
  First Amendment and, 302, 315
  in unified theory, 334, 344, 346,
    347
Medical model. *See* Surgical model
Medical technology, saving and
  prolonging lives with, 199–203
Meese, Edwin, 281
Mental patients, 200
Mexico City, 208
Military dictatorships, 204
Military intervention, 314–15
Minorities, anger and, 179
Mitral valve prolapse, 106
Moby Dick (Melville), 179
Mocking, 184–85
Moderation, 121
Monroe, Marilyn, 155, 220
Morgenthau, Hans, 305
Mother(s). *See also* Breastfeeding;
    Parents
  fear of abandonment and, 35–36,
    38–40, 44–45
  fear of non-being and, 58
  fights between fathers and, 176
  Jewish, 183
  love and, 145
  Ravel's relationship to his, 39, 40
  responses to newborns, 102
  romantic love and, 150, 154
  sexuality and, 155–57
  teenage, 206
  in unified theory, 326–27
Mothering
  therapy and, 234–37
  in unified theory of human
    motivation and behavior, 326–
    329
Mourning, 27
Munch, Edvard, 65
Murder, 135, 136
Myelin (myelination), 130–32
Mythology, 51

Nagasaki, atomic bombing of, 282,
    292
Narcissism, 60–61, 341. *See also*
    Self-coupling
National Council on Compensation
    Insurance, 134
National Public Radio (NPR), 300–
    301
Natural selection, 270
  human selection versus, 202–3
Nazis, 165, 166, 168
Neocortex, 125
Nerve impulses, in infants, 131–32
Nervous breakdowns, 134
Newborns. *See also* Birth
  animal nature of, 87–88
  attending to physical being of,
    218
  brain development in, 130–32
  as complex of physiologic
    reaction patterns, 325
  expectations of, 339
  experiences and reactions of, 75–
    78, 131
  fear of non-being in, 52, 54–57
  first experiences of, 322–26
  handicapped, 197–98
  helplessness (powerlessness) of,
    96–98
  life from perspective of, 95–98
  love between parents and, 153
  objective sources of knowledge
    about experiences of, 81–84
  screaming of, 96, 97
  in unified theory, 322–26, 338–
    341
  verification of experiences of,
    80–81
New mammalian brain, 125, 131,
    139
News leaks, 298–99
News media. *See* Media
New York City, graffiti in, 277
New Yorker, The, 140–41
New York Times, 256
Non-acting-out contract, 231–34,
    240–42
Non-aggression, 312
Non-being, fear of, 23, 50–59
  existence and nature of, 50–51
  fear of death distinguished from,
    50
  life after death and, 52

in newborns, 52, 54–57
physical closeness as means of
    relieving, 55–56
psychosis and, 56–57
sex and, 156
in unified theory, 324
withdrawal, autism and, 58–59
Nostalgia, 71–72, 192
Notes to the reader, 80, 118, 195,
    198, 292, 316
Nuclear war, 264
Numbness, in newborns, 131

Objectivity, 118
Old age, 135
love and, 145
Old mammalian brain, 124–25
Oral sex, 157
Organ transplantation, 200–201
Orgasm, 85
difficulties in reaching, 43
peace and relaxation that follow,
    157
"Other directed" people, 335
Overidentification
with handicapped children, 195,
    197–203
with lawbreakers, 269, 280, 301
in unified theory, 329, 333–34
Overpopulation, 205–11
Overprotected children, 185, 193

Pahlavi, Mohammed Riza (Shah of
    Iran), 284
Pain, emotional. See Hurt, feeling
    of
Panic. See also Fear
in animals, 88
in unified theory, 299–300
Parents (parenting), 98. See also
    Child rearing; Fathers; Mothers
anger and, 176–78
love of their children by, 152
love that children have for, 147
principles for good, 217–19
Passivity, television as promoting,
    295
Patients' rights, 200
Penal system, 268
Penis, women's sucking of, 157–
    158
Pessimistic view, 91
Pets, 186–87

Phobias, earliest experiences and,
    83–84, 90
Physical abuse, 85
Physical closeness. See also
    Touch(ing)
fear of non-being and, 55–56
romantic love and, 150–51
yearnings for, 84–86
Physical illness. See also
    Physiology (physiologic
    reactions)
anger and, 173
depression and, 73–74
hurt and, 184
job-related, 134
susceptibility to, 89–90
Physiology (physiologic reactions)
changes in during therapy, 228
character and, 88–93
as confirmation of earliest
    experiences, 82–83
to perceived danger, 76–77, 80
in therapist, 253
in therapy, 221, 224–25
in unified theory, 323, 325
Pining, in romantic love, 154
Pity, 138
Political leaders (politicians), 89,
    134, 276–77, 315–16
educational function of, 278
hate and, 165, 166
Political movements, 92. See also
    Protest movements
Politics, 113–14. See also
    Democracy (democratic
    societies); Political leaders
corrupting influence of feelings
    on, 204
hate and, 165–68
Polls, public opinion, 275, 334,
    346–47, 349
Population growth, 205–11
Power (powerlessness). See also
    Helplessness
delusions of, 185
of elected officials, 276–77
fear of engulfment and, 44–45, 48
of "the people," 276
romantic love and, 154–55
in unified theory, 321, 334–35,
    336–38, 340–41
Premature babies, handicapped,
    197–98

Preverbal hunger, 238
in unified theory, 340, 345, 346, 347, 349
Preverbal rage, 238
in unified theory, 340, 341, 345, 346, 347, 349
Price supports for agricultural products, 297–98
Primitive man, 101
Profanities, 174
Pro-life advocates, 207, 209
Protest movements, 92, 97–98
Psychoanalysis, 20, 129–30, 136
basic flaw of, 225
dreams and, 139–40
feelings and, 139
relationship between therapist and patients in, 222–23
Psychosis, fear of non-being and, 56–57
Psychotherapy. *See* Therapy
Ptolemaic system, 319
Puberty, 157
Public opinion polls, 275, 334, 346–347, 349
Public policy, maximizing justice and freedom in, 275–78, 345–349
"Pull of regression," 227
in unified theory, 326–29
"Push against progressing," 38, 83, 143, 227
in unified theory, 326–29
Pushing away versus clinging
in unified theory, 332–33

Qaddafi, Muammar, al-, 262, 280

Rage
expressions of, 173
internalized, 172
non-acting-out, 175
pre-verbal, 238, 340, 341, 345, 346, 347, 349
Rank, Otto, 74
Rationality
as goal in need of fulfillment, 113–16
investment in, 119, 321, 343–44
Rationalizations, 115, 343
Ravel, Maurice, 39, 40
Readers, personal note to, 80, 118, 195, 198, 292, 316

Reagan, Ronald, 205–6, 281, 283, 285, 307, 310, 311
Reality
individual views of, 114
parenting and, 218
Real relationship, 223, 236–37, 248
therapeutic relationship versus, 229–31
Rebelliousness, in therapy, 241
Recluses, 151
Reflexes, 123–24
"Regression, pull of," 326–30
Reich, Wilhelm, 21
Religion, 113, 295
Reptilian brain, 124, 127
Retreat, 120–21. *See also* Withdrawal
Revenge, 278
by ex-lovers, 153
Rigidity, 333
Rilke, Rainer Maria, 149
Rolland, Romain, 95
Romantic love, 144–46, 148–55
attention to needs and preferences of another in, 149
awakening from, 151
birth of a child and, 153–54
boundaries of self and, 150, 332
disappointment in, 153
exclusivity and, 153–54
fear of abandonment and, 26, 31, 149, 150, 152, 333
fear of engulfment and, 151, 332
forgiveness of faults and, 152
hate and, 164–65
as impoverishing both lovers, 149
mismatched lovers in, 152
power and, 154–55
real love versus, 158–60, 162
as self-coupling, 153
separation and, 148
sex and, 148–49
yearning in, 148–49, 158
Rousseau, Jean-Jacques, 268–69
Ruminating, 115–16
Runner, The (Conley), 109–11

Sadness, 133, 189–91
positive aspects of, 138, 190
showing, 138
Sado-masochistic relationships, fear of engulfment and, 47–48

SAVAK, 284
Screaming
  in anger, 174
  of newborns, 96, 97
Self-blame, anger and, 174
Self-care, 161
Self-concern, 161
Self-control, children and, 177–78
Self-coupling, 32, 58, 153
  selfishness versus, 160, 161
  self-love versus, 59–61, 160–61
Self-discipline, of children, 185
Self-help books, 93
Self-indulgence, 161, 185, 193, 213,
    266, 329, 346, 348
Selfishness, sensible, 160–61
Self-love, 138, 159
  self-coupling versus, 59–61
  selfishness and, 160
Self-mothering, 329
Self-observation, desirability and
    need for, 118
Self-respect, anger and, 171
Self-sacrifice, 161
Self-sufficient, wish to be and fear
    of being, 328, 329, 331
Sensitivity, as a liability, 104–5
Separation. See Individuation
  fear of abandonment and, 29–30,
    32
  hate and, 169–70
  panic and, 332
  physical and psychological, 330–
    331
  romantic love and, 148
Sermons, 93
Sex symbols, 155
Sexual activity (sexuality). See also
    Orgasm
  blondes and, 158
  breasts and, 156–57
  fear of engulfment, 151
  love and, 155–58
  oral, 157–58
  penis and, 157–58
  romantic love and, 148–49
  therapy and, 233
Sexual dysfunction, 85
Shame, 133, 342
  in therapy, 224
Sharon, Ariel, 308
Shower, bridal, 163–64
Sickly children, 184

Simpson, Wallis (later Duchess of
    Windsor), 32–35
Skin disorders, 173, 184
Sleep, newborns and, 131
Smiling, in newborns, 75
Social contract, 268–69
Social and psychological sciences,
    bias of the observer, 62–63
South Africa, 314
Soviet Union, 48, 49, 261–64, 280,
    299
  hate and, 167
  international law and, 306–7
Space shuttle Challenger, 283–84
"Space-time," 322
Sparta, 38, 59
Speech, freedom of, 315–16
Spies, 267
Spina bifida, 201
Spitz, René, 325
Stalin, 49, 167, 306
Starvation, mass, 261
"Star Wars" (Strategic Defense
    Initiative), 49, 308
Stethem, Robert, 274
Stoics, 187–88
Strategic Defense Initiative ("Star
    Wars"), 308
Stress. See also Anxiety;
    Depression
  actual, 301, 335
  definition of, 69
  emotional, 20, 65, 79, 80, 90, 98,
    117, 119, 344
  fallacy of environmental causes
    of, 70, 134
  test, 36
Stress management, 173
Subclinical depression, 341
Subversion, free societies' need to
    use, 282
Sudden infant death syndrome, 323
Suffering. See also Hurt, feeling of
  and public policy decisions, 275–
    278
Suicide, 53, 99–100
Sullivan, Harry Stack, 89
Superego, 139–40
Support groups, 225
Surgical model
  in the defense of the West, 282
  therapy and, 221–22, 224, 253
Survival, hate and, 169

Sympathy, efforts to elicit, 183
Symptom substitution, 108

Teachers, 134
Tearing, 142
Teenage mothers, 206
Television, 134, 204, 295–302
Tension, chronic, 117
Terrorism, 260–63
  casualties as inevitable in war
    against, 280–85
  experts on, 293–94
  feelings in fight against, 285–89
  fighting, 274–92
  hate and, 167
  subversion and cunning in war
    against, 282
  in total war against the West,
    279–80
Thatcher, Margaret, 311
Therapeutic contract, 232–34, 240–
  242
Therapeutic relationship, 222–23,
  236
  real relationship versus, 229–31
Therapy, 18
  anger and, 175, 233
  by the non-licensed and
    unqualified, 254–56
  child-parent relationship as
    model for, 246
  choosing therapists, 256–57
  combined individual and group,
    225
  confrontations in, 223
  contract in, 232–34, 240–42
  cost of, 251–53
  decisions in, 242
  demands of patients in, 238–
    240
  of depression, 105–12
  educational principles of, 246
  emotional dependency and, 226–
    227, 246–49
  fathering and limit setting in,
    238–46
  fear of non-being as manifested
    in, 50–51
  group, 249–50
  hate and, 170
  hurt and, 187–88, 233
  love in, 234–37
  marathon sessions in, 250–51

Therapy (cont.)
  mothering and "holding" in,
    234–37
  with multiple therapists, 226
  need for more competent
    therapists, 253–54
  need for sense of safety in, 231–
    234, 236–37
  objectives and basic principles of,
    220–27
  overidentification with the
    patient, 221–22
  patients' consent and, 227–28
  payment of money in, 236
  rebelliousness in, 241
  relationship between therapist
    and patients, 222–24
  setting for, 230–34
  sex and, 233
  surgical model and, 221–22
  terminating, 240, 241, 244
  touching and, 233
  trust and, 223–24
  using chapter on therapy as a
    guide to, 254–58
  working with feelings in, 224
  working with the body in, 225,
    228
  working with thinking in, 224–
    225
Thinking (thoughts). See also
    Rationality
  biases and distortions of feelings
    and, 117
  children and, 218–19
  compromise and, 121
  confusion in, 140–43
  feelings masquerading as, 117–18
  learning to think, 142, 224–25,
    343
  need to separate feelings from,
    142
  ruminating versus, 115–16
  therapy and, 224–25
  unified theory on feelings versus,
    342–45
Third World, 207, 265
Thought disorders, 141
Thumb sucking, 55
Tibet, 261–62
Time (magazine), 66–68, 208, 281–
  282
Tortoises, 327

Totalitarian regimes (dictatorships), 204, 261, 265
  characteristics of, 266–67
  fear of authority in, 277
  the media and, 299–300
  in unified theory, 331–32, 336, 345–49
Touch(ing), 85. See also "Holding"; Physical closeness
  in therapy, 225
  therapy and, 233
Tragedies, classical, 190
Transference, 222, 228
Tree of Knowledge, 101
Tripartite model of the human brain, 124–25
Truman, Harry, 282, 292, 294, 305
Trust, 95
  love and, 145
  therapy and, 223–24
Truth, 119–21
  necessity for lies in democracy and, 307–8
Tuchman, Barbara, 303
Type A personality, 174

Ulcers, 173, 184
Unconscious, the, 129, 139
Understanding, 139. See also Rationality; Feelings, masquerading as thoughts
Unified theory of human motivation and behavior, 19, 318–49
  on basic wants of infants and of adults, 338–41
  boundaries of the self in, 330–36
  clinging in, 332–33
  fear of abandonment in, 332–33
  fear of engulfment in, 332–33
  fear of non-being in, 324
  on feelings versus thinking, 342–345
  first experiences of newborns in, 322–26
  on free societies, 345–49
  on newborns, 322–26
  overidentification in, 329, 333–34
  on power and powerlessness, 336–38, 340–41
  "pull of regression" and "push against progressing" in, 326–30
  on wish to be mothered, 326–27

United Nations, 306
United States, changes recommended for, 315–16

Validation. See also Social and psychological sciences
  of international treaties, 322
  of theory, 17, 322
Vance, Cyrus, 178, 305, 311
Vietnam war, 309
Violence, 135
  anger and, 172
  of children of violent parents, 176
  hate and, 165, 167, 168
Virgil, 181, 189
Visceral brain, 57–58, 125, 126, 131, 132, 221, 227, 239
  dreams and, 138–40
Vulnerability, 104

Walker spy scandal, 298–99
Walking erect, 130
Wall Street Journal, 281
War against Western civilization, 279–80
Wars, 179–80
Wayne, John, 104
Weaning, 43, 327
Weber, Max, 336
Weinberger, Caspar, 290–91
Western civilization, 204, 259–317
  casualties as inevitable in defense of, 280–85
  code of conduct for international relations and, 311–15
  current necessity for lies in, 307–311
  dictatorship of feelings as root problem of, 263–67
  "fairness," principles in, 280, 289–92, 300–301, 303
  justice and freedom in policies of, 275–78
  law of the jungle and, 268–73, 309, 312–13
  the media in, 293–302, 308–10, 315
  need to ignore feelings in crisis, 285–89
  subversion and cunning to be used by, 282

Western civilization (*cont.*)
  undeclared state of war against,
    262–63, 279–80
  in unified theory, 336, 345–49
West Germany, 281
Whitworth, Jerry A., 298–99
Will, 128
  failure of, 309, 346
Wilson, Woodrow, 302–4, 306–9
Windsor, Duke and Duchess of, 32–
  35, 185
Wisdom, sadness and, 189–90
Withdrawal. *See also* Retreat
  fear of abandonment and, 32
  fear of non-being and, 58–59
  lowering anxiety through, 88–89
  of newborn into itself, 325

Womb
  Garden of Eden as metaphor for,
    101
  wish to return to, 76, 77
Women's liberation movement,
  104
World War I, 302–4
World War II, 287, 306

Yearning, romantic love and, 148–
  149
  for physical closeness, 85
Yellow Pages, 256
Young people, disappointment felt
  by, 260

Zen Buddhism, 21, 143

About the Author

Born in Berlin, raised in Tel Aviv, Dr. Bar-Levav studied in New York and Detroit, earning degrees in economics, political science, and medicine. A seeker, he dropped out of high school to work on a kibbutz, became a Socialist, apprenticed in journalism, joined the underground "Haganah," lectured, taught, and eventually resumed his studies. A father of three, he is a writer, an editor of *The Detroit Medical News*, an occasional painter, a teacher, and a practitioner of psychotherapy. He regards himself not only as a healer but also as one fighting to expand the domain of individual freedom by diminishing the insidious dictatorship of feelings.